The Quick Python Book

The Quick Python Book

DARYL HARMS
KENNETH MCDONALD

MANNING

Greenwich
(74° w. long.)

For electronic browsing and ordering of this and other Manning books,
visit http://www.manning.com. The publisher offers discounts on this book
when ordered in quantity. For more information, please contact:

> Special Sales Department
> Manning Publications Co.
> 32 Lafayette Place   Fax: (203) 661-9018
> Greenwich, CT 06830   email: orders@manning.com

Harms, Daryl D.
     The Quick Python book / Daryl Harms, Kenneth McDonald.
        p. cm.
     Includes bibliographical references.
     ISBN 1-884777-74-0   (alk. paper)
     1. Python (Computer program language)   I.   McDonald, Kenneth,
1964-   . II. Title.
QA76.73.P98H37 1999
005.13'3--dc21   99-38928
                          CIP

M Manning Publications Co.   Copyeditor: Elizabeth Martin
     32 Lafayette Place   Typesetter: Dottie Marsico
     Greenwich, CT 06830   Cover designer: Leslie Haimes

Printed in the United States of America
1 2 3 4 5 6 7 8 9 10 – CM – 02 01 00 99

brief contents

contents

preface

This is a simple yet powerful book about a simple but definitely powerful language, Python. We wrote it because we wanted learning Python to be as easy as using it. Our goal is to teach the fundamentals of Python programming in no more than a few hours, and to expose you to some of the really powerful Python libraries.

Python offers an ease of use and expressive power that may be unmatched by any other language available today. It is suited for short scripts and large programs, and handily beats Perl, C, C++, Java, and every other language we've ever seen, in terms of programmer productivity. It's an exciting time to be learning Python, too. The language is available in a mature, stable form for all major platforms and has an interface to a very powerful multiplatform Graphical User Interface (GUI) toolkit. It is bundled with its own integrated development environment and many new libraries are becoming available. It has even made its debut integrated into the Java language.

To learn Python from this book, you should already know some computer language in reasonable detail. C, C++, Pascal, Perl, Visual Basic, Java, or many others will provide sufficient background. You don't need to be an expert; an understanding of basics such as strings, arrays, loops, conditional (if-then) statements, and so forth, will be fine.

Familiarity with object-oriented programming is a plus. However, if you don't know anything about OOP (and perhaps don't want to), that's all right. Python is also an excellent procedural language.

Python may also be one of the easiest programming languages to learn. This book is designed so that you can use it to quickly become proficient. Our intent is to provide more than just a beginner's tutorial. Our plan is that even after you've become a more experienced Pythoneer, it will continue to be very valuable to you as an indexed cache of information for those concepts and constructs you will most often want to review.

special thanks

One of the pleasures of writing a book on Python has been the opportunity it has presented for interacting with members of the Python community. Many of its key members spared time from their work of continuing the development of the Python language itself to give freely and enthusiastically of their expertise to enrich this book.

Foremost we must thank those who contributed four of the key advanced topic chapters to the book. Andy Robinson, who wrote the chapter on COM; Guido van Rossum and Kirby Angell, the Jpython chapter; Robin Friedrich, the chapter on HTMLgen; and Brian Lloyd and Amos Latteier, the chapter on ZOPE. These individuals contributed their work in the full sense and due to their efforts 20% of the royalties for the book will go to the Python Software Activity (PSA).

Next we want to thank our technical reviewers: Brian Benjamin, Fred L. Drake, John Grayson, Garret G. Hodgson, Jeremy Hylton, Daniel Larsson, Fredrik Lundh, Ken Manheimer, Mike Meyer, William Park, Tim Peters, Robert J. Roberts, Guido van Rossum, Michael Smus, Barry Warsaw and Jean-Claude Wippler. Their detailed feedback has resulted in significant improvements to this book both in its form and its content.

Finally, we need to thank all the friendly people at Manning Publications who turned it into an actual book. This list includes publisher Marjan Bace, who spearheaded the project; Ted Kennedy, who coordinated the review efforts; Mary Piergies, who saw it through the production phase; Elizabeth Martin, the copyeditor, and Dottie Marsico, the book's effective typesetter.

about the authors

DARYL HARMS holds a Ph.D. in computer science. He has been working on the design and the development (or the management of the development) of small and large software systems since the mid-1980s. He is currently a software development consultant working out of Calgary, Alberta and can be reached at ddharms@yahoo.com.

KENNETH MCDONALD holds a B.Sc. and M.Sc. in computer science, and has studied programming languages extensively. He is currently a Technical Writer at Be, Inc., in Menlo Park, California. Among other duties, he is implementing a C++ automatic documentation system entirely in—of course—Python! Previous to this he worked at Washington University in St. Louis on the Human Genome Project as a programmer/analyst.

Contributors

KIRBY W. ANGELL began using Python and JPython in August 1998. He is a Microsoft certified solution developer, a consultant, and technology writer living in Oklahoma City, Oklahoma. He can be reached at kirbyangell@hotmail.com.

ROBIN FRIEDRICH has been a Python enthusiast since 1993 and founded Python Professional Services Inc. in 1997. Since graduating from Georgia Tech with a degree in aerospace engineering in 1984, his primary career has been space shuttle trajectory design as well as computer systems engineering at Johnson Space Center in Houston, Texas. He helped make Python a standard scripting language for engineering automation tasks at JSC. He also wrote and maintains HTMLgen—a class library for the creation of web pages with Python.

AMOS LATTEIER is a software engineer working for Digital Creations Inc. a web software company known for its contributions to the Python community. Digital Creations publishes Zope and develops commercial solutions based on Zope. Latteier has written extensively about Zope.

BRIAN LLOYD is also a software engineer working for Digital Creations Inc. He is the original author of Python CE, a version of Python for PDAs and other handheld devices.

ANDY ROBINSON is an independent consultant specializing in object-oriented analysis and design in the financial sector. He started programming with a Sinclair ZX80 eighteen years ago.

In the past decade he has worked in advertising, in a large investment bank, and spent three years as the finance director of a startup business. Having noticed that, whatever his official job, he always ended up having to fix the computers in his office, he bowed to the inevitable and has been developing software full-time for three years.

GUIDO VAN ROSSUM created Python in the early 1990s and still manages its development. He works as a researcher for the Corporation for National Research Initiatives, where he uses Python to develop infrastructural software for the Internet of the future.

about the cover illustration

The cover illustration of this book is from the 1805 edition of Sylvain Maréchal's four-volume compendium of regional dress customs. This book was first published in Paris in 1788, one year before the French Revolution. Its title alone required no fewer than 30 words.

Costumes Civils actuels de tous les peuples connus dessinés d'après nature gravés et coloriés, accompagnés d'une notice historique sur leurs coutumes, moeurs, religions, etc., etc., redigés par M. Sylvain Maréchal

The four volumes include an annotation on the illustrations: "gravé à la manière noire par Mixelle d'après Desrais et colorié." Clearly, the engraver and illustrator deserved no more than to be listed by their last names—after all they were mere technicians. The workers who colored each illustration by hand remain nameless.

The colorful variety of this collection reminds us vividly of how culturally apart the world's towns and regions were just 200 years ago. Dress codes have changed everywhere and the diversity by region, so rich at the time, has faded away. It is now hard to tell the inhabitant of one continent from another. Perhaps we have traded cultural diversity for a more varied personal life—certainly a more varied and exciting technological environment. At a time when it is hard to tell one computer book from another, Manning celebrates the inventiveness and initiative of the computer business with book covers based on the rich diversity of regional life of two centuries ago, brought back to life by Maréchal's pictures. Just think, Maréchal's was a world so different from ours people would take the time to read a book title 30 words long.

author online

Purchase of *The Quick Python Book* includes free access to a private Internet forum where you can make comments about the book, ask technical questions, and receive help from the author and from other Python users. To access the forum, point your Web browser to http://www.manning.com/Harms. There you will be able to subscribe to the forum. This site also provides information on how to access the forum once you are registered, what kind of help is available, and the rules of conduct on the forum.

Source code for the major examples provided in this book is available from the publisher's website.

Starting out 1

C H A P T E R   1

About Python

Read this chapter if you want to know how Python compares to other languages, and its place in the Grand Scheme of Things. Skip this chapter if you want to start learning Python right away. The information in this chapter is a valid part of this book—but it's certainly not necessary for programming with Python.

1.1 Why should I use it?

Python is a modern programming language developed by Guido van Rossum. It is in use by hundreds of thousands of programmers around the world, and the number is at least doubling every year.

Python is attracting new users for a variety of reasons. It can be used to develop applications far more rapidly than traditional languages such as C, C++, or Java. It is a true cross-platform language, running equally well on Windows, UNIX, Macintosh, and OS/2. It can be used to develop small applications or scripts, but scales well to permit development of large programs. It offers access to a powerful and easy-to-use graphical user interface (GUI) toolkit. It's free.

1.2 A look at languages

Everyone has a favorite programming language. Mine is obviously Python.* However, each language has its own advantages and disadvantages, and only by understanding these strengths and weaknesses can we be sure of selecting the tool that's right for us.

Table 1.1 defines important properties of various languages on a scale of Poor, Fair, Good, or Excellent. Poor means that if the given property is important to you, you probably don't want to use this language. Fair means you can use the language if the given property is important to you but you may encounter some frustrations. Good means the property is well implemented or available to the language. Excellent denotes best of breed—you can't do significantly better than this.

A table like this is subjective, and I realize it includes my biases, both in the ratings and the choices of categories (i.e., it does not illuminate Java's advantages over other languages in its portability and distribution capabilities). See the notes after the table for an explanation of how I define and evaluate each property.

Table 1.1 A comparison of languages

	(1) Execution speed	(2) Coding speed	(3) Object-orientation	(4) GUI coding	(5) Dev. Environ.	(6) Suitability for large tasks	(7) Libraries available
Python	Fair	Excellent	Excellent	Good*	Fair	Excellent	Good
Perl	Fair	Excellent	Fair	Good*	Fair	Fair	Excellent
Tcl/Tk	Fair	Good	Fair	Excellent	Good	Poor	Good
Vis. Basic	Good	Excellent	Fair	Excellent	Excellent	Poor	Fair
C	Excellent	Poor	Poor	n/a	Excellent	Good	Good
C++	Excellent	Fair	Excellent	n/a	Excellent	Excellent	Good
Java	Fair	Good	Excellent	Good	Excellent	Excellent	Good

* Using the Tk GUI package.

1 How fast your program will execute is one of the important aspects of a programming language. Python and Perl function similarly with respect to speed, while Tcl is slower. These languages are fast for "byte-compiled" code, but much slower than good C or C++ programs, which lead in the speed competition. Java gets a fair rating because it still is not living up to the performance claims that have been made for it. Perhaps this will change in the future.

---

* An unrelated note about the book's format: we collaborated on some segments, but often wrote portions separately. We used personal pronouns and did not indicate which of us had written the subsection or chapter. Our working assumption that differentiation between us was not important to the understanding of the information and would not likely be of significant interest to the reader.

2   Coding speed refers to how quickly you can do a project in the language. This measures the "expressiveness" and design of the language. Languages that permit you to perform powerful actions with little code usually win this competition. Perl and Python get top marks. Tcl offers less expressivity but the difference isn't large. Visual Basic uses visual programming to make implementation very fast, if the task is one for which the language is suited. C and C++ bring up the rear, since they require far more detailed code to accomplish most tasks. Java is a noticeable improvement in this regard, as it learned from some of the flaws of C and C++.

3   Object-oriented programmers are unlikely to want to work without OO features in their languages, which leaves out C and Tcl. Add-ons such as IncrTcl provide OO support, but are not always compatible with the most recent version of Tcl. Python, C++, and Java were all designed as OO languages and provide excellent support. Visual Basic has been modified to support some degree of OO programming, but is not ideal.

4   The ability to implement a good GUI is crucial to many programs. This was a tough section to rate and I expect to get the most disagreements here. Perl, Python, and Tcl can all use the excellent Tk GUI package to develop GUIs. But using Tk from Perl and Python is typically more difficult than using it from Tcl. Visual Basic offers a visual development environment which lets you "draw" your GUI, instead of coding it, a feature which appeals to many. There is no standard GUI package for C and C++, so your experience will depend on the package you use; hence, I give no rating. Implementing a GUI in Java has come a long way since the early days with AWT 1.0, and has the potential to reach excellent. However, as of this writing, it faces stability issues and its tools and libraries are still maturing.

5   A development environment consists of things like a special-purpose editor, interactive debugger, code management system, and so forth, preferably all in an integrated package. Perl and Python suffer in the context of a development environment; something like Emacs can be used, but it is not as convenient or as easy to use as more modern GUI-based development environments. However, as IDLE (Python's new integrated development environment) matures, Python is poised to move up in this category. Scriptics, the company started by the originator of Tcl, offers products for supporting Tcl development. Mature GUI-based development environments are available for Visual Basic, C, C++, and Java.

6   Suitability for large tasks is another metric of a language design, i.e., whether a language has features that support the complexity as programs grow in size. Tcl is specifically intended for use in relatively small programs, though some have pushed the envelope. Perl has more features to support programming-in-the-large, but is not ideal for this, due to syntactic complexity, and a lack of certain features such as structured exceptions. Visual Basic is intended for quickly building interfaces to other programs, and can run into code management problems when used for larger projects. Python, C, C++, and Java all have good support for large scale programming, though the age of C in some respects (e.g., no object orientation) can be a drawback.

7   The availability of good packages and libraries for use with a language can significantly enhance the productivity of using that language. Perl is the leader here because

of the number of packages available for download, organized by the Comprehensive Perl Archive Network (CPAN) web sites. Python and Tcl also fare well; they have less available, but still have most of the breadth of the Perl offerings, and generally the libraries offered are of high quality. VB suffers somewhat because most of the good libraries offered for it are commercial. This is not necessarily bad, but it adds to the cost, and, more importantly, it is very difficult for a second-party commercial library to become standard in the field, which means many of those commercial libraries will probably become obsolete in the foreseeable future. C, C++, and Java all have large numbers of packages available, but finding and evaluating an appropriate package can be so much trouble that people often resort to writing their own.

1.3 A comparison of Python and other languages

The next subsections attempt to give an idea of what Python feels like in relation to other languages. These subsections are certainly not complete comparisons. The information is offered to help you decide if you will be comfortable with Python.

1.3.1 Python versus C, Pascal, C++, and Java

Traditional computer languages such as C and Pascal share characteristics which give them a similar feel: strong typing, static typing, complex (and typically lengthy) compile cycles, and the need for large amounts of code to accomplish relatively small tasks. Java is new, but shares most of these characteristics, and so is included in this category.

Programmers familiar with traditional languages will find it easy to learn Python. All of the familiar constructs such as loops, conditional statements, arrays, and so forth are included, but many are easier to use in Python. Here are a few of the reasons why:

- Memory management is completely automatic.
  There is no need to worry about allocating or deallocating memory, and no danger of dangling references. Java is the only one of the aforementioned traditional-style languages to offer this.
- Types are associated with objects, not variables.
  A variable can be assigned a value of any type, and a list can contain objects of many different types. It also means that type casting is usually not necessary. Traditional languages do not offer this, although Java comes close.
- Python operations are typically carried out at a much higher level of abstraction.
  This is partly a result of the way the language is built, and partly the result of an extensive standard code library that comes with the Python distribution. A program to download a web page can be done in two or three lines!
- Syntax rules are very simple.

Python permits rapid application development. It isn't unusual for coding an application in Python to take one-fifth the time it would if coded in C, and take up as little as one-fifth the lines of the equivalent C program. This is dependent on the particular application, of course; for a numerical algorithm performing mostly integer arithmetic in `for` loops, there would be much less of a productivity gain. For the average application, the productivity gain can be significant.

A possible drawback with Python is its speed of execution. It is not a fully compiled language. Instead, it is first semi-compiled to an internal byte-code form, which is then executed by a Python interpreter. For some tasks for which very efficient implementations are built into Python, such as string parsing using regular expressions, it can be as fast as, or faster than, any C program you are likely to write, but, in general, using Python will result in slower programs. However, keep this in perspective. Modern computers have so much computing power that for the vast majority of applications, the speed of the language is irrelevant. Java, like Python is a byte-compiled language and is slower than Python at many things, yet people are using it for everything. In addition, it is very easy to extend Python with modules written in C or C++, which can be used to run the CPU-intensive portions of a program.

1.3.2 Python versus Visual Basic

This is a somewhat specialized comparison, but I've included it for a reason. Visual Basic is so entrenched in many corporate environments that new programmers may be unaware that there are alternatives. This is unfortunate, because, while Visual Basic has some definite strengths, it also has some weaknesses.

Comparing Python and Visual Basic is a difficult exercise. Both are often classified as *scripting* languages, that is, languages aimed at smaller projects, or as ancillary languages in a larger project. While Python may not have the execution speed needed for computationally intensive tasks, it is a highly structured language, and well-suited for building large programs which are not CPU bound, with CPU-intensive modules possibly implemented in C/C++. Visual Basic has more emphasis on speed. Depending on how verbose programmers are with their declarations, VB programs have at least the potential for faster execution than Python programs, but VB lacks the structuring mechanisms to be suitable for large-scale programming.

Let's start with the three most obvious differences:

- Visual Basic is a visual development language; Python is a more traditional editor-driven development language.
  Both languages are capable of building complex GUIs, but VB's entire development environment is based around the idea of drawing things on screen. Python has nothing like this, although various projects are in the works. Some people will prefer the nonvisual approach, but most will probably benefit from VB's visual development environment. Drawing controls on screen is intuitive, can proceed quickly, and reduces certain types of errors. On the other hand, doing everything with code gives the programmer much finer control over the program, encourages data abstraction, and permits much that simply can't be done using a purely visual development environment. To a certain extent, this is a personal preference call, but Visual Basic has the advantage here.
- Visual Basic costs money; Python is free.
  You can install copies of Python on every machine in your network, and not pay a dime.

- Visual Basic is limited to one operating system; Python is a true cross-platform language. If Java is any indication, this is a big draw for many people. If you are only a Windows shop this doesn't matter, and if you are only a UNIX shop, ditto. Many places have a mixture. It isn't so much that machines can share programs, as that programmers can learn (and become expert at) a common language, which they can carry with them no matter what environment they need to program in.

There is a deeper difference between Python and VB which has come about because of the ways in which they were developed. VB has been designed by many people over a period of time and has suffered a degree of bloat and inconsistency as a result. Microsoft has done a good job maintaining backward compatibility and adding language features to VB. However, VB is no longer a clean language, which makes it difficult to learn and to use.

Python has a cleaner design. It can accomplish the same tasks as VB, but with significantly less code:

- In Python, any type of data object can be stored in any variable, and any data object can be written to or read from a file with just two lines of code. This is not possible in VB.
- Exceptions (errors) are handled more cleanly in Python than in Visual Basic. In VB, each error handler must explicitly check each error to see if it is the sort the handler is interested in.
- Python syntax is more consistent than VB syntax.

Realistically, you probably won't be faced with choosing between Python and VB. Visual Basic is clearly not adequate as a system administration or scripting language; it is too complex, and can't be used without a GUI. If you are designing relatively small programs that are primarily GUI-based on Windows machines and are working in a team where most people already know VB, I can guess what your choice will be. If this is your situation, please don't stop reading now. At least check out "Have your language and Python too!" (section 1.5) before making any decisions of that nature!

1.3.3 Python versus Tcl

Tcl and Tk, a pair of scripting tools originally developed by John Ousterhout, have gained a significant following. Tk is a powerful and easy-to-use GUI toolkit, accessible from many languages. Tcl is a scripting language, intended as an improved replacement for the Bourne or C-shell scripting languages.

Tcl is a definite improvement over shell scripting, but is less suited than Python for large programming projects, due to its design. The designer of Tcl intended it as a high-level glue language, as opposed to more general languages such as Python and Perl, which can be used in any role, provided execution speed is not a bottleneck. In fact, Ousterhout specifically excluded object-oriented features from the Tcl language, in significant part because he did not want it used as a general-purpose language.

In spite of this, Tcl has gained a following among people who use it for projects of all sizes. A significant part of its appeal is the availability of the Tk GUI add-on for Tcl, which provides a wonderful library for developing GUI-based programs. Tk is so popular that it is available for many other languages, including Perl and Python, but it is easiest to learn and to use in the context of Tcl. Several good add-ons are available to permit object-oriented programming in Tcl.

For medium to large projects, Python is definitely better than Tcl, and for small projects, such as system administration scripts, the two languages are roughly comparable. The major advantage offered by Tcl is its Tk add-on, and, as I've mentioned, Tk can be used from Python.

1.3.4 Python versus Perl

Of the languages discussed here, Python is closest to Perl. The two can be used in similar roles, although the philosophies that determined the designs of the languages are quite different. I knew and liked Perl long before I knew Python. I now use Python for everything I previously used Perl for, so that should give you some idea of what this section will say. Without being critical of Perl, I believe Python is the natural successor to Perl.

Both languages offer lists, hash tables, object-oriented programming, excellent string handling, and other high-level features.

The major difference is conceptual simplicity. Python was built from the ground up as an extensible, structured, object-oriented language; it draws on languages such as C++ and Modula-3 for foundations. Perl was built initially as a replacement for UNIX shell languages, and draws on languages such as Bourne shell, sed, and awk for inspiration. Higher-level features were added later, as it became apparent the language was being used in arenas far beyond what had originally been envisioned.

This difference shows up in many aspects of the two languages:

- In Python, everything—numbers, strings, lists, hashes, file-objects, and compiled code—is an object, and can be passed around easily; in Perl, lists and hashes must be cast to scalars to pass them into a function, and then must be cast back to lists or hashes to be used.
- In Python, exceptions and exception handlers are an integral part of the language; Perl can achieve the same effect only by encapsulating a call in an `eval` statement, which produces more awkward code.
- In Perl, only a string may be used as a key into a hash table; in Python, almost anything can be used.
- Passing arguments into functions is cleaner and more powerful in Python than in Perl; Python permits named arguments, default argument values, and a number of other things that Perl does not provide.

What does this means in terms of actual code? Below are two short programs, one in Perl and one in Python. They both take two equal sized lists of numbers, and return the pairwise sum of those lists. I think the Python code is more readable than the Perl code; it is visually cleaner, and contains fewer inscrutable symbols.

```
# Python version.
def pairwiseSum(list1, list2):
    result = []
    for i in range(len(list1)):
        result.append(list1[i] + list2[i])
    return result
```

```
# Perl version.
sub pairwiseSum {
    my($arg1, $arg2) = @_;
    my(@result) = ();
    @list1 = @$arg1; @list2 = @$arg2;
    for($i=0; $i < length(@list1); $i++) {
        push(@result, $list1[$i] + $list2[$i]);
    }
    return(\@result);
}
```

This is not to say that Perl's syntax and semantics do not offer advantages. The Perl example is probably more verbose than necessary, because I was trying to make the code as clear as possible. There are instances where quickness of coding is more important than clarity, such as with throwaway system administration scripts. This is an area where Perl excels; a programmer can implement in a few lines what might take a page in another language.

In addition, Perl is in wide use and there is an incredible selection of Perl packages for almost any task under the sun. Python has similar modules for most things, but lacks some of the most specialized packages, and does not offer the same depth of selection in the most generally used packages.

In spite of all of this I will answer "Yes" if asked, "Is Python what Perl should have been?" Python is cleaner, easier to learn, and far more suited to large programming projects than is Perl. The languages are roughly equivalent in speed and capability, though Python possesses some significant features that are difficult or impossible to emulate in Perl. The converse is not true, to my knowledge. Perl is better than Python at its original task—fast system administration scripting—but Python can be easily used in this capacity.

1.4 What's the catch?

Python isn't the perfect solution to everything. As already mentioned, its drawback, which it shares with other rapid application development languages, is execution speed. To evaluate this factor, and come to a real decision as to whether or not Python will be useful to you, an understanding of the lower-level issues is needed.

Rapid Application Development (RAD) languages take care of many aspects of programming that, in traditional languages, need to be handled explicitly by the programmer's code. As an example, with a traditional language such as C, a programmer must explicitly declare an array before using it, giving both the type of the data to be stored in it and the size of the array. This permits extremely efficient allocation of the necessary memory, because the amount needed is known before the program is ever run—a block of memory of the appropriate size is simply reserved for that use. In Python, the array may expand (or shrink) as needed during the running of the program and any sort of object may be stored in it. This imposes two hidden costs. If the array grows beyond the space initially allocated, the entire array must be copied to a location where there is more free memory (or something equivalent will need to be done.) Also, since any type of object may be stored, Python doesn't know what it has when it extracts something from an array. If that object is used with a + operator, Python will have to check to see if the object is a number (in which case the + means addition) or a string (in which case the + means string concatenation.) Both factors will slow execution of the Python program. On the other hand, the flexibility offered by this approach greatly eases the programming process.

In real terms, this typically means execution speed between functionally equivalent Python and C programs differs by several factors, with 3x – 5x being not unusual. Many things can influence this. For highly numerical computations, a C program may be 10x faster or more. For intensive text processing, if you make use of the extremely efficient string facilities built into Python, your Python program will often execute at the same speed as a C program, while taking a fraction of the time to implement. Using the advanced canvas widget in the Tkinter GUI library will let you develop a highly efficient object-oriented paint program that would take a lot of effort if implemented directly in C.

As a general rule, implement CPU-bound tasks in C/C++ or a similar language. For almost anything else, Python is a viable language.

1.5 *Have your language and Python too!*

Of course, you can take a mixed approach, and get the best of both worlds.

You can develop most of your program in Python, but write the computationally intensive parts in C/C++ modules that interface directly with your code by extending the Python language. This is easy and efficient. After the application is complete, it can be collected into a single run-time file for distribution, using Python's freeze utility. Modules for certain computationally intensive tasks, such as matrix arithmetic, exist for Python, so you may not need to write any C/C++ code. A chapter on extending Python with C/C++ is included in this book (chapter 23).

It is also possible to meld Java and Python. The ability has been developed to compile Python code to Java bytecode. One can seamlessly interface Python and Java. It, in effect, allows one to use Python's higher level RAD and scripting capabilities in Java projects. The end result is 100% Java and runs on any Java virtual machine (JVM). This is described further in chapter 24.

Finally, using a nice Component Object Model (COM) package developed for Python, it is possible to integrate it with Visual Basic. This can be used to add Python's logic handling, scripting or web authoring capabilities to Visual Basic programs. This can be a great option to consider when a simple program grows beyond what was originally envisaged and what is easily developed in Visual Basic. Andy Robinson walks you through this in chapter 22. This is not limited to Visual Basic. Any COM compliant language implementation (i.e., Visual C++ or Delphi) can be interfaced to in the same manner.

1.6 *Python and open source software*

Python was originally, and continues to be, developed under the Open Source model and it's freely available.

Although this is changing, some people are still leery of free software because of concerns about a lack of support, fearing they lack the clout of a paying customer.

Python is a very stable, reliable, and well-supported product. It has a very active and knowledgeable user group. You'll get an answer to even the most difficult Python question more quickly on the Python internet newsgroup than you will on most tech-support phone lines, and the Python answer will be free and correct.

There really are no guarantees of getting all of your problems solved. This is software after all! The above applies to the core Python language. At some point you may find the robustness or functionality of one of its auxiliary modules and packages or the level of free support available for it not up to the level you need for your specific purposes. But the fact that the source is open means that you do have the ability, if something is critical to you, of going in yourself (or hiring someone to go in and get it solved for you). This is an option you rarely have at any reasonable cost with proprietary software.

The following is for those whom this will be their first foray into the world of Open Source software. You are free to use Python to produce both free and/or proprietary software with it. You will be welcome to ask questions on the Python newsgroup about problems you encounter. When you are first learning, you probably will not have that much to contribute. Also, your work and personal time constraints and priorities may curtail you from being involved in the community. However, if at some point you find yourself in a position to give back, definitely consider it. Something of significant value is being created here, and you have an opportunity to contribute to it.

This contribution may be financial. You may join the Python Software Advisory (PSA) individually or convince your company to sign up. It may be technical. You may begin answering questions on the newsgroup, joining one of the Special Interest Groups (SIGs), and/or testing and giving feedback on releases of the Python core or one of the auxiliary modules. You might even find yourself in a position to contribute some of what you or your company develops back to the community. There is also always the opportunity to get involved in the development and enhancement of the existing modules and packages. The level of your contribution (if any) is, of course, totally up to you.

1.7 Summary

Python is a modern, high-level language, with many features:

- Automatic memory management.
- Dynamic typing.
- Simple, consistent syntax and semantics.
- Multiplatform.
- Well-planned design and evolution of features.
- Highly modular.
- Suited for both scripting and large-scale programming.
- Reasonably fast and easily extended with C or C++ modules for higher speeds.
- Easy access to various GUI toolkits.
- Built-in advanced features such as persistent object storage, advanced hash tables, expandable class syntax, universal comparison functions, and so forth.
- Powerful libraries such as numeric processing, image manipulation, user interfaces, web scripting, and others.
- Supported by a dynamic Python community.
- Can be integrated with a number of other languages to let you take advantage of the strengths of both while obviating their weaknesses.

CHAPTER 2

About this book

2.1 How to use this book

There is nothing quite so tedious as an overly long technical book. A number of measures have been taken to make *Quick Python* as, well, as quick as possible, but this does require some explanation.

2.1.1 Organization

Basic topics come first, both in the book and within each chapter; advanced topics come later.

The book is organized so you can start reading from the front and, more or less, continue reading until you know as much as you want or need to know. The most basic and important information is at the beginning of the book, with later chapters becoming more specialized. Within each chapter basics are described before anything else, and if you reach a point in a chapter where the content is no longer of interest, skip ahead to the next chapter.

It's impossible in any technical book to avoid referring to language details that are described only later in the text, and this work is no exception. Where forward references

13

do occur, they are clearly indicated, and usually a simplified definition of a future concept is presented, so that you can avoid skipping ahead.

2.1.2 Sidenotes

Use sidenotes to skim through a chapter.

To make it *really* easy to go through a chapter rapidly, sidenotes describing the core aspects of Python have been inserted into the text. These sidenotes can be used to obtain a clear idea of what is in a chapter, without reading any of the body text. Sidenotes tersely describe a significant point, without going into details. Use them to easily skim a section whose contents are somewhat familiar, or to rapidly locate a precise piece of information within a chapter.

2.1.3 The alert marker

!!!

The triple exclamation points alert marker shown in the margin indicates a section in the book which is critical to understanding and making effective future use of either Python, or the book itself. When you see these explanation marks, *please* read the accompanying text. If I could make the alert marker flash, I would.

2.2 *Learning Python by example*

!!!

Please read this section and the following section. This book relies heavily on code examples, most of which can be executed at your computer as you read. The following sections describe how to use the examples, and various conventions which have been adopted to make examples clearer.

Python can be used interactively.

One of the great things about learning Python is that it can be used in a completely interactive mode. Instead of writing a program, compiling, and running it to see what happens, you can type in a Python command and see the result immediately. This feature is also the easiest way to resolve a question that is not adequately answered by documentation. Becoming comfortable with the Python interactive mode is strongly recommended.

2.3 *Formatting conventions for code examples*

Code examples are the single most important element in illustrating a new programming language. Code examples found in many computer books often use an unattractive, monospaced font, can be overly dense, and bury nuggets of desirable information in a large amount of uninteresting code. I've tried to make the examples in *Quick Python* more approachable by using small examples and by using formatting to clarify the presentation. The interactive nature of the Python language is a big help in this. One is usually able to focus directly on what one is trying to learn, without needing a lot of the support code that may be necessary with other languages.

2.3.1 Interactive examples

There are two types of code examples in *Quick Python*. The first, and most common, is the interactive example, which illustrates Python features via a sample interactive session.

Every interactive example will start with a little box containing the Python command prompt,

```
>>>
```

This indicates that you can type the example into your computer and get the indicated result, if I haven't goofed.

Additionally, I'll use different font styles within interactive examples, to make clear input, **output**, and the *result of evaluating an expression*. Here is a small example of the different font styles you might see; a brief description of each is given in the example, and a longer explanation afterwards:

```
>>>
```

```
>>> print "Your command does here"        ❶ Input font
Your command goes here                     ❷ Output font
>>> x=3000
>>> y=4000
>>> x + y
⇒   7000        ❸ Result font
>>>print x + y
7000
```

❶ Statements to be entered by you are given in input font, and start with the same command prompt ">>>" you'd see on the screen.

❷ Text printed to the screen as a result of executing commands is printed in **output** font. You'll see this on screen, even if the commands were executed noninteractively.

❸ Some code returns a result which can be seen when using Python interactively, but which would not be printed to the screen by a running program. Such results are shown using *result* font.

The difference between what you type to the screen (nonbold) and what the computer displays on the screen in response (bold) is obvious, but the difference between something printed in *result* font and something printed in **output** font requires explanation. Using the print command prints something to the screen, regardless of whether that command is executed in a program, or interactively at the >>> prompt—this is what is shown in **output** font. However, when you're using Python interactively, there's something else that looks like printing to the screen, but isn't.

Like any other computer language, Python supports *expressions*. An expression is a piece of code that is evaluated and returns a value. For example, the code "3 + 4" evaluates to and returns the value 7. It doesn't actually do anything; the value it returns has to be used by whatever Python code contained the original expression. If the Python interactive interpreter contained that expression, then Python automatically prints that result to the screen, so you can see what that result was. This is what we show using *result* font. In a program, the result of that expression, instead of being printed to the screen, would be used internally in the program by the containing code.

Sometimes it will be convenient to break up a long interactive example or series of related examples with explanatory text. To make clear that an interactive session is intended as a continuation of the previous interactive session, we'll preface it with a box containing ellipses:

Ellipses in a box indicates a continued interactive example.

```
...
```

```
>>> z = x + y
```

Also, in this book we will most often use single-letter variable names in the interactive examples. This is not to suggest that this is a good coding standard to emulate in actual code. Rather, the purpose is to have the syntax and keywords of the language stand out while you are learning the language.

2.3.2 Noninteractive examples

Most examples in this book are of the small, interactive variety, but more complex concepts sometimes require actual pieces of code, such as might be seen in a real Python program. I use special formatting for these noninteractive examples, too, but it's different than the formatting used with the interactive examples, because the intent is to draw your attention to the points being illustrated by the code.

Noninteractive code examples use boldface to highlight relevant code, and may include placeholders representing other code. Comments are given in an italic Roman font.

The noninteractive code examples can be easily identified because they do not start with a small box with the Python command prompt. In addition, **boldface code** font is used to highlight those parts of the code that relate to the topic of discussion; other comments may appear in a *comment* font. You may also see instances of *placeholders* in long code examples—these are words which, in a real code example, would be replaced with other code.

As an example of the sort of thing you'll see in noninteractive examples, here is a bit of code pulled from an example later in the book.

```
# Replace 'filename' with an expression which returns
# an appropriate file name.
f = open(filename, 'r')
occurrences = {}
for word in f.readlines():
    if occurs.has_key(word):
        occurs[word] = occurs[word] + 1
    else:
        occurs[word] = 1
```

In its original context, the code elements, which were of particular relevance, were the braces, brackets, and the has_key function. Only those parts of the code were in bold.

The examples in this book will probably be smaller than you are used to from other programming language books. Don't let this fool you into thinking you are not learning anything significant. The built-in features and interpreted nature of Python allow its concepts and constructs to be shown with smaller code segments than is possible for many other languages.

Note also that the intention of these examples is usually to introduce, illustrate, or facilitate the understanding of specific features of the language. They are not generally intended to be cookbook examples of production code. The fact that Python is an open source project means that there are already lots of examples of Python code available to you in electronic form anyway.

2.4 *What you will find in this book*

This book has been designed to allow the reader who is new to Python to quickly obtain a solid working understanding of the Python language. However, it also covers a number of more advanced topics so as to still be of value at different stages of the reader's exploration and use of the language. This section gives a brief synopsis of each of the chapters in this book. Use it as a guide for planning your use of the book.

PART 1 puts in all the initial groundwork to prepare you to get the most out of this book and be in a position to start learning Python.

Chapter 1 discusses the strengths and weaknesses of Python in comparison with the most popular languages currently in wide use.

Chapter 2 describes the mechanics of how this book is organized and what it covers. Its purpose is to provide suggestions on how to use the rest of the book.

Chapter 3 covers downloading, installing, and starting up the Python interpreter and IDLE, its integrated development environment.

PART 2 is the heart of the book. It covers the ingredients necessary for obtaining a working knowledge of Python as a general purpose programming language. The chapters are designed to allow the readers who are beginning to learn Python to work their way sequentially through, picking up knowledge of the key points of the language. They also contain some more advanced sections, allowing the reader to return to find in one place all the necessary information about a construct or topic. First-time readers are informed when the topic of a section is not necessary on a first pass.

A suggested plan if you are new to Python is to start by reading chapter 4 to obtain an overall perspective, then work through the rest of the chapters that are applicable. Enter in the interactive examples as they are introduced. This will immediately reinforce the concepts. You can also easily go beyond the examples in the text to answer questions about anything that may be unclear. This has the potential to amplify the speed of your learning and the level of your comprehension. If you are not familiar with OOP, or simply don't need it for your application, skip most of chapter 16. If you are not interested in developing a GUI, skip chapter 17.

Those familiar with Python should also start with chapter 4. It will be a good review and will introduce differences between our terminology and what may be more familiar. It's a reasonable test of whether you're ready to move on to the advanced chapters in section 4 of this book. You can also quickly browse through any of the chapters using the side notes.

It is possible that some readers, who, although new to Python, will have enough experience with other programming languages to be able to pick up the bulk of what they need to get going from chapter 4 and the appendix reference.

Chapter 4 begins with a short overview of the Python language. This should provide a basic idea of the philosophy, syntax, semantics, and capabilities of the language.

Chapter 5 starts with the basics of Python. It introduces Python variables, expressions, strings, and numbers. It also introduces Python's block structured syntax.

Chapters 6, 7, and 8 describe the four powerful built-in Python data types: lists, tuples, strings, and dictionaries.

Chapter 9 introduces Python's control flow syntax and use (loops and `if-else` statements).

Chapter 10 describes function definition in Python along with its flexible parameter-passing capabilities.

Chapter 11 describes Python modules. They provide an easy mechanism for segmenting the program namespace.

Chapter 12 describes how to work and navigate through the files and directories of the filesystem. It shows how to write code which is as independent as possible of the actual operating system being worked on.

Chapter 13 introduces the mechanisms for reading and writing files in Python. These include the basic capability to read and write strings (or byte streams), the mechanism available for reading binary records, and the ability to read and write arbitrary Python objects.

Chapter 14 discusses the use of exceptions, the error handling mechanism used by Python. It doesn't assume the reader has any prior knowledge of exceptions, although a reader who has previously used them in C++ or Java will find them familiar.

Chapter 15 discusses the creation and execution of scripts (or programs) in Python. The chapter also covers the support available for command line options, arguments and I/O redirection.

Chapter 16 introduces Python's support for writing object-oriented programs.

Chapter 17 focuses on the available Tk interface and ends with an introduction to some of the other options available for developing GUIs.

PART 3 introduces advanced language features of Python, elements of the language which are not essential to its use, but which can certainly be a great help to a serious Python programmer.

Chapter 18 introduces the package concept in Python for structuring the code of large projects.

Chapter 19 covers the simple mechanisms available to dynamically discover and work with data types in Python.

Chapter 20 introduces the use of Python's special method attributes mechanism. This is similar to but more general than operator overloading.

Chapter 21 discusses the regular expression capabilities available for Python.

PART 4 describes more advanced or specialized topics. The focus is on interfacing Python to the rest of the world. Readers may read these chapters or not, depending on their needs.

In chapter 22, contributor Andy Robinson walks the reader through examples using the excellent PythonCOM package created by Mark Hammond. He shows how easily the reader can create a PythonCOM server which can be used by a Visual Basic client. He also shows how to pull data from a Python server into an Excel session and how to use Python on the client side of COM to enter and retrieve data from Access, or launch Excel or Word and push data to them. Next he shows how Python scripts can be run from the Windows Scripting Host, then he introduces some of the other miscellaneous capabilities of PythonCOM (such as its ODBC connectivity, its MFC wrappers, and Sam Rushing's extension for calling Windows DLLs from Python).

Chapter 23 discusses the excellent support for writing extensions to Python in C or C++.

Chapter 24, contributed by Guido van Rossum (the originator of Python) and Kirby Angell, illustrates the value of combining Java and Python. It introduces JPython,* which allows the compilation of Python code to Java bytecode. It runs on any JVM and lets you use Python's RAD and scripting capabilities in Java projects.

Chapter 25, contributed by Robin Friedrich, takes the user through examples of the use of HTMLgen, which he wrote. HTMLgen is very effective for the automatic generation of static web pages and simple CGI programming.

Chapter 26, written by Brian Lloyd and Amos Latteier, is a tutorial introducing the ZOPE system and showing examples of its use. ZOPE is a powerful web building environment. It is excellent for sites that require the interactive presentation and manipulation of data.

Chapter 27 is a very short chapter which mentions some of the other Python modules and packages which are available but were not covered in this book.

The *appendix* is a semiformal reference summarizing the Python language constructs covered in the chapters of parts 2 and 3.

2.5 *Where to find more information*

The intention of this book is to first focus on giving a solid grounding in the core of the Python language. Next, it is an initial guide that introduces the library modules that are expected to be of most interest and value to the majority of its readers. It provides everything required to write serious programs in Python. It should also serve as an effective indexed reference to the material covered.

The number of modules and packages available for Python precludes including descriptions here of everything that is available. Fortunately, there are a lot of other resources available to you for this. Python is a well documented language.

In the text of this book you may be specifically referred to the *Python Library Reference* to obtain further details on various functions or modules. It comes in HTML format with the Python installation. Use it also to find details about any of the other library modules (those that come with Python and can be accessed through the `import` statement) that may be of interest to you.

There is also the excellent *Python Tutorial*, which comes in HTML format with Python, as well as a number of articles which are linked to off of the Python home page.

The official Python home page is http://www.python.org. This is where you obtain the Python source and executables. It contains a FAQ entry and an effective search engine.

The Python Internet newsgroup is comp.lang.python. It is active and a conduit to tap into the wealth of knowledge available from the people around the world who are developing and using Python. Its archives can be readily searched at http://www.dejanews.com

---

* If your interest is solely to use JPython, we suggest that you first read the beginning of the JPython chapter to get perspective on how you will be able to use JPython. Next, return to chapter 4 and work your way through part 2 of this book. Obtaining a solid understanding of Python's constructs will equip you with the tools to make the most effective use of the power it can provide you in your JPython developments. Once you have this grounding, you can return to the JPython chapter to be introduced to the JPython specifics which allow you to integrate with Java code. At the time of this writing there are not yet any JPython specific development environments. However, you can use IDLE or Emacs for editing your code, then cut and paste into the JPython shell.

If you don't have access to post news or are not comfortable broadcasting to the newsgroup, email your questions to python-help@python.org. Your message will be sent to a small group of volunteers.

There are also a number of special interest groups (SIGs) that focus on specialized topics (i.e. databases, string-processing, and XML) and maintain their own mailing lists. Descriptions of them and their archives can be found on the Python home page.

If this is your first experience with an interpreted language be sure to make full use of the interactive mode to try out more than just the examples we introduce in this book.

Also, take advantage of the fact that this is an Open Source project and you can easily obtain, look through, and learn from other people's code. You can start by using IDLE, Python's integrated development environment, to browse through the library modules.

2.6 Feedback

Any feedback is most welcome. Of special interest are any concepts you found confusing or topics or points you wished had been included. Feel free to send your comments to ddharms@yahoo.com.

CHAPTER 3

Getting started

This chapter guides you through downloading, installing, and starting up Python and IDLE. At the time of this writing, the Python language itself is fairly mature. It is going through what would be more aptly called refinement rather than major change. Further these enhancements are being developed with concern to avoid impacting an already significant existing code base. Therefore, the text of parts 2 and 3 will not likely become dated any time soon. However, the details of this chapter are subject to more change. IDLE, for example, is new with the 1.5.2 release. It will no doubt evolve significantly as it matures. However, I suspect that since this will be an evolution, what is presented here will still be useful as a base from which to work.

3.1 *Installing Python*

The most recent Python release will be at http://www.python.org.

Installing Python is a simple matter, regardless of which platform you are using. The first step is to obtain a recent distribution for your machine; the most recent one can always be found at http://www.python.org. This book is based on 1.5.2.

Some platform-specific descriptions for the Python installation are given below. There are instructions on the download pages and with the various versions. You are also probably already familiar with installing software on your particular machine, so I'll keep these descriptions short.

- *Microsoft Windows* Python can be installed in Windows 95, 98, or NT by using the Python installer program, currently called py152.exe. Just download it, execute it, and follow instructions (answer yes if asked if you want to install Tcl/Tk as this is necessary for IDLE). There are also older versions of Python that will run under DOS, and previous versions of Windows. If possible, avoid these; they are not as up-to-date, and installation is more difficult. If you're installing on Windows NT, you should be logged in as administrator to run the install. If you're on a network and don't have the administrator password, ask your system administrator to do the installation for you.
- *Macintosh* There are several different Python distributions for the Macintosh. Some support all Macintoshes, some reduce memory requirements by supporting only PowerPC Macintoshes. Some reduce resource requirements even further by stripping out a few of the most resource-intensive packages, typically the GUI and image-related packages. For anyone using a reasonably modern Macintosh, the correct distribution is probably the full distribution for PowerPC Macintoshes. Simply download it, decompress it, and run it. We won't be giving much specific information for Macintosh users in the rest of this book. This information can be found by following the links off of the Python home page. (Specifically, see Jack Jansen's page.)
- *UNIX* There are precompiled versions of Python for some of the different UNIXs out there. However, it is usually very easy to compile, so probably the best thing to do is just download the source, uncompress it, and follow the instructions in the README file. If you're a Linux user, you may even already have it. Red Hat typically comes with Python. If not, there are RPMs available. If you're networked, you can of course ask your system administrator to install it.

There are versions available for running Python under many other operating systems: Amiga, OS/2, BeOS, QNX, VMS, and Windows CE. See the web pages for specifics.

3.2 IDLE and the basic interactive mode

With the April 1999 release of version 1.5.2 of Python, there are two built-in options for obtaining interactive access to the Python interpreter: the original basic (command line) mode and IDLE. At the time of this writing, IDLE is available on the UNIX and Windows platforms. It still may not be available on others. You may need to do more work to get IDLE running, but it will be worth it as it is a large step up from the basic interactive mode. Even if you normally use IDLE, there still will likely be times you will want to fire up the basic mode. It will be useful to be familiar enough to start and use either one.

3.2.1 The basic interactive mode

The basic interactive mode is a rather primitive environment. However, the interactive examples in this book are generally quite small and at a later point in this book, you will also learn how to easily bring code you've placed in a file into your session (using the module mechanism).

Starting a basic session on Windows: for version 1.5.2 of Python, you navigate to the Python (command line) entry of the Python 1.5 submenu of the Programs folder of the Start menu and click on it. You can alternatively directly find the Python.exe executable (i.e. in `C:\Program Files\Python`) and double click on it. This should bring up a window (figure 3.1).

Starting a Basic Session on UNIX: type python at a command prompt. A version message similar to the one in figure 3.1 followed by the Python prompt ">>>" should appear in your current window.

On many of the UNIX and some of the other platforms there is a command line editing and a command history mechanism. (See "Basic Python interactive mode summary" at the end of the appendix.) This would be all you need to work your way through this book as you're learning Python. But IDLE is a significant improvement over it. So I suggest you use it instead if it is available to you. Another option is to use the excellent Python mode available for Emacs, which, among other things, provides access to the interactive mode of Python through an integrated shell buffer.

On Windows 95/98, this basic mode is more bare bones. It does not have command history and the only line editing functionality is the backspace character. However, your favorite editor can be used with the "cut and paste from clipboard" functionality. (Again, see "Basic Python interactive mode summary" in the appendix for more details.) You could get by with this as you work through this book while you learn Python. However, I strongly suggest that you use IDLE as it is such a nice step up.

Figure 3.1 The basic interactive mode on Windows 95/98

3.2.2 The IDLE Integrated Development Environment

Starting IDLE on Windows: for version 1.5.2 of Python, you navigate to the IDLE (Python GUI) entry of the Python 1.5 submenu of the Programs folder of your Start menu and click on it. You can alternatively directly find the idle.pyw executable (i.e. in `C:\Program Files\Python\Tools\idle`) and double click on it. This should bring up a window (figure 3.2).

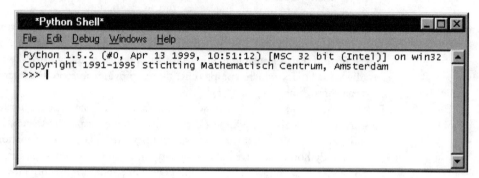

Figure 3.2 IDLE on Windows

If the window does not appear, Tcl/Tk may not be properly set up on your PATH. To fix this in Windows 95/98, open up `C:\autoexec.bat`* in NOTEPAD and find the line that sets your PATH variable:

```
set PATH=c:\windows;c:\windows\COMMAND
```

Add ;C:\PROGRA~1\Tcl\bin to this line:

```
set PATH=c:\windows;c:\windows\COMMAND;C:\PROGRA~1\Tcl\bin
```

Be sure to include the single semicolon between what is on the existing line and this addition. Save the file. You need to restart your computer for this to take effect.

In Windows NT, you can modify your PATH through the System Control Panel.

Starting IDLE on UNIX: just type idle at a command prompt. This should bring up a Window similar to the one above.

IDLE is the exciting addition to version 1.5.2 of Python. Its name is an acronym of Integrated DeveLopment Environment (of course, it might also have been influenced by the last name of a certain cast member of a particular British television show).

It is being actively developed by Guido van Rossum and will likely evolve significantly from where it stands at the time of this writing. Because it is continuing to mature, I will not go into the full details of all of its screens and the specifics of their use. I will instead maintain a web document detailing its use which you can access as a link from this book's web page (http://www.manning.com/Harms). The web page will be kept up to date for new releases of IDLE.

---

* Note that autoexec.bat may be on another drive on your particular machine.

To begin, I suggest you stick with the Python Shell window. It is the one that is first brought up. It is all you will need to use to work through the code examples in this book until you reach "Modules and scoping rules" (chapter 11). There I will discuss using IDLE to open up editor windows for writing your own modules, and a number of its other functions.

3.3 Hello, world

'>>>' is the Python command prompt.

Regardless of how you are accessing Python's interactive mode, you should see a prompt consisting of three angle braces: >>>. This is the Python command prompt, and indicates you can type in a command to be executed, or an expression to be evaluated. Start with the obligatory "Hello, World" program, which is a one-liner in Python. (End each line you type with a carriage return, and of course, don't type the ← arrows or anything after them.)

```
>>> print "Hello, World"    ← This is the command prompt and what you type after it.
Hello, World                ← This is what is printed to the screen.
```

Executing the `print` statement causes its argument to be printed to the standard output, usually the screen. If the command had been executed while Python was running a Python program from a file, exactly the same thing would have happened, that is "Hello, World" would have been printed to the screen. Congratulations! You've just written your first Python program, and we haven't even started talking about the language.

To exit IDLE choose Exit from the File menu. To exit from a basic session, type a CTRL-Z (if you are on Windows); or a CTRL-D (if you are on UNIX) at a command prompt.

3.4 Using IDLE's Python Shell window

The Shell window (figure 3.3) will open when you fire up IDLE. It provides automatic indentation and colorizes your code as you type it in, based on Python syntax types.

You can move around the buffer using the mouse, the arrow keys, the Page Up/Page Down keys, and/or a number of the standard Emacs key bindings. Check the Help menu for the details.

Everything in your session is buffered. You can scroll or search up and place the cursor on any line, hit enter or carriage return and that line will be copied to the bottom where you can edit it and then send it to the interpreter by hitting the Enter key again. Or, leaving the cursor at the bottom, you can toggle your way up and down through the previously entered commands using ALT-P and ALT-N. This will successively bring copies of the lines to the bottom. When you have the one you want, you can again edit it and then send it to the interpreter by hitting the Enter key. Python keywords or user-defined values will be completed by entering ALT-/.

If you ever find yourself in a situation where you seem to be hung and cannot get a new prompt, the interpreter is likely in a state where it is waiting for you to enter something specific. Hitting CTRL-C will send an interrupt and should get you back to a prompt. It can also be used to interrupt any running command.

The Edit menu is the one you'll likely be using the most to begin with. Like any of the other menus, you can tear it off by double clicking on the dotted line at its top and leave it up beside your window (figure 3.3).

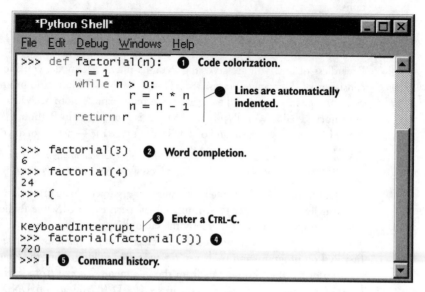

Figure 3.3 Python Shell window

❶ Code is automatically colorized (based on Python syntax) as it is typed in.

❷ Just had to type "f" here followed by and ALT-/ and automatic completion finished off "factorial".

❸ Lost the prompt, so entered a CTRL-C to interrupt the interpreter and get the prompt back (a closed bracket would have worked here as well).

❹ Placing the cursor on any previous command and pressing the Enter key causes it and the cursor to be moved to the bottom where you can edit it and then hit Enter again to send it to the interpreter.

❺ Placing the cursor at the bottom, you can toggle up and down through the history of previous commands using ALT-P and ALT-N. When you have the one you want, edit it as desired, hit Enter and it will be sent to the interpreter.

The essentials 2

CHAPTER 4

The Quick Python overview

4.1 About this chapter

The purpose of this chapter is to give you a basic feeling for the syntax, semantics, capabilities, and philosophy of the Python language. It has been designed to provide you with an initial perspective or conceptual framework upon which you will be able to add details as you encounter them in the rest of the book.

On an initial read, you needn't be concerned about working through and understanding the details of the code segments. You will be doing just fine if you simply pick up a bit of an idea of what is being done. The subsequent chapters of this book will walk you through the specifics of these features and won't assume prior knowledge. You can always return and work through the examples in the appropriate sections as a review, once you've read the later chapters.

4.2 Python synopsis

Python has a number of built-in data types such as integers, long integers, floats, complex numbers, strings, lists, tuples, dictionaries, and file objects. These can be manipulated using language operators, built-in functions, library functions, or a data type's own methods.

Programmers can also define their own classes and instantiate their own class instances.* These can be manipulated by programmer-defined methods as well as the language operators and built-in functions for which the programmer has defined the appropriate special method attributes.

Python provides conditional and iterative control flow through an `if-elif-else` construct along with `while` and `for` loops. It allows function definition with flexible argument passing options. Exceptions (errors) can be raised using the `raise` statement and caught and handled using the `try-except-else` construct.

Variables do not have to be declared and can have any built-in data type, user-defined object, function, or module assigned to them.

4.3 Built-in data types

4.3.1 Numbers

Python's four number types are: integers, long integers, floats, and complex numbers:

integers:	1, –3, 42, 355
long integers:	42L, 888888888888888L, –7777777777L
floats:	3.0, 31e12, –6e-4
complex numbers:	3 + 2j, –4- 2j, 4.2 + 6.3j

They can be manipulated using the arithmetic operators: + (addition), – (subtraction), * (multiplication), / (division), ** (exponentiation), and % (modulus).

Integers

```
>>> x = 5 + 2 - 3 * 2
>>> x
⇒ 1
>>> 5/2
⇒ 2
>>> 5 % 2
⇒ 1
>>> 2**8
⇒ 256
```

● **Integers are based on the longs in C. Integer division results in truncation.**

Long integers

```
>>> 1000000001L ** 3
1000000003000000003000000001L
```

● **Long integers are of unlimited precision. (They will grow as large as you need them to.)**

---

* The Python documentation and this book use the term "object" to refer to instances of any Python data type, not just for class instances.

Floats

```
>>> x = 4.3 ** 2.4
>>> x
⇒    33.1378473777
>>> 3.5e30 * 2.77e45
⇒    9.695e+075
>>> 1000000001.0 ** 3
⇒    1.000000003e+027
```

● Floats are based on the doubles in C. You can use long integers to emulate many floating point operations when you need precise accuracy. However, floats are more efficient and quicker.

Complex numbers

```
>>> (3 + 2j) ** (2 + 3j)
⇒    (0.681766519089-2.12074577662j)
>>> x = (3+2j) * (4+9j)
>>> x
⇒    (-6+35j)
>>> x.real
⇒    -6
>>> x.imag
⇒    35.0
```

● Variable "x" has been assigned to a complex number. Its "real" part can be obtained using the "attribute" notation x.real

There are a number of built-in functions that can operate on numbers. There is also the library module cmath (that contains functions for complex numbers) and the library module math (that contains functions for the other three types):

```
>>> round(3.49)
⇒    3.0
>>> import math
>>> math.ceil(3.49)
⇒    4.0
```

❶ Built-in function

❷ Library module function

❶ Built-in functions are always available and are called using a standard function calling syntax. Here round is called with a float as its input argument.

❷ The functions in library modules are made availalable using the import statement. Here the math library module is imported and its ceil function is called using attribute notation: module.function(arguments).

4.3.2 Lists

Python has a powerful built-in list type.

```
[ ]
[1]
[1, 2, 3, 4, 5, 6, 7, 8, 12]
[1, "two", 3L, 4.0, ["a", "b"], (5,6)]
```

● A list can contain a mixture of other types as its elements, including strings, tuples, lists, dictionaries, functions, fileobjects, and any type of number.

A list can be indexed from its front or back. One is also able to refer to a subsegment or "slice" of a list using slice notation.

```
>>> x = ["first", "second", "third", "fourth"]
>>> x[0]
⇒    'first'
>>> x[2]
```

● Index from the front using positive indices (starting with 0 as the first element).

```
⇒    'third'
>>> x[-1]
⇒    'fourth'
>>> x[-2]
⇒    'third'
>>> x[1:-1]
⇒    ['second', 'third']
>>> x[0:3]
⇒    ['first', 'second', 'third']
>>> x[-2:-1]
⇒    ['third']
>>> x[:3]
⇒    ['first', 'second', 'third']
>>> x[-2:]
⇒    ['third', 'fourth']
```

● Index from the back using negative indices (starting with -I as the last element).

● Obtain a "slice" using [m:n], where m is the starting point and n is the ending point (see table below).

● An [:n] slice will start at its beginning, and an [m:] slice will go to a list's end.

Table 4.1 List indices

x =	[		"first"	,	"second"	,	"third"	,	"fourth"		]
		↑		↑		↑		↑		↑	
Positive indices		0		1		2		3		4	
Negative indices		−4		−3		−2		−1			

This notation can be used to add, remove, and replace elements from a list or to obtain an element or a new list which is a slice from it:

```
>>> x = [1,2,3,4,5,6,7,8,9]
>>> x[1] = "two"
>>> x[8:9]
>>> x
⇒    [1, 'two', 3, 4, 5, 6, 7, 8]
>>> x[5:7] = [6.0, 6.5, 7.9]
>>> x
⇒    [1, 'two', 3, 4, 5, 6.0, 6.5, 7.0, 8]
>>> x[5:]
⇒    [6.0, 6.5, 7.0, 8]
```

● The size of the list will be increased or decreased if the new slice is bigger or smaller than the slice it is replacing.

Some built-in functions (len, max, and min), some operators (in, +, and *), the del statement, and the list methods (append, count, extend, index, insert, pop, remove, reverse, and sort) will operate on lists. A number of these repeat functionality that can be performed with slice notation but improve code readability.

```
>>> x = [1,2,3,4,5,6,7,8,9]
>>> len(x)
⇒    9
>>> [-1,0] + x
```

● The operators + and * will each create a new list leaving the original unchanged.

```
⇒    [-1, 0, 1, 2, 3, 4, 5, 6, 7, 8, 9]
>>> x.reverse()
>>> x
⇒    [9, 8, 7, 6, 5, 4, 3, 2, 1]
```

● **A list's methods are called using attribute notation on the list itself: `x.method(arguments)`.**

4.3.3 Tuples

Tuples are similar to lists but are *immutable*, that is they cannot be modified once they have been created. The operators (`in`, `+`, and `*`) and built-in functions (`len`, `max`, and `min`), operate on them the same as they do on lists, as none of them modify the original. Index and slice notation works the same for obtaining elements or slices, but cannot be used to add, remove, or replace elements. There are also no tuple methods. A major purpose of tuples is for use as keys for dictionaries. They are also more efficient to use when you don't need modifiability.

```
( )
(1,)
(1, 2, 3, 4, 5, 6, 7, 8, 12)
(1, "two", 3L, 4.0, ["a", "b"], (5,6)) ❶
```

● **A one element tuple needs a comma.**

❶ A tuple, like a list, can contain a mixture of other types as its elements, including strings, tuples, lists, dictionaries, functions, fileobjects, and any type of `number`.

A list can be converted to a tuple using the built-in function `tuple`:

```
>>> x = [1.2.3.4]
>>> tuple(x)
⇒    (1,2,3,4)
```

Conversely, a tuple can be converted to a list using the built-in function `list`:

```
>>> x = (1,2,3,4)
>>> list(x)
⇒    [1,2,3,4]
```

4.3.4 Strings

String processing is one of Python's strengths. There are many options for delimiting them:

```
"A string in double quotes can contain 'single quote' characters."
'A string in single quotes can contain "double quote" characters.'
'''\tThis string starts with a tab, ends with a newline character.\n'''
"""this is a triple double quoted string. The only kind which can
contain real newlines""" ❶
```

❶ Strings can be delimited by single (' '), double (" "), triple single (''' ''') or triple double (""" """) quotations and can contain tab `\t` and newline `\n` characters.

Strings are also immutable. The operators and functions that work with them return new strings derived from the original. The operators (`in`, `+`, and `*`) and built-in functions (`len`, `max`, and `min`), operate on strings as they do on lists and tuples. Index and slice notation works the same for obtaining elements or slices, but cannot be used to add, remove, or replace elements. There are two major library modules (`string` and `re`) which contain functions for working with strings.

```
>>> import string                          ❶ The string module
>>> x = "live and     let \t   \tlive"
>>> string split(x)
⇒ ['live', 'and', 'let', 'live']
>>> string replace(x, "    let \t  \tlive", "enjoy life")
⇒ 'live and enjoy life'
>>> string translate(x, string.maketrans{'i','o'), '\t')
⇒ 'love and     let     love'

>>> import re                               ❷ The re module
>>> regExpr = re.compile(r"[\t ]+")
>>> regEpr.sub(" ", x)
⇒ 'live and let live'
```

❶ The `string` module has functions for such things as splitting a string into its constituent words, finding and/or replacing strings, translating characters in a string, and capitalizing or changing the case of words in a string.

❷ The `re` module provides regular expression functionality. It provides more sophisticated pattern extraction and replacement capability than the `string` module.

The `print` statement will output strings. Other Python data types can be easily converted to strings and formatted:

```
>>> e = 2.718                                                              ❶
>>> x = [1, "two", 3L, 4.0, ["a", "b"], (5,6)]
>>> print "The constant e is: ", e, " and the list x is: ", x
The constant e is: 2.718 and the list x is: [1, 'two', 3L, 4.0,
 ['a', 'b'], (5, 6)]
>>> print "the value of %s is: %.2f" % ("e", e)    ❷
the value of e is: 2.72
```

❶ Objects are automatically converted to string representations for printing.

❷ The modulus (%) operator provides a formatting capability similar to that of C's sprintf.

4.3.5 Dictionaries

Python's built-in dictionary data type provides an associative array functionality implemented using hash tables. The built-in `len` function will return the number of key-value pairs in a dictionary. The `del` statement can be used to delete a key-value pair. As is the case for lists, there are also a number of dictionary methods (`clear`, `copy`, `get`, `has_key`, `items`, `keys`, `update`, and `values`) available.

```
>>> x = { 1:"one", 2:"two"}              'Keys' must be immutable.
>>> x["first"] = "one"                   Values' may be any kind of
>>> x[("Delorme", "Ryan", 1995)] = (1,2,3) ❶ object.
>>> x.keys()
⇒ ['first', 2, 1, ('Delorme', 'Ryan', 1995)]
>>> x[1]
⇒ 'one'
>>> x.get(1, "not available")
```

```
⇒    'one'
>>> x.get(4,"not available")      ❷ The get dictionary
⇒    'not available'                   method
```

❶ "Keys" must be of a nonmodifiable (immutable) type. This includes numbers, strings, and tuples. "Values" can be of any kind of object, including mutable types such as lists and dictionaries.

❷ The dictionary method get optionally returns a user-definable value when a key is not in a dictionary.

4.3.6   File objects

A file is accessed through a Python file object.

```
>>> f = open("myfile", "w")      ❶ Open "myfile" in write mode.
>>> f.write("First line with necessary newline character\n")
>>> f.write("Second line to write to the file\n")
>>> f.close()
>>> f = open("myfile", "r")      ● After writing two lines to it and closing
>>> line1 = f.readline()            it, the same file is opened again, this
>>> line2 = f.readline()            time in the read ("r") mode.
>>> f.close()
>>> print line1, line2
First line with necessary newline character
Second line to write to the file

>>> import os                    ❷ The os module
>>> print os.getcwd()
c:\My Documents\test            Here, we move to another directory. ●
>>> os.chdir(os.path.join("c:","My Documents", "images"))
>>> FileName = os.path.join("c:", "My Documents",      ● But by referring
...    "test", "myfile")                                  to the file by an
>>> print FileName                                        absolute
c:\My Documents\test\myfile                               pathname we
>>> f = open(FileName, "r")                               are still able to
>>> print f.readline()                                    access it.
First line with necessary newline character

>>> f.close()
```

❶ The open statement creates a file object. Here the file "myfile" in the current workng directory is being opened in write ("w") mode.

❷ The os module provides a number of functions for moving around the file system and working with the pathnames of files and directories.

There are a number of other available input/output capabilities. The built-in input and raw_input functions can be used to prompt and respectively obtain a Python expression or string from the user. The sys library module allows access to stdin, stdout, and stderr. The struct library module provides support for reading and writing files that were generated by or are to be used by C programs. The cPickle library module delivers data persistence through the ability to easily read and write the Python data types to and from files.

4.4 Control flow structures

4.4.1 Boolean values and expressions

Python does not have a specific Boolean data type. Instead, 0, the Python nil value `None`, and empty values (i.e., the empty list [ ] or empty string"") are all taken as `false`. Anything else is considered `true`.

Comparison expressions can be created using the comparison operators (`<, <=, ==, >, >=, !=, <>, is, is not, in, not in`) and the logical operators (`and, not, or`) which all will return a `1` for a `true` and `0` for a `false` value.

4.4.2 The if-elif-else statement

The block of code after the first `true` condition (of an `if` or an `elif`) is executed. If none of the conditions are `true`, the block of code after the `else` is executed.

```
x = 5
if x < 5:
    y = -1
    z = 5
elif x > 5:
    y =1
    z = 11
else:
    y = 0
    z = 10
print x, y, z
```

● The `elif` and `else` clauses are optional and there can be any number of `elif` clauses.

Python uses indentation to delimit blocks. No explicit delimiters such as brackets or braces are necessary. Each block consists of one or more statements separated by newlines. These statements must all be at the same level of indentation.

4.4.3 The while loop

The `while` loop is executed as long as the condition (which here is x>y) is `true`.

```
u, v, x, y = 0, 0, 100, 30
while x > y:
    u = u + y
    x = x - y
    if x < y +2:
        v = v + x
        x = 0
    else:
        v = v + y +2
        x =x -y -2
print u, v
```

● This is a shorthand notation. Here u and v are assigned a value of zero, x is set to 100, and y obtains a value of 30.

● The loop block. It's possible for it to contain `break` (which ends the loop) or `continue` statements (which abort the current iteration of the loop).

The output here would be `60  40`.

4.4.4 The for loop

The `for` loop is simple but quite powerful as it is possible to iterate over any group of items that can be in a list or tuple. The following loop finds the first occurrence of an integer that is divisible by seven:

```
ItemList = [3, "string1", 23, 14.0, "string2", 49, 64, 70]
for x in ItemList:              ●  x is sequentially assigned
    if type(x) != type(1):          each value in the list.
        continue            ❶

    if not x % 7:
        print "found an integer divisible by seven: %d" % (x)
        break               ❷
```

❶ If x is not an integer, then the rest of this iteration is aborted by the continue statement. Flow control continues with x set to the next item from the list.

❷ Once the first appropriate integer is found, the loop is ended by the break statement.

The output here would be

```
found an integer divisible by seven: 49
```

4.4.5 Function definition

Python provides flexible mechanisms for passing arguments to functions.

```
def funct1(x, y, z):            ●  Functions are defined using
    value = x + 2*y + z**2          the def statement.
    if value > 0:
        return x + 2*y + z**2   ❶  The return statement
    else:
        return 0

>>> u, v = 3,4
>>> funct1(u, v, 2)
⇒  15
>>> funct1(u, z=v, y=2)         ❷  Named arguments
⇒ 23

def funct2(x, y=1, z=1):        ❸  Parameters defined with defaults
    return x + 2*y + z**2

>>> funct2(3, z=4)
⇒  21

def funct3(x, y=1, z=1, *tup):  ●  A special parameter can be defined
    print (x,y,z)+ tup             which will collect all extra positional
                                   arguments in a function call into a tuple.
>>> funct3(2)
⇒  (2, 1, 1)
>>> funct3(1,2,3,4,5,6,7,8,9)
⇒  (1, 2, 3, 4, 5, 6, 7, 8, 9)

def funct4(x, y=1, z=1, **dict): ●  Likewise, a special parameter can
    print x, y, z, dict             be defined which will collect all
                                    extra keyword arguments in a
>>> funct4(1, 2, m=5, n=9, z=3)     function call into a dictionary.
⇒  1 2 3 {'n': 9, 'm': 5}
```

❶ The return statement is what a function uses to return a value. This value can be of any type. If no return statement is encountered, Python'sNone value will be returned.

② Function arguments can be entered either by position or by name (keyword). Here z and y are entered by name.

③ Function parameters can be defined with defaults that are used if a function call leaves them out.

4.4.6 Exceptions

The built-in exceptions (errors) can be caught and handled using the `try-except-else` compound statement. It can also catch and handle exceptions we define and raise ourselves. Any exception that is not caught will cause the program to exit.

```
class EmptyFileError(Exception): ❶
    pass

FileNames = ["myfile1","nonExistent", "emptyFile", "myfile2"]
for file in FileNames:                    ❷
    try:
        f = open(file,'r')              ⌐
        line = f.readline()             ❸
        if line == "":
            f.close()
            raise EmptyFileError("%s: is empty" % (file))
    except IOError, error:
        print "%s: could not be opened: %s" % (file, error[1])
    except EmptyFileError, error:
        print error[0]
    else:
        print "%s: %s" % (file, f.readline())
        f.close()
```

Here we raise the EmptyFileError. ●

else clause (optional) ❹

❶ Here we define our own exception type inheriting from the base Exception type.

❷ If an `IOError` or `EmptyFileError` occurs during the execution of the statements in the `try` block, the associated `except` block will be executed.

❸ This is where an `IOError` might be raised.

❹ The `else` clause is optional. It is executed if no exception occurs in the `try` block (note that in this example `continue` statements in the `except` blocks could have been used instead).

4.5 Module creation

It is very easy to create one's own modules, which can be imported and used in the same way as Python's built-in library modules. The following example is a simple module with one function which prompts the user to enter a file name and determines the number of times words occur in this file.

File wo.py

```python
"""wo module. Contains function: WordsOccur()"""    ❶ Documentation string

# other modules used by this module                 ● Comments are anything beginning
import string                                          with a # character.

# interface functions

def WordsOccur():
    """WordsOccur() - count the occurrences of words in a file."""

    # Prompt user for the name of the file to use.
    fileName = raw_input("Enter the name of the file: ")

    # Open the file, read it and store its words in a list.
    f = open(fileName, 'r')
    wordList= string.split(f.read())    ❷
    f.close()

    # Count the number of occurrences of each word in the file.
    occursDict = {}
    for word in wordList:
        # increment the occurrences count for this word
        occursDict[word] = occursDict.get(word, 0) + 1

    # Print out the results.
    print "File %s has %d words (%d are unique)" \    ❸
        % ( fileName, len(wordList), len(occursDict) )
    print occursDict

if __name__ == '__main__':
    WordsOccur()
```

Documentation string ❶

Comments are anything beginning with a # character.

This allows the program to also be run as a script by typing "python wo.py" at a command line.

❶ Documentation strings are a standard way of documenting modules, functions, methods, and classes.

❷ read will return a string containing all the characters in a file and split will return a list of the words of a string "split out" based on whitespace.

❸ A \ can be used to break a long statement across multiple lines.

If a file is placed in one of the directories on the module search path, which can be found in sys.path, then it can be imported like any of the built-in library modules using the import statement.

```
>>> import wo
>>> wo.WordsOccur()
⇒
```

Our function is called using the same attribute syntax as used for library module functions.

Note that if you change the file wo.py on disk, import will not bring your changes in to the same interactive session. You use the built-in reload function in this situation:

```
>>> reload(wo)
⇒    <module 'wo'>
```

For larger projects, there is a generalization of the module concept called *packages*. This allows you to easily group a number of modules together in a directory or directory subtree and import and hierarchically refer to them using a `package.subpackage.module` syntax. This entails little more than the creation of a possibly empty initialization file for each package or subpackage.

4.6 Object-oriented programming

Python provides full support for OOP. Below is an example that might be the start of a simple shapes module for a drawing program. It is intended mainly to serve as reference for readers already familiar with object-oriented programming. The callout notes relate Python's syntax and semantics to the standard features found in other languages.

File sh.py

```
"""sh module. Contains classes Shape, Square and Circle"""

class Shape:
    """Shape class: has method move"""

    def __init__(self, x, y):
        self.x = x
        self.y = y

    def move(self, deltaX, deltaY):
        self.x = self.x + deltaX
        self.y = self.y + deltaY

class Square(Shape):
    """Square Class:inherits from Shape"""

    def __init__(self, side=1, x=0, y=0):
        Shape.__init__(self, x, y)
        self.side = side

class Circle(Shape):
    """Circle Class: inherits from Shape and has method area"""

    pi = 3.14159

    def __init__(self, r=1, x=0, y=0):
        Shape.__init__(self, x, y)
        self.radius = r

    def area(self):
        """Circle area method: returns the area of the circle."""
        return self.radius * self.radius *self.pi

    def __str__(self):
        return "Circle of radius %s at coordinates (%d, %d)"\
               % (self.radius, self.x, self.y)
```

- ● **Classes are defined using the `class` key word.**
- ● **The instance initializer method (constructor) for a class is always called `__init__`.**
- ● **Instance variables x and y are created and initialized here.**
- ● **Class `Circle` inherits from class `Shape`.**
- ● **Similar to, but not exactly like a standard class variable.**
- ● **A class must, in its initializer, explicitly call the initializer of its base class.**

❶ Methods, like functions, are defined using the `def` keyword. The first argument of any method is by convention called `self`. When the method is invoked, `self` is set to the instance which invoked the method.

❷ The __str__ method is used by the print statement. Other special attribute methods permit operator overloading or are employed by built-in methods such as the length (`len`) function.

Importing this file makes these classes available.

```
>>> import sh
>>> c1 = sh.Circle()
>>> c2 = sh.Circle(5,15,20)
>>> print c1
Circle of radius 1 at coordinates (0, 0)
>>> print c2
Circle of radius 5 at coordinates (15, 20)
>>> c2.area()
⇒ 78.53975
>>> c2.move(5,6)
>>> print c2
Circle of radius 5 at coordinates (20, 26)
```

● **The initializer is implicitly called and a circle instance is created.**

● **The `print` statement implicitly uses the special __str__ method.**

❶

● **Here we see that the `move` method of `Circle`'s parent class `Shape` is available.**

❶ A method is called using attribute syntax on the object instance: `object.method()`. The first (`self`) parameter is set implicitly.

4.7 Summary

This ends our overview of Python. Don't worry if some parts were confusing. You only need to have an understanding of the broad strokes at this point. The rest of the chapters here in section 2 and in section 3 won't assume prior knowledge of their concepts and will walk you through these features in detail. You can also think of this as an early preview of what your level of knowledge will be when you are ready to move on to the chapters in part 4. You may find it valuable to return here and work through the appropriate examples as a review once you cover the features in subsequent chapters.

If this was mostly a review, or there were only a few features you would like to learn about more, jump ahead, using the index, the table of contents, or the appendix, or the sidenotes. You can always slow down if anything catches your eye. You probably should have an understanding of Python to the level where you have no trouble understanding most of this chapter before you move on to chapters in part 4.

C H A P T E R 5

The absolute basics

This chapter describes the absolute basics in Python: assignments and expressions, how to type a number or a string, how to indicate comments in code, and so forth. It starts out with a discussion of how Python block-structures its code, which is different from any other major language.

5.1 *Indentation and block-structuring*

!!! Python differs from most other programming languages because it uses white space and indentation to determine block structure (i.e., determine what constitutes the body of a loop, the `else` clause of a conditional, etc.). Most languages use braces of some sort to do this. Here is C code that calculates the factorial of 9, leaving the result in the variable r:

```
/* This is C code */
int n, r;
n = 9;
r = 1;
while (n > 0) {
```

42

```
    r = r * n;
    n--;
}
```

The { and } delimit the body of the `while` loop, the code that is executed with each repetition of the loop. The code is usually indented more or less as shown, to make clear what's going on, but it could also be written:

```
/* And this is C code with arbitrary indentation */
    int n, r;
        n = 9;
        r = 1;
    while (n > 0) {
r = r * n;
n--;
}
```

and still execute correctly, even though it is rather difficult to read.

Here is the Python equivalent:

```
# This is Python code. (Yea!)
n = 9
r = 1
while n > 0:
    r = r * n
    n = n - 1
```

The block-structure of a Python program is determined by its indentation.

Python does not use braces to indicate code structure; instead, the indentation itself is used. The last two lines of the above code are the body of the `while` loop because they come immediately after the `while` statement and are indented one level further than the `while` statement. If they weren't indented, they wouldn't be a part of the body of the `while`.

Using indentation to structure code, rather than braces, may take some time getting used to. There are some significant benefits:

1   It is impossible to have missing or extra braces. You will never need to hunt through your code for the brace near the bottom that matches the one a few lines from the top.

2   The visual structure of the code reflects its real structure. This makes it easy to grasp the "skeleton" of code just by looking at it.

3   Python coding styles are mostly uniform. In other words, you're unlikely to go crazy from dealing with someone's idea of "aesthetically pleasing" code. Their code will look pretty much like yours.

You probably use consistent indentation in your code already, so this won't be a big step for you. If you are using IDLE, it will automatically indent lines. You just need to backspace out of levels of indentation when desired. Emacs provides this functionality as well. One thing that may trip you up once or twice until you get used to it is that the Python interpreter will return an error message if you have a space (or spaces) preceding the commands you enter at a prompt.

5.2 Comments

Comments begin with #.

For the most part, anything following a # symbol in a Python file is a comment, and is disregarded by the language. The obvious exception is a # in a string, which is just a character of that string.

```
# Assign 5 to x
x = 5
x = 3      # Now x is 3
x = "# This is not a comment"
```

We'll put comments into Python code quite frequently, but when we do, we'll also italicize them, to make it obvious they're just comments

5.3 Variables and assignments

Assignments take the form var=value. *Variables will come into existence as needed.*

The most commonly used command in Python is assignment, which looks pretty close to what you might've used in other languages. Python code to create a variable called 'x' and assign the value 5 to that variable is:

```
x = 5
```

In Python, neither a variable type declaration, nor an end of line delimiter is necessary unlike in many other computer languages. The line is ended by the end of the line. Variables are created automatically when they are first assigned.

Python variables can be set to any object, unlike C or most other languages' variables, which can store only the type of value they are declared as. The following is perfectly legal Python code:

```
>>>
>>> x = "Hello"
>>> print x
⇒   Hello
>>> x = 5
>>> print x
⇒   5
```

x starts out referring to the string object "Hello" and ends by referring to the integer object 5. Of course, this feature can be abused. Arbitrarily assigning the same variable successively to different data types can make code confusing to understand.

A new assignment will clear a variable of its previous contents. The del statement will delete the variable itself. Trying to print its contents after deleting it will give an error the same as if it had never been created in the first place.

```
>>> x = 5
>>> print x
5
>>> del x
>> print x
Traceback_(innermost last):
  File "<stdin>", line 1, in ?
```

```
NameError: x
>>>
```

A traceback will tell us what type of error (called an exception) occurred.

Here we have our first look at a *traceback*, which is printed when an error, called an *exception*, has been detected. The last line tells us what exception was detected, which in this case is a `NameError` exception on x. After its deletion, x is no longer a valid variable name. In this example the trace returns only: `line 1 in ?` as we only have the single line that has been sent in the interactive mode. In general, the full dynamic call structure of the existing function calls at the time of the occurrence of the error will be returned. If you are using IDLE you will obtain the same information with some small differences as it may look something like this:

```
Traceback (innermost last):
  File "<pyshell#3>", line 1, in ?
    print x
NameError: x
```

The chapter on *Exceptions* will describe this mechanism in more detail. There is a full listing of the possible exceptions and what causes them in the appendix of this book. Use the index to find any specific exception (such as `NameError`) you receive.

Variable names are case sensitive and can include any alphanumeric character as well as underscores, but must start with a letter or underscore.

5.4 Expressions

Python supports arithmetic and similar expressions; these will be quite familiar to most readers. The following code calculates the average of 3 and 5, leaving the result in the variable z.

```
x = 3
y = 5
z = (x + y)/2.0
```

Note the use of the floating-point divisor in the above expression. Python's arithmetic rules follow those of C in terms of type coercions, which means that arithmetic operators involving only integers always return an integer. Using 2.0 as the divisor coerces the result to a floating-point number, so the fractional part is not truncated.

Standard rules of arithmetic precedence apply; if we'd left out the parentheses in the last line, it would've been calculated as `x+(y/2.0)`.

Expressions don't have to involve just numerical values; strings, Boolean values, and many other types of objects can be used in expressions in various ways. These will be discussed in more detail as they are used.

5.5 Strings

You've already seen that Python, like most other programming languages, indicates strings through the use of double quotes, . This line leaves the string "Hello, World" in the variable x.

```
x = "Hello, World"
```

Backslashes in
strings can be
used to escape
characters.

Backslashes can be used to escape characters, to give them special meanings. \n means the newline character, \t means the tab character, \\ means a single normal backslash character, and \" is just a plain double quote character. It doesn't end the string.

```
x = "\tThis string starts with a \"tab\"."
x = "This string contains a single backslash(\\)."
```

Strings can be
enclosed in single
quotes or double
quotes.

Single quotes can be used instead of double quotes; the following two lines do the same thing:

```
x = "Hello, World"
x = 'Hello, World'
```

The only difference is that you don't need to backslash " characters in single-quoted strings, or ' characters in double-quoted strings:\

```
x = "Don't need a backslash"
x = 'Can\'t get by without a backslash'
x = "Backslash your \" character!"
x = 'You can leave the " alone'
```

You can't split a "normal" string across lines; this code won't work:

```
# This Python code will cause an ERROR—you can't split the string across two lines.
x = "This is a misguided attempt to
put a newline into a string without using backslash-n"
```

However, Python offers triple-quoted strings, which will let you do this, and permit single and double quotes to be included without backslashes:

```
x = """Starting and ending a string with triple " characters
permits embedded newlines, and the use of " and ' without
backslashes"""
```

Now x is the entire sentence between the """ delimiters. (And you could also use triple single quotes—'''—instead of triple double quotes, to do the same thing.)

Python offers enough string-related functionality that a chapter is devoted to the topic.

5.6 Numbers

!!!

Because the reader is likely familiar with standard numeric operations from other languages, this book does not contain a separate chapter describing Python's numeric abilities. This section describes the unique features of Python numbers, and the reference appendix lists the available functions.

Python offers four kinds of numbers; *integers*, *long integers*, *floats*, and *complex numbers*. An integer is just written as an integer; 0, –11, +33, 123456. A float can be written with a decimal point, or using scientific notation; 3.14, –2E-8, 2.718281828. The precision of these values is governed by the underlying machine, but is typically equal to long (32-bit) and double (64-bit) types in C. A Python long integer is written as an integer followed by a lowercase or capital L; 3L, 12l, 144L, –256L. It behaves like a normal integer, but has unlimited precision. Complex numbers are probably of limited interest, and are discussed separately, later in the section.

Arithmetic is much like it is in C. Operations involving two integers always produce an integer; operations involving a float always produce a float. Operations involving an integer and a long integer produce a long integer. Operations involving two normal integers will not automatically produce a long integer if the result is too large for a normal integer. Instead, an error will result. Here are a few examples:

```
>>>
>>> 5 +2 - 3 * 2
⇒  1
>>> 5/2          # Two integers produce an integer result with truncation.
⇒  2
>>> 5/2.0        # Involve a float to produce a nontruncated floating point result.
⇒  2.5
>>> 30000000000  # This can't be represented as an integer!
Overflow: integer literal too large
>>> 30000000000L     # It's fine as a long integer, though.
⇒  30000000000L
>>> 30000000000L * 3
⇒  90000000000L
>>> 30000000000L * 3.0
⇒  90000000000.0
>>> 2.0e-8       # Scientific notation gives back a float.
2e-008
>>> 3000000 * 3000000
Traceback_(innermost last):
  File "<stdin>", line 1, in ?
Overflow: integer multiplication
>>> int(200.2)
⇒  200
>>> int(200L)
⇒  200
>>> long(2e2)
⇒  200L
>>> long(200)
⇒  200L
>>> float(200)
⇒  200.0
```

● Integers don't automatically convert to long integers when necessary—multiplying two large normal integers just gives an error.

● The functions int, long, and float can be used to explicitly convert between types. int and long will truncate float values.

5.6.1 Built-in numeric functions

A small number of numeric functions are in the Python core.

Python provides the following number-related functions as part of its core; see the reference appendix for details.

abs, divmod, cmp, coerce, float, hex, int, long, max, min, oct, pow, round.

5.6.2 Advanced numeric functions

More advanced numeric functions such as the trig and hyperbolic trig functions, as well as a few useful constants, are not built into the Python core, but are provided in a standard module called math. Modules will be explained in detail later; for now, it is sufficient to know that the math functions in this section must be made available by starting your Python program or interactive session with the statement:

```
from math import *
```

The `math` module provides the following functions and constants; see the reference appendix for details.

```
acos, asin, atan, atan2, ceil, cos, cosh, e, exp, fabs, floor, fmod,
frexp, hypot, ldexp, log, log10, mod, pi, pow, sin, sinh, sqrt, tan,
tanh.
```

5.6.3 Numeric computation

The core Python installation is not well-suited to intensive numeric computation, due to speed constraints. However, the powerful Python extension NumPy, provides highly efficient implementations of many advanced numeric operations. The emphasis is on matrix operations, including multidimensional matrices and more advanced functions such as the Fast Fourier Transform. NumPy is mentioned briefly later in this book, but you will want to read the documentation included in the NumPy package to get a good idea of what it can do. You should be able to find NumPy (or links to it) at http://www.python.org.

For more specialized needs, it may be appropriate to implement a C extension to Python. This process is discussed later in the book.

5.6.4 Complex numbers

j represents the square root of –1 in Python; complex numbers are of the form `x+yj`.

Complex numbers are created automatically whenever an expression of the form `nj` is encountered, with n having the same form as a Python integer or float. `j` is, of course, standard engineering notation for the imaginary number equal to the square root of –1. For example:

```
>>>
```

```
>>> (3+2j)
⇒   (3+2j)
```

Note that Python expresses the resultant complex number in parentheses, as a way of indicating that what is printed to the screen represents the value of a single object.

```
...
```

```
>>> 3 + 2j - (4 + 4j)
⇒   (-1-2j)
>>> (1 + 2j) * (3 + 4j)
⇒   (-5+10j)
>>> 1j*1j
⇒   (-1+0j)
```

The real and imaginary parts of a complex number can be accessed by dot-suffixing the number with `real` *or* `imag`.

Calculating `j * j` does give the expected answer of –1, but the result remains as a Python complex number object. Complex numbers are never converted automatically to equivalent real or integer objects. However, their real and imaginary parts can be easily accessed with `real` and `imag`:

```
>>> z = 3+5j
>>> z.real
⇒   3.0
>>> z.imag
⇒   5.0
```

Note that real and imaginary parts of a complex number are always returned as floating-point numbers.

!!!

Advanced complex-number functions are contained in the cmath module.

The functions in the math module do not apply to complex numbers; the rationale is that most users want the square root of −1 to generate an error, not an answer! Instead, similar functions, which can operate on complex numbers, are provided in the cmath module:

acos, acosh, asin, asinh, atan, atanh, cos, cosh, e, exp, log, log10, pi, sin, sinh, sqrt, tan, tanh.

In order to make clear in the code that these are rather special-purpose complex-number functions, and to avoid name conflicts with the more normal equivalents, it is probably best to import the cmath module by saying*

```
import cmath
```

and then to explicitly refer to the cmath package when using the function, for example:

```
>>>
```

```
>>> import cmath
>>> cmath.sqrt(-1)
⇒   1j
```

See the "Modules and scoping rules" chapter for more details on how to use modules and module names.

5.7 *The None value*

!!!

None represents the empty or unknown value in Python.

In addition to standard types such as strings and numbers, Python has a special basic data type, which defines a single special data object called None. As the name suggests, None is used to represent an empty value. This appears in various guises throughout Python. For example, a procedure in Python is just a function that does not explicitly return a value, which means that, by default, it returns None.

None is often useful in day-to-day Python programming as a placeholder, to indicate a point in a data structure where meaningful data will eventually be found, even though that data has not yet been calculated. The presence of None can easily be tested for, since there

---

* This is a good example of why it's best to minimize one's use of the from <module> import * form of the import statement. If first the math and then the cmath modules were imported using it, the commonly named functions in cmath would override those of math. It also is more work for someone reading your code to figure out the source of the specific functions you use. There are some modules which are explicitly designed to use this form of import. This will be discussed in the "Modules and scoping rules" chapter.

is only one instance of None in the entire Python system (all references to None point to the same object), and None is equivalent only to itself.

5.8 Built-in operators

Python provides various built-in operators, from the standard (such as +, *, etc.) to the more esoteric, such as operators for performing bit shifting, bitwise logical functions, and so forth. Most of these operators are no more unique to Python than to any other language, and hence will not be explained in the main text. A complete list of the Python built-in operators can be found in the appendix.

CHAPTER 6

Lists and tuples

This chapter discusses the two major Python sequence types: lists and tuples. Lists are a good deal more flexible than the arrays found in most languages.

There is a typed `array` module available in Python which provides arrays based on C data types. Information on its use can be found in the *Python Library Reference*. I suggest you only look into it if you run into a situation where you really need the performance improvement.

Tuples are like lists that can't be modified—you can think of them as a restricted type of list, or as a basic record type. Why we would need such a restricted data type will be discussed later in the chapter.

Most of the chapter is devoted to lists, since, if you understand lists, you pretty much understand tuples. The last part of the chapter will discuss the differences between lists and tuples, in both functional and design terms.

6.1 Lists are like arrays

Use [and] to create a list.

A list in Python is much the same thing as an array in Java or C or any other language. It's an ordered collection of objects. Lists are created by enclosing a comma-separated list of elements in square brackets, like so:

```
# This assigns a three-element list to x
x = [1, 2, 3]
```

Note that we don't have to worry about declaring the list, or fixing its size ahead of time. The line above creates the list as well as assigning it, and a list will automatically grow or shrink in size as needed.

Unlike many other languages, Python lists can contain different types of elements; in fact, a list element can be any Python object. Here's a list that contains a variety of elements:

```
# The first element is a number, the second a string, and the third element is another list.
x = [2, "two", [1, 2, 3]]
```

len returns the length of a list.

Probably the most basic built-in list function is the `len` function, which returns the number of elements in a list:

```
>>>
>>> x = ["This", "list", "has", 5, "elements"]
>>> len(x)
⇒  5
```

6.2 List indices

!!!

Understanding how list indices work will make Python much more useful to you. Please read the whole section!

List elements are 0-indexed.

Elements can be extracted from a Python list using a notation like C's array indexing. Like C and many other languages, Python starts counting from 0; asking for element 0 will return the first element of the list, asking for element 1 will return the second element, and so forth. Here are a few examples:

```
>>>
>>> x = ["first", "second", "third", "fourth"]
>>> x[0]
⇒  'first'
>>> x[2]
⇒  'third'
```

Negative indices count from the end of the list; -1 is the last element of a list.

However, Python indexing is more flexible than C indexing; if indices are negative numbers, they indicate positions counting from the end of the list, with −1 being the last position in the list, −2 being the second-to-last, and so forth. Using the same list x as above, we can do the following:

```
...
>>> a = x[-1]
>>> a
```

CHAPTER 6 LISTS AND TUPLES

```
⇒   'fourth'
>>> x[-2]
⇒   'third'
```

For operations involving a single list index, it is generally satisfactory to think of the index as pointing at a particular element in the list. For more advanced operations, it's more correct to think of list indices as indicating positions *between* elements. In the list `["first", "second", "third", "fourth"]`, you can think of the indices as pointing like this:

x =	[	"first",	"second",	"third",	"fourth"	]
		↑	↑	↑	↑	
Positive indices	0		1	2	3	
Negative indices	−4		−3	−2	−1	

This is irrelevant when extracting a single element, but Python can extract or assign to an entire sublist at once, an operation known as *slicing*. Instead of entering `list[index]` to extract the item just after `index`, enter `list[index1:index2]` to extract all items between `index1` and `index2` into a new list. Here are some examples:

```
>>>
>>> x = ["first", "second", "third", "fourth"]
>>> x[1:-1]
⇒   ['second', 'third']
>>> x[0:3]
⇒   ['first', 'second', 'third']
>>> x[-2:-1]
⇒   ['third']
```

It might seem reasonable that if the second index indicates a position in the list *before* the first index, this would return the elements between those indices in reverse order—but this isn't what happens. Instead, this will return an empty list.

```
...
>>> x[-1:2]
⇒   []
```

When slicing a list, it is also possible to leave out `index1` or `index2`. Leaving out `index1` means go from the beginning of the list, and leaving out `index2` means go to the end of the list.

```
...
>>> x[:3]
⇒   ['first', 'second', 'third']
>>> x[2:]
⇒   ['third', 'fourth']
```

Omitting both indices makes a new list that goes from the beginning to the end of the original list; that is, it copies the list. This is useful when you wish to make a copy that you can modify, without affecting the original list.

```
...
```

```
>>> y = x[:]
>>> y[0] = '1 st'
>>> y
⇒  ['1 st', 'second', 'third', 'fourth']
>>> x
⇒  ['first', 'second', 'third', 'fourth']
```

6.3 *Modifying lists*

Assign to an existing list index to change the value stored at that index.

List index notation can be used to modify a list, as well as to extract an element from it. Simply put the index on the left side of the assignment operator:

```
>>>
```

```
>>> x = [1, 2, 3, 4]
>>> x[1] = "two"
>>> x
⇒  [1, 'two', 3, 4]
```

Slicing can be used to replace a sublist with another list. This can be used to append to the start or end of a list.

Slice notation can be used here too. Saying something like listA[index1:index2] = listB causes all elements of listA between index1 and index2 to be replaced with the elements in listB. listB can have more or fewer elements than are removed from listA, in which case the length of listA will be altered. Slice assignment can be used to do a number of different things, as shown below:

```
>>>
```

```
>>> x = [1, 2, 3, 4]
>>> x[len(x):] = [5, 6, 7]          #Append a list to the end of a list.
>>> x
⇒  [1, 2, 3, 4, 5, 6, 7]
>>> x[:0] = [-1,0]                  #Append a list to the front of a list.
>>> x
⇒  [-1, 0, 1, 2, 3, 4, 5, 6, 7]
>>> x[1:-1] = []                    #Remove elements from a list.
>>> x
⇒  [-1, 7]
```

append adds a single element to the end of a list.

Appending a single element to a list is such a common operation that there is a special append method to do it:

```
>>>
```

```
>>> x = [1, 2, 3]
>>> x.append("four")
>>> x
⇒  [1, 2, 3, 'four']
```

insert *inserts a*
new element at a
given position in
the list.

There is also a special `insert` method to insert new list elements between two existing elements, or at the front of the list. `insert` is used as a method of lists, and takes two additional arguments; the first is the index position in the list where the new element should be inserted, and the second is the new element itself.

```
>>>
>>> x = [1, 2, 3]
>>> x.insert(2, "hello", 3)
>>> print x
[1, 2, "hello", 3]
>>> x.insert(0, "start")
>>> print x
['start', 1, 2, 'hello', 3]
```

`insert` understands list indices as discussed in the section on slice notation but, for most uses, it is easiest to think of *list*.insert(*n, elem*) as meaning insert *elem* just before the *n*th element of *list*. `insert` is really just a convenience method. Anything that can be done with `insert` can also be done using slice assignment; that is, *list*.insert(*n, elem*) is the same thing as *list*[n:n]=[*elem*] when *n* is nonnegative. Using `insert` makes for somewhat more readable code, **but, insert does not handle negative indices—** a negative index will be taken as 0.

List elements or
slices can be
deleted with del.

The `del` statement is the preferred method of deleting list items or slices. It doesn't do anything that can't be done with slice assignment, but it is usually easier to remember and easier to read:

```
>>>
>>> x = ['a', 2, 'c', 7, 9, 11]
>>> del x[1]
>>> x
⇒   ['a', 'c', 7, 9, 11]
>>> del x[:2]
⇒   [7, 9, 11]
```

In general, `del` *list*[n] does the same thing as *list*[n:n] = [], while `del` *list*[m:n] does the same thing as *list*[m:n] = [].

remove searches
for and removes a
given value from
a list.

The `remove` method is not the converse of `insert`. While `insert` inserts an element at a specified location, `remove` looks for the first instance of a given value in a list, and removes that value from the list:

```
>>>
>>> x = [1, 2, 3, 4, 3, 5]
>>> x.remove(3)
>>> x
⇒   [1, 2, 4, 3, 5]
>>> x.remove(3)
>>> x
⇒   [1, 2, 4, 5]
>>> x.remove(3)
Traceback (innermost last):
```

```
File "<stdin>", line 1, in ?
ValueError: list.remove(x): x not in list
```

If remove can't find anything to remove, it raises an error. You can catch this error using the exception-handling abilities of Python, or you can avoid the problem by using in to check for the presence of something in a list, before attempting to remove it.

reverse
reverses a list.

The reverse method is a more specialized list modification method. It efficiently reverses a list, in-place.

```
>>>
```

```
>>> x = [1, 3, 5, 6, 7]
>>> x.reverse()
>>> x
⇒   [7, 6, 5, 3, 1]
```

6.4 Sorting

sort sorts a list
(in-place).

Lists can be sorted using the built-in Python sort method:

```
>>>
```

```
>>> x = [3, 8, 4, 0, 2, 1]
>>> x.sort()
>>> x
⇒   [0, 1, 2, 3, 4, 8]
```

This does an in-place sort—that is, it changes the list being sorted. To sort a list without changing the original list, make a copy of it first.

```
>>>
```

```
>>> x = [2, 4, 1, 3]
>>> y = x[:]
>>> y.sort()
>>> y
⇒   [1, 2, 3, 4]
>>> x
⇒   [2, 4, 1, 3]
```

Use the bisect
module to segment
and add elements
to sorted lists.

Using the insort method of the bisect module, new items can be placed in an already sorted list in the proper place to maintain it in sorted order. Its bisect method (bisect.bisect) will return the position where a value would be added. It can be used to partition a sorted list.

```
>>>
```

```
>>> import bisect
>>> z = [1, 3, 5, 6, 7]
>>> bisect.insort(z, 4.5)
>>> z
⇒   [1, 3, 4.5, 5, 6, 7]
>>> z[bisect.bisect(z, 4):]
⇒   [4.5, 5, 6, 7]
```

Sorting works with strings, too:

```
>>>
>>> x = ["Life", "Is", "Enchanting"]
>>> x.sort()
>>> x
⇒ ['Enchanting', 'Is', "Life']
```

sort can sort lists of any element types, because Python can compare objects of any type.

In fact, the sort method can sort just about anything, because Python can compare just about anything. We can sort a list of lists, for example:

```
>>>
>>> x = [[3,5], [2,9], [2,3], [4,1], [3,2]]
>>> x.sort()
>>> x
⇒ [[2, 3], [2, 9], [3, 2], [3, 5], [4, 1]]
```

According to the built-in Python rules for comparing complex objects (delineated in detail in the reference at the end of this book), the sublists are sorted first by ascending first element, then by ascending second element.

sort is even more flexible than this—it's possible to use your own comparison function to determine how elements of a list are sorted.

6.4.1 Custom sorting

This is an advanced topic you may want to skip if you are just learning the language. It will be here for your future reference when you want to use this feature.

To use custom sorting, you need to be able to define functions, something we haven't talked about. In this section we'll also use the fact that len(*string*) returns the number of characters in a string. String operations are discussed more fully in the *Strings* chapter.

You can tell sort *exactly how to order a list, by passing in your own ordering function.*

By default, sort uses the built-in Python comparison function cmp to determine ordering, which is satisfactory for most purposes. There will be times, though, when you want to sort a list in a way that doesn't correspond to this default ordering. For example, let's say we wish to sort a list of words by the number of characters in each word, in contrast to the lexicographic sort that would normally be carried out by Python.

To do this, write an ordering function defining your ordering, and use it with the sort method. An ordering function in the context of sort is a function which takes two arguments and returns -1 if the first argument is less than the second argument, 0 if the two arguments are equivalent, and 1 if the first argument is greater than the second argument. (Try out Python's built-in cmp function with various pairs of arguments to see how this works in the normal case.)

For our number of characters ordering, a suitable comparison function could be :

```
def compareNumOfChars(string1, string2):
 return cmp(len(string1), len(string2))
```

This comparison function is really quite trivial. It passes the length of each string through to the cmp function, rather than the strings themselves.

Once the comparison function is defined, using it is simply a matter of passing it to the sort method. Because functions are Python objects, they can be passed around like any other Python object. Here is a small program I wrote to illustrate the difference between a default sort and our custom sort:

```
def compareNumOfChars(string1, string2):
 return cmp(len(string1), len(string2))

wordList = ['Python', 'is', 'better', 'than', 'C']
wordList.sort()
print wordList

wordList = ['Python', 'is', 'better', 'than', 'C']
wordList.sort(compareNumOfChars)
print wordList
```

The results of running this program were the following two lines of output:

```
['C', 'Python', 'better', 'is', 'than']
['C', 'is', 'than', 'Python', 'better']
```

The first list is a lexicographic order (with uppercase coming before lowercase), while the second list is ordered by ascending number of characters.

Sorting with a custom ordering function can be slow.

Custom sorting is very useful; it is not very fast. In fact, compared to Python's default sorting, it is very slow, because the built-in cmp function is implemented in C, while a custom ordering function that you pass in is (usually) implemented in Python. As a result, a custom sort is suitable for lists involving hundreds or even thousands of elements, but perhaps not for sorts involving hundreds of thousands or millions of elements. (On my Pentium 150 system, hardly a speed demon, a custom sort of 10,000 numbers executed in a fraction of a second—but sorts with more complex conditions would take longer).

reverse a normally sorted list to obtain a descending sort.

One particular place to avoid custom sorts is where you want to sort a list in descending, rather than ascending, order. In this case, sort the list normally, then use the reverse method to invert the order of the resulting list. These two operations together—the standard sort and the reverse—will still be much faster than a custom sort.

6.5 *Other common list operations*

There are a number of other list methods which are frequently useful, but don't fall into any specific category.

6.5.1 List membership with the in operator

Use in and not in to treat a list as a set and perform set membership tests.

It's easy to test if some value is in a list using the in operator, which returns a Boolean value. The converse, the not in operator, can also be used:

```
>>>
>>> 3 in [1, 3, 4, 5]
⇒ 1
>>> 3 not in [1, 3, 4, 5]
⇒ 0
>>> 3 in ["one", "two", "three"]
```

```
⇒   0
>>> 3 not in ["one", "two", "three"]
⇒   1
```

6.5.2   List concatenation with the + operator

+ can be used to concatenate lists..

To create a list by concatenating two existing lists, use the + (list concatenation) operator. This will leave the argument lists unchanged.

```
>>>
    <<< z = [1, 2, 3] + [4, 5]
    >>> z
⇒   [1, 2, 3, 4, 5]
```

6.5.3   List initialization with the * operator

* can be used to define a new initialized list of a given size, or to replicate a list many times.

Use the * operator to produce a list of a given size, which is initialized to a given value. This is a common operation for working with large lists whose size is known ahead of time. While `append` could be used to add elements and automatically expand the list as needed, greater efficiency can be obtained by using * to correctly size the list at the start of the program. A list which does not change in size will not incur any memory reallocation overhead.

```
>>>
    >>> z = [None] * 4
    >>> z
⇒   [None, None, None, None]
```

When used with lists in this manner, * (which in this context is called the list multiplication operator) replicates the given list the indicated number of times, and joins all of the copies to form a new list. This is the standard Python method for defining a list of a given size ahead of time. A list containing a single instance of `None` is commonly used in list multiplication, but the list can be anything:

```
>>>
    >>> z = [3,1] * 2
    >>> z
⇒   [3, 1, 3, 1]
```

6.5.4   List minimum or maximum with min and max

min and max return the smallest or largest elements in a list.

`min` and `max` can be used to find the smallest or largest element in a list. You'll probably use these mostly with numerical lists, but they can be used with lists containing any type of element. The maximum object in a set of objects of different types, is somewhat arbitrary, but consistent.

```
>>>
    >>> min([3, 7, 0, -2, 11])
⇒   -2
```

```
>>> max([4, "Hello",[1, 2]])
⇒  'Hello'
```

6.5.5 List search with index

index finds the position of a value in a list.

If you wish to find where in a list a value can be found (rather than only wanting to know if the value is in the list), use the index method. It searches through a list looking for a list element equivalent to a given value, and returns the position of that list element:

```
>>>
>>> x = [1, 3, "five", 7, -2]
>>> x.index(7)
⇒  3
>>> x.index(5)
Traceback (innermost last):
 File "<stdin>", line 1, in ?
ValueError: list.index(x): x not in list
```

Attempting to find the position of an element that doesn't exist in the list at all will raise an error, as shown above. This can be handled in the same manner as the analogous error that can occur with the remove method (i.e., by testing the list with in, before using index).

6.5.6 List matches with count

count counts the number of times a value occurs in a list.

count also searches through a list, looking for a given value, but it returns the number of times that value was found in the list, rather than positional information.

```
>>>
>>> x = [1, 2, 2, 3, 5, 2, 5]
>>> x.count(2)
⇒  3
>>> x.count(5)
⇒  2
>>> x.count(4)
⇒  0
```

6.6 Nested lists and deep copies

This is again an advanced topic that you may want to skip if you are just learning the language.

Lists can be nested. One application of this is to represent two-dimensional matrices. The members of these can be referred to using two-dimensional indices. Indices for these work as follows:

```
>>>
>>> m = [ [0,1,2], [10,11,12], [20,21,22] ]
>>> m[0]
⇒  [0, 1, 2]
```

```
>>> m[0][1]
⇒   1
>>> m[2]
⇒   [20, 21, 22]
>>> m[2][2]
⇒   22
```

This mechanism scales to higher dimensions in the manner one would expect.

Most of the time this is all you will need to concern yourself with. However, there is an issue with nested lists that you may run into. This is the result of the combination of the way variables refer to objects and the fact that some objects (such as lists) can be modified (they are mutable). An example is the best way to illustrate it.

```
>>>
```

```
>>> nested = [0]
>>> original = [ nested, 1]
>>> original
⇒   [[0], 1]
```

What this looks like is:

The value in the nested list can now be changed either using the nested or the original variables.

```
>>>
```

```
>>> nested[0] = 'zero'
>>> original
⇒   [['zero'], 1]
>>> original[0][0] = 0
>>> nested
⇒   [0]
>>> original
⇒   [[0], 1]
```

However, if nested is set to another list, the connection between them is broken

```
>>> nested = [2]
>>> original
⇒   [['ZERO'], 1]
```

This now looks like:

We have seen that we can obtain a copy of a list by taking a full slice (i.e., x[:]). You can also obtain a copy of a list using the + or * operators (i.e., x + [] or x * 1). These are slightly less efficient than the slice method. All three create what is called a *shallow* copy of the list. This is probably what you want most of the time. However, if your list has other lists nested in it, you may want to make a *deep* copy. This can be done with the deepcopy function of the copy module.

```
>>> original = [ [0], 1]
>>> shallow = original[:]
>>> import copy
>>> deep = copy.deepcopy(original)
```

What this looks like is:

The lists pointed at by the original or shallow variables are connected. Changing the value in the nested list through either one of them will affect the other.

```
>>> shallow[1] =2
>>> shallow
⇒   [[0], 2]
>>> original
⇒   [[0], 1]
>>> shallow[0][0] = 'zero'
>>> original
⇒   [['zero'], 1]
```

The deep copy is independent of the original and no change to it will have any effect on the original list.

```
>>> deep[0][0] = 5
>>> deep
⇒   [[5], 1]
>>> original
⇒   [['zero'], 1]
```

This behavior will be the same for any other nested objects in a list which are modifiable (i.e., dictionaries).

6.7 Tuples

Tuples are data structures which are very similar to lists, but they can't be modified. They can only be created. In fact, tuples are so much like lists that you might wonder why Python bothers including them. Tuples actually have important roles that can't be efficiently filled by lists, as keys for dictionaries.

6.7.1 Tuple basics

Tuples use (and), not [and].

Creating a tuple is similar to creating a list: assign a sequence of values to a variable. A list is a sequence which is enclosed by [and], a tuple is a sequence which is enclosed by (and):

```
>>>
        >>> x = ('a', 'b', 'c')          # Create a three-element tuple.
```

Once a tuple is created, using it is so much like using a list that it's easy to forget they are different data types:

```
...
        >>> x[2]
        ⇒  'c'
        >>> x[1:]
        ⇒  ('b', 'c')
        >>> len(x)
        ⇒  3
        >>> max(x)
        ⇒  'c'
        >>> min(x)
        ⇒  'a'
        >>> 5 in y
        ⇒  0
        >>> 5 not in y
        ⇒  1
```

Tuples cannot be modified.

The main difference between tuples and lists is that tuples are immutable. An attempt to modify a tuple will result in a confusing error message, which is Python's way of saying it doesn't know how to set an item in a tuple.

```
...
        >>> x[2] = 'd'
        Traceback (innermost last):
         File "<stdin>", line 1, in ?
        TypeError: object doesn't support item assignment
```

You can create tuples from existing ones by using the + and * operators.

```
...
        >>> x + x
        ⇒  ('a', 'b', 'c', 'a', 'b', 'c')
        >>> 2 * x
```

```
⇒  ('a', 'b', 'c', 'a', 'b', 'c')
```

A copy of a tuple can be made in any of the same ways as for lists:

```
...
```

```
>>> x[:]
⇒  ('a', 'b', 'c')
>>> x * 1
⇒  ('a', 'b', 'c')
>>> x + ()
⇒  ('a', 'b', 'c')
```

If you didn't read the previous subsection "Nested lists and deep copies," you can skip the rest of this paragraph. Tuples themselves cannot be modified. However, if they contain any mutable objects (i.e., lists or dictionaries) these might be changed if they are still assigned to their own variables. Tuples that contain mutable objects are not allowed as keys for dictionaries.

One-element tuples

One-element tuples must be written with a comma.

There's a small syntactical point associated with using tuples. Since the square brackets used to enclose a list aren't used elsewhere in Python,* it's clear that [ ] means an empty list and [1] means a list with one element. The same thing isn't true with the parentheses used to enclose tuples. Parentheses can also be used to group items in expressions, in order to force a certain evaluation order. If we say (x+y) in a Python program, do we mean that x and y should be added and then put into a one-element tuple, or that the parentheses should be used to force x and y to be added, before any expressions to either side come into play?

This is only a problem for tuples with one element, because tuples with more than one element will always include commas to separate the elements, and the commas tell Python the parentheses indicate a tuple, not a grouping. In the case of one-element tuples, Python requires that the element in the tuple be followed by a comma, to disambiguate the situation. In the case of zero-element (empty) tuples, there is no problem. An empty set of parentheses must be a tuple, because it is meaningless otherwise.

```
>>>
```

```
>>> x = 3
>>> y = 4
>>> (x + y)         # This just adds x and y.
⇒  7
>>> (x + y,)        # Including a comma indicates the parentheses deonote a tuple.
⇒  (7,)
>>> ()              # To create an empty tuple, just use an empty pair of parentheses.
⇒  ()
```

---

* That isn't quite true. [and] are also used in regular expressions (discussed in chapter 21), but in that case they appear only in strings.

6.7.2 Tuple packing and unpacking

Tuples can be used to perform multiple assignments simultaneously.

As a convenience, Python permits tuples to appear on the left-hand side of an assignment operator, in which case variables in the tuple receive the corresponding values from the tuple on the right-hand side of the assignment operator. Here's a simple example:

```
>>>
>>> (one, two, three, four) = (1, 2, 3, 4)
>>> one
⇒   1
>>> two
⇒   2
```

This can be written even more simply, because Python will recognize tuples in an assignment context, even without the enclosing parentheses. The values on the right-hand side are packed into a tuple and then unpacked into the variables on the left-hand side:

```
one, two, three, four = 1, 2, 3, 4
```

One line of code has replaced the following four lines of code:

```
one = 1
two = 2
three = 3
four = 4
```

Tuples provide a convenient way to swap variable contents.

This is a convenient way to swap values between variables. Instead of saying

```
temp = var1
var1 = var2
var2 = temp
```

just say,

```
var1, var2 = var2, var1
```

Packing and unpacking can be performed using list delimiters as well:

```
>>>
>>> [a, b] = [1, 2]
>>> [c, d] = 3, 4
>>> [e, f] = (5, 6)
>>> (g, h) = 7,8
>>> i, j = [9, 10]
>>> k, l = (11, 12)
>>> a
⇒   1
>>> [b, c, d]
⇒   [2, 3, 4]
>>> (e, f, g)
⇒   (5, 6, 7)
>>> h, i, j, k, l
⇒   (8, 9, 10, 11, 12)
```

6.7.3 Converting between lists and tuples

Tuples can be easily converted to lists with the `list` function (which takes any sequence as an argument and produces a new list with the same elements as the original sequence). Similarly, lists can be converted to tuples with the `tuple` function (which does the same thing, but produces a new tuple instead of a new list).

```
>>>
>>> list((1, 2, 3, 4))
⇒   [1, 2, 3, 4]
>>> tuple([1, 2, 3, 4]}
⇒   (1, 2, 3, 4)
```

As an interesting side note, `list` is a convenient way to break up a string into characters:

```
>>>
>>> list("Hello")
⇒   ['H', 'e', 'l', 'l', 'o']
```

This works because `list` (and `tuple`) apply to any Python sequence, and a string is just a sequence of characters. (Strings are discussed fully in the next section.)

6.8 Summary

Lists are a basic and highly useful data structure built into the Python language. In addition to fairly standard array-like behavior, lists possess additional functionality, such as automatic resizing, the ability to use slice notation, and a good set of convenience functions, methods, and operators. Note that there are a few more list methods than were covered in this chapter. You will find the details on these in the appendix.

Tuples are similar to lists, but cannot be modified. They take up slightly less memory, and are faster to access. They are not as flexible but are more efficient than lists. Their normal use (from the point of view of a Python coder) is to serve as dictionary keys, which is discussed in a later chapter.

C H A P T E R   7

Strings

This chapter discusses the standard string and string-related operations in Python.

7.1 Strings as sequences of characters

Strings are sequences of characters.

For purposes of extracting characters and substrings, strings can be considered as sequences of characters, which means we can use index or slice notation:

>>>

```
>>> x = "Hello"
>>> x[[0]
⇒ 'H'
>>> x[-1]
⇒ 'o'
>>> x[1:]
⇒ 'ello'
```

Indexing (including slices) can be used to extract characters or substrings from a string.

One use for slice notation with strings is to chop the newline off the end of a string, usually a line that's just been read from a file:

```
>>>
>>> x = "Goodbye\n"
>>> x = x[:1]
>>> x
⇒ 'Goodbye'
```

Use len *to find the number of characters in a string.*

You can also determine how many characters are in the string by using the len function, just like finding out the number of elements in a list:

```
>>>
>>> len("Goodbye")
⇒ 7
```

Strings cannot be modified.

However, strings are not lists of characters. The most noticeable difference between strings and lists is that, unlike lists, *strings cannot be modified.* Attempting to say something like string.append('c') or string[0] = 'H' will result in an error. You'll notice in the example above that we stripped off the newline from the string by creating a string that was a slice of the previous one, not by modifying the previous string directly. This is a basic Python restriction, imposed for efficiency reasons.

7.2 Basic string operations

Concatenate strings with +

The simplest (and probably most common) way of combining Python strings is to use the string concatenation operator **+**:

```
>>>
>>> x = "Hello" + "World"
>>> x
⇒ 'Hello World'
```

There is an analogous string multiplication operator which I have found sometimes, but not often, useful:

```
...
>>> 8 * "x"
⇒ 'xxxxxxxx'
```

7.3 Special characters and escape sequences

Escape sequences are (sub)strings beginning with a \. They generally represent special characters.

You've already seen a few of the character sequences Python regards as special when used within strings: "\n" represents the newline character, and "\t" represents the tab character. Sequences of characters which start with a backslash and which are used to represent other characters, are called *escape sequences*. Escape sequences are generally used to represent *special characters*, that is, those characters (such as tab and newline) which do not have a standard one-character printable representation. This section covers escape sequences, special characters, and related topics in more detail.

7.3.1 Basic escape sequences

Basic escape sequences are \n, \t, \\, \', \", \a, \b, \f, \r, and \w.

Python provides a brief list of two-character escape sequences to use in strings (table 7.1).

Table 7.1 Escape sequences

Escape Sequence	Character Represented
\'	single-quote character
\"	double-quote character
\\	backslash character
\a	bell character
\b	backspace character
\f	formfeed character
\n	newline character
\r	carriage return character (not the same as \n)
\t	the tab character
\v	the vertical tab character

The ASCII character set, which is the character set used by Python, and the standard character set on almost all computers, defines quite a few more special characters. They are accessed by the numeric escape sequences, described in the next section.

7.3.2 Numeric (octal and hexadecimal) escape sequences

Any character can be represented by a numeric escape sequence.

You can include any ASCII character in a string by using an octal (base 8) or hexadecimal (base 16) escape sequence corresponding to that character. An octal escape sequence is a backslash followed by three digits defining an octal number; the ASCII character corresponding to this octal number is substituted for the octal escape sequence. A hexadecimal escape sequence is similar, but starts with "\x" rather than just "\", and can consist of any number of hexadecimal digits. The escape sequence is terminated when a character is found that is not a hexadecimal digit. For example, in the ASCII character table, the character 'm' happens to have decimal value 109. This is octal value 155, and hexadecimal value 6D, so:

```
>>>
>>> 'm'
⇒   'm'
>>> '\155'
⇒   'm'
>>> '\x6D'
⇒   'm'
```

All three expressions evaluate to a string containing the single character 'm'. However, these forms will normally be used to represent characters that have no printable representation. The newline character '\n', for example, has octal value 012 and hexadecimal value 0A

```
>>>
>>> '\n'
⇒   '\012'
>>> '\012'
⇒   '\012'
>>> '\x0A'
⇒   '\012'
```

7.3.3 Printing vs. evaluating strings with special characters

We talked before about the difference between evaluating a Python expression interactively, and printing the result of the same expression using the `print` statement. Although the same string is involved, the two operations can produce screen outputs that look very different. A string that is simply evaluated at the top level of an interactive Python session will be shown with all of its special characters as octal escape sequences which makes clear what is in the string. Meanwhile the print command passes the string directly to the terminal program, which may interpret special characters in special ways. For example, here's what happens with a string consisting of an 'a' followed by a newline, a tab, and a 'b':

```
>>>
>>> 'a\n\tb'
⇒   'a\012\011b'
>>> print 'a\n\tb'
a
    b
```

A comma after the string will prevent print *from adding a newline.*

In the first case, the newline and tab are shown explicitly in the string: in the second, they are actually used as newline and tab characters.

A normal `print` statement will also add a newline to the end of the string. There are times (i.e., when we have lines from files that already end with newlines) where we may not want this. A comma after a string will cause the `print` statement to not append the newline.

```
>>> print "abc\n"
⇒   abc
⇒
>>> print "abc\n",
⇒   abc
>>>
```

7.4 The 'string' module

Because string *is a module, it must be imported before use.*

Most of the other Python string functions (along with some useful constants) come in the standard `string` module. *

---

* In version 1.6 of Python there will be string methods that will provide the functionality of this module. You may see new code that uses these (and be able to find descriptions of the methods) in the *Python Library Reference*. However, due to the size of the existing code *base,* this module will continue to be available as well. Code you have written using it will continue to work, and you will be able to continue using it. There will also be two new methods: `startswith` and `endswith`.

Modules will be discussed in detail in a later chapter. For the purposes of this section, you need only remember that any Python program that uses functions in the `string` module must have the line

```
import string
```

at or near the beginning of the program, and that functions and data values in the string module are always referred to as `string.function` or `string.data`; that is, they are prepended with `string` followed by a period.

None of the functions in `string` *actually modify a string.*

Because strings are immutable, the functions in the string module are all functions in the truest sense of the word, that is, they are used only to obtain their return value, and do not modify any of their arguments in any way.

I will start off with those operations from the string module which are the most useful and commonly used, and then go on to discuss some less commonly used, but still useful, operations. At the end I'll discuss a few miscellaneous points related to the string module. Not all of the string module is documented here. See the reference at the end of the book for a complete list of the string module contents.

7.4.1 string.split and string.join

Anyone who works with strings is almost certain to find the functions `string.split` and `string.join` invaluable. They are inverses of one another—`string.split` takes a string and returns a list of substrings, and `string.join` takes a list of strings and puts them together to form a single string. Typically, these two functions use whitespace as the delimiter within the strings they are splitting or joining, but that can be changed via an optional argument.

Join multiple strings with `string.join`

String concatenation using '+' is useful, but not efficient for joining large numbers of strings into a single string, because each time '+' is applied, a new string object is created. Our previous "Hello, World" example produced two string objects, one of which was immediately discarded. A better option is to use the `join` function.

```
>>> import string
>>> string.join(["join", "puts", "spaces", "between", "elements",
...    "by", "default"])
⇒ 'join puts spaces between elements by default'
```

By passing an optional second argument to `join`, you can put anything you want between the joined strings:

```
 ...
```

```
>>> string.join(["Separated", "with", "colons"],"::")
⇒ 'Separated::with::colons'
```

Split strings apart with `string.split`.

The most common use of `string.split` is probably as a very simple parsing mechanism for string-delimited records stored in text files. By default, `split` splits on any whitespace, not just a single space character, but it can also be told to split on a particular sequence, by passing it an optional second argument:

```
>>> import string
>>> string.split("You\t\t can have tabs\t\n \t and newlines \n\n " \
                 "mixed in")
⇒   ['You', 'can', 'have', 'tabs', 'and', 'newlines', 'mixed', 'in']
>>> string.split("Mississippi", "ss")
⇒   ['Mi', 'i', 'ippi']
```

`string.join` and `string.split` are not precise inverses: when the optional second argument is omitted, `string.split` will split on any run of whitespace (not necessarily just a single space), but `string.join` will only insert a single space character between joined substrings.

You can have `string.split` *produce only a certain number of substrings.*

Sometimes it's useful to permit the last field in a joined string to contain arbitrary text, including, perhaps, substrings that might match what `string.split` splits on when reading in that data. This can be done by specifying how many splits `string.split` should perform when it is generating its result, via an optional third argument. If you specify n splits, then `string.split` will go along the input string until it has performed n splits (generating a list with $n+1$ substrings as elements), or until it runs out of string. Here are some examples:

```
>>> import string
>>> string.split('a b c d', ' ', 1)
⇒   ['a', 'b c d']
>>> string.split('a b c d', ' ', 2)
⇒   ['a', 'b', 'c d']
>>> string.split('a b c d', ' ', 9)
⇒   ['a', 'b', 'c', 'd']
```

When using `string.split` with its optional third argument, you must supply a second argument. To get it to split on runs of whitespace while using the third argument, use `"None"` as the second argument.

I use `string.split` and `string.join` extensively, usually when working with text files generated by other programs. You should know, however, that if you are able to define your own data file format, for use solely by your Python programs, then there is a much better alternative to storing data in text files. It will be discussed later in the book when we talk about the `cPickle` module.

7.4.2 Converting strings to numbers

string.atoi, string.atol, and string.atof can convert strings to numbers, but...

The functions `string.atoi`, `string.atol`, and `string.atof` can be used to convert strings into integer, long integer, or floating-point numbers, respectively. If they are passed a string that cannot be interpreted as a number of the given type, they will raise a `ValueError` exception. Exceptions are explained in chapter 14. In addition, `string.atoi` or `string.atol` may be passed an optional second argument, specifying the numeric base to use when interpreting the input string.

```
>>> string.atof('123.456')
⇒   123.456
```

```
>>> string.atof('xxyy')
Traceback (innermost last):
 File "<stdin>", line 1, in ?
ValueError: invalid literal for atof(): xxyy
>>> string.atoi('3333')
⇒  3333
>>> string.atoi('123.456')
Traceback (innermost last):
 File "<stdin>", line 1, in ?
ValueError: invalid literal for atoi(): 123.456
>>> string.atoi('10000', 8)
⇒  4096
>>> string.atoi('123456', 6)
Traceback (innermost last):
 File "<stdin>", line 1, in ?
ValueError: invalid literal for atoi(): 123456
```

● **Can't have a decimal point in an integer**

● **Interpret 10000 as an octal number**

● **Can't interpret 123456) as a base 6 number!**

Did you catch the reason for that last error? We requested that the string be interpreted as a base six number, but the digit 6 can never appear in a base six number. Sneaky!

...int, long, and float are probably more convenient.

You need to know about the string numeric conversion functions because if you do have to work with octal, hexadecimal, or other base-numeric strings, that's the way to go. However, if I'm going to be converting strings to numbers, I prefer to use Python's built-in type conversion functions: int, long, or float. They are easier to remember, and provide similar functionality to that of string.atoi, string.atol, and string.atof respectively. However, int and long only work with base ten numbers.

7.4.3   Getting rid of extra whitespace

The strip functions will get rid of whitespace on the ends of strings.

A trio of simple functions that are surprisingly useful are the string.strip, string.lstrip, and string.rstrip functions. string.strip takes a single string as argument, and returns a new string which is the same as the original string, except that any whitespace at the beginning or end of the string has been removed. string.lstrip and string.rstrip work similarly, except that they only remove whitespace at the left or right end of the original string, respectively:

```
>>>

import string
>>> string.strip(" Hello,    World\t\t ")
⇒  'Hello,    World'
>>> string.lstrip(" Hello,    World\t\t ")
⇒  'Hello,    World\011\011 '
>>> string.rstrip(" Hello,    World\t\t ")
⇒  ' Hello,    World'
```

All the characters that Python considers as whitespace are in the string.whitespace constant.

In the above example tab characters are considered to be whitespace. The exact meaning may differ across different operating systems, but you can always find out what Python considers to be whitespace by accessing the string.whitespace constant. On my Windows system, it gives the following:

```
>>> string.whitespace
⇒  '\011\012\013\014\015 '
>>>"\t\n\v\f\r "
⇒  '\011\012\013\014\015 '
```

The characters given in backslashed octal (\nnn) format represent the tab, newline, and so forth. The space character is in there as itself, right after the '5' in \015. It may be tempting to change the value of this variable, to try to attempt to affect how `string.strip` and so forth, work—but don't. Such an action isn't guaranteed to give you the results you're looking for.

The most common use for these functions is as a quick way of cleaning up strings which have just been read in. This is particularly helpful when reading lines from files (discussed in a later chapter), as Python always reads in an entire line, including the trailing newline, if it exists. Once you get around to processing the line read in, you typically don't want the trailing newline. `string.rstrip` is a convenient way to get rid of it.

7.4.4 String searching

The `string` module provides a number of functions to perform simple string searches. Before I describe them, though, let me talk a bit about another module in Python, the `re` module, which will be discussed in "Regular expressions" chapter 21.

The re module provides more powerful string searches than the 'string' module.

The `re` module also does string searching, but in a far more flexible manner. Rather than searching for a single specified substring, an `re` search can look for a string pattern. You could look for substrings which consisted entirely of digits, for example.

Why am I mentioning this, when `re` is discussed fully later on? In my experience, many uses of basic string searches, such as those found in the `string` module, are inappropriate. The programmer would benefit from a more powerful searching mechanism but isn't aware that one exists, and so doesn't even look for something better. Perhaps you have an urgent project involving strings, and don't have time to read this entire book. If basic string searching will do the job for you, great. But be aware that there is a more powerful alternative.

There are four basic string searching functions in the `string` module, which are all similar; `string.find`, `string.rfind`, `string.index`, and `string.rindex`. There is also a related function `string.count` that simply counts how many times a substring can be found in another string. We'll describe `find` in detail, and then describe how the other functions differ from it.

Find the location of a substring in a string with `string.find`

`string.find` takes two required arguments: the first, *string*, is the string being searched, and the second, *substring*, is the substring being searched for. `string.find` returns the position of the first character of the first instance of *substring* in *string*, or -1 if *substring* does not occur in *string*.

```
>>> import string
>>> string.find("Mississippi", "ss")
⇒  2
>>> string.find("Mississippi", "zz")
```

$$\Rightarrow \quad \textit{-1}$$

find can also take one or two additional, optional arguments. The first of these, if present, is an integer *start*, and causes find to ignore all characters before position *start* in *string*, when searching for *substring*. The second optional argument, if present, is an integer *end*, and causes find to ignore characters at or after position *end* in string.

> [···]

```
>>> string.find("Mississippi", "ss", 3)
⇒  5
>>> string.find("Mississippi", "ss", 0, 3)
⇒  -1
```

string.rfind is almost the same as find, except that it starts its search at the end of *string*, and so returns the position of the first character of the last occurrence of *substring* in *string*.

> [···]

```
>>> string.rfind("Mississippi", "ss")
⇒  5
```

string.rfind can also take one or two optional arguments, with the same meanings as those for string.find.

string.index and string.rindex are identical to string.find and string.rfind, respectively, except for one difference: if string.index or string.rindex fail to find an occurrence of *substring* in *string*, they do not return -1, but rather raise a ValueError exception. Exactly what this means will be clear after you read the "Exceptions" chapter.

string.count is used identically to any of the above four functions, but returns the number of nonoverlapping times the given substring occurs in the given string:

```
>>> string.count("Mississippi", "ss")
⇒  2
```

7.4.5 Modifying strings

Strings are immutable, but the string module provides a number of functions which take a string as an argument and return a new string which is a modified version of the argument string. This provides much the same effect as direct modification, for most purposes. A more complete description of these functions may be found in the reference section at the back of the book.

Further string module functions perform substring replacement...

string.replace may be used to replace occurrences of *substring* (its second argument) in *string* (its first argument) with *newstring* (its third argument). It also takes an optional fourth argument. See the reference section for details.

> [···]

```
>>> string.replace("Mississippi", "ss", "+++")
⇒  'Mi+++i+++ippi'
```

As with the string search functions, the `re` module provides a much more powerful method of substring replacement.

The functions `string.maketrans` and `string.translate` may be used together to translate characters in strings into different characters. Though rarely used, these functions can simplify your life when they are needed.

Let's say, for example, that you are working on a program that translates string expressions from one computer language into another. The first language uses '~' to mean logical not, while the second language uses '!'; the first language uses '^' to mean logical and, while the second language uses '&'; and, the first language uses '(' and ')' where the second language uses '[' and ']'. So, in a given string expression, you need to change all instances of '~' to '!', all instances of '^' to '&', all instances of '(' to '[', and all instances of ')' to ']'. This could be done using multiple invocations of `string.replace`, but an easier and more efficient way is:

```
>>> table = string.maketrans("~^()", "!&[]")
>>> string.translate("~x^(y % z)", table)
⇒ '!x & [y % z]'
```

The first line uses `string.maketrans` to make up a translation table from its two string arguments. The two arguments must each contain the same number of characters, and a table will be made such that looking up the *n*th character of the first argument, in that table, gives back the *n*th character of the second argument.

Then, the table produced by `string.maketrans` is passed to `string.translate`, along with a string to be translated. `string.translate` goes over each of the characters in its first string argument, and checks to see if they can be found in the table given as the second argument. If a character can be found in the translation table, `string.translate` replaces that character with the corresponding character looked up in the table, to produce the translated string.

An optional argument may be given to `string.translate`, to specify characters that should be removed from the string entirely. See the reference for details.

Other functions in the string module perform more specialized tasks. `string.lower` converts all alphabetic characters in a string to lowercase, while `string.upper` does the opposite. `string.capitalize` capitalizes the first character of a string, and `string.capwords` capitalizes all words in a string. `string.swapcase` converts lowercase characters to uppercase and uppercase to lowercase, in the same string. `string.expandtabs` gets rid of tab characters in a string, by replacing each tab with a specified number of spaces. `string.ljust`, `string.rjust`, and `string.center` pad a string with spaces, to justify it in a certain field width. `string.zfill` left-pads a numeric string with zeroes. Refer to the reference section for details of these functions.

7.4.6 Modifying strings with list manipulations

Because strings are immutable objects, there is no way to directly manipulate them in the same way you can lists. While the operations which operate on strings to produce new strings (leaving the original strings unchanged) are useful for many things, sometimes you want to be able to manipulate a string as if it were a list of characters. In that case, just turn it into a list of characters, do whatever you want, and turn the resulting list back into a string:

```
>>>
>>> import string
>>> text = "Hello, World"
>>> wordList = list(text)
>>> wordList[6:] = []                    ● Remove everything
>>> wordList.reverse()                     after the comma.
>>> text = string.join(wordList, "")     ● Join the characters with
>>> print text                             no space between them.
⇒ olleH,
```

Although `string.split` can be used to turn your string into a list of characters, the type-conversion function **list** is easier to use and to remember (and, for what it's worth, you can turn a string into a tuple of characters using the built-in **tuple** function). To turn the list back into a string, use `string.join`.

Operating on strings in this manner is relatively expensive, so you shouldn't go over-board with this method. Processing hundreds or thousands of strings in this manner probably won't have much of an impact on your program. Processing millions probably will.

7.4.7 Useful constants

Some useful string constants

Finally, the `string` module defines some useful constants. We've already seen `string.whitespace`, which is a string made up of the characters Python thinks of as whitespace on your system. `string.digits` is the string `'0123456789'`. `string.hex-digits` includes all the characters in `string.digits`, as well as `'abcdefABCDEF'`, the extra characters used in hexadecimal numbers. `string.octdigits` contains `'01234567'`—just those digits used in octal numbers. `string.lowercase` contains all lowercase alphabetic characters, `string.uppercase` contains all uppercase alphabetic characters; `string.letters` contains all of the characters in `string.lowercase` and `string.uppercase`.

Remember, strings are sequences of characters, so you can use the convenient Python `in` operator to test for a character's membership in any of these strings.

You might be tempted to try assigning to these constants, to change the behavior of the language. Python will let you get away with this, but it would probably be a Bad Idea.

7.5 Converting from objects to strings

!!!

Anything can be converted to a string.

In Python, almost anything can be converted to some sort of a string, using the built-in `repr` function. Lists are the only complex Python data types we're familiar with so far, so let's turn some lists into strings:

```
>>>
>>> repr([1, 2, 3])
⇒ '[1, 2, 3]'
>>> x = [1]
```

```
>>> x.append(2)
>>> x.append([3, 4])
>>> repr(x)
⇒ '[1, 2, [3, 4]]'
```

`obj` returns obj
in string form.

The ability to obtain a string representation for almost anything is so useful that Python has a special shortcut for it, the *backquotes* notation. Putting an expression into backquotes is just like surrounding it with a call to repr:

```
>>>

>>>x = [1, 2, 3]
>>> str = "The list " + `x` + " has " + `len(x)` + " elements."
>>> str
⇒ 'The list [1, 2, 3] has 3 elements.'
```

Note the difference between back quotes (`x`) and single quotes ('x'). Surrounding an item in single quotes will only create a string out of its name.

In the example, we used `` to convert the list x and the number len(x) into strings, which were then concatenated with other strings to form the final string. Without the use of ``, this wouldn't have worked. In an expression like "string" + [1, 2] + 3, are we trying to add strings, or add lists, or just add numbers? Python doesn't know what you want in such a circumstance, and will do the safe thing (raise an error), rather than make any assumptions. In the example above, all the elements had to be converted to strings before the string concatenation would work.

Lists are the only "complex" Python objects that have been described to this point, but `` can be used to obtain some sort of string representation for almost any Python object. To see this, try backquotes around a built-in complex object—an actual Python function. Try this:

```
>>>

>>> `len`
⇒ '<built-in function len>'
```

Python hasn't actually produced a string containing the code which implements the len function, but it has at least returned a string—<built-in function len>—which describes what that function is. If you keep the `` operator in mind, and try it out on each Python data type (dictionaries, tuples, classes, etc.) as we get to them in the book, you'll see that no matter what type of Python object you have, you can get a string saying something about that object.

This is great for debugging programs. If you're in doubt as to what's held in a variable at a certain point in your program, just use `` and print out the contents of that variable.

repr returns a
full, formal repre-
sentation of an
object—this may
not be what you
want for
debugging.

We have covered how Python can convert any object into a string that describes that object. The truth is, Python can do this in one of two different ways. The repr function always returns what might be loosely called the *formal string representation* of a Python object. More specifically, repr returns a string representation of a Python object from which the original object can be rebuilt. For large, complex objects, this may not be the sort of thing you wish to see in debugging output or status reports.

To return a more human-friendly representation of an object, Python provides the built-in `str` function. `str` can be applied to any Python object to return what might be called the *informal string representation* of the object. A string returned by `str` need not define an object fully. It is intended to be read by humans, not by Python code.

You won't notice any difference between `repr` and `str` when you first start using them, because until you start using the object-oriented features of Python, there is none. In fact, `str` applied to any built-in Python object always calls `repr` to calculate its result. It is only when you start defining your own classes that the difference between `str` and `repr` becomes important. This will be discussed later in the book.

So why talk about this now? Basically, I wanted you to be aware that there is more going on behind the scenes with `repr` than being able to easily write `print` statements for debugging. As a matter of good style, you might want to get into the habit of using `str` rather than `repr` or `` ` `` when creating strings for displaying information.

7.6 *Formatting strings*

Use % to format strings precisely for output.

This section covers a single Python string operator, the *string modulus* ('%') operator. It's used to combine Python values into formatted strings, for printing or other use. C users will notice a strange similarity to the `printf` family of functions.

An example:

```
>>>
>>> "%s is the %s of %s" % ("Ambrosia", "food", "the gods")
⇒ 'Ambrosia is the food of the gods'
```

The % operator substitutes substrings for formatting sequences in a larger string.

The string modulus operator (the bold % that occurs in the middle, not the three %'s that come before it in the example above) takes two parts; the left-hand side, which is a string, and the right-hand side, which is a tuple. The string modulus operator scans the left-hand string for special *formatting sequences*, and produces a new string by substituting the values on the right-hand side for those formatting sequences, in order. In this example, the only formatting sequences on the left-hand side are the three instances of `"%s"`, which stands for "stick a string in here."

Passing in different values on the right-hand side produces different strings:

```
>>>
>>> "%s is the %s of %s" % ("Nectar", "drink", "gods")
⇒ 'Nectar is the drink of the gods'
>>> "%s is the %s of the %s" % ("Brussels Sprouts", "food",
…    "foolish")
⇒ 'Brussels Sprouts is the food of the foolish'
```

The members of the tuple on the right will have `str` applied to them automatically by `%s`, so they do not have to already be strings:

```
>>>
>>> x = [1, 2, "three"]
```

```
>>> "The %s contains: %s"%("list", x)
⇒ "The list contains: [1, 2, 'three']"
```

7.6.1 Using formatting sequences

Formatting sequences can specify field width, justification, and number of decimal places.

All formatting sequences are substrings contained in the string on the left-hand side of the central "%". Each formatting sequence begins with a percent sign, and is followed by one or more characters which specify what is to be substituted for the formatting sequence, and how the substitution is accomplished. The '%s' formatting sequence used above is the simplest formatting sequence, and indicates that the corresponding string from the tuple on the right-hand side of the central "%" should be substituted in place of the '%s'.

Other formatting sequences can be more complex. This one specifies the field width (total number of characters) of a printed number to be six, number of characters after the decimal point to be two, and left justifies the number in its field. I've put in angle brackets so you can see where extra spaces are inserted into the formatted string:

```
>>>
```

```
>>> "Pi is <%-6.2f>" % 3.14159 # use of the formatting sequence: %-6.2f
⇒ 'Pi is <3.14  >'
```

All of the options for characters that are allowable in formatting sequences are given in the reference at the end of the book. There are quite a few options, but none are particularly difficult to use. Remember, you can always try out a formatting sequence interactively in Python, to see if it does what you expect it to do.

7.6.2 Named parameters and formatting sequences

Finally, there is one additional feature available with the string modulus operator that can be quite useful in certain circumstances. Unfortunately, to describe it, we're going to have to make use of a Python feature we haven't used yet—dictionaries, commonly called hashtables or associative arrays by other languages. You can skip ahead to the next chapter "Dictionaries" to learn about dictionaries, skip this section for now and come back to it later, or read straight through, trusting to the examples to make things clear.

Formatting sequence substitution can be done by name.

Formatting sequences can specify what should be substituted for them by name, rather than by position. When this is done, each formatting sequence has a name in parentheses, immediately following the initial % of the formatting sequence, like so:

"%(pi).2f" # *Note the name in parentheses—given in bold, here*

In addition, the argument to the right of the % operator is no longer given as a single value or tuple of values to be printed, but rather as a dictionary of values to be printed, with each named formatting sequence having a correspondingly named key in the dictionary. So, using the above formatting sequence with the string modulus operator, we might produce code like this (with the new parts—the formatting sequence name and dictionary—given in bold):

```
>>> dict = { 'e' : 2.718, 'pi' : 3.14159 }
>>> print "%(pi).2f - %(pi).4f - %(e).2f" % dict
⇒ 3.14 - 3.1416 - 2.72
```

This is particularly useful for using the string modulus operator with strings that perform a large number of substitutions, because one no longer has to keep track of the positional correspondences of formatting sequences and elements of a tuple on the right-hand side. The order in which elements are defined in the dict argument is irrelevant, and the template string may use values from dict more than once (as it does with the 'pi' entry).

C H A P T E R   8

Dictionaries

This chapter discusses dictionaries, Python's name for associative arrays, which it implements using hash tables. Dictionaries are amazingly useful, even in simple programs.

Because dictionaries are less familiar to many programmers than other basic data structures such as lists and strings, some of the examples illustrating dictionary use are slightly more complex than the corresponding examples for other built-in data structures. It may be necessary to read parts of the next chapter, "Control flow", to fully understand some of the examples in this chapter.

8.1   What is a dictionary?

A dictionary is an indexed structure in which the indices are not restricted to integers.

If you've never used associative arrays or hash tables in other languages, then a good way to start understanding the use of dictionaries is to compare them with lists. In some ways, dictionaries are a generalized form of lists; in other ways, dictionaries are more restrictive than lists:

- Values in lists are accessed by means of integers called *indices*, which indicate where in the list a given value is found.

Dictionaries access values by means of integers, strings, or other Python objects called *keys*, which indicate where in the dictionary a given value is found. In other words, both lists and dictionaries provide indexed access to arbitrary values, but the set of items which can be used as dictionary indices is much larger than, and contains, the set of items which can be used as list indices.

- Both lists and dictionaries can store objects of any type.

Dictionaries are not ordered.

- Values stored in a list are implicitly *ordered* by their position in the list, because the indices that access these values are consecutive integers; the programmer may or may not care about this ordering, but it can be used if desired. Values stored in a dictionary are not implicitly ordered relative to one another, because dictionary keys are not just numbers. Note that a programmer using a dictionary can define an ordering on the items in a dictionary by using another data structure (often a list) to store such an ordering explicitly; this does not change the fact that dictionaries have no implicit (built-in) ordering.

Create a dictionary by using {}.

In spite of the differences between them, use of dictionaries and lists often appears alike. As a start, an empty dictionary is created much like an empty list, but with curly braces instead of square brackets:

Dictionary assignments take the form `dict[key] = value.`

```
>>>
>>> x = []  # create a new, empty list and assign it to x.
>>> y = {}  # create a new, empty DICTIONARY, and assign it to y.
```

Once a dictionary has been created, values may be stored in it as if it were a list:

Positions in a dictionary are created as necessary.

```
...
>>> y[0] = 'Hello'
>>> y[1] = 'Goodbye'
```

Even in the above assignments, there is already a significant operational difference between the dictionary and list usage. Trying to do the same thing with a list would result in an error, because in Python it is illegal to assign to a position in a list that does not already exist. For example, if we try to assign to the 0th element of the list x:

```
...
>>> x[0] = 'Hello'
Traceback (innermost last):
  File "<stdin>", line 1, in ?
IndexError: list assignment index out of range
```

Elements in dictionaries are accessed similarly to elements in lists.

This is not a problem with dictionaries; new positions in dictionaries are created as necessary.

Having stored some values in the dictionary, we can now access and use them:

```
...
>>> print y[0]
Hello
>>> y[1] + ", Friend."
⇒ 'Goodbye, Friend'
```

All in all, this makes a dictionary look pretty much like a list. Now for the big difference; let's store (and use) some values under keys that are not integers:

```
    ...

>>> y["two"] = 2
>>> y["pi"] = 3.14
>>> y["two"] * y["pi"]
⇒  6.28
```

This is definitely something that can't be done with lists! While list indices must be integers, dictionary keys are much less restricted—they may be numbers, strings, or one of a wide range of other Python objects. This makes dictionaries a natural for jobs that lists can't do. For example, it would make more sense to implement a telephone directory application with dictionaries than with lists, because the phone number for a person can be stored indexed by that person's last name.

8.1.1   Why dictionaries are called dictionaries

A dictionary is a way of mapping from one set of arbitrary objects to an associated, but equally arbitrary set of objects. Actual dictionaries, thesauri, or translation books are a good analogy in the real world. To see how natural this correspondence is, here is the start of a English to French color translator:

```
    >>>

>>> EnglishToFrench = {}                       # Create an empty dictionary.
>>> EnglishToFrench['red'] = 'rouge'           # Store three words in it.
>>> EnglishToFrench['blue'] = 'bleu'
>>> EnglishToFrench['green'] = 'vert'
>>> print "red is ", EnglishToFrench['red']   # Obtain the value for 'red'.
red is rouge
```

8.2   *Other dictionary operations*

Besides basic element assignment and access, dictionaries support a number of other operations. Dictionaries may be defined explicitly as a series of `key:value` pairs separated by commas:

```
    >>>

>>> EnglishToFrench = {'red':'rouge','blue':'bleu','green':'vert'}
```

`len` returns the number of entries in a dictionary.

```
    ...

>>> len(EnglishToFrench)
⇒  3
```

A list of all the keys in the dictionary can be obtained with the **keys** method. This is often used to iterate over the contents of a dictionary using Python's `for` loop, described later in the book.

```
>>> EnglishToFrench.keys()
⇒  ['green', 'blue', 'red']
```

The order of the keys in a list returned by `keys` has no meaning—they are not necessarily sorted, and they do not necessarily occur in the order they were created. In fact, your Python might print out the keys in a different order than my Python did. If you need keys sorted, you can store them in a list variable, and then sort that list.

values returns a list of all values in a dictionary.

It is also possible to obtain a list of all the values stored in a dictionary, using `values`:

```
>>> EnglishToFrench.values()
⇒  ['vert', 'bleu', 'rouge']
```

This method isn't used nearly as often as `keys`.

items returns a list of all key/value tuples in a dictionary.

The `items` method can be used to return all keys and their associated values as a list of tuples:

```
>>> EnglishToFrench.items()
⇒  [('green', 'vert'), ('blue', 'bleu'), ('red', 'rouge')]
```

del will remove an entry from a dictionary.

Like `keys`, this is often used in conjunction with a `for` loop to iterate over the contents of a dictionary.

The `del` statement can be used to remove an entry (key/value pair) from a dictionary:

```
>>> EnglishToFrench.items()
⇒  [('green', 'vert'), ('blue', 'bleu'), ('red', 'rouge')]
>>> del EnglishToFrench['green']
>>> EnglishToFrench.items()
⇒  [('blue', 'bleu'), ('red', 'rouge')]
```

has_key tests if a key exists in a dictionary.

Attempting to access a key that isn't in a dictionary is an error in Python. There are two ways to handle this. First, you can test the dictionary for the presence of a key with the `has_key` method, which returns a true value if a dictionary has a value stored under the given key, and false otherwise:

```
>>> EnglishToFrench.has_key('red')
⇒  1
>>> EnglishToFrench.has_key('orange')
⇒  0
```

get returns a value associated with a key, or a configurable value if the given key doesn't exist in the dictionary.

Alternatively, you can use the `get` function. It returns the value associated with a key, if the dictionary contains that key, but returns its second argument if the dictionary doesn't contain the key.

```
>>> print EnglishToFrench.get('blue', 'No translation')
bleu
>>> print EnglishToFrench.get('chartreuse', 'No translation')
No translation
```

Use copy to obtain a copy of a dictionary.

The second argument is optional. If it is not included, `get` will return None if the dictionary doesn't contain the key. (As an unrelated point, the interested reader may find it a challenge to figure out why `print` was used in the last example above.)

A copy of a dictionary can be obtained using the `copy` method.

```
>>>
>>> x = {0 :'zero', 1 :'one'}
>>> y = x.copy
>>> y
⇒   {1: 'one', 0: 'zero'}
```

This will make a shallow copy of the dictionary. This will likely be all you will need in most situations. For dictionaries that contain any modifiable objects as values (i.e., lists or other dictionaries), you might want to make a deep copy using the `copy.deepcopy` function. See "Nested lists and deep copies" (subsection 6.6) of "Lists and tuples" (chapter 6) for an introduction to the concept of shallow and deep copies.

The `update` method will update a first dictionary with all the key-value pairs of a second dictionary. For keys that are common to both, the values from the second dictionary will override those of the first.

Use update to combine the entries of two dictionaries.

```
>>>
>>> z = { 1: 'One', 2: 'Two'}
>>> x = {0 :'zero', 1 :'one'}
>>> x.update(z)
>>> x
⇒   {2: 'Two', 1: 'One', 0: 'zero'}
```

8.3 Word counting

Assume we have a file which contains a list of words, one word per line. We want to know how many times each word occurs in the file. Dictionaries can be used to do this very easily, (dictionary-specific code given in bold):

```
import string
SampleString = "To be or not to be"
occurrences = {}
for word in string.split(SampleString):
    occurrences[word] = occurrences.get(word, 0) + 1
for word in occurrences.keys():
    print "The word", word, "occurs", \
          occurrences[word], \
          "time(s) in the string"
```

Increment the occurrences count for this word. ●

This is simpler than the simplest list-based approach I could think up. It is also probably much faster.

If you try out this example, remember that the indentation is necessary in Python. If you type it directly into the basic interactive mode or IDLE's Python Shell window you will also need to add an extra line before the second for loop (as this extra line is always needed here for the outermost indentation level). This is not necessary if you type this into a file (i.e. module or script).

8.4 What can be used as a key?

Any immutable object may be used as a key.

In the examples above, strings were used as keys, but Python permits more than just strings to be used in this manner. Any Python object that is immutable can be used as a key to a dictionary.

In Python, as discussed earlier, any object that can be modified is called *mutable*. Lists are mutable, because list elements can be added, changed, or removed. Dictionaries are also mutable, for the same reason. Numbers are immutable. If a variable x is holding the number 3, and you assign 4 to x, you've changed the value in x, but you haven't changed the number 3; 3 is still 3. Strings are also immutable. `list[n]` returns the nth element of `list`, `string[n]` returns the nth character of `string`, and `list[n]` = `value` changes the *n*th element of `list`—but `string[n]` = `character` is illegal in Python, and causes an error.

The reason for this restriction on dictionary keys is efficiency. Dictionaries can perform lookups quickly when their keys are known to be immutable. Allowing mutable keys would make dictionaries so slow that they would be useless.

Unfortunately, this means that lists can't be used as dictionary keys. However, there are many instances when it would be convenient to have a list-like key. For example, it's convenient to store information about a person under a key consisting of both their first and last names, which could be easily done if we could use a two-element list as a key.

Lists can't be used as dictionary keys, but tuples can.

Python solves this difficulty by providing tuples, which are basically immutable lists—they're created and used similarly to lists, except that once you've got them, you can't modify them. However, there is one further restriction necessary to ensure they don't change. Only tuples that don't contain any mutable objects nested within them are valid to use as keys for dictionaries. Tuples have been discussed in a previous chapter. The next sections give examples illustrating how tuples and dictionaries can work together.

8.5 Sparse matrices

In mathematical terms, a *matrix* is a two-dimensional grid of numbers, usually written in textbooks as a grid with square brackets on each side, like so:

$$\begin{bmatrix} 3 & 0 & -2 & 11 \\ 0 & 9 & 0 & 0 \\ 0 & 7 & 0 & 0 \\ 0 & 0 & 0 & -5 \end{bmatrix}$$

A fairly standard way to represent such a matrix is by means of a list of lists. In Python, it would be presented like this:

```
matrix = [[3, 0, -2, 11], [0, 9, 0, 0], [0, 7, 0, 0], [0, 0, 0, -5]]
```

Elements in the matrix can then be accessed by row and column number:

```
element = matrix[rownum][colnum]
```

However, in some applications, such as weather forecasting, it is common for matrices to be very large—thousands of elements to a side, meaning millions of elements in total. It is also common for such matrices to contain many zero elements. In some applications, all but a small percentage of the matrix elements may be set to zero. In order to conserve memory, it is common for such matrices to be stored in a form where only the nonzero elements are actually stored. Such representations are called *sparse matrices*.

It is simple to implement sparse matrices using dictionaries with tuple indices. For example, the sparse matrix above could be represented as follows:

```
matrix = {(0, 0):3, (0, 2):-2, (0, 3):11,
          (1, 1):9, (2, 1):7, (3, 3):5}
```

Now, an individual matrix element at a given row and column number can be accessed by the following bit of code:

```
if matrix.has_key((rownum, colnum)):
    element = matrix[(rownum, colnum)]
else:
    element = 0
```

A slightly less clear (but more efficient) way of doing this is to use the dictionary get method, which can be told to return 0 if it can't find a key in the dictionary, and otherwise returns the value associated with that key. This avoids two dictionary lookups.

```
element = matrix.get((rownum, colnum), 0)
```

If you are considering doing extensive work with matrices, you might want to look into the NumPy, numeric computation package.

8.6 Dictionaries as caches

The following is an example of how dictionaries can be used as *caches*, data structures that store results to avoid recalculating those results over and over. A short while ago, I wrote a function called sole, which took three integers as arguments, and returned a result. It looked something like this:

```
def sole(m, n, t):
    #... do some time-consuming calculations ...
    return(result)
```

The problem with this function was that it really was time-consuming, and because I was calling sole tens of thousands of times, the program ran too slowly.

However, sole was called with only about two hundred different combinations of arguments during any program run. That is, I might call sole(12, 20, 6) fifty or more times during the execution of my program, and similarly for many other combinations of arguments. By eliminating the recalculation of `sole` on identical arguments, I'd save a huge amount of time. I used a dictionary with tuples as keys, like so:

```
sole_cache = {}

def sole(m, n, t):
    if sole_cache.has_key((m, n, t)):
        return sole_cache[(m, n, t)]
    else:
        # . . . do some time-consuming calculations . . .
        sole_cache[(m, n, t)] = result
        return result
```

The rewritten `sole` function uses a global variable to store previous results. The global variable is a dictionary, and the keys of the dictionary are tuples corresponding to argument combinations that have been given to `sole` in the past. Then, anytime `sole` passed an argument combination for which a result has already been calculated, it simply returns that stored result, rather than recalculating it.

!!!

Using dictionaries as caches can speed up your program.

This particular instance provides a good example of why one can't assume a byte-compiled language such as Python is inherently slower than a fully compiled language such as C. The original sole code was written in C, and C is much faster than Python at basic mathematical calculations. Yet, my Python implementation of the program actually runs significantly faster than the C program. What happened?

C has no equivalent of built-in dictionaries, so there was no easy way for the original programmer to cache `sole` values for later reuse.* As a result, the C program does a complete sole calculation every time its `sole` function is called. An actual sole calculation is much slower in the Python program, but the benefits of caching and reusing results make this irrelevant, and the Python code ends up being far faster.

8.7 *Efficiency of dictionaries*

Dictionary lookups are very fast.

Programmers from a traditional compiled-language background might hesitate to use dictionaries, due to a worry that they are less efficient than lists (arrays). This was a worry of mine for awhile. The truth is the Python dictionary implementation is very fast. A lot of the internal language features rely on dictionaries and a lot of work has gone into making them efficient. It will take longer (on average) to look up an element in a dictionary than to look it up in a list, but the difference is probably not as large as you might think. If the problem can be solved more easily and cleanly by using a dictionary than by using a list, do it that way.

---

* There are libraries available that provide hash table functionality for C.

C H A P T E R   9

Control flow

Python provides a complete set of control flow elements, with loops and conditionals.

9.1   The while loop

The while loop is fairly standard, but does have an 'else' clause.

You've come across the basic while loop several times already. The full while loop looks like this:

```
while condition:
    body
else:      # The 'else' is optional—it isn't used much.
    post-code
```

condition is an expression that evaluates to a true or false value. As long as it is true, the *body* will be executed repeatedly. If it evaluates to false, the while loop will execute the *post-code* section and then terminate. If the condition starts out by being false, the *body* won't be executed at all, just the *post-code*. The *body* and *post-code* are each sequences of one or more Python statements that are separated by newlines and are at the same level of indentation. The Python interpreter uses this level to delimit them. Thus no other delimiters, such as braces or brackets, are necessary.

break *and*
continue *can*
modify the
behavior of a
while *(or other*
type of) loop.

The two special statements break and continue can be used in the *body* of a while loop. If break is executed, it immediately terminates the while loop and not even the *post-code* will be executed. If continue is executed, it causes the remainder of the *body* to be skipped over; the condition is evaluated again, and the loop proceeds as normal.

Note that the else part of the while loop is optional and not often used. That's because, as long as there is no break in the *body*, this loop

```
while condition:
    body
else:
    post-code
```

and this loop

```
while condition:
    body
post-code
```

do the same things—and the second is simpler to understand. I probably wouldn't have mentioned the else clause except that if you didn't learn about it now, you may have found it confusing if you found this syntax in another person's code. Also, there are some situations where it is useful.

9.2 The if-elif-else statement

The if *statement*
can have multi-
ple 'elif' clauses.

The most general form of the if-then-else construct in Python is

```
if condition1:
    body1
elif condition2:
    body2
elif condition3:
    body3
    .
    .
    .
elif condition(n-1):
    body(n-1)
else:
    body(n)
```

It says: if *condition1* is true, execute *body1*; otherwise, if *condition2* is true, execute *body2*; otherwise . . ., and so on, until it either finds a condition that evaluates to true, or hits the else clause, in which case it executes *body(n)*. As for the while loop, the *bodies* are again each sequences of one or more Python statements that are separated by newlines and are at the same level of indentation.

Of course, you don't need all that luggage for every conditional. You can leave out the elif parts, or the else part, or both. If a conditional can't find any body to execute (no conditions evaluate to true, and there is no else part), it does nothing.

The body after the if statement is required. However, you can use the pass statement here (as you can anywhere in Python where a statement is required). It performs no action:

```
if x < 5:
    pass
else:
    x = 5
```

There is no case (or switch) statement in Python.

9.3 The for loop

for iterates over a list of values. It has an optional else *clause.*

A for loop in Python is quite different from a for loop in C. Instead of incrementing and testing a variable on each iteration, which is what C for loops usually do, Python iterates over a sequence of values. The sequence can be a list, a tuple, or a string. This can be quite powerful. The general form is

```
for variable in sequence:
    body
else:                    # the 'else' part is optional
    post-code
```

body will be executed once for each element of *sequence:*. *variable* is set to be the first element of *sequence*, and *body* is executed; then *variable* is set to be the second element of *sequence*, and *body* is executed; and so on, for each remaining element of the sequence.

The else part is optional. As with the else part of a while loop, it is rarely used. break and continue do the same thing in a for loop as in a while loop.

This small loop prints out the reciprocal of each number in x:

```
x = [1.0, 2.0, 3.0]
for n in x:
    print 1/n
```

9.3.1 The range function

Use range *to iterate over the indices of a list.*

There are times when you need to loop with explicit indices (to know the position at which values occur in a list). The range command can be used together with the len command on lists, to generate a sequence of indices for use by the for loop. This code prints out all the positions in a list where it finds negative numbers:

```
x = [1, 3, -7, 4, 9, -5, 4]
for i in range(len(x)):
    if x[i] < 0:
        print "Found a negative number at index ", i
```

range can also provide control over starting and stepping values in an interation.

Given a number *n*, range(*n*) returns a sequence 0, 1, 2, . . ., *n*–2, *n*–1. So, passing it the length of a list (found using len) produces a list of the indices for that list's elements.

Two variants on the range function can be used to gain more control over the sequence it produces. If range is used with two numeric arguments, the first argument is the starting number for the resulting sequence, and the second number is the number the resulting sequence goes up to (but doesn't include). Here are a few examples:

```
range(3, 7)
⇒ [3, 4, 5, 6]
```

```
range(2, 10)
⇒  [2, 3, 4, 5, 6, 7, 8, 9]
range(5, 3)
⇒  []
```

This still doesn't allow us to count backwards, which is why the value of range(5, 3) is an empty list. To count backwards, or to count by any amount other than 1, we need to use the optional third argument to range, which gives a step value by which counting proceeds:

```
range(0, 10, 2)
⇒  [0, 2, 4, 6, 8]
range(5, 0, -1)
⇒  [5, 4, 3, 2, 1]
```

Lists returned by range always include the starting value given as an argument to range, and never include the ending value given as an argument.

xrange is like range but uses only a small amount of memory.

One final variant on range is the xrange function, which gives exactly the same results, but which doesn't build a Python list—it just appears to. This is useful when using explicit loops to iterate over really large lists. range(10000000) actually builds a list with ten million elements in it, which will take up quite a bit of memory. xrange(10000000) doesn't build a list, and takes up only a small amount of memory, but can be used in the same manner as range(10000000) in a for loop. As is often the case, there is a speed versus memory tradeoff here. You should be aware that xrange is much slower than range and thus you probably want to use it only when you absolutely have to.

9.3.2 The for loop and tuple unpacking

Tuple unpacking can be used to make some for loops cleaner. The following code takes a list of two-element tuples, and calculates the value of the sum of the products of the two numbers in each tuple (a moderately common mathematical operation, in some fields):

```
list = [(1, 2), (3, 7), (9, 5)]
result = 0
for t in list:
    result = result + (t[0] * t[1])
```

Items in the sequence may be unpacked into multiple variables

Here is the same thing, but cleaner:

```
list = [(1, 2), (3, 7), (9, 5)]
result = 0
# On each iteration of the for loop, 'x' will contain element 0 of the current tuple from 'list', and
# 'y' will contain element 1 of the current tuple from 'list'.
for x, y in list:
 result = result + (x * y)
```

In the latter example, we have used a tuple x, y immediately after the for keyword, instead of the usual single variable. Using a tuple in this manner is a convenience of Python, and doing this indicates to Python that each element of the list is expected to be a tuple of appropriate size to unpack into the variable names mentioned in the tuple after the for.

9.4 Statements, blocks, and indentation

Since the control flow constructs we encountered in this chapter are the first to make use of blocks and indentation, this is a good time to revisit the subject.

The `if-elif-else` construct, `while` loops and `for` loops are compound statements.

Python uses the indentation of the statements to determine the delimitation of the different blocks (or *bodies*) of the flow control constructs. A block consists of one or more statements, which are usually separated by newlines. Examples of Python statements are the assignment statement, function calls, the `print` statement, the placeholder `pass` statement, and the `del` statement. The control flow constructs (`if-elif-else`, `while` and `for` loops) are compound statements.

```
compound statement clause:
    block
compound statement clause:
    block
```

A compound statement contains one or more clauses that are each followed by indented blocks.

Compound statements can appear in blocks just like any other statement. When they do, they create nested blocks.

There are also a couple of special cases you may encounter. Multiple statements may be placed on the same line if they are separated by semicolons. A block containing a single line may be placed on the same line after the semicolon of a clause of a compound statements.

Statements separated by semicolons may be placed on the same line and a single line statement block may be placed on the same line after a colon (:).

```
>>>
>>> x = 1; y = 0; z = 0
>>> if x > 0: y = 1; z = 10
...    else: y = -1
...
>>> print x, y, z
1, 1, 10
```

Improperly indented code will result in a `SyntaxError` exception being raised. There are two forms of this that you may encounter. The first is:

Incorrectly indented code will result in a SyntaxError.

```
>>>
>>>
>>> x = 1
⇒   File "<stdin>", line 1
⇒       x =1
⇒       ^
⇒   SyntaxError: invalid syntax
>>>
```

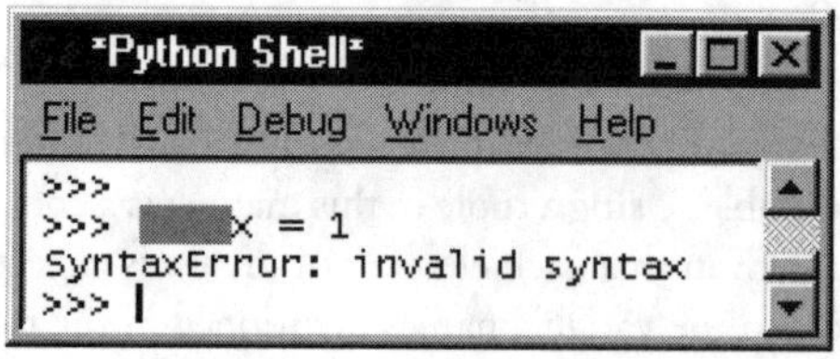

Figure 9.1 Indentation error

We indented a line that should not have been indented. In the basic mode, the carat (^) indicates the spot where the problem occurred. In the IDLE Python Shell (figure 9.1), the invalid indent is highlighted. The same message would occur if we didn't indent where necessary (i.e., the first line after a compound statement clause).

There is a situation where this can occur that can be quite confusing. If you are using an editor that displays tabs in four space increments (or the Windows interactive mode which indents the first tab only four spaces in from the prompt) and indent one line with four spaces and then the next line with a tab, the two lines may look to you to be at the same level of indentation. But you will receive this exception because Python maps the tab to eight spaces.

On the subject of the basic interactive mode and the IDLE Python Shell, you will likely have noticed that you need an extra line after the outermost level of indentation:

```
>>>
>>> x = 1
>>> if x ==1:
...         y = 2
...         if v > 0:
...             z = 2
...         v = 0
...
>>> x = 2
```

No line is necessary after the line z = 2, but one is needed after the line v = 0. This line is not necessary if you are placing your code in a module in a file.

The second form of exception will occur if you indent a statement in a block less than the legal amount:

```
>>>
>>>     x = 1
>>>     if x ==1:
...             y = 2
...         z = 2
⇒   inconsistent dedent
⇒       File "<stdin>", line 3
⇒         z=2
⇒           ^
    SyntaxError: invalid token
```

Here, the line containing z = 2 is not lined up properly under the line containing y = 2. This form is rare, but I mention it again because in a similar situation, it might be confusing.

Actually, Python will allow you to indent any amount and won't complain regardless of how much you vary it as long as you are consistent within a single block. However, please don't take improper advantage of this. The accepted standard is to simply use four spaces (or a tab) for each level of indentation.

Statements can be broken across lines by placing a \ as the last character. You can also break between any two tokens when in (), [], or {} brackets.

Before leaving indentation, I'll cover breaking up statements across multiple lines. This of course is necessary more often as the level of indentation increases. You can explicitly break up a line using the backslash character. You can also implicitly break any statement between tokens when within a set of (), {}, or [] delimiter (i.e., when typing a set of values in a list, a tuple, or a dictionary, or a set of arguments in a function call or any expression within a set of brackets). You can indent the continuation line of a statement to any level you desire.

```
>>>
```

```
>>> print 'string1', 'string2', 'string3' \
...   ,'string4', 'string5'
string1 string2 string3 string4 string5
>>> x =  100 + 200 +300 \
...        + 400 + 500
>>> x
⇒  1500
>>> v = [100, 300, 500, 700, 900,
...        1100, 1300]
>>> v
⇒  [100, 300, 500, 700, 900, 1100, 1300]
>>> max(1000, 300, 500,
...        800, 1200)
⇒  1200
>>> x=(100 + 200 + 300
...        + 400 + 500)
>>> x
⇒  1500
```

Split strings across lines using the \ outside of the delimiters to avoid including indentation tabs.

A string can be broken with a \ as well. However, any indentation tabs or spaces will become part of the string. To avoid this you can use the fact that any set of string literals separated by white space is automatically concatenated.

```
>>> "strings separated by whitespace "       \
    """"are automatically""" ' concatenated'
⇒  'strings separated by whitespace are automatically concatenated'
>>> x = 1
>>> if x > 0:
...      string1 = "this string broken by a backslash will end up \
...      with the indentation tabs in it"
...
>>> string1
⇒  'this string broken by a backslash will end up \011\011\011with
    the indentation tabs in it'
>>> if x > 0:
...      string1 = "this can be easily avoided by splitting the " \
...          "string in this way"
...
>>> string1
⇒  'this can be easily avoided by splitting the string in this way'
```

9.5 Boolean values and expressions

The examples of control flow used conditional tests in a fairly obvious manner, but never really explained what constitutes true or false in Python, nor what expressions can be used where a conditional test is needed. This section describes aspects of Python.

9.5.1 Most Python objects can be used as booleans

Python is similar to C with respect to Boolean values, in that it does not have any special values to mean true or false. C uses the integer 0 to mean false, and any other integer to mean true. Python generalizes this idea; zero or empty values are false, and any other values are true. In practical terms, this means that:

Zero or empty values are `false`*; anything else is* `true`*.*

1   The numbers 0, 0.0, 0L and 0+0j are all `false`; any other number is `true`.
2   The empty string "" is `false`; any other string is `true`.
3   The empty list `[]` is `false`; any other list is `true`.
4   The empty dictionary `{}` is `false`, any other dictionary is `true`.
5   The special Python value `None` is always `false`.

There are some Python data structures we haven't looked at yet, but generally the same rule applies; if the data structure is empty or zero, it will be taken to mean false in a Boolean context, otherwise it will be taken to mean true. There are some objects, such as fileobjects and code objects, that don't have a sensible definition of a zero or empty element, and these objects shouldn't be used in a Boolean context.

9.5.2 Comparison and boolean operators

The normal complement of comparison operators is provided. and, or, *and* not *are the Boolean operators.*

Objects can be compared using normal operators: `<`, `<=`, `>`, `>=`, and so forth. `==` is the equality test operator, and either `!=` or `<>` may be used as the "not equal" to test. There are also `in` and `not in` operators to test membership in sequences (i.e., lists, tuples, strings, or dictionaries) as well as `is` and `is not` operators to test if two objects are the same.

Expressions which return a Boolean value may be combined into more complex expressions using the `and`, `or`, and `not` operators. This code snippet checks to see if a variable is within a certain range:

```
if 0 < x and x < 10:
    ...
```

Comparisons may be chained.

Python offers a nice shorthand for this particular type of compound statement; you can write it as you would in a math paper:

```
if 0 < x < 10:
    ...
```

Various rules of precedence apply, but when in doubt you can use parentheses to make sure Python interprets an expression the way you want it to. This is probably a good idea for complex expressions, regardless of whether it's necessary, because it makes it clear to future maintainers of the code exactly what is happening. See the reference appendix for more details on precedence.

The rest of this section is more advanced information and if this is your first read through this book as you are learning the language you may want to skip over it.

The and and or operators actually return objects. The and operator returns either the first false object (i.e., that an expression evaluates to) or the last object. Similarly, the or operator will return either the first true object or the last object. As with many other languages, evaluation will stop as soon as a true expression is found for the or operator or a false expression is found for the and operator.

```
>>>
```

```
>>> [2] and [3,4]
⇒   [3, 4]
>>> [] and 5
⇒   []
>>> [2] or [3,4]
⇒   [2]
>>> [] or 5
⇒   5
>>>
```

is tests whether two objects are the same while == tests whether they have the same value.

The ==, !=, and <> operators test if their operands contains the same value(s). They are used in most situations. The is and is not operators test if their operands are the same object.

```
>>> x = [0]
>>> y = [x, 1]
>>> x is y[0]          ● Here they reference the same object.
⇒   1
>>> x = [0]            ● Now x has been assigned to a new
>>> x is y[0]             object. So, although the values are
⇒   0                    the same, the objects are different.
>>> x == y[0]
⇒   1
```

Revisit "Nested lists and deep copies" (subsection 6.6) of "Lists and tuples" (chapter 6) if the above example is not clear to you.

C H A P T E R   1 0

Functions and procedures

This chapter assumes the reader is familiar with function definitions in at least one other computer language, and with the concepts that go along with function definitions, arguments, parameters, and so forth.

10.1 **Basic function and procedure definitions**

Use the def *key-word to define functions or procedures.*

The basic syntax for a Python function or procedure definition is

```
def name(parameter1, parameter2, . . .):
    body
```

As with control structures, Python uses indentation to delimit the body of the function definition. The following simple example puts the factorial code from a previous section into a function body, so we can simply call a fact function to obtain the factorial of a number:

Indentation delimits the function body.

```
def fact(n):
    """Return the factorial of the given number."""
```

```
r = 1
while n > 0:
    r = r * n
    n = n - 1
return r
```

The second line is the optional *documentation string*. Its value can be obtained by printing `fact.__doc__`. The intention of documentation strings is to describe the external behavior of a function, while internal information is left to comments.

There are browsing tools that extract the first line of document strings. It is a standard practice for multiline documentation strings to give a synopsis of the function in the first line, follow this by a blank second line, and end with the rest of the information being presented.

Procedures are just functions that do not return a value.

The only difference between a function and a procedure is the presence or absence of a `return` statement. In fact, all Python procedures are functions; if no explicit `return` is executed in the procedure body, then the special Python value `None` is returned, and if `return arg` is executed, then the value `arg` is immediately returned. Nothing else in the function body is executed once a `return` has been executed.

10.2 Assigning functions to variables

A function can be assigned to a variable.

Functions can be assigned, like other Python objects, to variables as shown in the following example:

```
>>>
>>> def FtoKelvin(degreesF): return 273.15 + (degreesF - 32) * 5/9.0
...
>>> def CtoKelvin(degreesC): return 273.15 + degreesC
...
>>> AbsTemperature = FtoKelvin
>>> AbsTemperature(32)
⟹  273.15
>>> AbsTemperature = CtoKelvin
>>> AbsTemperature(0)
⟹  273.15
```

They can thus be placed in lists, tuples, or dictionaries:

```
>>> t = { 'FtoK':FtoKelvin, 'CtoK:CtoKelvin }
>>> t['FtoK'](32)
⟹  273.15
>>> t['CtoK'](0)
⟹  273.15
```

10.3 Lambda expressions

Short functions like those above can also be defined using `lambda` expressions of the form

lambda *parameter1, parameter2, ...: statement*

These are unnamed functions that can be defined *in situ*. This is used in some cases to save having to declare simple functions in a separate place from where they are used. Our dictionary in the previous subsection could have been defined all in one place with:

```
>>> t2 = { 'FtoK':lambda, degF: 273.15+(degF-32)*5/9.0,
...     'CtoK':lambda, degC: 273.15+degC }
>>> t2['FtoK'](32)
⇒   273.15
```

10.4 *Function parameter options*

Python provides flexible options for defining function parameters. These are outlined below.

10.4.1 Default values

Function param-
eters can have
default values;
the default will
be used if the call
invoking the
function does not
pass in an argu-
ment for that
parameter.

Function parameters can have default values, which are declared by assigning a default value in the first line of the function definition, like so:

```
def fun(arg1, arg2=default2, arg3=default3, . . .)
```

Any number of parameters can be given default values. Parameters with default values must be defined as the last parameters in the parameter list. This is a result of the fact that Python, like most languages, pairs up arguments with parameters on a positional basis. There must be enough arguments to a function that the last parameter in that function's parameter list that does not have a default value gets an argument. See the next section, "Passing arguments by parameter name," for a more flexible mechanism.

The function below computes x to the power of y. However, if y isn't given in a call to the function, the default value of 2 is used, and the function is just the square function.

```
def power(x, y = 2):
    r = 1
    while y > 0:
        r = r * x
        y = y - 1
    return r
```

We can see the effect of the default argument in the following interactive session:

```
>>>
```

```
>>> power(3, 3)
⇒   27
>>> power(3)
⇒   9
```

10.4.2 Passing arguments by parameter name

Arguments can be passed by parameter name, instead of positionally.

Arguments can also be passed into a function using the name of the corresponding function parameter, rather than its position. Continuing with the interactive example just above, we can type

```
...
```

```
>>> power(2, 3)
⇒  8
>>> power(3, 2)
⇒  9
>>> power(y=2, x=3)
⇒  9
```

Because the arguments to power in the final invocation of it are named, their order is irrelevant; the arguments are associated with the parameters of the same name in the definition of power, and we get back 3^2. This type of argument passing is called *keyword passing*.

Keyword passing, in combination with the default argument capability of Python functions, can be highly useful when defining functions with large numbers of possible arguments, most of which have common defaults. For example, consider a function which is intended to produce a list with information about files in the current directory, and which uses Boolean arguments to indicate whether that list should include information such as file size, last modified date, and so forth, for each file. We could define such a function along these lines:

```
def listFileInfo(size=0, create_date=0, mod_date=0, ...):
    ...get file names...
    if size == 1:
        # code to get file sizes goes here
    if create_date == 1:
        # code to get create dates goes here
    .
    .
    .
    return fileinfostructure
```

and then call it from other code using keyword argument passing to indicate that we only wished certain information (in this example, the file size and modification date, but *not* the creation date):

```
fileinfo = listFileInfo(size=1, mod_date=1)
```

This type of argument handling is particularly suited for functions with very complex behavior, and one place such functions occur is in graphical user interfaces. If you ever use the Tkinter package to build GUIs in Python, you'll find that the use of optional, keyword-named arguments like this is invaluable.

10.4.3 Variable numbers of arguments

Python functions can also be defined to handle variable numbers of arguments. In fact, there are two different ways in which this can be done. One way handles the relatively

There are two different ways of defining Python functions that take a variable number of arguments.

'Excess' function arguments can be collected into a tuple structure.

familiar case where we wish to collect an unknown number of arguments at the end of the argument list into a list structure. The other method can collect an arbitrary number of keyword-passed arguments, which have no correspondingly named parameter in the function parameter list, into a dictionary. These two mechanisms are discussed below.

Dealing with an indefinite number of positional arguments

Prefixing the final parameter name of the function with a '*' causes all excess nonkeyword arguments in a call of a function (i.e., those positional arguments not assigned to another parameter) to be collected together, and assigned as a tuple to the given parameter. Here's a simple way to implement a function to find the maximum in a list of numbers. First, implement the function:

```
def maximum(*numbers):
    if len(numbers) == 0:
        return(None)
    else:
        max = numbers[0]
        for n in numbers[1:]:
            if n > max: max = n
        return max
```

Now, test out the behavior of the function:

```
>>>
```

```
>>> maximum(3, 2, 8)
⇒   8
>>> maximum(1, 5, 9, -2, 2)
⇒   9
```

Dealing with an indefinite number of arguments passed by keyword

'Excess' keyword-passed arguments can be collected into a dictionary.

An arbitrary number of keyword arguments can also be handled. If the final parameter in the parameter list is prefixed with '**', it will collect all excess *keyword-passed* arguments into a dictionary. The index for each entry in the dictionary will be the keyword (parameter name) for the excess argument. The value of that entry is the argument itself. An argument passed by keyword is excess in this context if the keyword by which it was passed does not match one of the parameter names of the function.

For example:

```
def exampleFun(x, y, **other):
    print "x:", x, "y:", y, ",keys in 'other':",other.keys()
    otherTotal = 0
    for k in other.keys():
        otherTotal = otherTotal + other[k]
    print "The total of values in 'other' is", otherTotal
```

Trying out this function in an interactive session reveals that it can handle arguments passed in under the keywords foo and bar, even though these are not parameter names in the function definition:

```
>>> exampleFun(2, y="1", foo=3, bar=4)
x:2 y:1 ,keys in 'other': ['foo', 'bar']
The total of values in 'other' is 7
```

10.4.4 Mixing argument-passing techniques

It is possible to use all of the argument-passing features of Python functions at the same time, although it can be confusing if not done with care. There are rules governing what you can do. See the appendix for the details.

10.5 Mutable objects as arguments

Changing a mutable object that has been passed in as a parameter will affect the corresponding argument. Reassignment will not.

Arguments are passed in by object reference. The parameter becomes a new reference to the object. For immutable objects (i.e., tuples, strings, and numbers), what is done with a parameter will have no effect outside the function. However, if you pass in a mutable object (i.e., list, dictionary, or class instance), any change made to the object itself will change what the argument is referencing outside the function. Reassigning the parameter will, however, not affect the argument:

```
def f(n, list1, list2):
    list1.append(3)
    list2 = [4, 5, 6]
    n = n+1

>>> x = 5; y = [1, 2]; z = [4, 5]
>>> f(x, y, z)
>>> x, y, z
⇒  (5, [1, 2, 3], [4, 5])
```

Only y sees a change because the actual list it points at was changed.

10.6 Local and global variables

Returning to our definition of fact from the beginning of this chapter:

```
def fact(n):
    """Return the factorial of the given number."""
    r = 1
    while n > 0:
        r = r * n
        n = n - 1
    return r
```

Function parameters and variables created within a function are local to the function body. Global variables may be explicitly accessed with the global *statement.*

The variables r and n are both *local* to any particular call of the factorial function; changes to them made when the function is executing have no effect on any variables outside the function. Any variables in the parameter list of a function, and any variables created within a function by an assignment (like "r = 1" in fact), are local to the function.

A variable may explicitly be made global by declaring it so at the beginning of a function using the global statement. Global variables can be accessed and changed by the function. They exist outside the function, and can also be accessed and changed by other functions which declare them global, or by code which is not within a function. Let's take a look at an example to see the difference between local and global variables:

```
def fun():
    global a
    a = 1
    b = 2
```

This defines a function which treats a as a global variable and b as a local variable, and attempts to modify both a and b.

Now, test this function:

n fun is an assignment to the global variable a also existing [...] hat global variable to hold the value 1 instead of the value [...] r b—the local variable called b inside fun is different from [...]

to a variable existing outside a function, you must explicitly [...]. However, if you are simply accessing a variable which exists [...] t need to declare it global. If Python cannot find a variable [...] e, it will attempt to look up the name in the global scope. [...] les will automatically be sent through to the correct global [...] mmend using this shortcut. It is much clearer to a reader if [...] declared as global. Further, the use of global variables at all [...] mething you want to limit to only rare occasions.

tes, which are functions without an explicit `return` state-ment, [...] exible. There is no need to declare internal function vari-[...] during the execution of a function body are local to that [...] iables can easily be accessed using the `global` statement. [...] exceedingly powerful argument-passing features:

- Default values may be provided for function parameters.
- Arguments may be passed positionally or by parameter name.
- Functions can collect arguments into tuples, giving the ability to define functions that take an indefinite number of arguments.
- Functions can collect arguments into dictionaries, giving the ability to define functions that take an indefinite number of arguments passed by parameter name.

CHAPTER 11

Modules and scoping rules

Modules are used to organize larger Python projects. The Python language itself is split into modules to make it more manageable. You don't need to organize your own code into modules, but if you're writing any programs more than a few pages long, or any code that you want to reuse, you should probably do so.

11.1 What is a module?

A module is just a single file containing related functions, constants, and so forth.

A module is a file containing code. A module defines a group of Python functions or other objects. The name of the module is derived from the name of the file.

Modules will most often contain Python source code, but they can also be compiled C or C++ object files. Compiled modules and Python source modules are used in the same way.

As well as grouping related Python objects, modules help avoid name clash problems. For example, you might write a module for your program called `MyModule`, which defines a function called `reverse`. In the same program you might also wish to make use of somebody else's module called `OtherModule`, which also defines a function called `reverse`, but which does something different from your `reverse` function. In a language without modules, it would be impossible to use two different reverse functions. In Python, it's trivial— you simply refer to them in your main program as `MyModule.reverse` and `OtherModule.reverse`.

Modules are also used to make Python itself more manageable. Most standard Python functions are not built into the core of the language, but instead are provided via specific modules, which the programmer can load as needed.

11.2 *A first module*

The best way to learn about modules is probably to make one, so...

Create a text file called mymath.py, and in that text file, enter the following Python code (if you are using IDLE, just select New window (figure 11.1) from the File menu and start typing):

File mymath.py

```python
"""mymath - our example math module"""
pi = 3.14159

def area(r):
    """area(r): return the area of a circle with radius r."""
    global pi
    return(pi * r * r)
```

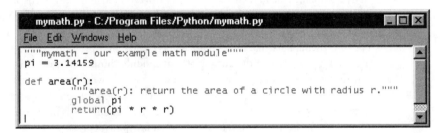

Figure 11.1 An IDLE edit window provides the same editing functionality as the shell window including automatic indentation and colorization.

Save this for now in the directory where your Python executable is. This code merely defines a constant and a function. The .py filename suffix is mandatory for all Python code files. It identifies that file to the Python interpreter as consisting of Python source code. As with functions, we have the option of putting in a document string as the first line of our module. Now start up the Python Shell, and type

```
>>>
```

```
>>> pi
Traceback (innermost last):
 File "<stdin>", line 1, in ?
NameError: pi
>>> area(2)
Traceback (innermost last):
 File "<stdin>", line 1, in ?
NameError: area
```

In other words, Python doesn't have the constant pi or the function area built in. Now, type:

```
...
```

```
>>> import mymath
>>> pi
Traceback (innermost last):
File "<stdin>", line 1, in ?
NameError: pi
>>> mymath.pi
⇒  3.14159
>>> mymath.area(2)
⇒  12.56636
>>> mymath.__doc__
⇒  'mymath - our example math module'
>>> mymath.area.__doc__
⇒  'area(r): return the area of a circle with radius r.'
```

Modules are made accessible to other code with the `import` *statement. The other code then refers to names within that imported module by prepending the internal names with the module's name.*

We've brought in the definitions for `pi` and `area` from the mymath.py file, using the `import` statement (which automatically adds on the .py suffix when it searches for the file defining the module named `"mymath"`). However, the new definitions aren't directly accessible; typing `pi` by itself gave an error, and typing `area(2)` by itself would give an error. Instead, we access `pi` and `area` by *prepending* them with the name of the module which contains them. This guarantees name safety. There may be another module out there which also defines `pi` (maybe the author of that module thinks that pi is 3.14, or 3.14159265), but that is of no concern. Even if that other module were imported, its version of `pi` will be accessed by *othermodulename.pi*, which is different from `mymath.pi`. This form of access is often referred to as *qualification* (i.e., the variable `pi` is being qualified by the module `mymath`). We may also refer to `pi` as an *attribute* of `mymath`.

Names within a module can be explicitly imported into other code, which means the other code can refer to those names without prepending the module name.

Definitions within a module can access other definitions within that module, without prepending the module name. The `mymath.area` function accesses the `mymath.pi` constant as just `pi`.

If we want to, we can also specifically ask for names from a module to be imported in such a manner that we don't have to prepend them with the module name. Type:

```
...
```

```
>>> from mymath import pi
>>> pi
```

```
⇒    3.14159
>>> area(2)
Traceback (innermost last):
 File "<stdin>", line 1, in ?
NameError: area
```

The name `pi` is now directly accessible because we specifically requested it using `from module import name`.

The function `area` still needs to be called as `mymath.area`, though, because it was not explicitly imported.

Using `import` *again won't pick up changes made to a module, but* `reload` *will.*

You may want to use the basic interactive mode or IDLE's Python Shell to incrementally test a module as you are creating it. However, if you change your module on disk, retyping the `import` command will not cause it to load again. You need to use the `reload` function for this.

```
>>>
```

```
>>> import mymath

>>> reload(mymath)
⇒   <module 'mymath'>
```

When a module is reloaded (or imported for the first time), all of its code is parsed. So a syntax exception will be raised if an error is found. On the other hand, if everything is okay, a .pyc file (i.e., `mymath.pyc`) containing Python byte code will be created.

Reloading a module does not put you back into exactly the same situation as when you start a new session and import it for the first time. However, the differences will not normally cause you any problems. If interested, you can look up `reload` in the built-in functions section of the *Python Language Reference* to find the details.

Of course, modules don't need to be used from the interactive Python shell. They can also be imported into scripts, or other modules for that matter; just enter suitable `import` statements at the beginning of your program file. Also, internally to Python, the interactive session and a script are considered modules as well.

To summarize:

- A module is a file defining Python objects.
- If the name of the module file is *modulename*`.py`, then the Python name of the module itself is *modulename*.
- A module named *modulename* can be brought into use with the "`import` *modulename*" statement. After this statement is executed, objects defined in the module can be accessed as *modulename.objectname*.
- Specific names from a module can be brought directly into your program using the "`from` *modulename* `import` *objectname*" statement. This makes *objectname* accessible to your program without needing to prepend it with *modulename*, and is useful for bringing in names that are often used.

11.3 *The import statement*

There are three different forms of the `import` statement. The most basic,

```
import modulename
```

simply searches for a Python module of the given name, parses its contents, and makes it available. The importing code can make use of the contents of the module, but any references by that code to names within the module must still be prepended with the module name. If the named module is not found, an error will be generated. Exactly where Python looks for modules will be discussed shortly.

You can explicitly import objects (names) from a module, and then refer to those objects directly.

The second form permits specific names from a module to be explicitly imported into the code:

```
from modulename import name1, name2, name3, . . .
```

Each of *name1*, *name2*, and so forth, from within *modulename* are made available to the importing code; code after the import statement can make use of any of *name1*, *name2*, *name3*, . . ., without prepending the module name.

You can explicitly import all names from a module, and refer to them directly.

Finally, there's a general form of the from . . . import . . . statement:

```
from modulename import *
```

The '*' stands for all of the names in *modulename*. This imports almost all names from *modulename*, and makes them available to the importing code, without the necessity of prepending the module name.

This particular form of importing should be used with some care. If two modules both define a name, and you import both modules using this form of importing, you'll end up with a name clash. It also makes it more difficult for readers of your code to determine where names you are using originate. When using either of the two previous forms of the import statement you give your reader explicit information about where they are from.

However, some modules (such as Tkinter and types, which will be covered later) name their functions such as to make it obvious where they originate, and to make it quite unlikely there will be name clashes. It is standard practice to use this form to import them.

11.4 *The module search path*

Python searches the list of directories given in sys.path, when looking for requested modules.

Exactly where Python looks for modules is defined in a variable called path, which is accessible to the programmer through a module called sys. Do the following:

```
>>>
```

```
>>> import sys
>>> sys.path
⇒ _list of directories in the search path_
```

The value shown in place of where I've said ...list of directories in the search path... will depend on the configuration of your system. Regardless of the details, the string indicates a list of directories that are searched by Python (in order), when attempting to execute an import statement. The first module found which satisfies the import request is used. If there is no satisfactory module in the module search path, an ImportError exception is raised.

If you are using IDLE, you can graphically look at the search path and the modules on it using the Path Browser window, which you can start from File menu of the Python Shell window.

The `sys.path` variable is initialized from the value of the environment (operating system) variable `PYTHONPATH`, if it exists, or from a default value which is dependent on your installation. In addition, whenever a Python script is run, the `sys.path` variable for that script will have the directory containing the script inserted as its first element—this provides a convenient way of determining where the executing Python program is located. In an interactive session such as the one just above, the first element of `sys.path` will be set to the empty string, which Python takes as meaning that it should first look for modules in the current directory.

11.4.1   Where to place your own modules

In the example that started this chapter, the `mymath` module was accessible to Python because: (1) when you execute Python interactively, the first element of sys.path is `" "`, telling Python to look for modules in the current directory; and (2) you were executing Python in the directory which contained the `mymath.py` file. In a production program, neither of these conditions will typically be true. You will not be running Python interactively, and Python code files will not be located in your current directory. In order to ensure that modules coded by you can be used by your programs, you need to do one of the following:

- Place your modules into one of the directories that Python normally searches for modules.
- Place all of the modules used by a Python program into the same directory as the program.
- Create a directory (or directories) which will hold your modules, and modify the `sys.path` variable so that it includes this new directory.

Of these three options, the first is apparently the easiest, and is also an option that should *never* be chosen because it can cause trouble. For example, what if you place new modules in a standard Python directory, and then you or someone else installs a new version of Python on top of that? Your modules would disappear and your programs would stop working, even if a new installation were done more carefully and you still had the old directory with your modules. You would still have to remember which ones were yours and copy them to their new residence.

Note that it's possible that your version of Python includes local code directories in its default module search path. Such directories are specifically intended for site-specific code, and are not in danger of being overwritten by a new Python install, because they are not part of the Python installation. If your `sys.path` refers to such directories, put your modules there.

The second option is a good choice for modules that are associated with a particular program. Just keep them with the program.

The third option is the right choice for site-specific modules that will be used in more than one program at that site. You can modify `sys.path` in various ways. You can assign to it in your code, which is easy, but hard-codes directory locations right into your program code; you can set the PYTHONPATH environment variable, which is relatively easy, but may not apply to all users at your site; or you can add to the default search path using using a .pth file.

See the section on environment variables in the appendix for examples of how to set PYTHONPATH. The directory or directories you set it to are prepended to the `sys.path` variable. If you use it be careful that you do not define a module with the same name as one of the existing library modules that you are using or is being used for you. Your module will be found before the library module. In some cases this may be what you want, but probably not often.

You can avoid this issue using the .pth method. In this case, the directory or directories you added will be appended to `sys.path`. The last of these mechanisms is best illustrated by a quick example. On Windows you can place this in the directory pointed to by `sys.prefix`. Assume your `sys.prefix` is `c:\program files\python`, and you place the following file in that directory.

File myModules.pth

```
mymodules
c:\My Documents\python\modules
```

Then the next time a Python interpreter is started, sys.path will have `c:\program files\python\mymodules` and `c:\My Documents\python\modules` added to it, if they exist. You can now place your modules in these directories. Note that the `mymodules` directory still runs the danger of being overwritten with a new installation. The `modules` directory is safer. You also may have to move or create a mymodules.pth file when you upgrade Python. See the description of the `site` module in the *Python Library Reference* if you want more details on using .pth files

11.5   *Private names in modules*

We mentioned that you could say `from module import *` to import *almost* all names from a module. The exception to this is that names in the module beginning with an underscore cannot be imported in this manner so that people can write modules which are intended for importation with `from module import *`. By leading off all internal names (i.e., names which should not be accessed outside the module) with an underscore, the module writer can ensure that `from module import *` brings in only those names which the user will want to access.

To see this in action, let's assume we have a file called modtest.py, containing the following code:

File modtest.py

```
"""modtest: our test module"""
def f(x):
    return x

def _g(x):
    return x

a = 4
_b = 2
```

Now, start up an interactive session, and try the following:

```
>>>

>>> from modtest import *
>>> f(3)
⇒   3
>>> _g(3)
Traceback (innermost last):
  File "<stdin>", line 1, in ?
NameError: _g
>>> a
⇒   4
>>> _b
Traceback (innermost last):
  File "<stdin>", line 1, in ?
NameError: _b
```

As you can see, the names f and a were imported, but the names _g and _b remain hidden outside of modtest. Note that this behavior occurs only with from … import *. We can do the following to access _g or _b:

```
>>>

>>> import modtest
>>> modtest._b
⇒   2
>>> from modtest import _g
>>> _g(5)
⇒   5
```

The convention of leading underscores to indicate private names is used throughout Python, and not just in modules. You'll encounter it in classes and packages, later in the book.

11.6 *Library and third-party modules*

It was mentioned at the beginning of this chapter that the standard Python distribution is itself split into modules, to make it more manageable. Once Python has been installed, all of the functionality in these library modules is available to the Python programmer. All that is needed is to import the appropriate modules, functions, classes, and so forth explicitly, before using them.

Many of the most common and useful standard modules are discussed throughout this book. However, the standard Python distribution includes far more than what this book describes. At the very least, you should browse through the table of contents of the *Python Library Reference*.

In IDLE you can also easily browse to and look at those written in Python using the Path Browser window. You can also search for example code which uses them with the Find in Files dialog, which can be opened from the Edit menu of the Python Shell window. You can search through your own modules as well in this way.

Available third-party modules, and links to them, are identified on the Python home page. These simply need to be downloaded and placed in a directory in your module search path in order to make them available for import into your programs.

11.7 Python scoping rules and namespaces

Python's scoping rules and namespaces will become more interesting as your experience as a Python programmer grows. If you are new to Python, you probably don't need to do anything more than quickly read through the text to get the basic ideas. For more details, consult the *Python Language Reference*.*

A namespace maps names to variables, modules, functions, or objects.

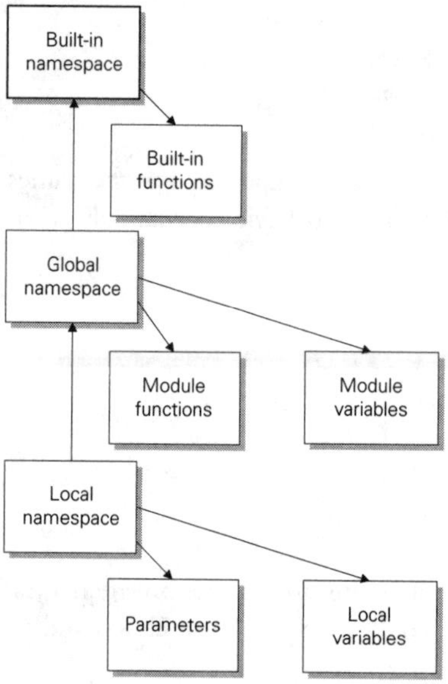

Its local, global and built-in namespaces are searched in that order when a name is encountered in a block of code.

An entry in a namespace is called a binding.

The core concept here is that of a *namespace*. A namespace in Python is a mapping from identifiers to objects and is usually represented as a dictionary. When a block of code is executed in Python it will have three namespaces: *local, global,* and *built-in* (figure 11.1).

When an identifier is encountered during execution, Python first looks in the *local namespace* for it. If it is not found, the *global namespace* is looked in next. If it still has not been found the *built-in namespace* is checked. If it does not exist there, this is considered an error and a `NameError` exception occurs.

For a module, a command executed in an interactive session or a script running from a file, the global and local namespaces are the same. The creation of any variable or function or importing anything from another module will result in a new entry or *binding* being made in this namespace.

However, when a function call is made, a local namespace is created and a binding is entered in it for each parameter of the call. A new binding is then entered into this local namespace whenever a variable is created within the function. The global namespace of a function is the global namespace of the containing block of the function (that of the module, script file, or interactive session). It is independent of the dynamic context from which it is called and there is no nested scoping.

In all of the above situations, the built-in namespace will be that of the `__builtin__` module. This is the module that contains, among other things, all the built-in functions we've encountered (such as `len`, `min`, `max`, `int`, `float`, `long`, `list`, `tuple`, `cmp`, `range`, `str`, and `repr`) and the other built-in classes in Python such as the exceptions (like `NameError`).

One thing that sometimes catches new Python programmers is the fact that you can override items in the built-in module. If, for example, you created a list in your program

Figure 11.1 The namespace

---

* You can find the appropriate section by looking up "namespaces" in its index.

and put it in a variable called `list`, you would not subsequently be able to use the built-in `list` function. The entry for your list would be found first. There is no differentiation between names for functions and modules and other objects. The first occurrence of a binding for a given identifier will be used.

Enough talk, time to explore this with some examples. We use two built-in functions, **locals** and **globals**. They return dictionaries containing the bindings in the local and global namespaces respectively.

Starting a new interactive session:

```
>>>
>>> locals()
{'__doc__': None, '__name__': '__main__', '__builtins__':
      <module '__builtin__'>}
>>> globals()
{'__doc__': None, '__name__': '__main__', '__builtins__':
      <module '__builtin__'>}
>>>
```

The local and global namespaces for this new interactive session are the same. They have three initial key/value pairs that are for internal use: (1) an empty documentation string __doc__, (2) the main module name __name__ (which for interactive sessions and scripts run from files is always __main__), and (3) the module used for the built-in namespace __builtins__ (the module __builtin__).

Now, if we continue by creating a variable and importing from modules, we will see a number of bindings created:

```
...
>>> z = 2
>>> import math
>>> from cmath import cos
>>> globals()
{'math': <module 'math'>, '__doc__': None, 'z': 2, 'cos':
<built-in function cos
>, '__name__': '__main__', '__builtins__': <module '__builtin__'>}
>>> locals()
{'math': <module 'math'>, '__doc__': None, 'z': 2, 'cos':
<built-in function cos>, '__name__': '__main__', '__builtins__':
<module '__builtin__'>}
>>> math.ceil(3.4)
4.0
```

As expected, the local and global namespaces continue to be equivalent. Entries have been added for z as a number, `math` as a module, and `cos` from the `cmath` module as a function.

We can use the `del` statement to remove these new bindings from the namespace (including the module bindings created with the `import` statements).

```
...
>>> del z, math, cos
```

```
>>> locals()
{'__doc__': None, '__name__': '__main__', '__builtins__':
<module '__builtin__'>}
>>> math.ceil(3.4)
Traceback (innermost last):
  File "<stdin>", line 1, in ?
NameError: math
>>> import math
>>> math.ceil(3.4)
⇒   4
```

The result was not drastic, as we were able to import the `math` module and use it again. Using `del` in this manner can be handy when in the interactive mode. *

For the trigger happy, yes it is also possible to use `del` to remove the __doc__, __main__, and __builtins__ entries. But resist doing this, as it would not be good for the health of your session!

Now let's take a look at a function created in an interactive session:

```
...
```

```
>>> def f(x):
...         print "global: ",globals()
...         print "Entry local: ",locals()
...         y = x
...         print "Exit local: ",locals()
...
>>> z = 2
>>> globals()
{'f': <function f at 793d0>, '__doc__': None, 'z': 2, '
__name__': '__main__', '__builtins__': <module '__builtin__'>}
>>> f(z)
global:  {'f': <function f at 793cd0>, '__doc__': None, '
z': 2, '__name__': '__main__', '__builtins__': <module
'__builtin__'>}
Entry local:  {'x': 2}
Exit local:  {'x': 2, 'y': 2}
>>>
```

If we dissect this apparent mess, we see that, as expected, upon entry the parameter x is the original entry in f's local namespace but y is added later. The global namespace is the same as that of our interactive session, as this is where f was defined. Note that it contains z, which was defined after f.

In a production environment we will normally be calling functions that are defined in modules. Their global namespace will be that of the module they are defined in. Assume we've created the following file:

---

* Using `del` and then `import` again will not pick up changes made to a module on disk. It is not actually removed from memory and then loaded from disk again. The binding is simply taken out of and then put back in your namespace. You still need to use `reload` if you want to pick up changes made to a file.

```
"""scopetest: our scope test module"""
v = 6

def f(x):
    """f: scope test function"""
    print "global: ", globals().keys()
    print "entry local:", locals()
    y = x
    w = v
    print "exit local:", locals()
```

Note that we will be only printing the keys (identifiers) of the dictionary returned by globals. This will reduce the clutter in the results. It was very necessary in this case due to the fact that in modules as an optimization, the whole __builtin__ dictionary is stored in the value field for the __builtins__ key.

>>>

```
>>> import scopetest
>>> z = 2
>>> scopetest.f(z)
global:  ['v', '__doc__', 'f', '__file__', '__name__',
'__builtins__']
entry local: {'x': 2}
exit local: {'w': 6, 'x': 2, 'y': 2}
```

The global namespace is now that of the scopetest module and includes the function f and integer v (but not z from our interactive session). Thus, when creating a module you have complete control of the namespaces of its functions.

We've now covered local and global namespaces. Next, let's move on to the built-in namespace. We'll introduce another built-in function, **dir**, which, given a module, returns a list of the names defined in it.

>>>

```
>>> dir(__builtins__)
⇒  ['ArithmeticError', 'AssertionError', 'AttributeError',
    'EOFError', 'Ellipsis', 'EnvironmentError', 'Exception',
    'FloatingPointError', 'IOError', 'ImportError', 'IndexError',
    'KeyError', 'KeyboardInterrupt', 'LookupError', 'MemoryError',
    'NameError', 'None', 'NotImplementedError', 'OSError',
    'OverflowError', 'RuntimeError', 'StandardError',
    'SyntaxError', 'SystemError', 'SystemExit', 'TypeError',
    'ValueError', 'ZeroDivisionError', '_', '__debug__', '__doc__',
    '__import__', '__name__', 'abs', 'apply', 'callable', 'chr',
    'cmp', 'coerce', 'compile', 'complex', 'delattr', 'dir',
    'divmod', 'eval', 'execfile', 'exit', 'filter', 'float',
    'getattr', 'globals', 'hasattr', 'hash', 'hex', 'id', 'input',
    'int', 'intern', 'isinstance', 'issubclass', 'len', 'list',
    'locals', 'long', 'map', 'max', 'min', 'oct', 'open', 'ord',
    'pow', 'quit', 'range', 'raw_input', 'reduce', 'reload', 'repr',
```

```
'round',  'setattr',  'slice',  'str',  'tuple',  'type',  'vars',
'xrange']
```

You can easily print the document string of any built-in function.

There are a lot of entries here. Those ending in Error and System Exit are the names of the exceptions built-in to Python. These will be discussed in "Exceptions" (chapter 14).

The last group (from `abs` to `xrange`), are built-in functions of Python. We have already seen many of these in this book and will see more. However, they won't all be covered here. When interested, you can find details on the rest in the *Python Library Reference*. You can also at any time easily obtain the documentation string for any of them:

```
...
```

```
>>> print max.__doc__
max(sequence) -> value
max(a, b, c, ...) -> value

With a single sequence argument, return its largest item.
With two or more arguments, return the largest argument.
>>>
```

Beware of accidentally overriding a built-in function.

As mentioned earlier, it is not unheard of for a new Python programmer to inadvertently override a built-in function.

```
>>>
```

```
>>> list("Peyto Lake")
⇒  ['P', 'e', 'y', 't', 'o', ' ', 'L', 'a', 'k', 'e']
>>> list = [1,3,5,7]
>>> list("Peyto Lake")
Traceback (innermost last):
 File "<stdin>", line 1, in ?
TypeError: call of non-function (type list)
```

Functions and modules can be set to variables and thus their names can be overridden as well.

The Python interpreter will not look beyond our new binding for list as a `list`, even though we are using function syntax.

The same thing will of course happen if we try to use the same identifier twice in a single namespace. The previous value will be overwritten, regardless of its type:

```
>>> import string
>>> string = "Mount Rundle"
>>> string.split("Bow Lake")
Traceback (innermost last):
  File "<stdin>", line 1, in ?
AttributeError: 'string' object has no attribute 'split'
```

Once aware of this, it isn't a significant issue. Reusing identifiers, even for different types of objects, wouldn't make for the most readable code anyway. If we do inadvertently make one of these mistakes when in interactive mode, it's easy to recover. We can use `del` to remove our binding, to regain access to an overridden built-in, or import our module again, to regain access.

```
...
```

```
>>> del list
```

```
>>> list("Peyto Lake")
⇒   ['P', 'e', 'y', 't', 'o', ' ', 'L', 'a', 'k', 'e']
>>> import string
>>> string.split("Bow Lake")
⇒   ['Bow', 'Lake']
```

The `locals` and `globals` functions can be quite useful as simple debugging tools. The **dir** function doesn't give the current settings but if called without parameters, it returns a sorted list of the identifiers in the local namespace. This will help catch the mistyped variable error that compilers may usually catch for you in languages that require declarations:

```
>>>
>>> x1 = 6
>>> x1 = x1 - 2
>>> x1
⇒   6
>>> dir()
⇒   ['__builtins__', '__doc__', '__name__', 'x1', 'x1']
```

The debugger that is bundled with IDLE has settings where you can view the local and global variable settings as you step through your code, and what it displays is the output of the `locals` and `globals` functions.

CHAPTER 12

Using the filesystem

Working with files involves one of two things: basic I/O (described in the next chapter, "Reading and writing files") and working with the filesystem (e.g., naming, creating, moving, or referring to files), which is a bit tricky, because different operating systems have different filesystem conventions.

It would be easy enough to learn how to perform basic file I/O without learning all the features Python has provided to make crossplatform filesystem interaction as easy as possible—but I wouldn't recommend it. Instead, read at least the first part of this chapter. This will give you the tools you need to refer to files in a manner which does not depend on your particular operating system. Then, when you use the basic I/O operations, you can open the relevant files in this manner.

12.1 Paths and pathnames

Pathnames are strings referring to files or directories in the filesystem.

All operating systems refer to files and directories with strings naming a given file or directory. Strings used in this manner are usually called *pathnames* (or sometimes just *paths*), which is the word we'll use for them. The fact that pathnames are strings introduces possible complications into working with them. Python does a good job of providing functions that help avoid these complications, but to make use of these

Python functions effectively, you need an understanding of what the underlying problems are. This section discusses these details.

Pathname semantics are similar (but not identical) across different operating systems.

Pathname semantics across different operating systems are very similar, because the file system on almost all operating systems is modeled as a tree structure, with a disk being the root and folders, subfolders, and so forth, being branches, subbranches, and so on. This means that most operating systems refer to a specific file in fundamentally the same manner; with a pathname which specifies the path to follow from the root of the filesystem tree (the disk), to the file in question. (This characterization of the root corresponding to a hard disk in an oversimplification. But it is close enough to the truth to serve for this chapter.)

This pathname just consists of a series of folders to descend into, in order to get to the desired file.

Pathname syntax differs across operating systems; Python provides functions to 'hide' these differences.

Different operating systems have made different choices about the precise syntax of pathnames. For example, the character used to separate sequential file or directory names in a UNIX pathname is '/', while the character used to separate file or directory names in a Windows pathname is '\'. In addition, the UNIX file system has a single root (which is referred to by having a '/' character as the very first character in a pathname), while the Windows file system has a separate root for each drive, labeled 'a:\', 'b:\', 'c:\', and so forth (with c: usually being the 'main' drive). Because of these differences, files will have different pathname representations on different operating systems. For example, a file called `C:\data\myfile` in MS Windows might be called `/data/myfile` on UNIX, and `HD:data:myfile` on the Macintosh. Python provides functions and constants that allow you to perform common pathname manipulations without worrying about such syntactic details. With a little care, you can write your Python programs in such a manner that they will run correctly no matter what the underlying filesystem happens to be.

12.1.1 Absolute and relative paths

These operating systems allow two different types of pathnames. *Absolute* pathnames specify the exact location of a file in a file system, without any ambiguity; they do this by listing the entire path to that file, starting from the root of the filesystem. *Relative* pathnames specify the position of a file relative to some other point in the filesystem, and that other point is not specified in the relative pathname itself; instead, the absolute starting point for relative pathnames is provided by the context in which they are used.

As examples of this, here are two Windows absolute pathnames:

```
c:\Program Files\Doom
a:\backup\June
```

two UNIX absolute pathnames:

```
/bin/Doom
/floppy/backup/June
```

two Windows relative pathnames:

```
mydata\project1\readme.txt
games\tetris
```

and two UNIX relative pathnames:

```
mydata/project1/readme.txt
games/tetris
```

Relative paths need context to anchor them. This is typically provided in one of two ways. The simplest is merely to append the relative path to an existing absolute path, producing a new absolute path. For example, we might have a relative Windows path, `Start Menu\Programs\Explorer`, and an absolute path, `c:\winnt\Profiles\Administrator`. By appending the two, we have a new absolute path `c:\winnt\Profiles\Administrator\Start Menu\Programs\Explorer` which refers to a specific file in the file system. By appending the same relative path to a different absolute path (say, `c:\winnt\Profiles\kmcdonald`), we produce a path which refers to the Explorer program in a different user's (kmcdonald's) Profiles directory.

The second way in which relative paths may obtain a context is via an implicit reference to the *current working directory*, which is where the particular directory a Python program considers itself to be at any point during its execution. Python commands may implicitly make use of the current working directory when they are given a relative path as an argument. For example, if you use the `os.listdir(path)` command with a relative path argument, the anchor for that relative path will be the current working directory, and the result of the command will be a list of the file names in the directory whose path is formed by appending the current working directory with the relative path argument.

12.1.2 The current working directory

Whenever you edit a document on a computer, you have a concept of where you are in that computer's file structure because you are in the same directory (folder) as the file you are working on. Similarly, whenever Python is running, it has a concept of where in the directory structure it is at any moment. This is important, because the program might ask for a list of files stored in the current directory. The directory that a Python program is in is called the *current working directory* for that program. This may be different from the directory the program itself resides in.

os.getcwd returns the path-name to the current working directory.

To see this in action, start Python and use the `os.getcwd` (get current working directory) command.

```
>>>
```

```
>>> import os
>>> os.getcwd()
```

to find out what Python's initial current working directory is. Note that `os.getcwd` is used as a zero-argument function call, to emphasize the fact that the value it returns is not a constant, but will change as you issue commands which change the value of the current working directory.* (It will probably be either the directory the Python program itself resides in,

---

* On a Windows machine, you might see something like `c:\\users\\mcdonald`. There aren't really doubled backslashes in the string. Python simply prints it out this way as a result, because you would need to type it in this way (i.e. escape the backslashes) to get such a string correctly into Python, due to the fact that backslashes in Python strings have a special meaning. Backslashes in Python strings signal the beginning of an escape sequence (see chapter 7), and the escape sequence '\\' represents a single backslash in the string. To see what the string really is, use `print`, i.e., do something like `print; os.listdir(os.getcwd())`. For this example, you would get `c:\users\mcdonald`, which is how the path is stored internally in Python.

or the directory you were in when you started up Python. On my UNIX machine, the result is `"/home/mcdonald"`, which is my home directory.) On Windows machines, you'll see extra backslashes inserted into the path—this is because Windows uses "\" as its path separator, and in Python strings, \ has a special meaning unless it is itself backslashed.

Now, type

```
...
```

```
>>> os.listdir(os.curdir)
```

The constant `os.curdir` returns whatever string your system happens to use as the same directory indicator. On both UNIX and Windows, this happens to be a single period, but to keep your programs portable, you should always use `os.curdir` instead of typing '.'. This string is a relative path, meaning that `os.listdir` will append it to the path for the current working directory, giving the same path. This command will return a list of all of the files or folders inside the current working directory. Choose some folder `folder`, and type

```
...
```

```
>>> os.chdir(folder)    # The "change directory" function
>>> os.getcwd()
```

os.chdir changes the current working directory.

As you can see, Python has moved into the folder specified as an argument of the `os.chdir` function. Another call to `os.listdir(os.curdir)` would return a list of files in *folder*, since `os.curdir` would then be taken relative to the new current working directory. Many Python filesystem operations (discussed later in this chapter) make use of the current working directory in this manner.

12.1.3 Manipulating pathnames

The os.path sub-module works with file names in an abstract manner.

Now that we have the background for understanding file and directory pathnames, it's time to look at the facilities Python provides for manipulating these pathnames. These facilities consist of a number of functions and constants in the `os.path` submodule, which can be used to manipulate paths without explicit use of any operating-system-specific syntax. Paths are still represented as strings, but the programmer need never think of them or manipulate them as such.

Let's start out by constructing a few pathnames on different operating systems, using the `os.path.join` function. Note that importing `os` is sufficient to bring in the `os.path` submodule also. There is no need for an explicit `import os.path` statement.

First, let's start up Python under Windows NT:

```
...
```

```
>>> import os
>>> print os.path.join('bin', 'utils', 'disktools')
bin\utils\disktools
```

os.path.join can be used to form file paths without worrying about the underlying os.

The `os.path.join` function interprets its arguments as a series of directory or file names, which are to be joined to form a single string understandable as a relative path by the underlying operating system. In a Windows system, that means path component names should be joined together with backslashes, which is what was produced.

Now, try the same thing in UNIX:

```
>>>
```

```
>>> import os
>>> print os.path.join('bin', 'utils', 'disktools')
bin/utils/disktools
```

The result was the same path, but using the UNIX convention of forward slash separators, rather than the Windows convention of backwards slash separators. In other words, os.path.join lets you form file paths from a sequence of directory or file names, without any worry about the conventions of the underlying operating system. os.path.join is the fundamental way by which file paths may be built in a manner which does not constrain the operating systems on which your program will run.

os.path.join can also be used to joins paths into longer paths.

The arguments to os.path.join do not need to be single directory or file names; they may also be subpaths which are then joined together to make a longer pathname. The example below illustrates this in the MS Windows environment and is also a case where we find it necessary to use double backslashes in our strings. Note that we could have entered the pathname with forward slashes (/) as well as Python converts them before accessing the Windows operating system.

```
>>>
```

```
>>> import os
>>> print os.path.join('mydir\\bin', 'utils\\disktools\\chkdisk')
mydir\bin\utils\disktools\chkdisk
```

Of course, if you always use os.path.join to build up your paths, you will rarely need to worry about this. To write the above example in a truly portable manner, we should have said,

```
...
```

```
>>> path1 = os.path.join('mydir', 'bin');
>>> path2 = os.path.join('utils', 'disktools', 'chkdisk')
>>> print os.path.join(path1, path2)
mydir\bin\utils\disktools\chkdisk
```

Absolute and relative paths are treated differently by os.path.join.

The os.path.join command also has some understanding of *absolute* versus *relative* path names. In UNIX, an absolute path always begins with a '/' (as a single slash denotes the topmost directory of the entire system, which contains everything else, including the various floppy and CD drives that might be available). A relative path in UNIX is any legal path that does *not* begin with a slash. Under any of the Windows operating systems, the situation is more complicated, because the way in which MS Windows handles relative and absolute paths is messier. Rather than going into all of the details, the best way to handle this is to work with the following simplified rules for Windows paths:

- A pathname beginning with a drive letter followed by a backslash and then a path is an absolute path: c:\Program Files\Doom. (Note that c: by itself, without a trailing backslash, cannot reliably be used to refer to the top-level directory on c: drive.

You must use `c:\` to refer to the top-level directory on c. This is a result of DOS conventions, not Python design.)

- A pathname beginning with neither a drive letter nor a backslash is a relative path: `mydirectory\letters\business`.
- Anything else can be considered as an invalid pathname.*

os.path.join does not perform validity checks.

Regardless of the operating system used, the `os.path.join` command does not perform sanity checks on the names it is constructing. It is quite possible to construct path names containing characters which, according to your OS, are forbidden in path names. If such checks are a requirement, probably the best solution is to write a small path validity checker function yourself.

os.path.split splits a path after the last slash, returning both parts.

The `os.path.split` returns a two element tuple splitting the basename of a path (the single file or directory name at the end of the path from the rest of the path). For example, on my Windows NT system:

```
>>>
>>> import os
>>> print os.path.split(os.path.join('some','directory', 'path'))
⇒ ('some\\directory', 'path')
```

os.path.basename returns the last component of a pathname.

The `os.path.basename` function, just returns the "basename" of the path and the `os.path.dirname` function, returns the path up to but not including the last name. For example:

os.path.dirname returns the entire pathname except for the last component.

```
>>>
>>> import os
>>> os.path.basename(os.path.join('some', 'directory', 'path.jpg'))
⇒ 'path.jpg'
>>> os.path.dirname(os.path.join('some', 'directory', 'path.jpg'))
⇒ 'some\\directory'
```

os.path.splitext splits out filename dotted extensions.

To handle the dotted extension notation used by most filesystems to indicate file type (the Macintosh is a notable exception), Python provides `os.path.splitext`:

```
...
>>> os.path.splitext(os.path.join('some', 'directory', 'path.jpg'))
⇒ ('some/directory/path', '.jpg')
```

Other useful pathname manipulation functions in `os.path` are `commonprefix`, `expanduser`, and `expandvars`.

The last element of the returned tuple will contain the dotted extension of the indicated file (if there was a dotted extension.) The first element of the returned tuple contains everything from the original argument except for the dotted extension.

There are also more specialized functions that can be used to manipulate pathnames. `os.path.commonprefix(path1, path2, …)` can be used to find the common prefix (if any) for a set of paths. This is useful if you wish to find the lowest-level directory which contains all in a set of files. `os.path.expanduser` will expand out username shortcuts in

---

* MS Windows allows some other constructs. However, it's probably best to stick to the given definitions.

paths, i.e., for UNIX. Similarly, `os.path.expandvars` will do the same for environment variables. For example, on my Windows NT system,

```
>>>
```

```
>>> import os
>>> os.path.expandvars('$HOME\\temp')
⇒ 'c:\\winnt\\profiles\\administrator\\personal\\temp'
```

12.1.4 Useful constants and functions

os.curdir and os.pardir are constants containing current directory and parent directory symbols for your OS.

You can access a number of useful path-related constants and functions to make your Python code more system-independent than it otherwise would be.

The most basic of these constants are `os.curdir` and `os.pardir`, which respectively define the symbol used by the operating system for the directory and parent directory path indicators. (In both Windows and UNIX, these happen to be '.' and '..' respectively.) These can be used as normal path elements; for example

```
os.path.isdir(os.path.join(path, os.pardir, os.pardir))
```

asks if the parent of the parent of *path* is a directory. `os.curdir` is particularly useful for requesting commands on the current working directory, for example

```
os.listdir(os.curdir)
```

os.name contains a string allowing you to identify the type of the operating system.

returns a list of file names in the current working directory (because `os.curdir` is a relative path and `os.listdir` always takes relative paths as being relative to the current working directory).

The `os.name` constant returns the name of the Python module imported to handle the operating system-specific details. For example, on my Windows NT system,

```
>>>
```

```
>>> import os
>>> os.name
⇒ 'nt'
```

On a Mac, we would get `mac`, and on UNIX, the response would be `posix`. This can be used to perform special operations depending on the platform we are working on.

```
import os
if os.name == 'posix': rootDir = "/"
elif os.name == 'nt': rootDir = "c:\\"
else: print "Don't understand this operating system!"
```

You may also see programs use `sys.platform`, which gives more exact information. On Windows 95/98/NT, it is set to win32. On Linux, you might see linux2 while on Solaris, it could be set to sunos5 depending on the versions you are running.

Environment variables are available through a dictionary called os.environ.

All of your environment variables, and the values associated with them, are available in a dictionary called `os.environ`; in most operating systems this includes variables related to paths, typically search paths for binaries and so forth. If what you are doing requires this, you know where to find it now.

At this point, you have received a grounding in the major aspects of working with pathnames in Python. If your immediate need is to open files for reading or writing, you can jump directly to the next chapter. Continue reading for further information about pathnames, testing what they point to, useful constants, and so forth.

12.2 *Getting information about files*

File paths are supposed to indicate actual files and directories on your hard drive, and of course, you are probably passing a path around because you wish to know something about what it points to. There are various Python functions to do this.

!!!

The examples in this section work as indicated on my machine, but because they depend on the directory structure of the machine, they may not give the same results on your machine.

os.path.exists, os.path.isfile, and os.path.isdir test if a path exists, is a regular file, or is a directory.

The most commonly used Python path information functions are os.path.exists, os.path.isfile, and os.path.isdir, which all take a single path as an argument. os.path.exists returns 1 if its argument is a path corresponding to something that actually exists in the file system. os.path.isfile returns 1 if and only if the path it is given indicates a normal data file of some sort (executables would fall under this heading), and it returns 0 otherwise, including the possibility that the path argument does not indicate anything in the file system at all. os.path.isdir returns 1 if and only if its path argument indicates a directory, and it returns 0 otherwise. These examples are valid on my system. You may need to use different paths on yours, to investigate the behavior of these functions:

```
>>>
```

```
>>> import os
>>> os.path.exists('c:\\My Documents')
⇒ 1
>>> os.path.exists('c:\\My Documents\\Letter.doc')
⇒ 1
>>> os.path.exists('c:\\My Documents\\ljsljkflkjs')
⇒ 0
>>> os.path.isdir('c:\\My Documents')
⇒ 1
>>> os.path.isfile('c:\\My Documents')
⇒ 0
>>> os.path.isdir('c:\\My Documents\\Letter.doc')
⇒ 0
>>> os.path.isfile('c:\\My Documents\\Letter.doc')
⇒ 1
```

Other useful functions in os.path are islink, ismount, samefile, and isabs.

A number of similar functions provide more specialized queries. os.path.islink and os.path.ismount are useful in the context of UNIX and other operating systems which provide file links and mount points. They return 1 if, respectively, a path indicates a file which is a link or a mount point. os.path.islink does *not* return 1 on MS Windows shortcuts files (files ending with .LNK), for the simple reason that such files are not true links. The OS does not assign them a special status, and programs cannot transparently use them as if they were the actual file. os.path.samefile(*path1*, *path2*) returns true if and only if the two path arguments point to the same file. os.path.isabs(*path*) returns `true` if its argument is an absolute path, `false` otherwise. `os.path.get-size`(*path*), `os.path.getmtime`(*path*), and `os.path.getatime`(*path*) return the size, last modify time, and last access time of a pathname, respectively.

12.3 More filesystem operations

In addition to obtaining information about files, Python lets you perform certain file system operations directly. This is accomplished through a set of basic but highly useful commands in the `os` module.

!!!

I will only describe those operations that are true crossplatform operations. Many operating systems—UNIX and Windows NT in particular—also have access to more advanced filesystem functions. For details, see the main Python library documentation.

We've already seen that to obtain a list of files in a directory, we use `os.listdir`:

`os.listdir` returns a list of filenames in a directory.

```
>>> os.chdir(os.path.join('c:','my documents', 'tmp'))
>>> os.listdir(os.curdir)
⇒ ['book1.doc.tmp', 'a.tmp', '1.tmp', '7.tmp', '9.tmp',
    'registry.bkp']
```

Note that unlike the list directory command in many other languages or shells, Python does *not* include the `os.curdir` and `os.pardir` indicators in the list returned by `os.listdir`.

The `glob.glob` function will expand wildcard characters and sequences into matched file names.

The `glob.glob` function will expand UNIX Shell style wildcard characters and character sequences in a pathname, returning the files in the current working directory that match. A `*` matches any sequence of characters. A `?` matches any single character. A character sequence ([h,H] or [0-9]) matches any single character in that sequence.

```
>>> import glob
>>> glob.glob("*")
⇒ ['book1.doc.tmp', 'a.tmp', '1.tmp', '7.tmp', '9.tmp',
    'registry.bkp']
>>> glob.glob("*bkp")
⇒ ['registry.bkp']
>>> glob.glob("?.tmp")
⇒ ['a.tmp', '1.tmp', '7.tmp', '9.tmp']
>>> glob.glob("[0-9].tmp")
⇒ ['1.tmp', '7.tmp', '9.tmp']
```

Rename (i.e. move) a file using `os.rename`.

To rename (move) a file or directory, use `os.rename`:

```
>>> os.rename('registry.bkp', 'registry.bkp.old')
>>> os.listdir(os.curdir)
⇒ ['book1.doc.tmp', 'a.tmp', '1.tmp', '7.tmp', '9.tmp',
    'registry.bkp.old']
```

This command may be used to move files across directories, as well as within directories. Remove or delete a data file with `os.remove`:

```
>>> os.remove('book1.doc.tmp')
>>> os.listdir(os.curdir)
⇒ ['a.tmp', '1.tmp', '7.tmp', '9.tmp', 'registry.bkp.old']
```

Note that `os.remove` cannot be used to delete directories. This is a safety feature, to ensure that you don't accidentally delete an entire directory substructure by mistake.

Create directories
with os.mkdir
or os.makedirs.

Files can be created simply by writing to them, as we saw in the last chapter. To create a directory, use `os.makedirs` or `os.mkdir`. The difference between them is that `os.mkdir` won't create any necessary intermediate directories but `os.makedirs` will.

```
>>> os.makedirs('mydir')
>>> os.listdir(os.curdir)
⇒ ['mydir', 'a.tmp', '1.tmp', '7.tmp', '9.tmp', 'registry.bkp.old']
>>> os.path.isdir('mydir')
⇒ 1
```

To remove a directory use `os.rmdir`. This will remove only empty directories. Attempting to use it on a nonempty directory will raise an exception.

```
>>> os.rmdir('mydir')
>>> os.listdir(os.curdir)
⇒ ['a.tmp', '1.tmp', '7.tmp', '9.tmp', 'registry.bkp.old']
```

To remove nonempty directories, use the `shutil.rmtree` function. It will recursively remove all files in a directory tree. See the appendix for the details of its use.

12.4 *Processing all files in a directory subtree*

Recursively
traverse an entire
directory struc-
ture, applying a
function of your
choice to each
node, using
os.path.walk.

Finally, a specialized but highly useful function for manipulating recursive directory structures is the `os.path.walk` function. It can be used to walk through an entire directory tree.

`os.path.walk` is called with three arguments: `os.path.walk(`*directory, function, arg*`)`. *directory* is a starting directory path, *function* is a function that can be applied to every directory and subdirectory during the walk; and *arg* is a parameter made available to the programmer that will simply be passed to *function* whenever *function* is invoked. When `os.path.walk` is invoked, it in turn successively calls *function* in each subdirectory with three arguments: *function(arg, subdirectory, names)*, where *arg* is the argument passed into the original invocation `os.path.walk`; *subdirectory* is the current subdirectory, and *names* is a list of names generated by a call to `os.listdir(`*subdirectory*`)`. At this point *function* can do anything it wants to. Generally, it might do something with the list of files given by *names*.

After this initial application of *function*, os.path.walk recursively applies itself to all of the directories contained in the *names* parameter. In other words, for each subdirectory *subdir* in *names*, *os.path.walk* recursively invokes a call to itself, of the form os.path.walk(*subdir, function, arg*). Note that the previous invocation of *function* might have modified the value in *names* (using any of the list modification operators or methods), which can be used to control into which—if any—subdirectories os.path.walk will descend.

This is complex, and if you want to use os.path.walk to its fullest extent, you should probably play around with it quite a bit to understand the details of what is going on. To start, I recommend simply passing in a function which prints out its three arguments. However, a very simple example will illustrate the power of os.path.walk. To list the current working directory and all of its subdirectories along with a count of the number of entries in each of them we need only the following:

```
import os
def printFunction(arg, directory, names):
    print directory, len(names)

os.path.walk(os.getcwd(), printFunction, None)
```

The copytree function of the shutil module will recursively make copies of all the files in a directory and all of its subdirectories preserving permission mode and stat (i.e., access/modify times) information. It also has the already mentioned rmtree function, for removing a directory and all of its subdirectories, as well as a number of functions for making copies of individual files. See the appendix for details.

12.5 Summary

Handling filesystem references (pathnames) and filesystem operations in a manner independent of the underlying operating system is always a difficult task. Fortunately, Python provides a group of functions and constants which make this task much easier. More advanced filesystem operations which typically are tied to a certain operating system or systems were not discussed here, and if your needs are more advanced and specialized, take a look at the main Python documentation for the os and posix modules.

CHAPTER 13

Reading and writing files

13.1 *Opening files and file objects*

Use open to open a file for reading or writing. open returns a file object.

Probably the single most common thing you will want to do with files is open and read them. In Python, opening and reading a file is accomplished using the built-in open function, and various different built-in reading operations. This following short Python program reads in one line from a text file named "myfile":

```
fileobject = open("myfile", 'r')
line = fileobject.readline()
```

open doesn't actually read anything from the file; instead it returns an abstract object called a *file object*, representing the opened file. All Python file I/O is done using file objects, rather than file names.

131

The first call to `readline` returns the first line in the file object, everything up to and including the first newline character, or all of the file if there is no newline character in the file; the next call to `readline` would return the second line, and so on. So, a file object is something that keeps track of a file and how much of the file has been read, or written.

The first argument to the open function is a pathname. In the above example we are opening what we expect to be an already existing file in the current working directory. The following would open a file at the given absolute location:

```
import os
fileName = os.path.join("c:", "My Documents", "test", "myfile")
fileobject = open(fileName,'r')
```

13.2 Closing files

Once all data has been read from or written to a file object, it should be closed. Closing a file object frees up system resources, allows the underlying file to be read or written to by other code, and, in general, makes the program more reliable. In small scripts, not closing a file object will generally not have much of an effect; file objects are automatically closed when the script or program terminates. In larger programs, too many open file objects may exhaust system resources, causing the program to abort.

Use close *to close a file object once you are done with it.*

Closing file objects is done using the `close` method, after the file object is no longer needed. The short program above then becomes this:

```
fileobject = open("myfile", 'r')
line = fileobject.readline()
#... any further reading on the fileobject ...
fileobject.close()
```

13.3 Opening files in write or other modes

open will open a file for reading, (over)writing, or appending, depending on the value if its second argument, which can be 'r'*,* 'w'*, or* 'a'*.*

The second argument of the open command is a single character denoting how the file should be opened. `'r'` means open the file for reading: `'w'` means open the file for writing (any data already in the file will be erased): and `'a'` means open the file for writing (new data will be appended to the end of any data already in the file). If you want to open the file for reading, you can leave out the second argument. `'r'` is the default. The following short program writes "Hello, World" to a file:

```
fileobject = open("myfile", 'w')
fileobject.write("Hello, World\n")
fileobject.close()
```

Depending on the operating system, open may also have access to additional file modes. In general, these are not necessary for most purposes. As you write more advanced Python programs, you may wish to consult the Python reference manuals for details.

As well, open can take an optional third argument, which defines how reads or writes for that file are *buffered*. Buffering is the process of holding data in memory until enough has been requested or written to justify the time cost of doing a disk access. Again, this is not something you typically need to worry about, but as you become more advanced in your use of Python, you may wish to read up on it.

13.4 Functions to read and write text or binary data

The readline *method reads and returns a single line from a file object, up to and including the next newline.*

The most common text file-reading function, readline, was presented above. It reads and returns a single line from a file object, including any newline character on the end of the line. If there is nothing more to be read from the file, readline returns an empty string. This makes it easy to, for example, count the number of lines in a file:

```
fileobject = open("myfile", 'r')
count = 0
while fileobject.readline() != "":
    count = count + 1
print count
fileobject.close()
```

readlines *can be used to read in all lines from a file object, and return them as a list of strings.*

For this particular problem, an even shorter way of counting all of the lines is using the built-in readlines method, which reads *all* of the lines in a file, and returns them as a list of strings, one string per line (with trailing newlines still included):

```
fileobject = open("myfile", 'r')
print len(fileobject.readlines())
fileobject.close()
```

An optional argument to readline *or* readlines *can limit the amount of data they read in at any one time.*

Of course, if you happen to be counting all of the lines in a particularly huge file, this might cause your computer to run out of memory, since it does read the entire file into memory at once. It is also possible to overflow memory with readline, if you have the misfortune to try to read a line from a huge file that contains no newline characters, although this is highly unlikely. To handle such circumstances, both readline and readlines can take an optional argument affecting the amount of data they read at any one time. See the Python reference documentation for details.

Use the read *method to read a byte sequence from a file— either the entire file, or a fixed number of bytes.*

Use binary mode (i.e., "rb" *or* "wb"*) when working with binary files.*

On some occasions, you might wish to read all of the data in a file into a single string, especially if the data is not actually a string, and you simply want to get it all into memory so you can treat it as a byte sequence. Or you might wish to read data from a file as strings of a fixed size. For example, you might be reading data without explicit newlines, where each line is assumed to be a sequence of characters of a fixed size. To do this, use the read method. Without any argument, it will read all of the rest of a file and return that data as a string. With a single integer argument, it will read that number of bytes, or less, if there is not enough data in the file to satisfy the request, and return a string of the given size. A possible problem may arise due to the fact that on Windows and Macintosh machines text mode translations will occur if you use the open command. On Macintosh any "\r" will be converted to "\n", while on Windows "\r\n" pairs will be converted to "\n" and "\32" will be taken as an EOF character. Use the 'b' (binary) argument open("file",'rb') or open("file",'wb'), to open the file in binary mode to eliminate this issue. This will work transparently on UNIX platforms.

```
# Open a file for reading.
input = open("myfile", 'rb')
# Read the first four bytes as a header string.
header = input.read(4)
```

```
# Read the rest of the file as a single piece of data.
data = input.read()
input.close()
```

Use write *to write a string or byte sequence to a file, and* writelines *to write a list of strings to a file.*

The converses of the `readline` and `readlines` methods are the `write` and `write-lines` methods. Note that there is no writeline function. `write` writes a single string, which could span multiple lines if newline characters are embedded within the string, for example something like:

```
myfile.write("Hello")
```

`write` does not write out a newline after it writes its argument; if you want a newline in the output, you must put it there yourself. If you open a file in text mode (using w), any '\n' characters will be mapped back to the platform-specific line endings (i.e., '\r\n' on Windows or '\r' on Macintosh platforms). Again opening the file in binary mode (i.e., 'wb') will avoid this.

`writelines` is something of a misnomer; it doesn't necessarily write lines—it simply takes a list of strings as an argument, and writes them, one after the other, to the given file object, without writing newlines. If the strings in the list end with newlines, they will be written as lines, otherwise they will be effectively concatenated together in the file. However, `writelines` is a precise inverse of `readlines`, in that it can be used on the list returned by `readlines` to write a file identical to the file `readlines` read from. For example, assuming `myfile.txt` exists and is a text file, this bit of code will create an exact copy of `myfile.txt` called `myfile2.txt`:

```
input = open("myfile.txt", 'r')
lines = input.readlines()
input.close()
output = open("myfile2.txt", 'w')
output.writelines(lines)
output.close()
```

13.5 *Screen input/output and redirection*

raw_input can prompt for and read in a string.

The built-in `raw_input` method can be use to prompt for and read an input string.

```
>>> x = raw_input("enter file name to use:")
enter file name to use:myfile
>>> s
⇒ 'myfile'
```

The prompt line is optional and the newline at the end of the input line is stripped off. We could read in numbers with `raw_input`, obtaining a string version that we convert.

```
>>> x = int(raw_input("enter your number:"))
enter your number: 39
>>> x
⇒ 39
```

A more general approach is to use another built-in function, `input`.

```
>>> x = input("enter your number:")
enter your number: 39
```

```
>>> x
⇒  39
```

With `input` we have excellent flexibility as it can actually read in any valid Python expression. Thus, we can read in a floating point or complex number or a delimited string. Anything that is not a valid expression will result in a `syntaxError` exception being raised.

input can prompt for and read in any valid Python expression.

```
>>> x = input("enter your number:")
enter your number: 47+3j
>>> x
 ⇒  (47+3j)
>>> x = input()
4 + 10/2.0                    ● Any valid Python expression
>>> x                            can be input.
 ⇒  9.0
>>> x = input("enter a delimited string:")
enter a delimited string: 'Here is my delimited string.'
>>> x
 ⇒  'Here is my delimited string.'
>>> input("enter expression:")
enter expression:an undelimited string   ● An undelimited string is not a
Traceback (innermost last):                  valid Python expression so a
  File "<stdin>", line 1, in                  SyntaxError is raised.
  File "<string>", line 1
    an undelimited string
                  ^
SyntaxError: invalid syntax
```

The specialized file objects `sys.stdin`, `sys.stdout`, and `sys.stderr` are set to the standard input, standard output and standard error, respectively.

Both `raw_input` and `input` write their prompt to the *standard output* and read from the *standard input*. Lower level access to these and *standard error* can be had using the `sys` module. It has `sys.stdin`, `sys.stdout`, and `sys.stderr` attributes. These can be treated as specialized file objects.

For `sys.stdin` we have `read`, `readline`, and `readlines` methods. For `sys.stdout` and `sys.stderr` there are the `write` and `writelines` methods. These operate as they do for other file objects.

```
>>> import sys
>>> sys.stdout.write("Write to the standard output.\n")
Write to the standard output.
>>> s = sys.stdin.readline()
An input line
>>> s
⇒  'An input line\012'
```

We can redirect standard input to read from a file. Similarly, standard output or standard error can be set to write to files. They can also be subsequently programmatically restored to their original values using `sys.__stdin__`, `sys.__stdout__`, and `sys.__stderr__`:

```
>>> import sys
>>> f= open("outFile.txt",W)
>>> sys.stdout = f
```

```
>>> sys.stdout.writelines(["A first line.\n","A seconde line.\n"])
>>> print "A line from the print statement""
>>> 3+4
>>> sys.stdout = sys.__stdout__
>>> f.close()
>>> 3+4
⇒    7
```

sys.stdin,
sys.stdout,
and sys.stderr
can be redirected
to files.

While the standard output was redirected, we received prompts and we would have received any tracebacks from errors, but no other output. If you are using IDLE, these examples using sys.__stdout__ will not work as indicated. You will have to use the interpreter's interactive mode directly.

This would normally be used when you are running from a script or program. However, if you are using the interactive mode on Windows you might want to temporarily redirect standard output in order to capture what might otherwise scroll off the screen. The following short module implements a set of functions that provide this capability. Here, CaptureOutput() will redirect standard output to a file that defaults to "capture-File.txt". The function RestoreOutput() will restore standard output to the default. Also PrintFile() will print this file to the standard output and ClearFile() will clear it of its current contents.

File mio.py

```
"""myIO: module, (contains functions CaptureOutput, RestoreOutput,
        PrintFile, and ClearFile )"""
import sys
_fileObject = None

def CaptureOutput(file="captureFile.txt"):
    """CaptureOutput(file='captureFile.txt'): redirect the standard
    output to 'file'."""
    global _fileObject
    print "output will be sent to file: %s" % (file)
    print "restore to normal by calling 'mu.RestoreOutput()'"
    _fileObject= open(file, 'w')
    sys.stdout = _fileObject

def RestoreOutput():
    """RestoreOutput(): restore the standard output back to the
        default (also closes the capture file)"""
    global _fileObject
    sys.stdout = sys.__stdout__
    _fileObject.close()
    print "standard output has been restored back to normal"

def PrintFile(file="captureFile.txt"):
    """PrintFile(file="captureFile.txt"): print the given file to the
        standard output"""
    f = open(file,'r')
    print f.read()

def ClearFile(file="captureFile.txt"):
```

```
"""ClearFile(file="captureFile.txt"): clears the contents of the
    given file"""
f = open(file,'w')
f.close()
```

13.6 The struct module

Generally speaking, when working with your own files, you probably don't want to read or write binary data in Python. For very simple storage needs, it is usually best to use textual input and output as described above. For more sophisticated applications, Python provides the ability to easily read or write arbitrary Python objects, pickling, described later in this chapter. This ability is much less error-prone than directly writing and reading your own binary data, and so is highly recommended.

However, there is at least one situation in which you will likely need to know how to read or write binary data, and that is when dealing with files which are generated or used by other programs. This section gives a short description of how to do this using the struct module. Refer to the Python reference documentation for more details.

Use the above-mentioned read/write methods to read or write byte sequences, and process those sequences with the struct module.

Python does not actually support explicit binary input or output. Instead, in keeping with its philosophy of modularization, it simply reads and writes strings, which are really just byte sequences, and provides the standard struct module to permit you to treat those strings as formatted byte sequences with some specific meaning.

Assume that we wish to read in a binary file called data, containing a series of records generated by a C program. Each record consists of a C short integer, a C double float, and a sequence of four characters that should be taken as a four-character string. We wish to read this data into a Python list of tuples, with each tuple containing an integer, floating-point number, and a string.

struct functions understand format strings which define how binary data is packed.

The first thing to do is to define a *format string* understandable to the struct module, which tells the module how the data in one of our records is packed. The format string uses characters meaningful to struct to indicate what type of data is expected where in a record. For example, the character 'h' indicates the presence of a single C short integer, and the character 'd' indicates the presence of a single C double-precision floating-point number. Not surprisingly, 's' indicates the presence of a string, and may be preceded by an integer to indicate the length of the string; '4s' indicates a string consisting of four characters. For our records, the appropriate format string is therefore 'hd4s'. struct understands a wide range of numeric, character, and string formats. See the *Python Library Reference* for details.

Before we start reading records from our file, we need to know how many bytes to read at a time. Fortunately, struct includes a calcsize function, which simply takes our format string as argument and returns the number of bytes used to contain data in such a format.

To read each record, we will simply use the read method described previously. Then, the struct.unpack function conveniently returns a tuple of values by parsing a read record according to our format string. The program to read our binary data file is remarkably simple:

```
import struct
    recordFormat = 'hd4s'
    recordSize = struct.calcsize(recordFormat)
```

```
                resultList = []
                input = open("data", 'rb')
                while 1:
                      # Read in a single record.
                      record = input.read(recordSize)
                      # If the record is empty, it indicates we have reached the end of file, so quit the loop.
                      # Note that we have made no provision for checking for file consistency,
                      # i.e. that the file contains a number of bytes which is an integer multiple
                      # of the record size. However, if the last record is an "odd" size, the
                      # struct.unpack function will raise an error.
                      if record == '':
                         input.close()
                         break
                      # Unpack the record into a tuple, and append that tuple to the result list.
                      resultList.append(struct.unpack(recordFormat, record))
```

As you might already have guessed, struct also provides the ability to take Python values and convert them into packed byte sequences. This is accomplished through the struct.pack function, which is almost, but not quite, an inverse of struct.unpack. The "almost" comes from the fact that while struct.unpack returns a tuple of Python values, struct.pack does not take a tuple of Python values; rather, it takes a format string as its first argument, and then enough additional arguments to satisfy the format string. So, to produce a binary record of the form used in the above example, we might do something like this:

```
>>>
```

```
>>> import struct
>>> recordFormat = 'hd4s'
>>> struct.pack(recordFormat, 7, 3.14, 'gbye')
⇒   '\007\000\000\000\000\000\000\000\037\205\353Q\270\036\011@gbye'
```

struct gets even better than this; you can insert other special characters into the format string to indicate that data should be read/written in big-endian, little-endian, or machine-native-endian format (default is machine-native), and to indicate that sizes of things like C short integer should either be sized as native to the machine (the default), or as standard C sizes. But, if you need these features, it's nice to know they exist. See the *Python Library Reference* for details.

13.7 *Pickling objects into files*

Pickling is a *major* benefit in Python. Use this ability!

Python can write any data structure into a file, and read that data structure back out of a file and re-create it, with just a few commands. This is an unusual ability, but one that is highly useful. It can save the programmer many pages of code which do nothing but dump the state of a program into a file (and can save a similar amount of code which does nothing but read that state back in).

Write an arbitrary Python object with cPickle.dump.

Python provides this ability via the cPickle module. cPickle is actually a C language rewrite of the original pickle module. We are using it in our examples here as it is a thousand times faster than the pickle module. Pickling is very powerful but very simple to use. For example, assume that the entire state of a program is held in three variables: a, b, and c. We can save this state to a file called "state" as follows:

```
import cPickle
.
.
.
file = open("state", 'w')
cPickle.dump(a, file)
cPickle.dump(b, file)
cPickle.dump(c, file)
file.close()
```

It doesn't matter what was stored in a, b, and c. It might be as simple as numbers, or as complex as a list of dictionaries containing instances of user-defined classes. cPickle.dump will save everything.

Now, to read that data back in on a later run of the program, just say

Retrieve an arbitrary Python object with cPickle.load.

```
import cPickle
file = open("state", 'r')
a = cPickle.load(file)
b = cPickle.load(file)
c = cPickle.load(file)
file.close()
```

Any data that was previously in the variables a, b, or c will have been restored to them by cPickle.load.

cPickle can handle just about any Python object.

The cPickle module can store almost anything in this manner. The cPickle module can handle lists, tuples, numbers, strings, dictionaries, and just about anything made up of these types of objects, which includes all class instances. It also handles shared objects, cyclic references, and other complex memory structures correctly, storing shared objects only once, and restoring them as shared objects, not as identical copies. However, code objects (what Python uses to store byte-compiled code) and system resources (like files or sockets) cannot be pickled.

A convenient way of using cPickle is to save your state variables into a dictionary, and then cPickle the dictionary.

More often than not, you won't want to save your entire program state with cPickle. For example, most applications can have multiple documents open at one time. If you saved the entire state of the program, you would effectively save all open documents in one file. An easy and effective way of saving and restoring only data of interest is to write a save function which stores all data you wish to save into a dictionary, and then uses cPickle to save the dictionary. Then, a complementary restore function can be used to read the dictionary back in (again using cPickle), and to assign the values in the dictionary to the appropriate program variables. This also has the advantage that there is no possibility of reading values back in an incorrect order, that is, an order different from the order in which they were stored. Using this approach with the above example, we would get code looking something like this:

```
import cPickle
.
.
.
```

```
def saveData():
    global a, b, c
    file = open("state", 'w')
    data = {'a' : a, 'b' : b, 'c' : c}
    cPickle.dump(data, file)
    file.close()

def restoreData():
    global a, b, c
    file = open("state", 'r')
    data = cPickle.load(file)
    file.close()
    a = data['a']
    b = data['b']
    c = data['c']
    .
    .
    .
```

Now this is a somewhat contrived example. You probably won't be saving the state of the top-level variables of your interactive mode very often.

A real life application is an extension of the cache example given in the dictionary chapter. Recall that there we were calling a function that performed a time intensive calculation based on its three arguments. During the course of a program run many of our calls to it ended up being with the same set of arguments. We were able to obtain a significant performance improvement by caching the results in a dictionary, keyed by the arguments that produced them. However, it was also the case that many different sessions of this program were being run many times over the course of days, weeks, and months. Therefore, by pickling the cache we were able to keep from having to start over with every session. Following is a pared down version of the module for doing this.

File sole.py

```
"""sole module: contains function sole, save, show"""

import cPickle

_soleMemCacheD = {}
_soleDiskFileS = "solecache"

# This initialization code will be executed when this module is first loaded.
file = open(_soleDiskFileS, 'r')
_soleMemCacheD = cPickle.load(file)
file.close()

# Public functions
def sole(m, n, t):
    """sole(m,n,t): perform the sole calculation using the cache."""
    global _soleMemCacheD
    if _soleMemCacheD.has_key((m, n, t)):
        return _soleMemCacheD[(m, n, t)]
    else:
        #... do some time-consuming calculations ...
        _soleMemCacheD[(m, n, t)] = result
```

```
        return result
def save():
    """save(): save the updated cache to disk."""
    global _soleMemCacheD, _soleDiskFileS
    file = open(_soleDiskFileS, 'w')
    cPickle.dump(_soleMemCacheD, file)
    file.close()

def show():
    """show(): print the cache"""
    global _soleMemCacheD
    print _soleMemCacheD
```

This code assumes the cache file already exists. If you want to play around with it, use the following to initialize the cache file:

```
>>> import cPickle
>>> file = open("solecache",w)
>>> cPickle.dump({}, file)
```

You will also, of course, need to replace the comment "# . . . *do some time-consuming calculations*" with an actual calculation. Note that for production code, this is a situation where you probably would use an absolute pathname for your cache file. Also, concurrency is not being handled here. If two people run overlapping sessions, you will only end up with the additions of the last person to save. If this were an issue, you could limit this overlap window significantly by using the dictionary update method in the save function.

13.8 *Shelving objects*

The shelve module permits you to pickle Python objects into files which appear as dictionaries. This is very useful for large data sets.

This is a somewhat advanced topic, but certainly not a difficult one. This section is likely of most interest to people whose work involves storing or accessing pieces of data in large files, because the Python shelve module does exactly that—it permits the reading or writing of pieces of data in large files, without reading or writing the entire file. For applications which perform many accesses of large files (such as database applications), the savings in time can be spectacular. Like the cPickle module (which it makes use of), the shelve module is very simple.

Let's explore it through an address book. This is the sort of thing that is usually small enough so that an entire address file could be read in when the application is started, and written out when the application is done. If you're an extremely friendly sort of person, and your address book is too big for this, better to use shelve and not worry about it.

We'll assume that each entry in our address book consists of a tuple of three elements, giving the first name, phone number, and address of a person. Each entry will be indexed by the last name of the person the entry refers to. This is so simple that our application will just be an interactive session with the Python shell.

First, import the shelve module, and open the address book. shelve.open will create the address book file if it does not exist:

```
>>>
```

```
>>> import shelve
```

```
>>> book = shelve.open("addresses")
```

Now, add a couple of entries. Notice that we're treating the object returned by `shelve.open` as a dictionary (though it is a dictionary which can only use strings as keys):

```
...
```

```
>>> book['flintstone'] = ('fred', '555-1234', '1233 Bedrock Place')
>>> book['rubble'] = ('barney', '555-4321', '1235 Bedrock Place')
```

Finally, close the file and end the session:

```
...
```

```
>>> book.close()
```

So what? Well, in that same directory, start Python again, and open the same address book:

```
>>>
```

```
>>> import shelve
>>> book = shelve.open("addresses")
```

But now, instead of entering something, let's see if what we put in before is still around:

```
...
```

```
>>> book['flintstone']
⇒   ('fred', '555-1234', '1233 Bedrock Place')
```

The "addresses" file created by `shelve.open` in the first interactive session has acted just like a persistent dictionary. The data we entered before was stored to disk, even though we did no explicit disk writes. That's exactly what `shelve` does.

Shelf objects are effectively persistent, string-indexed dictionaries.

More generally, `shelve.open` returns a shelf object which permits basic dictionary operations, key assignment or lookup, `del`, and the `has_key` and `keys` methods. However, unlike a normal dictionary, shelf objects store their data on disk, not in memory. Unfortunately, shelf objects do have one significant restriction as compared to dictionaries. They can only use strings as keys, versus the wide range of key types allowable in dictionaries.

Shelf objects do NOT read an entire file into memory—this can be a major advantage.

It's important to understand the advantage shelf objects give you over dictionaries when dealing with large data sets. `shelve.open` makes the file accessible; it does not read an entire shelf object file into memory. File accesses are done only when needed, typically when an element is looked up, and the file structure is maintained in such a manner that lookups are very fast. Even if your data file is really large, only a couple of disk accesses will be required to locate the desired object in the file. This can improve your program in a number of ways. It may start faster, since it does not need to read a potentially large file into memory. It may execute faster, since there is more memory available to the rest of the program, and thus less code will need to be swapped out into virtual memory. You can operate on data sets that are otherwise too large to fit in memory at all.

Shelf objects are not necessarily written to disk until they are closed.

There are a few restrictions when using the `shelve` module. As previously mentioned, shelf object keys can only be strings; however, any Python object that can be pickled can be stored under a key in a shelf object. Also, shelf objects are not really suitable for multiuser databases, because they provide no control for concurrent access.

!!!   Finally, make sure to `close` a shelf object when you are done—this is sometimes required in order for changes you've made (entries or deletions) to be written back to disk.

As written, the cache example of the previous section would be an excellent candidate to be handled using shelves. You would not, for example, have to rely on the user to explicitly save his work to the disk. The only possible issue is that it would not have the low-level control when you write back to the file.

13.9 Summary

File input and output in Python is a remarkably simple but powerful feature of the language. You can use various built-in functions to open, read, write, and close files. For very simple uses, you'll probably want to stick with reading and writing text, but the `struct` module does give you the ability to read or write packed binary data. Even better, the `cPickle` and `shelve` modules provide simple, safe, and powerful ways of saving and accessing arbitrarily complex Python data structures, which means you may never again need to worry about defining file formats for your programs.

C H A P T E R   1 4

Exceptions

This chapter will discuss *exceptions*, which are a language feature specifically aimed at handling unusual circumstances during the execution of a program. The most common use for exceptions is to handle errors which arise during the execution of a program, but they can also be used effectively for many other purposes. Python provides a comprehensive set of exceptions, and new ones can be defined by users for their own purposes.

The concept of exceptions as an error-handling mechanism has been around for quite some time. However, C and Perl, the most commonly used systems and scripting languages, do not provide any exception capabilities, and even programmers who use languages such as C++, which do include exceptions, are often unfamiliar with them. As a result, this chapter will not assume familiarity with exceptions on the part of the reader, but instead provides detailed explanation. Programmers already familiar with exceptions can skip directly to "Exceptions in Python" (section 14.2).

14.1 Introduction to exceptions

The following sections provide an introduction to exceptions, and how they are used. You may feel free to skip them if you're already familiar with exceptions from other languages.

14.1.1 General philosophy of errors and exception handling

Any program may encounter errors during its execution. For the purposes of illustrating exceptions we'll look at the case of a word processor which writes files to disk, and which therefore may run out of disk space before all of its data is written. There are various ways of coming to grips with this problem.

Solution one: don't handle the problem

The simplest way of handling this disk-space problem is to assume that there will always be adequate disk space for whatever files we write, and we needn't worry about it. Unfortunately, this seems to be the most commonly used option. It will usually be tolerable for small programs dealing with small amounts of data, but is completely unsatisfactory for more mission-critical programs. For several months while I was writing this book, my officemate spent hours every day cleaning up files that had become corrupt when a program written by someone else ran out of disk space and crashed. Eventually he went into the code and put in some checks, which took care of most of the problem; even now, he still has to do occasional disk cleanups. Since the original program wasn't written cleanly with exceptions, the checks he put in could only do a partial job.

Solution two: all functions return success/failure status

The next level of sophistication in error handling is to realize that errors will occur, and define a methodology using standard language mechanisms for detecting and handling them. There are various ways of doing this, but a typical one is to have each function or procedure return a status value which indicates if that function or procedure call executed successfully. Normal results can be passed back in a call-by-reference parameter.

Let's look at how this might work with our hypothetical word-processing program. We will assume that the program invokes a single high-level function, saveToFile, to save the current document to file. This will call various subfunctions to save different parts of the entire document to the file, for example, saveTextToFile to save the actual document text, savePrefsToFile to save user preferences for that document, saveFormatsToFile to save user-defined formats for the document, and so forth. Any of these may in turn call their own subfunctions, which save smaller pieces to the file. At the bottom will be built-in system functions, which write primitive data to the file, and report on the success or failure of the file-writing operations.

We could put error-handling code into each and every function that might get a disk-space error, but that doesn't make much sense. The only thing the error handler will be able to do is to put up a dialog telling the user that there is no more disk space, and asking that the user remove some files and save again. It wouldn't make sense to duplicate this code everywhere we do a disk write. Instead, we will put one piece of error-handling code into the main disk-writing function, saveToFile.

Unfortunately, for saveToFile to be able to determine when to call this error-handling code, each and every function it calls which writes to disk, must itself check for disk space errors, and return a status value indicating success or failure of the disk write. Additionally, the saveToFile function must explicitly check each and every call to a function which writes to disk, even though it doesn't actually care about which function fails. The code, using a C-like syntax, looks something like this:

```
const ERROR = 1;
const OK = 0;
int saveToFile(filename) {
    int status;
    status = savePrefsToFile(filename);
    if (status == ERROR) {
        ...handle the error...
    }
    status = saveTextToFile(filename);
    if (status == ERROR) {
        ...handle the error...
    }
    status = saveFormatsToFile(filename);
    if (status == ERROR) {
        ...handle the error...
    }
    .
    .
    .
}

int saveTextToFile(filename) {
    int status;
    status = ...lower-level call to write size of text...
    if (status == ERROR) {
        return(ERROR);
    }
    status = ...lower-level call to write actual text data...
    if (status == ERROR) {
        return(ERROR);
    }
    .
    .
    .
}
```

and so on for `savePrefsToFile`, `saveFormatsToFile`, and all other functions that either write to `filename` directly or that (in any way) call functions that write to `filename`.

Under this methodology, code to detect and handle errors can become a significant portion of the entire program, because each and every function and procedure containing calls that might result in an error needs to contain code to check for an error. Often, programmers do not have the time or the energy put in this type of complete error-checking; as a result, programs end up being unreliable and crash-prone.

Solution three: the exception mechanism

... or use exceptions.

It's obvious that most of the error checking code in the above type of program is largely repetitive code in the file-writing functions, which simply checks for errors on each attempted file write, and passes an error status message back up to the calling procedure if an error is detected. The disk space error is only handled in one place, the top-level `saveToFile`. In other words, most of the error-handling code is really just plumbing code, which connects the place an error is generated with the place it is handled. What we really want to do is to get rid of this plumbing, and write code that looks something like this:

```
void saveToFile(filename) {
    try to execute the following block {
        saveTextToFile(filename);
        saveFormatsToFile(filename);
        savePrefsToFile(filename);
        .
        .
        .
    } except that, if the disk runs out of space while
          executing the above block, do this {
          ...handle the error...
    }
}
void saveTextToFile(filename) {
    ...lower-level call to write size of text...
    ...lower-level call to write actual text data...
    .
    .
    .
}
```

Exceptions permit a direct connection between the source of an error and the code that handles that error.

The error-handling code is completely removed from the lower-level functions; an error (if it occurs) will be generated by the built-in file writing routines and will propagate directly to the `saveToFile` routine, where the programmer's error-handling code will (presumably) take care of it. Unfortunately, there is no way of doing this in languages such as C, which is why some of the code is in our italicized comment-style. We simply can't write this code in C! Fortunately, languages that offer exceptions permit exactly this sort of behavior, and, of course, Python is one such language.

14.1.2 A more formal definition of exceptions

Generating an exception is called raising or throwing an exception. Detecting a thrown exception, and calling code to act on it, is called catching an exception. The called code is the exception handler.

The act of generating an exception is called *raising* or *throwing* an exception. In the example above, all exceptions were raised by the built-in disk-writing functions, but exceptions can also be raised by any other built-in functions, or can be explicitly raised by your own code. This will be discussed in more detail shortly. In the above example, it would be the low-level disk-writing functions (not seen in the code above) which would throw an exception if the disk were to run out of space.

The act of responding to an exception is called *catching* an exception, and the code which actually handles an exception is called *exception-handling code*, or just an *exception handler*. In the above example, it is the *except that...* line which catches the disk-write exception, and the code that would be in place of the

```
...handle the error...
```

line would be an exception handler for disk-write (out of space) exceptions. There may be other exception handlers for other types of exceptions, or even other exception handlers for the same type of exception but at another place in your code.

14.1.3 User-defined exceptions

Depending on exactly what event causes an exception, a program may wish to take different actions. For example, an exception raised when disk space is exhausted needs to be handled quite differently from an exception that is raised if we run out of memory, and both are completely different from an exception that arises when a divide-by-zero error occurs. One way of handling these different types of exceptions would be to globally record an error message indicating the cause of the exception, and to have all exception handlers examine this error message and take appropriate action. In practice, a different method has proven to be much more flexible.

Different types of exceptions may be raised in response to different error conditions.

Rather than defining a single kind of exception, Python, like most modern languages which implement exceptions, defines different types of exceptions, corresponding to various problems which may occur. So, depending on the underlying event, different types of exceptions may be raised. In addition, the code that catches exceptions may be told only to catch certain types. This feature was used in the pseudocode above when we said, *except that, if the disk runs out of space, do this*, we were specifying that this particular exception handling code was only interested in disk-space exceptions. Another type of exception would not be caught by that exception handling code. It would either be caught by an exception handler that was looking for numeric exceptions, or, if there were no such exception handler, it would cause the program to exit prematurely with an error.

14.2 Exceptions in Python

The remaining sections of this chapter talk specifically about the exception mechanisms built into Python. The entire Python exception mechanism is built around an object-oriented paradigm, which makes it both flexible and expandable. Readers who are not familiar with OOP do not need to learn OO techniques, in order to make use of exceptions.

A Python exception is a Python data object; it can be generated internally or by the raise *statement.*

Like everything else in Python, an exception is merely a data object. It is generated automatically by Python built-in functions, or explicitly by the user with a `raise` statement. Once it is generated, the `raise` statement, which raises an exception, causes execution of the Python program to proceed in a manner differently than would normally occur. Instead of proceeding on with the next statement after the `raise`, or whatever generated the exception, the current call chain is searched for a handler which can handle the generated exception. If such a handler is found, it is invoked and may access the exception object for more information. If no suitable exception handler is found, the program aborts with an error message.

14.2.1 Types of Python exceptions

It is possible to generate different types of exceptions, to reflect the actual cause of the error or exceptional circumstance being reported. Python provides a number of difference exception types:

```
Exception
    SystemExit
    StandardError
        LookupError
            IndexError, KeyError
        ArithmeticError
            OverflowError, ZeroDivisionError, FloatingPointError
        EnvironmentError
            IOError, OSError
        RunTimeError
            NotImplementedError
        KeyboardInterrupt, ImportError, IOError, EOFError,
        RuntimeError, NameError, AttributeError, SyntaxError,
        TypeError, AssertionError, ValueError, SystemError, MemoryError
```

The Python exception set is hierarchically structured, as reflected by the indentation in the list of exceptions above (the last group from `KeyboardInterrupt` to `MemoryError` are under `StandardError`). As we saw in a previous chapter, we can obtain an alphabetized list from the `__builtin__` module.

Each type of exception is a Python class, which inherits from its parent exception type. But if you're not into OOP yet, don't worry about that. For example, a `ZeroDivision-Error` is also a `NumberError`, and by inheritance a `StandardError` and also an `Exception`. An explanation of the meaning of each type of exception can be found in the appendix, but you will rapidly become acquainted with the most common types as you program!

14.2.2 Raising exceptions

Exceptions may be raised by built-in functions.

Exceptions are raised by many of the Python built-in functions. For example:

```
>>>
>>> list = [1, 2, 3]
>>> element = list[7]
Traceback (innermost last):
  File "<stdin>", line 1, in ?
IndexError: list index out of range
```

Error-checking code built into Python detects that the second input line above is requesting an element at a list index which does not exist, and raises an `IndexError` exception. This exception propagates all the way back to the top level (the interactive Python interpreter), which handles it by printing out a message stating that the exception has occurred.

Exceptions may be raised explicitly, with the raise *statement.*

Exceptions may also be raised explicitly in your own code, through the use of the `raise` statement. The most basic form of this statement is

raise *exception(args)*

The *exception(args)* part of the code creates an exception. The arguments to the new exception are typically values which aid the programmer in determining what happened, something we'll discuss shortly. Once the exception has been created, `raise` takes it and throws it upwards along the stack of Python functions which were invoked in getting to the line containing the `raise` statement. The new exception will be thrown up to the nearest (on the stack) exception catcher looking for that type of exception. If no catcher is found on the way to the top level of the program this will either cause the program to terminate with an error or, in an interactive session, will cause an error message to be printed to the console.

Try the following:

```
>>>
```

```
>>> raise IndexError("Just kidding")
Traceback (innermost last):
  File "<stdin>", line 1, in ?
IndexError: Just kidding
```

The use of `raise` here generates what, at first glance, looks similar to all of the Python list index error messages we've seen so far. Closer inspection reveals this not to be the case. The actual error reported isn't quite as serious as those other ones.

Most exceptions can take an optional string argument which describes the exception in more detail.

The use of a string argument when creating exceptions is common. Most of the built-in Python exceptions, if given a first argument, will assume it is a message to be shown to the programmer as an explanation of what happened. This is not always the case, though, since each exception type is its own class, and the arguments expected when a new exception of that class is created are determined entirely by the class definition. Also, programmer-defined exceptions, created by yourself or by other programmers, are often used for reasons other than error-handling, and as such, may not take any text message at all.

14.2.3 Catching and handling exceptions

The important thing about exceptions isn't that they cause a program to halt with an error message. Achieving that in a program is never much of a problem. What's special about exceptions is that they don't have to cause the program to halt. By defining appropriate exception handlers, the programmer can ensure that commonly encountered exceptional circumstances don't cause the program to fail; perhaps they display an error message to the user, or do something else, even fix the problem, but they don't crash the program.

Python catches and handles exceptions with try and except blocks.

The basic Python syntax for exception catching and handling is as follows, using the `try` and `except` and sometimes the `else` keywords:

```
try:
    body
except exceptionType1, var1:
    exceptionCode1
except exceptionType2, var2:
    exceptionCode2
  .
  .
  .
except:
    defaultExceptionCode
else:
    elseBody
```

If an exception occurs, a try *block will look at all of its associated* except *clauses to see if any of them can handle the exception.*

A `try` statement is executed by first executing the code in the *body* part of the statement. If this is successful (i.e., no exceptions are thrown to be caught by the `try` statement), then the *elseBody* is executed and the `try` statement is finished. Nothing else occurs. If an exception is thrown to the `try`, then the `except` clauses are searched sequentially for one whose associated exception type matches that which was thrown. If a matching `except` clause is found, the thrown exception is assigned to the variable named after the associated exception type, and the exception code body associated with the matching exception is executed. If the line `except` *exceptionType, var:* matches some thrown expression *exc*, the variable *var* will be created and *exc* will be assigned as the value of *var*, before the exception handling code of the `except` statement is executed. However, you don't need to put in *var*; you can just say something like `except` *exceptionType:*, which will still catch exceptions of the given type, but won't assign them to any variable.

If no matching `except` clause is found, then the thrown exception cannot be handled by that `try` statement, and the exception is thrown further up the call chain, in hopes that some enclosing `try` will be able to handle it.

The last except *clause in a* try *can be made to catch all exception types.*

The last `except` clause of a `try` statement can optionally refer to no exception types at all, in which case it will handle all types of exceptions. This can be convenient for some debugging and extremely rapid prototyping, but generally isn't a good idea, because all errors will be hidden by the `except` clause, which can lead to some very confusing behavior on the part of your program.

The `else` clause of a `try` statement is optional, and is rarely used. It is executed if and only if the *body* of the `try` statement executes without throwing any errors.

14.2.4 Defining new exceptions

A basic new exception can be easily created with two lines of code.

You can easily define your own exception. The following two lines will do this for you.

```
class MyError(Exception):
    pass
```

What this is doing is creating a class that inherits everything from the base `Exception` class. But you don't have to worry about that if you don't want to.

You can raise, catch, and handle it like any other exception. If you give it a single argument (and you don't catch and handle it), this will be printed at the end of the traceback.

```
>>> raise MyError, "Some information about what went wrong"
Traceback (innermost last):
  File "<stdin>", line 1, in ?
__main__.MyError: Some information about what went wrong
```

This argument will of course be available to a handler you write as well.

```
try:
    raise MyError, "Some information about what went wrong"
except MyError, error:
    print "Situation:", error
```

The result here would be:

```
Situation: Some information about what went wrong
```

If you raise your exception with multiple arguments, these will be delivered to your handler as a tuple:

```
try:
    raise MyError("Some information", "myFilename",3)
except MyError, error:
    print "Situation: problem %d with file %s: %s" % (error[2],
        error[1], error[0])
```

giving the result:

```
Situation: problem 3 with file myFilename: Some information
```

In older code you might see exceptions defined as plain strings. These can be raised and possibly passed as single, but not multiple, arguments.

Some older Python code will use exceptions defined simply as strings.

```
>>> MyError2 = "My Error Occurred"
>>> raise MyError2
Traceback (innermost last):
  File "<stdin>", line 1, in ?
My Error Occurred
>>> raise MyError2, "at x"
Traceback (innermost last):
  File "<stdin>", line 1, in ?
My Error Occurred: at x
```

The following paragraph introduces the use of object-oriented nature of exceptions when defining your own. It's here to make this section complete for your future reference. You don't have to worry about this on a first read of the book. You can always come back to it after you've read "Classes and object-oriented programming" (chapter 16).

Because an exception type is a regular class in Python and happens to inherit from the root `Exception` class, it is a simple matter to create you own sub-hierarchy of exception types for use by your own code. Exactly how you do this depends on your particular needs. If you are writing a small program which might generate only a few unique errors or exceptions, simply subclass the main `Exception` class as we've done above. If, on the other hand, you are writing a large, multifile code library with a special goal in mind—say, weather forecasting—you might decide to define a unique class called `WeatherLibraryException`, and then to define all of the unique exceptions of the library as subclasses of `WeatherLibraryException`.

14.2.5 Debugging programs with the assert statement

The `assert` statement is a specialized form of the `raise` statement.

```
assert expression, argument
```

Use `assert` statements to print debug information.

The `AssertionError` exception with the optional *argument* will be raised if the *expression* evaluates to false and the system variable __debug__ is true. The __debug__ variable defaults to true. It is turned off by either starting up the Python interpreter with the -O or -OO options or by setting the system variable PYTHONOPTIMIZE to true (see the "Environment variables" section in the appendix for description of how to set system variables).

The code generator creates no code for assertion statements if __debug__ is false. So you can use assert statements to instrument your code with debug statements during development and leave them in the code for possible future use with no run-time cost during regular use.

```
>>> x = (1, 2, 3)
>>> assert len(x)>5
Traceback (innermost last):
  File "<pyshell#1>", line 1, in ?
    assert len(x) >5
AssertionError:
```

Notice that the assert statement itself is printed in the traceback.

14.2.6 The exception inheritance hierarchy

Now let's expand on an earlier notion that Python exceptions were hierarchically structured and on what it means in terms of how except clauses catch exceptions.

The following code

```
try:
    body
except LookupError, error:
    exception code
except IndexError, error:
    exception code
```

catches two different types of exceptions: IndexError and LookupError. However, it just so happens that IndexError is a subclass of LookupError. If body throws an IndexError, that error will first be examined by the except LookupError, error: line, and since an IndexError is a LookupError by inheritance, the first except will succeed. The second except clause will never be used because it is subsumed by the first except clause.

On the other hand, flipping the order of the two except clauses could potentially be useful; the first clause would then handle IndexError exceptions, and the second clause would handle any LookupError exceptions which are not IndexError errors.

14.2.7 Example: our disk writing program in Python

Let's revisit our example of a word processing program which needs to check for disk out of space conditions as it writes a document to disk.

```
def saveToFile(filename) :
    try:
        saveTextToFile(filename)
        saveFormatsToFile(filename)
        savePrefsToFile(filename)
        .

        .
    except IOError:
        ...handle the error...
```

```
def saveTextToFile(filename):
    ...lower-level call to write size of text...
    ...lower-level call to write actual text data...
    .
    .
    .
```

Notice how unobtrusive the error-handling code is. It is simply wrapped around the main sequence of disk-writing calls in the `saveToFile` function. None of the subsidiary disk-writing functions need any error-handling code at all. It would be quite easy to develop the program first, and then to add error-handling code later. That is often what is done, although this is not the optimal ordering of events.

As another note of interest, the above code doesn't respond specifically to disk-full errors; rather, it responds to `IOError` exceptions, which Python built-in functions raise automatically whenever they cannot complete an I/O request, for whatever reason. That is probably satisfactory for our needs, but if you really need to identify disk-full conditions, you could do a couple of different things. The `except` body could simply check to see how much room is available on disk; if the disk is out of space, clearly it is a disk-full problem and should be handled in this `except` body, otherwise the code in the `except` body could throw the `IOError` further up the call chain, to be handled by some other `except`. If that wasn't sufficient, you could do something more extreme, like going into the C source for the Python disk-writing functions, and raising your own `DiskFull` exceptions as necessary. This latter option isn't a course I'd recommend, but it is nice to know the possibility exists, if you really need to make use of it.

14.2.8   Example: exceptions in normal evaluation

Exceptions are most often used in error-handling, but can also be remarkably useful in certain situations involving what we would think of as normal evaluation. An example I encountered recently involved a spreadsheetlike program I was implementing. Like most spreadsheets, it permits arithmetic operations involving cells and it permits cells to contain values other than numbers. For my application, I wanted blank cells used in a numerical calculation to be considered as containing the value 0, and cells containing any other non-numeric string to be considered as invalid, which I represented as the Python value `None`. Any calculation involving an invalid value should return an invalid value.

The first step was to write a function which would evaluate a string from a cell of the spreadsheet, and return an appropriate value:

```
def cellValue(string):
    try:
        return float(string)
    except ValueError:
        if string == "":
            return 0
        else:
            return None
```

Python's exception-handling ability made this a simple function to write. I simply tried to convert the string from the cell into a number and return it, in a `try` block using the `float` built-in function. `float` raises the `ValueError` exception if it can't convert its string argument to a number, so I caught that, and returned either `0` or `None` depending on whether the argument string was empty or non-empty.

The next step was to handle the fact that some of my arithmetic might have to deal with a value of `None`. In a language without exceptions, the normal way to do this would be to define a custom set of arithmetic functions, which checked their arguments for `None`, and then to use those functions rather than the built-in arithmetic functions, to perform all of the spreadsheet arithmetic. This is time-consuming, error-prone, and leads to slow execution, because you are effectively building an interpreter in your spreadsheet. I took a different approach. All of my spreadsheet formulas were actually Python functions which took as arguments the *x* and *y* coordinates of the cell being evaluated, and the spreadsheet itself, and calculated the result for the given cell using standard Python arithmetic operators, using `cellValue` to extract the necessary values from the spreadsheet. I simply defined a function called `safeApply`, which took one of these formulas, applied it to the appropriate arguments in a `try` block, and returned either the formula's result or `None`, depending on whether the formula evaluated successfully or not:

```
def safeApply(function, x, y, spreadsheet):
    try:
        return apply(function, (x, y, spreadsheet))
    except TypeError:
        return None
```

These two changes were enough to integrate the idea of an empty (`None`) value into the semantics of my spreadsheet. It is a highly educational exercise to try to develop this ability without the use of exceptions.

14.2.9   Where to use exceptions

Exceptions are a natural choice for error-handling almost any error condition. It is an unfortunate fact that error-handling is often added after the rest of the program is largely complete, but exceptions are particularly good at intelligibly managing this sort of after-the-fact error-handling code (or, more optimistically, for the case where one is adding more of them after the fact).

Exceptions are also highly useful in circumstances where a large amount of processing may need to be discarded once it has become obvious that a computational branch in your program has become untenable. The spreadsheet example above was one such case; others are branch-and-bound algorithms and parsing algorithms.

Scripts

Up until now we've only been using the Python interpreter in interactive mode. For production use you will want to create Python programs. Python programs are run as *scripts*. A number of the sections in this chapter focus on command line scripts. If you come from a UNIX background, you are likely quite familiar with command line scripts which can be started from a command line and given arguments and options that can be used to pass in information, and possibly redirect their input and output. If you are from a Windows background, these things may be new to you and you might be more inclined to question their value. It is true that command line scripts are less convenient to use in a Windows environment. It will be well worth your time to read the bulk of this chapter at some point. You may find occasions when these techniques are useful or you may run across code that you need to understand that uses some of them.

15.1 *Creating a very basic script*

A simple script is a file containing a function definition and a call to that function.

A group of Python statements placed sequentially in a file can be used as a script. However, it is more standard and quite useful to introduce more structure. In its most basic form, this is a simple matter of creating a controlling function in a file and calling that function:

File script1.py

```
def main():      ● The controlling function main
    print "this is our first test script file"

main()           ● The call to the controlling function main
```

In this script, main is our controlling, and only, function. It is first defined, and then it is called.

15.1.1 Starting a script from a command line

If you are using UNIX, make sure Python is on your path and you are in the same directory as your script. Then type the following to your command line:

```
python script1.p      ● Starting a script from a UNIX command line   y
```

If you are using Windows, place your script on the desktop (if you are on Windows 95/98) or in the top level "C:" directory (if you are on Windows NT) and select Run from your start menu. Type in the following command and then click okay.

```
python -i script1.py   ● Starting a script from the Windows Run Box
```

The use of the -i option here will leave the Python interpreter and its window up after the script exits. If you leave it out, the window will close as soon as the script finishes. You might get a chance to quickly read it before it disappears. You certainly won't be able to study it at your leisure. Starting up another script will just open a new interpreter and window, so exit (with a CTRL-Z) once you're through. We will be looking at other options for calling scripts later in this chapter, but stick with this for now.

15.1.2 Command line arguments

Command line arguments are placed as a list of strings in sys.argv.

There is a simple mechanism available for passing in command line arguments.

File script2.py

```
import sys
def main():
    print "this is our second test script file"
    print sys.argv

main()
```

If we call this with the line (don't forget to add -i after python if you are on Windows):

```
python script2.py arg1 arg2 3
```

we will get

```
this is our second test script file
['script2.py', 'arg1', 'arg2', '3']
```

We see that the command line arguments have been stored in `sys.argv` as a list of strings.

15.1.3 Redirecting the input and output of a script

You can redirect the input and/or the output for a script using command line options. To show this we will use the following short script:

File replace.py

```
import string, sys

def main():
    sys.stdout.write( string.replace(sys.stdin.read(), sys.argv[1],
                      sys.argv[2]) )

main()
```

The input or output of a script can be redirected on the command line using '<' and '>' respectively.

This script will read its standard input and write to its standard output whatever it read, with all occurrences of its first argument replaced with its second argument. Called as follows, it will place in `outFile` a copy of `inFile` with all occurrences of `zero` replaced by `0`.

```
python replace.py zero 0 <inFile >outFile
```

Note that this will work on UNIX, but, on Windows, redirection of input and/or output will work only if you start a script from an MS-DOS Prompt window.*

In general the line,

```
python script.py arg1 arg2 arg3 arg4 <inFile >outFile
```

Redirecting output with '>>' will cause the file to be appended to, rather than overwritten.

will have the effect of having any `raw_input`, `input`, or `sys.stdin` operations directed out of `inFile` and any `print` or `sys.stdout` operations to be directed into `outFile`. The effect will be as if you had set `sys.stdin` to `inFile` with `'r'` (read) mode and `sys.stout` to `outFile` with `'w'` (write) mode except `__stdin__` and `__stdout__` will be set to `inFile` and `outFile` as well.

```
python replace.py a A <inFile >>outFile
```

This line will cause the output to be appended to `outFile` rather than overwrite it, as will happen in the previous example.

You can also *pipe* in the output of one command as the input of another command:

```
python replace.py 0 zero <inFile  |   python replace.py 1 one > outFile
```

This will end up with `outFile` containing the contents of `inFile` with all occurrences of `0` changed to `zero` and all occurrences of `1` changed to `one`.

---

* If you try this using the Windows Run box, input and output will not be redirected. You will be placed in the interpreter window where you can type lines of text. Ending this with a Ctrl-Z will cause the program to output what you just typed but with the replacements made (Ctrl-D would do the same on UNIX). Section 15.3 discusses starting a script from an MS-DOS prompt window.

15.1.4 The getopt module

A script can be configured to accept command line options as well as arguments. The `getopt` module provides support for parsing options and arguments. It delivers similar functionality to the `getopt` function in UNIX. The following example illustrates its use.

File script3.py

```
import getopt, sys

def main():
    (options, arguments) = getopt.getopt(sys.argv[1:], 'f:vx:y:z:')
    print "options:",options
    print "arguments:",arguments

main()
```
❶

❶ This is a string containing the valid option characters. A colon after a character indicates that argument requires an argument. Here the valid options are -f, -v, -x, -y and -z, with all but -v requiring an argument.

The `getopt` function returns two lists. The first contains tuples of the options found, along with their respective arguments represented as strings. An empty string indicates there was no argument for an option. The second is a list of the regular arguments found. Thus, if the previous script is called with the line:

```
python script3.py -x100 -v -y50 -f infile arg1 arg2
```
❶

❶ options come after the script name so as not to be considered to be options to the interpreter itself.

The `getopt` module can be used to parse out regular arguments as well as command line options and their arguments

The following output will result

```
options: [('-x', '100'), ('-v', ''), ('-y', '50'), ('-f', 'infile')]
arguments: ['arg1', 'arg2']
```

If an invalid option is found, or if an option that requires an argument isn't given one, `getopt` will raise an error.

```
python script3.py -x100 -r
```

The above line will result in the following response

```
getopt.error: option -r not recognized
```

The `getopt` function also can be used to parse GNU style long arguments. See the appendix for details.

15.1.5 Using the fileinput module

The `fileinput` module is also sometimes useful for scripts. It provides support for processing lines of input from one or more files. It will automatically read the command line arguments (out of `sys.argv`) and take them as its list of input files. It allows you to then sequentially iterate through these lines. The following simple example script (which will strip out any lines starting with ##) illustrates the module's basic use.

File script4.py

```
import fileinput
def main():
    for line in fileinput.input():
        if line[:2] != '##':
            print line,

main()
```

Now, assume we have the following data files:

File sole1.tst

```
## sole1.tst: test data for the sole function
0 0 0
0 100 0
##
0 100 100
```

File sole2.tst

```
## sole2.tst: more test data for the sole function
12 15 0
##
100 100 0
```

and that we make the following call:

```
python script4.py sole1.tst sole2.tst
```

We would obtain the following result with the comment lines stripped out and the data from the two files combined:

```
0 0 0
0 100 0
100 100 100
12 15 0
100 100 0
```

If no command line arguments are present, the standard input will be all that is read. If one of the arguments is a "-" the standard input will be read at that point.

The module provides a number of other functions. These allow you at any point to determine: the total number of lines that have been read (`lineno`); the number of lines that have been read out of the current file (`filelineno`); the name of the current file (`filename`); whether this is the first line of a file (`isfirstline`); and/or whether standard input is currently being read (`isstdin`). You can at any point skip to the next file (`nextfile`) or close the whole stream (`close`). The following short script (which combines the lines in its input files and adds file start delimiters) illustrates how these can be used:

File script5.py

```
import fileinput
def main():
    for line in fileinput.input():
        if fileinput.isfirstline():
            print "<start of file %s>" % fileinput.filename()
        print line,

main()
```

Using the call:

```
python script5.py file1 file2
```

will result in the following (where the dotted lines indicate the lines in the original files):

```
<start of file file1>
·················· . .
·················· . .
<start of file file2>
·················· . .
·················· . .
```

Finally, if you call `fileinput.input` with an argument of a single file name or a list of file names, they will be used as its input file(s) rather than the arguments in `sys.argv`. It also has an inline option that will leave its output in the same file as its input while optionally leaving the original around as a backup file. See the appendix for a description of this last option.

15.2   *Making a script directly executable on UNIX*

If you're on UNIX, you can easily make a script directly executable. Add the following line to its top and change its mode appropriately (i.e. `chmod +x replace.py`):

```
#! /usr/bin/env python
```

Then, if you place it somewhere on your path (in your bin directory), you can execute it regardless of the directory you are in by simply typing its name and the desired arguments:

```
replace zero 0 <inFile >outfile
```

On UNIX you will have input and output redirection and, if you are using a modern shell, command history and completion.

15.3   *Script execution options in Windows*

If you're on Windows, you have a number of options for starting a script that vary in their capability and ease of use. Unfortunately, none of them are as flexible or powerful as on UNIX.

15.3.1 Starting a script as a document or shortcut

A script can be opened (without command line arguments) on Windows by double clicking on it.

The window will disappear as soon as the script finishes.

If you don't want the interpreter window to appear at all, use the .pyw extension for your file's name.

The easiest way to start a script on Windows is to use its standard document opening technique. When you installed Python it should have registered the .py suffix to itself. Verify this by confirming that your ".py" files are shown with a green snake icon. If you double click on any .py file, Python will be automatically called with this file as its argument. It will also be entered onto the Documents list on your Start menu. However, you are not able to enter any arguments and the MS-DOS window that the interpreter is opened in will close as soon as the script exits. If you want to have the window stay up so you can read the output, you can place the following line at the bottom of your controlling function:

```
raw_input("Press the Enter key to exit")
```

This will leave the window up until you click Enter. You can also query the user for any input data you might have desired on the command line. Your current working directory at start up will be the one where your Python interpreter is located (`c:\Program Files\Python`).

If you do not want the interpreter window to open at all (when, for example, starting a GUI program using Tk), you can give the file the suffix .pyw. This will cause it to be opened by pythonw.exe. However, if you start a script this way, any output to `stdout` or `stderr` will be thrown away.

You have more flexibility and the ability to pass in more information to your script if you set it up as a Windows Shortcut (figure 15.1). Right-click on it and either select the Create Shortcut or the Send to Desktop as Shortcut option. You can move the shortcut to any location and rename it as desired. By right-clicking on it and selecting the Properties option you can set the directory it starts in, type in arguments that it will be called with, and specify a shortcut key that will call it. The following example illustrates this.

File script6.py

```
import sys, os
def main():
    print os.getcwd()
    print sys.argv
    raw_input("Hit return to exit")
main()
```

As a shortcut, a script can be placed anywhere and set to start with preset arguments in a preset directory, with a preset shortcut key, and with or without a window.

Creating the shortcut as shown in figure 15.1 and then calling this script (by typing CTRL ALT-J or double-clicking on its icon) brings up a Python window containing:

```
C:\My Documents\Images
['C:\\MYDOCU~1\\PYSCRI~1\\SCRIPT6.PY', 'arg1', 'arg2']
Hit return to exit
```

What happens is that the Python interpreter is implicitly called with the Target line (as it has registered for Python files). You can also explicitly put it in. You may do this if you want to also enter options for the interpreter itself:

```
"C:\Program Files\Python\Python.exe" -i
"C:\My Documents\pyScripts\script6.py" arg1 arg2*
```

---

* Please note that this should be entered as a single line with no line breaks on the target line.

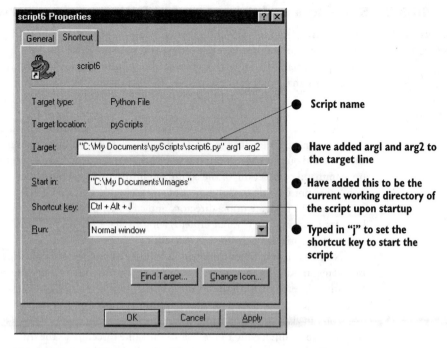

Figure 15.1 A Windows shortcut

Since you change the selection for the Run line to Minimized from the default Normal window, no MS-DOS window will be brought up, just as when you use the .pyw suffix for a document.

There is unfortunately no mechanism for redirecting the input or output for shortcuts.

15.3.2 Starting a script from the Windows run box

A script can be started from the Windows Run box with command line options and arguments (but not with I/O redirection).

This is the way we've been starting our scripts up to now—by placing the script on the desktop and typing:

```
python -i script.py arg1 arg2
```

More flexibility is available. Using the window obtained by selecting the browse button, you can search for scripts residing elsewhere (by selecting All Files for the Files type box at the bottom, as this defaults to Programs). This will result in the pathname to the script you selected being displayed in the Run box (C:\My Documents\book\script1.py). You will have to prepend this with python -i.

You can of course eliminate the need for using the -i option in the call by using a raw_input line in the same way as described in the previous section.

Also the selection button to the right of the text box will bring up a history of your past lines of entries, from which you can select a line to edit. The current working directory for any script started from the Run box will be the desktop.

15.3.3 Starting a script from an MS-DOS Prompt window

Scripts can be started from an MS-DOS Prompt with command line options and arguments and I/O redirection.

To run a script from the MS-DOS Prompt window, place the script in the same directory as your Python executable or a subdirectory of it (`C:\Program Files\Python\scripts`). Then open up an MS-DOS prompt near the bottom of your Start Menu and navigate to the directory that holds your executable. You can then enter in your commands.

```
python scripts\replace.py zero 0 <scripts\inFile >scripts\outFile
```

You don't need to use the `-i` option as the script will run in your existing window. This is the most flexible of the ways to run a script on Windows because it allows you to use input and output redirection. It is not all that convenient, as you don't have mouse editing, command completion, or the command history that you have in modern UNIX shells. It also does not provide the full power of an executable script on UNIX. It lacks the ability, for example, to navigate into a directory and call a script with a set of file names from that directory as arguments without either having to place the script in that directory or enter in the full pathname of the files or the script.

Note that if you are using input or output redirection, the default is for Windows to use the text mode. If you want your script to work with binary data, you either need to call the Python interpreter with the `-u` option set (`python -u script.py`) or set the environment variable `PYTHONUNBUFFERED=1` to turn off buffering and place it in a binary mode.

You can also add the directory where the Python interpreter is to your PATH variable. This frees you from having to move into the same directory as the interpreter or refer to it with a full pathname. To do this on Windows 95/98, open the file `C:\autoexec.bat` in NOTEPAD and find the line that sets your PATH variable:

```
set PATH=c:\windows;c:\windows\COMMAND;C:\PROGRA~1\Tcl\bin
```

Add `;C:\PROGRA~1\Python` to this line.

Be sure to include the single semicolon between what is on the existing line and this addition. Save the file. You need to shutdown and restart your computer for this to take effect. Now you just have to move to the directory containing the script and type python script.py. You also would only have to use `python -i` rather than `"C:\Program Files\Python\Python.exe" -i` in the Shortcut described earlier.

15.3.4 Other Windows options

There are other options to explore. If you are familiar with writing batch files, you can wrap your commands in them. There is a port of the GNU BASH shell which comes with the cygwin tool set, about which you can read at http://sourceware.cygnus.com/cygwin/. This provides a UNIX-like shell capability for Windows.

If you are on Windows NT, you can add .py as a magic extension making your scripts automatically executable:

```
PATHEXT=.COM;.EXE;.BAT;.CMD;.VBS;.JS;.PY
```

The PythonWin development environment provides the capability of calling a script with arguments. This functionality may also be added to a future version of IDLE.

164   CHAPTER 15   SCRIPTS

15.4 *Scripts on Windows versus scripts on UNIX*

The fact that the ease of use and functionality that you can obtain in calling scripts on Windows differs from that on UNIX can affect what kind of scripts you develop and how you write them. Let's revisit our initial script from the section describing the `fileinput` module. Making it directly executable might be the only change we would make to use it on UNIX:

File script4a.py

```
#! /usr/bin/env python import fileinpu          ● This line allows the script  t
def main():                                       to be executed on UNIX. It
    for line in fileinput.input():                has no effect on Windows.
        if line[:2] != '##':
            print line,

main()
```

On UNIX, once this has been made executable and placed on our path, we are then able to simply navigate into any desired directory and call this with wild cards and output redirection.

```
script4a.py sole*.tst > sole.data
```

This UNIX shell will find all files in the current directory that start with `sole` and end with `.tst`, and these will be sent in as command line arguments.

On Windows it's not so easy. As we've just discovered, using the convenient double-click mechanism, we can't pass in command line arguments. Using the Run Box we can pass in arguments, but not redirect the output. The closest we can come is to use the MS-DOS Prompt window, actually place the script in the desired directory, navigate into the directory, and then type:*

```
"C:\Program Files\Python\python.exe" script4a.py sole1.tst sole2.tst
sole4.tst sole15.tst > sole.data
```

or if you set your PATH as described in the previous section:

```
python script4a.py sole1.tst sole2.tst sole4.tst sole15.tst > sole.data
```

However, using the `glob.glob` function we can obtain the wildcard character functionality:

File script4b.py

```
#! /usr/bin/env python
import fileinput, glob, sys, os
```

---

* Please note that this should be entered as a single line with no line breaks. Due to space constraints, it could not be represented here in that manner.

```
def main():
    if os.name == 'nt':
        sys.argv[1:] = glob.glob(sys.argv[1])
    for line in fileinput.input():
        if line[:2] != '##':
            print line,

main()
```

This will be true if we are running under ● Windows 95/98/NT.

● We replace the single wildcarded filename string in the argument list with those files into which it expands.

Assuming that we have placed our script in the same directory as our .tst files and navigated to that directory in an MS-DOS Prompt window, we can now call our script with a single wildcarded argument:*

```
"C:\Program Files\Python\python.exe" script4b.py sole*.tst >
  sole.data
```

or, again, if your PATH has been modified:

```
python script4b.py sole*.tst > sole.data
```

With the use of copy and paste and storing the command text in a file, this might be acceptable for your situation. However, the script can be set up so that it can be started using the double-click open mechanism. This is often done for those scripts that will be run by end users.

When started with double-click, a script's working directory will be the directory where the Python interpreter resides, not where the script is. Fortunately, the directory where the script is will be appended as the first string in sys.path. The following script uses this fact and changes into that directory. It then prompts the user for a possibly wildcarded input file-name and expands it. Next it prompts for the name of the output file and redirects standard output to this file. Finally, it proceeds to the original script's functionality.

File script4c.py

```
#! /usr/bin/env python
import fileinput, glob, sys, os
def main():
    if os.name == 'nt':
        if sys.path[0]: os.chdir(sys.path[0])
        sys.argv[1:] = glob.glob(raw_input("Name of input file:"))
        sys.stdout = open(raw_input("Name of output file:"),'w')
    for line in fileinput.input():
        if line[:2] != '##':
            print line,

main()
```

Move to the appropriate ● directory.

Redirect the ● standard output.

Placing this script in the directory of our .tst files, we can double-click on it and enter in the requested information. The end result will be the same as if it had been run from a command line.

---

* Again, this should be on a single line.

```
Name of input file:sole*.tst
Name of output file:sole.data
```

This is not as nice as on UNIX but in many cases may do fine. If you are writing scripts that will be run on Windows only, be sure to also check out the section on the "Windows scripting host" in "Python, Windows and COM" (chapter 22).

15.5 Scripts and modules

For small scripts that contain only a few lines of code, a single function works well. However, if the script grows beyond this, separating your controlling function from the rest of the code is a good option to take. The rest of this section will illustrate this technique and some of its benefits. We start with an example using a simple controlling function. The following will return the English language name for a given number between 0 and 99.

File script7.py

```
#! /usr/bin/env python
import sys

# conversion mappings
_1to9Dict = {'0':'', '1':'one', '2':'two', '3':'three', '4':'four',
             '5':'five', '6':'six', '7':'seven', '8':'eight',
             '9':'nine'}
_10to19Dict = {'0':'ten', '1':'eleven', '2':'twelve', '3':
               'thirteen', '4':'fourteen', '5':'fifteen', '6':
               'sixteen', '7':'seventeen', '8':'eighteen',
               '9':'nineteen'}
_20to90Dict = {'2':'twenty', '3':'thirty', '4':'forty', '5':'fifty',
               '6':'sixty', '7':'seventy', '8':'eighty', '9':'ninety'}

def num2words(numString):
    if numString == '0': return('zero')
    if len(numString) > 2:
        return "Sorry can only handle 1 or 2 digit numbers"
    numString = '0' + numString  # pad on left in case it's a single digit number
    tens, ones = numString[-2], numString[-1]
    if tens == '0': return _1to9Dict[ones]
    elif tens == '1': return _10to19Dict[ones]
    else: return _20to90Dict[tens] + ' ' + _1to9Dict[ones]

def main():
    print num2words(sys.argv[1])

main()
```

● Our controlling function here simply calls the function num2words with the appropriate argument and prints the result.

If we call it with

```
python script7.py 59
```

we will get a result of

```
fifty nine
```

It's standard to have its call at the bottom, but sometimes you will see the controlling function's definition at the top of the file. I prefer it at the bottom, just above the call so I don't have to scroll back up to find it after going to the bottom to find out its name. This also cleanly separates the scripting plumbing from the rest of the file. This is useful when combining scripts and modules.

People combine scripts with modules when they want to make functions they've created in a script available to other modules or scripts. Also a module may be instrumented so it can run as a script either to provide a quick interface to it for users or to provide hooks for automated module testing.

Combining a script and a module is a simple matter of putting the following conditional test around the controlling function.

```
if __name__ == '__main__':
    main()
else
    # module specific initialization code if any
```

If it is called as a script, it will be run with the name __main__ and the controlling function, main, will be called. If it has been imported into an interactive session or another module, its name will be its filename.

When creating a script, I often set it as a module as well, right from the start. This allows me to import it into a session and interactively test and debug my functions as I create them. Only the controlling function needs to be debugged externally. If it grows, or I find myself writing functions I might be able to use elsewhere, I can separate those functions into their own module or have other modules import this module.

The following is an extension of our last script that has been set up to be able to be used as a module. The functionality has also been expanded to allow the entry of a number from 0 to 999999999999999 rather than just from 0 to 99. The controlling function (main) now does checking of the validity of its argument and also strips out any commas in it, allowing more user readable input like 1,234,567.

File n2w.py

```
#! /usr/bin/env python
"""n2w: number to words conversion module: contains function
   num2words. Can also be run as a script

usage as a script: n2w num
    (Convert a number to its English word description)
    num: whole integer from 0 and 999,999,999,999,999 (commas are
    optional)
example: n2w 10,103,103
    for 10,003,103 say: ten million three thousand one hundred three
"""

import sys, string

# conversion mappings
_1to9Dict = {'0':'', '1':'one', '2':'two', '3':'three', '4':'four',
             '5':'five', '6':'six', '7':'seven', '8':'eight',
             '9':'nine'}
```

● Usage message that includes an example.

```python
_10to19Dict = {'0':'ten', '1':'eleven', '2':'twelve', '3':
            'thirteen', '4':'fourteen', '5':'fifteen', '6':
            'sixteen', '7':'seventeen', '8':'eighteen',
            '9':'nineteen'}
_20to90Dict = {'2':'twenty', '3':'thirty', '4':'forty', '5':'fifty',
            '6':'sixty', '7':'seventy', '8':'eighty', '9':'ninety'}
_magnitudeList = [(0,''), (3,' thousand '), (6, ' million '),
            (9, ' billion '), (12, ' trillion '),(15,'')]

def num2words(numString):
    """num2words(numString): convert number to English words"""
    # handle the special conditions (number is zero or too large)
    if numString == '0': return('zero')
    numLength = len(numString)
    maxDigits = _magnitudeList[-1][0]
    if numLength > maxDigits:
        return "Sorry, can't handle numbers with more than  " \
            "%d digits" % (maxDigits)

    # working from least to most significant digit create a string containing the number
    numString = '00' + numString       # pad the number on the left
    wordString = ''                     # initiate string for number
    for mag, name in _magnitudeList:
        if mag  >= numLength: return wordString
        else:
            hundreds, tens, ones = numString[-mag-3], \
                    numString[-mag-2], numString[-mag-1]
            if not (hundreds == tens == ones == '0'):
                wordString =  _handle1to999(hundreds, tens, ones) + \
                        name + wordString

def _handle1to999(hundreds, tens, ones):
    if hundreds == '0': return _handle1to99(tens,ones)
    else: return _1to9Dict[hundreds] + ' hundred ' + \
        _handle1to99(tens,ones)

def _handle1to99(tens, ones):
    if tens == '0': return _1to9Dict[ones]
    elif tens == '1': return _10to19Dict[ones]
    else: return _20to90Dict[tens] + ' ' + _1to9Dict[ones]

def test():
    values = string.split(sys.stdin.read())
    for val in values:
        num  = string.replace(val, ',', '')
        print "%s = %s" % ( val, num2words(num) )

def main():
    if len(sys.argv) != 2 or sys.argv[1] == '+?':
        print __doc__
    elif sys.argv[1] == '+test':
        test()
    else:
        num = string.replace(sys.argv[1], ',', '')
```

● **Function for module test mode**

● Run in test mode if argument is '+test.'

● Remove any commas from the number.

```
    try:
        result = num2words(num)
    except KeyError:
        print __doc__
    else:
        print "For %s, say: %s" % (sys.argv[1], result)

if __name__ == '__main__':
    main()
else:
    print "n2w  loaded as a module"
```

● Catch KeyErrors due
  to the argument
  containing non-digits.

● If it is called as a script, the
  name will be __main__. If
  it is imported as a module,
  it will be named n2w.

Our main function above illustrates the purpose of a controlling function for a command line script, which, in effect, is to create a simplistic user interface for the user. The tasks it may handle are:

1 Ensure that there is the right number of command line arguments and that they are of the right types. Inform the user, giving him usage information if not. Here it ensures there was a single argument but it doesn't explicitly test to ensure that the argument contains only digits.

2 Possibly handle a special mode. Here, a '+test' argument will put us in a test mode.

3 Map the command line arguments to those required by the function(s) and call them in the appropriate manner. Here, commas were stripped and the single function num2words was called.

4 Possibly catch and print a more user friendly message for exceptions that may be expected. Here KeyErrors are caught, which will occur if the argument contains non-digits. *

5 Map the output if necessary to a more user-friendly form. This was done here in the print statement.

It should be noted that if this were a script to run on Windows, you would probably want to let the user open it with the double-click method. That is, to use the raw_input to query for the parameter, rather than having it as a command line option and keeping the screen up to display the output by ending the script with the line:

```
raw_input("Press the Enter key to exit")
```

However, you might still want to leave the test mode in as a command line option.

The test mode here is used to provide a regression test capability for the module and its num2words function. In this case it is used by placing a set of numbers in a file:

File n2w.tst

```
0 1 2 3 4 5 6 7 8 9 10 11 12 13 14 15 16 17 18 19 20 21 98 99 100
101 102 900 901 999
```

---

* A better way to do this would be to explicitly check for nondigits in the argument using the regular expression module that will be introduced later. This would ensure that we don't hide KeyErrors that occur due to other reasons.

```
.......................
.......................
999,999,999,999,999
1,000,000,000,000,000
```

then typing

```
python n2w.py +test <n2w.tst >n2w.txt
```

The output file can be easily checked for correctness. This was run a number of times during its creation and can be rerun anytime num2words or any of the functions it calls are modified. And, yes, although the dotted lines above do represent a number of lines that have not been printed here, full exhaustive testing certainly did not occur. I admit that there are still well over 999 trillion valid inputs for this program that have not been checked!

Often, the provision of a test mode for a module will be the only function of a script. I know of at least one company where it is part of its development policy to always create one for every Python module developed. Python's built-in data object types and methods usually make this quite easy and those who practice this technique seem to be unanimously convinced that it is well worth the effort.

Another option here would have been to create a separate file with just the portion of the main function which handles the argument and import n2w into this file. Then only the test mode would be left in the main function of n2w.py.

15.6 *Creating executable programs with freeze*

The freeze *tool can be used to create an executable Python program.*

You can distribute your scripts as source files (as .py files). You can also ship them as byte code (as .pyc or .pyo files). A byte code file will run under any platform as long as it has been written portably.

It is possible to create an executable Python program that will run on machines that do not have Python installed. This is done using the freeze tool. You will find the instructions for this in the Readme file in the freeze directory in the Tools subdirectory of your Python directory. If you are using Windows you will need to download the Python source distribution. If you are using JPython, instead of freeze, you will want to look at the jpythonc compiler.

In the process, you will be creating C files which are then compiled and linked using a C compiler which you will need. It will only run on the platform for which the C compiler you use provides its executables. Note that it will still be possible for someone to reverse engineer your Python code from the resulting output. This also does not always work in a straightforward manner. This is one situation where you may end up needing to obtain support from the Python newsgroup, depending on the specifics of your application and which C compiler you are using. Once you've got your executable, however, it generally will be quite robust.

15.7 *Summary*

Python scripts in their most basic form are simply a sequence of Python statements placed in a file. A slightly more structured way for organizing scripts that contain more than a few lines of Python code is presented here. This is a simple matter of using a control function to buffer out some of the control and interface logic. Modules can be instrumented to run as scripts, and scripts can be set up so they can be imported as modules. This provides a modular way to create quite large scripts and a simple mechanism to instrument a module with a regression test mode.

Scripts can be made executable on UNIX. They can be set up to support command line redirection of their input and output and with the `getopt` module it is easy to parse out complex combinations of command line options and arguments.

On Windows, there are a number of ways of calling scripts: opening them with a double-click, using the Run window, or using an MS-DOS Prompt window. It is possible to use command line options and arguments in the last two of these and redirection in the last, but this is not as convenient as UNIX. Therefore, on Windows, command line arguments and redirection are normally used only for special situations like test modes. This is also generally true for GUI programs on both Windows and UNIX platforms.

If you are writing administrative scripts on Windows, see "Windows Scripting Host" in "Python, Windows, and COM" (chapter 22) later in this book.

If you are writing administrative scripts on UNIX, there are a number of library modules available that you might find useful. These include `grp` for accessing the group database, `pwd` for accessing the password database, `resource` for accessing resource usage information, `syslog` for working with the syslog facility, and `stat` for working with information about a file or directory obtained from an `os.stat` call. You can find information on this in the *Python Library Reference*.

Finally, as an alternative to scripts, the freeze tool provides the capability to provide an executable Python program that will run on machines that do not contain a Python interpreter.

C H A P T E R   1 6

Classes and object-oriented programming

This chapter discusses Python classes, which can be used in a manner analogous to C structures or Pascal records, and which can also be used in a full object-oriented manner. For the benefit of readers who are not object-oriented programmers, use of classes as structures is discussed in the first two subsections.

The remainder of the chapter discusses OOP in Python. It is only a description of the constructs available in Python. It is not an exposition on object-oriented programming itself. There would not be room here to do the subject proper justice.

16.1 Defining classes

Define classes with the class *keyword.*

A *class* in Python is effectively a user-defined data type. It is defined with the `class` statement:

```
class Myclass:
    body
```

body is a list of Python statements, typically variable assignments and function definitions. No assignments or function definitions are required. The body can just be a single `pass` statement.

!!!

By convention, classes are capitalized, to make them stand out. Once defined, a new object of the class type (an instance of the class) can be created by calling the class name as a function:

```
instance = Myclass()
```

16.1.1 Using a class instance as a structure or record

Objects (instances of classes) can have fields, and so can act as a structure or record.

Class instances can be used as structures or records. Unlike C structures, the fields of an instance do not need to be declared ahead of time, but can be created on the fly. The following short example defines a class called Circle, creates a Circle instance, assigns to the `radius` field of the circle, and then uses that field to calculate the circumference of the circle.

```
class Circle:
    pass
myCircle = Circle()
myCircle.radius = 5
print 2 * 3.14 * myCircle.radius
```

Like C and many other languages, the fields of an instance/structure are accessed and assigned to, using dot notation.

Fields (and other aspects) of a newly created object can be initialized by defining an __init__ *method in the class.*

Fields of an instance can be initialized automatically by including an __init__ initialization function (constructor) in the class body. This function is run every time an instance of the class is created, with that new instance as its first argument. This example creates circles with a radius of 1 by default.

```
class Circle:
    # By convention, "self" is always the name of the first argument of __init__. "self" will be
    # set to the newly created circle instance, when __init__ is run.
    def __init__(self):
        self.radius = 1

# Now a bit of code to make use of the above class definition...

# Create a Circle instance object.
myCircle = Circle()
# This makes use of the fact that the radius field is already initialized
print 2 * 3.14 * myCircle.radius.
# The radius field can be overwritten.
myCircle.radius = 5
# This will print a different result than the previous print statement.
print 2 * 3.14 * myCircle.radius
```

A great deal more can be done by using true object-oriented programming. If you're not familiar with OO, I urge you to read up on it. It is one of the few real advances in programming in the last two decades. The object-oriented programming constructs of Python are the subject of the remainder of this chapter.

16.1.2 Objects, class instances, and instances of other Python types

In Python, the term object often refers to instances of any Python data type, not just class instances.

In the formal Python documentation, the term "object" is generally used to refer to instances of any Python data type. We use the term object in this context in many places in this book. In the literature at large, "object" is often used to refer only to what the Python documentation calls a class instance. In this chapter this terminology is used at times as well. The meaning should be clear from the context.

16.2 Instance variables

Instance variables are created whenever an assignment is made to an attribute of an object. This is usually (but not always) in the class __init__ method.

Instance variables are the most basic feature of object-oriented programming. Take a look at the Circle class again:

```
class Circle:
    def __init__(self):
        self.radius = 1
```

`radius` is an *instance variable* of Circle instances. That is, each instance of the Circle class has its own copy of `radius`, and the value stored in that copy may be different from the values stored in the `radius` variable in other instances. In Python, instance variables can be created as necessary, simply by assigning to a field of a class instance:

```
instance.variable = value
```

If the variable does not already exist, it will be created automatically. This is how `__init__` creates the `radius` variable.

!!!

All uses of instance variables—both assignment and access—require *explicit mention* of the containing instance, that is, ***instance**.variable*. A reference to *variable* by itself is not a reference to an instance variable, but rather to a local variable in the executing method. This is different from C++ or Java, where instance variables are referred to in the same manner as local method function variables. I rather like Python's requirement for explicit mention of the containing instance, because it clearly distinguishes instance variables from local function variables.

16.3 Methods

A method is just a function defined in (and hence associated with) a class.

A *method* is a function associated with a particular class. You've already seen the special `__init__` method, which is called on a new instance when that instance is first created. In the following example, we define another method, `area`, for the Circle class, which can be used to calculate and return the area for any Circle instance. Like most user-defined methods, `area` is called with a *method invocation syntax* which resembles instance variable access:

```
class Circle:
    def __init__(self):
        self.radius = 1
    def area(self):
        return self.radius * self.radius * 3.14159

>>> c = Circle()
>>> c.radius = 3
>>> # Method invocation syntax consists of an instance, followed by a period, followed by
>>> # the method to be invoked on the instance.
>>> print c.area()
28.27431
>>> # the above syntax is sometimes called "bound" method invocation.

>>> # area' can also be invoked as an "unbound" method by accessing it through its
>>> # containing class. This is less convenient than the above, and is almost never done.
>>> # When a method is invoked in this manner, its first argument _must_ be an instance of
>>> # the class in which that method is defined.
>>> print Circle.area(c)
28.27431
```

The first argument of any method is the instance the method is invoked on. This parameter is named 'self by convention.

Like __init__, the area method is defined as a function within the body of the class definition. The first argument of any method is the instance it was invoked by or on, named `self` by convention.

Methods can be invoked with arguments, if the method definitions accept those arguments. This version of `Circle` adds an argument to the __init__ method, so that we can create circles of a given radius, without the necessity of setting the radius after a circle is created:

```
class Circle:
    def __init__(self, radius):
        # Note the two uses of radius here! "self.radius" is the instance variable called 'radius'.
        # "radius" by itself is the local function variable called 'radius'. The two are not the
        # same! In practice, we'd probably call the local function variable something like 'r' or
        # 'rad', to avoid any possibility of confusion.
        self.radius = radius
    def area(self):
        return self.radius * self.radius * 3.14159
```

Methods can be invoked with arguments, if the method definition accepts them.

Using this definition of Circle, we can create circles of any radius with one call on the circle class:

```
# Create a Circle of radius 5
c = Circle(5)
```

The standard Python function argument passing features— default argument values, extra argument, keyword arguments, and so forth.—can be used with methods too.

All of the standard Python function features—default argument values, extra arguments, keyword arguments, and so forth—can be used with methods. For example, we could have defined the first line of __init__ above to be

```
    def __init__(self, radius=1):
```

and then calls to circle would work with or without an extra argument; `Circle()` would return a circle of radius 1, and `Circle(3)` would return a circle of radius 3.

There is nothing magical about method invocation in Python. It can be considered as shorthand for normal function invocation. Given a method invocation *instance*.

`method(arg1, arg2, . . .)`, Python transforms it into a normal function call by using the following rules:

1 Look up the class type *class* of *instance*. In the examples above, *class* is Circle—the type of the instance c.

2 Make a direct call to the normal Python function *class.method*, by using *instance* as the first argument of the function, and shifting all of the other arguments in the method invocation one space over to the right. So, *instance.method(arg1, arg2, . . .)* becomes *class.method(instance, arg1, arg2, . . .)*.

16.4 *Class variables*

Class variables in Python are subtly different from class variables in most OO languages.

A class variable is a variable associated with a class, not an instance of a class, and which is accessed by all instances of the class, in order to keep track of some class-level information, such as how many instances of the class have been created at any point in time. Python provides class variables, though using them requires slightly more effort than in most other languages. Also, there is an interaction between class and instance variables which you need to watch out for.

Class variables are created via an assignment in the class body, and may be accessed as attributes of the class.

A class variable is created by an assignment in the class body, not in the __init__ function, and once it has been created, it can be seen by all instances of the class. We can use a class variable to make a value for pi accessible to all instances of the Circle class:

```
class Circle:
    pi = 3.14159
    def __init__(self, radius):
        self.radius = radius
    def area(self):
        return self.radius * self.radius * Circle.pi
```

With the above definition entered, we can type

```
>>> Circle.pi
⇒   3.14159
>>> Circle.pi = 4
>>> Circle.pi
⇒   4
>>> Circle.pi = 3.14159
⇒   3.14159
```

This is exactly how we would expect a class variable to act. It is associated with and contained in the class which defines it. Notice in the above example that we are accessing `Circle.pi` before any circle instances have been created. Obviously `Circle.pi` exists independently of any specific instances of the Circle class.

A class variable can also be accessed from a method of a class, simply by accessing it through the class name. This is done in the definition of `Circle.area` above, where the `area` function makes specific reference to `Circle.pi`. In operation, this has the desired effect; the correct value for pi is obtained from the class and used in the calculation:

```
...
```

```
>>> c = Circle(3)
>>> c.area
⇒   28.27431
```

You may object to hard coding the name of a class inside that class's methods. This can be avoided through use of the special __class__ attribute, available to all Python class instances. This attribute simply returns the class of which the instance is a member. For example:

```
...
```

```
>>> Circle
⇒   <class __main__.circle at 861620>
>>> c.__class__
⇒   <class __main__.circle at 861620>
```

The class named Circle is represented internally by an abstract data structure, and that data structure is exactly what is obtained from the __class__ attribute of c, an instance of the Circle class. This lets us obtain the value of Circle.pi from c without ever explicitly referring to the Circle class name:

```
...
```

```
>>> c.__class__.pi
⇒   3.14159
```

Of course, we could use this internally in the area method to get rid of the explicit reference to the Circle class just replace Circle.pi with self.__class__.pi.

16.4.1   An oddity with class variables

There is a bit of an oddity with class variables which can trip you up if you are not aware of it. When Python is looking up an instance variable, if it cannot find an instance variable of that name, it will then try to find and return the value in a class variable of the same name. Only if it cannot find an appropriate class variable will it signal an error. This does make it efficient to implement default values for instance variables; just create a class variable with the same name and appropriate default value, and avoid the time and memory overhead of initializing that instance variable every time a class instance is created. However, this also makes it very easy to inadvertently refer to an instance variable rather than a class variable, without signaling an error. Let's take a look at how this operates in conjunction with the example from above.

First, this means that we can refer to the variable c.pi, even though c does not have an associated instance variable named pi; Python will first try to look for such an instance variable, but when it cannot find it, it will then look for a class variable pi in Circle, and find it:

```
...
```

```
>>> c.pi
⇒   3.14159
```

This may or may not be what you want; it is convenient, but can be prone to error, so be careful.

Now what happens if we attempt to use c.pi as a true class variable, by changing it from one instance with the intent that all instances should see the change? Again, using the above definition for Circle:

```
...
```

```
>>> c1 = Circle(1)
>>> c2 = Circle(2)
>>> c1.pi = 3.14
>>> c1.pi
⇒   3.14
>>> c1.pi
⇒   3.14159
>>> Circle.pi
⇒   3.14159
```

This hasn't worked as it would for a true class variable—c1 now has its own copy of pi, distinct from the `Circle.pi` accessed by c2. This is because the assignment to c1.pi *creates* an instance variable in c1; it does not affect the class variable `Circle.pi` in any way. So, subsequent lookups of c1.pi return the value in that instance variable, while subsequent lookups of c2.pi look for an instance variable pi in c2, fail to find it, and resort to returning the value of the class variable `Circle.pi`. If you want is to change the value of a class variable, access it through the class name, not through the instance variable `self`.

16.5 *Class methods*

Python does not provide class methods, but a class can be encapsulated in its own module to provide a similar effect.

Python doesn't have anything corresponding explicitly to class methods in a language such as Java. This is due to the restriction that Python always expects the first argument of any method to be an instance of a class, and, of course, class methods are often used before any class instances are created. This section will cover the best way to obtain the functionality of class methods in Python.

A simple (and to my knowledge, the only convenient) way of implementing class methodlike behavior is to include the entire class of interest in its own module, and then define the class methods as top-level functions within this module.

The example in this case will be a version of the Circle class with a class method which returns the current total area of all circles. Here is the code which defines the Circle class and associated class methods and class variables. This code should be in a file called circle.py.

File circle.py

```
"""circle module: contains the Circle class."""

class Circle:
    """Circle class"""

    # Variable containing a list of all circles which have been created.
    allCircles = []
    pi = 3.14159
```

```
        def __init__(self, r=1):
            """Create a Circle with the given radius"""
            self.radius = r
            self.__class__.allCircles.append(self)

        def area(self):
            """determine the area of the Circle"""
            return self.__class__.pi * self.radius * self.radius

    # This is a top-level function (not in the Circle class).
    def totalArea():
        total = 0
        for c in Circle.allCircles:
            total = total + c.area()
        return total
```

Now, interactively type

>>>

```
>>> import circle
>>> c1 = circle.Circle(1)
>>> c2 = circle.Circle(2)
>>> circle.totalArea()
⇒  15.70795
>>> c2.radius = 3
>>> circle.totalArea()
⇒  31.4159
```

The only inconvenience in using the `circle` module is the necessity to create circles by saying `circle.Circle(number)`, rather than just `Circle(number)`. This isn't too bad.

Also notice that documentation strings have been used. In a real module, one would probably put in more informative strings, indicating in the class string what methods are available, and in the method strings including usage information.

...

```
>>> circle.__doc__
⇒  'circle module: contains the Circle class.'
>>> circle.Circle.__doc__
⇒  'Circle class'
>>> circle.Circle.area.__doc__
⇒  'determine the area of the circle'
```

16.6 *Inheritance*

Inheritance in Python is simple.

Inheritance in Python is easier and more flexible than inheritance in compiled languages such as Java and C++, because the dynamic nature of Python doesn't force so many restrictions on the language.

To see how inheritance is used in Python, start with the Circle class given previously and generalize. We might want to define an additional class for squares:

```
class Square:
    def __init__(self, side=1):
```

```
        # "side" is the length of any side of the square.
        self.side = side
```

Now, if we want to use these classes in a drawing program, they will need to define some sense of where on the drawing surface each instance is. This can be done by defining an x and y coordinate in each instance.

```
class Square:
    def __init__(self, side=1, x=0, y=0):
        self.side = side
        self.x = x
        self.y = y

class Circle:
    def __init__(self, radius=1, x=0, y=0):
        self.radius = radius
        self.x = x
        self.y = y
```

This approach will work, but will result in a good deal of repetitive code as we expand the number of Shape classes, since each Shape will presumably want to have this concept of position. No doubt you know where we are going here. This is a standard situation for using inheritance in an object-oriented language. Instead of defining the x and y variables in each and every Shape class, abstract them out into a general Shape class, and have each class defining an actual shape inherit from that general class. In Python, that looks like this:

```
class Shape:
    def __init__(self, x, y):
        self.x = x
        self.y = y

# This line says 'Square' inherits from 'Shape'
class Square(Shape):
    def __init__(self, side=1, x=0, y=0):
        # Must make an explicit call to the __init__ method of 'Shape'
        Shape.__init__(self, x, y)
        self.side = side

# This line says 'Circle' inherits from 'Shape'
class Circle(Shape):
    def __init__(self, r=1, x=0, y=0):
        # Must make an explicit call to the __init__ method of 'Shape'
        Shape.__init__(self, x, y)
        self.radius = r
```

Inherited __init__ methods must be called explicitly.

There are (generally) two requirements in using an inherited class in Python, both of which can be seen in the bolded code in the Circle and Square classes above. The first requirement is defining the inheritance hierarchy, which is accomplished by giving the classes inherited from, in parentheses, immediately after the name of the class being defined with the class keyword. In the code above, Circle and Square both inherit from Shape. The second, and more subtle element, is the necessity to explicitly call the __init__ method of inherited classes. Python does not automatically do this for you. This is accomplished in the code above by the Shape.__init__(self, x, y) lines, which calls the

Shape initialization function with the instance being initialized, and the appropriate arguments. If this were not done, then in the example above, instances of Circle and Square would not have their x and y instance variables set.

Inheritance comes into effect when we attempt to use a method which isn't defined in the base classes, but which is defined in the superclass. To see this, let's define another method in the Shape class called move, which will move a shape by a given displacement. It will modify the x and y coordinates of the shape by an amount determined by arguments to the method. The definition for Shape now becomes

```
class Shape:
    def __init__(self, x, y):
        self.x = x
        self.y = y
    def move(self, deltaX, deltaY):
        self.x = self.x + deltaX
        self.y = self.y + deltaY
```

If you enter this definition for Shape, and the previous definitions for Circle and Square, you can then engage in the following interactive session:

```
>>>
>>> c = Circle(1)
>>> c.move(3, 4)
>>> c.x
⇒   3
>>> c.y
⇒   4
```

If you actually try this and are doing it in an interactive session be sure to reenter the Circle class after the redefinition of the Shape class.

The Circle class did not define a move method immediately within itself, but because it inherits from a class which implements move, all instances of Circle can make use of move.

16.7 Inheritance with class and instance variables

Inheritance allows an instance to inherit attributes of the class. Instance variables are associated with object instances, and only one instance variable of a given name exists for a given instance.

To see this, consider the following example. Using these class definitions:

```
class P:
    z = "Hello"
    def setP(self):
        self.x = "Class P"
    def printP(self):
        print self.x

class C(P):
    def setC(self):
        self.x = "Class C"
```

```
def printC(self):
    print self.x
```

execute the following code:

```
>>>
```

```
>>> c = C()
>>> c.setP()
>>> c.printP()
Class P
>>> c.setC()
Class P
>>> c.setC()
>>> c.printC()
Class C
>>> c.printP*()
Class C
```

The object c in the above example is an instance of class C. C inherits from P, but c does not inherit from some invisible instance of class P. It just inherits methods and class variables directly from P. Because there is only one instance (c), any reference to the instance variable x in a method invocation on c must refer to c.x. This is true regardless of which class defines the method being invoked on c. As can be seen above, when they are invoked on c, both setP and printP, defined in class P, refer to the same variable referred to by setC and printC when they are invoked on c.

In general, this is what is desired for instance variables because it makes sense that references to instance variables of the same name should refer to the same variable. Occasionally, somewhat different behavior is desired, which can be achieved using private variables. These are explained in the next subsection.

Class variables are inherited, but you should take care to avoid name clashes and be aware of a generalization of the same behavior we saw in the earlier subsection on class variables. In our example, a class variable z is defined for the superclass P. It can be accessed in three different ways: through the instance c, through the derived class C or directly through the superclass P:

```
>>>
```

```
>>> c.z; C.z; P.z
⇒   'Hello'
⇒   'Hello'
⇒   'Hello'
```

However, if we try setting it through the class C, a new class variable will be created for the class C. This has no effect on P's class variable itself (as accessed through P). However, future accesses through the class C or its instance c will see this new variable rather than the original.

```
>>> C.z = "Bonjour"
>>> c.z; C.z; P.z
⇒   'Bonjour'
⇒   'Bonjour'
⇒   'Hello'
```

Similarly, if we try setting z through the instance c, a new instance variable will be created and we'll end up with three different variables.

```
>>> c.z = "Ciao"
>>> c.z; C.z; P.z
⇒   'Ciao'
⇒   'Bonjour'
⇒   'Hello'
```

16.8 *Private variables and private methods*

A private variable or private method is one which can't be seen outside of the methods of the class in which it is defined. Private variables and methods are useful for a number of reasons. They enhance security and reliability by selectively denying access to important or delicate parts of an object's implementation. They avoid name clashes which can arise from the use of inheritance. A class might define a private variable and inherit from a class which defines a private variable of the same name, but this will not cause a problem, since the fact that the variables are private will ensure that separate copies of them are kept. Finally, private variables make it easier to read code, as they explicitly indicate what is used only internally in a class. Anything else is the class's interface.

Variables are private if their names begin with a double underscore. The same convention applies to methods.

Most languages which define private variables do so through the use of a private or other similar keyword. The convention in Python is quite a bit simpler, and also makes it easier to immediately see what is private and what isn't. Any method or instance variable whose name begins—but does not end—with a *double underscore* (__) is private; anything else is not private.

As an example, consider the following class definition:

```
class Mine:
    def __init__(self):
        self.x = 2
        # Define __y as private by using leading double underscores.
        self.__y = 3
    def printY(self):
        print self.__y
```

Using the above definition, create an instance of the class:

```
>>>
```

```
>>> m = Mine()
```

x is not a private variable, so it is directly accessible.

```
...
```

```
>>> printm.x
2
```

__y is a private variable. Trying to access it directly raises an error.

```
...
```

```
>>> print m.__y
```

```
Traceback (innermost last):
  File "<stdin>", line 1, in ?
AttributeError: __y
```

The `printY` method is not private, and because it is in the Mine class, it can access
__y and print it.

```
...
```

```
>>> m.printY()
3
```

Finally, it should be noted that the mechanism used to provide privacy is to "mangle"
the name of private variables and private methods. What specifically happens is that
_classname is appended to the variable name.

```
...
```

```
>>> dir(m)
⇒   ['_Mine__y', 'x']
```

The purpose is to avoid any accidental accesses. If someone really wanted to they could
access the value. However, by performing the mangling in this easily readable form, debugging is made easy.

16.9 Scoping rules and namespaces for class instances

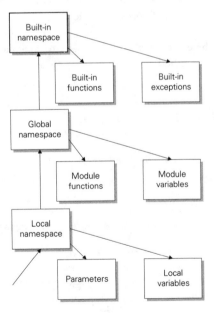

Figure 16.1 Direct namespaces

Now we have all the pieces to put together a picture of the scoping rules and namespaces for a class instance.

When we are in a method of a class, we have direct access to the *local namespace* (parameters and variables declared in the method), the *global namespace* (functions and variables declared at the module level), and the *built-in namespace* (built-in functions and built-in exceptions). These three namespaces are searched in the following order: local, global, and built-in (figure 16.1).

We also have access through the `self` variable to our *instance's namespace* (instance variables, private instance variables, and superclass instance variables), its *class's namespace* (methods, class variables, private methods, and private class variables) and its *superclass's namespace* (superclass methods and superclass class variables). These three namespaces are searched in the order instance, class, and then superclass (figure 16.2).

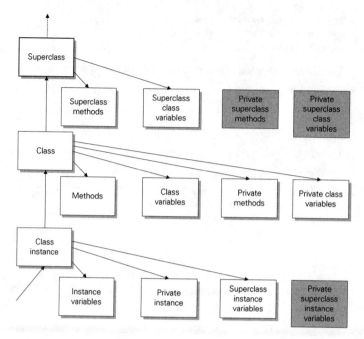

Figure 16.2 Self variable namespaces

Private superclass instance variables, private superclass methods, and private superclass class variables cannot be accessed using `self`. A class is able to hide these names from its children.

The following module puts these two together in one place to concretely demonstrate what can be accessed from within a method.

File cs.py

```
"""cs module: class scope demonstration module."""
mv ="module variable: mv"
def MF():
    return "module function (can be used like a class method in " \
            "other languages): MF()"

class SC:
    scv = "superclass class variable: self.scv"
    __pscv = "private superclass class variable: no access"
    def __init__(self):
        self.siv = "superclass instance variable: self.siv " \
                    "(but use SC.siv for assignment)"
        self.__psiv = "private superclass instance variable: " \
                        "no access"
    def SM(self):
        return "superclass method: self.SM()"
    def __SPM(self):
```

```
                  return "superclass private method: no access"
       class C(SC):
           cv = "class variable: self.cv (but use C.cv for assignment)"
           __pcv = "class private variable: self.__pcv (but use C.__pcv " \
                   "for assignment)"
           def __init__(self):
               SC.__init__(self)
               self.__piv = "private instance variable: self.__piv"
           def M2(self):
               return "method: self.M2()"
           def __PM(self):
               return "private method: self.__PM()"

           def M(self, p="parameter: p"):
               lv = "local variable: lv"
               self.iv = "instance variable: self.xi"
               print "Access local, global and built-in " \
                     "namespaces directly"
               print "local namespace:",locals().keys()
               print p          # parameter
               print lv         # instance variable
               print "global namespace:",globals().keys()
               print mv         # module variable
               print MF()       # module function
               print "Access instance, class, and superclass namespaces " \
                     "through 'self'"
               print "Instance namespace:",dir(self)
               print self.iv        # instance variable
               print self.__piv   # private instance variable
               print self.siv       # superclass instance variable
               print "Class namespace:",dir(C)
               print self.cv        # class variable
               print self.M2()     # method
               print self.__pcv   # private class variable
               print self.__PM()  # private module
               print "Superclass namespace:",dir(SC)
               print self.SM()     # superclass method
               print self.scv      # superclass variable through the instance
```

This output is considerable, so we'll look at it in pieces. In the first part below it can be seen that our method M's local namespace contains our parameters self (which is our instance variable) and p along with our local variable lv (all of which can be accessed directly).

```
>>> import cs
>>> c = cs.C()
>>> c.M()
Access local, global and built-in namespaces directly
local namespace: ['self', 'p', 'lv']
parameter: p
local variable: lv
```

Next, we see that the method M's global namespace contains the module variable mv and the module function MF, (which, as described in a previous section, we can use to provide a class method functionality). There are also the classes defined in the module (the class C and the superclass SC). These can all be directly accessed.

```
global namespace: ['__doc__', '__file__', '__name__',
              '__builtins__', 'mv', 'MF', 'C', 'SC']
module variable: mv
module function (can be used like a class method in other
                languages):  MF()
```

Our instance C's namespace, below, contains our instance variable iv and our superclass's instance variable siv (which, as described in a previous section, is really no different from our regular instance variable). It also has the mangled name of our private instance variable __piv (which we can access through self) and the mangled name of our superclass's private instance variable __psiv (which we cannot access).

```
Access instance, class, and superclass namespaces through 'self'
Instance namelist: ['_C__piv', '_SC__psiv', 'iv', 'siv']
instance variable: self.xi
private instance variable: self.__piv
superclass instance variable: self.siv
```

The class C's namespace contains the class variable cv and the mangled name of the private class variable __pcv: Both can be accessed through self, but to assign to them you need to use the class C. It also has the class's two methods M and M2, along with the mangled names of the private method __PM (which can be accessed through self).

```
Class namelist: ['M', 'M2', '_C__PM', '_C__pcv', '__doc__',
             '__init__', '__module__', 'cv']
class variable: self.cv (but use C.cv for assignment)
class variable: self.cv or C.cv
method: self.M2()
private class variable: self.__pcv (but use C.__pcv for assignment)
private class variable: self.__pcv or C.__pcv
private method: self.__PM()
```

Finally, we see that our superclass SC's namespace contains our superclass class variable scv (which can be accessed through self, but to assign to it you need to use the superclass SC) and our superclass method SM. It also contains the mangled names of the private superclass method __SPM and the private superclass class variable __spcv, neither of which can be accessed through self.

```
Superclass namelist: ['SM', '_SC__SPM', '_SC__pscv', '__doc__',
             '__init__', '__module__', 'scv']
superclass method: self.SM()
superclass class variable: self.scv or C.scv or SC.sc
superclass class variable: self.scv or C.scv or SC.sc
superclass class variable: self.scv or C.scv or SC.sc
```

This is a rather full example to decipher at first. You can use it as a reference or a base for your own exploration. As with most other concepts in Python, you can build a solid understanding of what is going on by playing around with a few simplified examples.

16.10 *Destructors and memory management*

Python will auto-matically free up the memory used by your class instances.

We've already seen class constructors (the __init__ methods). A destructor can be defined for a class as well. However, unlike for C++, creating and calling a destructor is not necessary to ensure that the memory used by your instance is freed. Python provides automatic memory management through a reference counting mechanism. That is, it keeps track of the number of references to your instance, and when this reaches zero, the memory used by your instance will be reclaimed and any Python objects referenced by your instance will have their reference counts decremented by one. *For the vast majority of your classes you will not need to define a destructor.*

Use an explicit cleanup method to perform any other necessary cleanup.

C++ destructors are sometimes used to also perform cleanup tasks such as releasing or resetting system resources unrelated to memory management. To perform these functions in Python, the definition of explicit cleanup or close methods for your classes is the best way to go.

A __del__ destructor method will be implicitly called just before your instance is reclaimed. It can be used to back up your cleanup method.

You can also define destructor methods for your classes. Python will implicitly call a class's destructor method __del__ just before an instance is removed upon its reference count reaching zero. This can be used as a backup to ensure your cleanup method is called. The following simple class illustrates this.

```
class SpecialFile:
    def __init__(self, fileName):
        self.__file = open(fileName, 'w')
        self.__file.write('***** Start Special File *****\n\n')
    def write(self, str):
        self.__file.write(str)
    def writelines(self, strList):
        self.__file.writelines(strList)

    def __del__(self):                  ● Destructor method,
        print "entered __del__"             __del__.
        self.close()

    def close(self):                    ● Clean up method, close.
        if self.__file:
            self.__file.write('\n\n***** End Special File *****')
            self.__file.close()
            self.__file = None
```

Notice that close is written so that it can be called more than once without complaint. This is what we generally want to do. Also the __del__ function has a print statement in it. But this is just for demonstration purposes. Take the following test function:

```
def test():
    f = SpecialFile('testfile')
    f.write('111111\n')
    f.close()

>>> test()
entered __del__
```

When the function test exits, f's reference count goes to zero and __del__ is called. Thus, in the normal case close is called twice, which is why we wanted close to be able to handle this. If we forgot the f.close() at the end of test the file would still be closed properly as we are backed up by the call to the destructor. This also happens if we reassign to the same variable without first closing the file.

```
>>> f = SpecialFile('testfile')
>>> f = SpecialFIle('testfile2')
entered __del__
```

As with the __init__ constructor, the __del__ destructor of a class's parent class needs to be called explicitly within a class's own destructor. Be careful when writing a destructor. If it's called when a program is shutting down, members of its global namespace may already have been deleted. Any exception that occurs during its execution will be ignored, other than a message being sent of the occurrence to sys.stderr. Also, there is no guarantee that destructors will be called for all still existing instances when the Python interpreter exits. Check the entries for destructors in the Python Language Manual and the Python FAQ for more details. They will also give you hints as to what may be happening in cases where you think all references to your object should be gone but its destructor has not been called.

Partly because of these issues, some people avoid using Python's destructors other than possibly to flag an error when they've missed putting in an explicit call. They prefer that cleanup always be done explicitly. There are times when they are worth using but only when the programmer knows the issues.

If you are familiar with Java you will be aware that this is what you have to do in that language. Java uses garbage collection and its finalize methods will not be called if this mechanism is not invoked, which may be never in some programs. Python's destructor invocation is more deterministic. When the references to an object go away, it will be individually removed. On the other hand, if you have structures with cyclical references, they will not be removed automatically. You have to go in and do this yourself. In Java, these are found and removed automatically by its garbage collection mechanism.

The following example illlustrates the effect of a cyclical reference in Python and how you might break it. The purpose of the __del__ method in this example is only to indicate when an object is removed.

To avoid memory leaks, explicitly break cyclical references when you are through with objects.

```
class Circle:
    def __init__(self, name, parent):
        self.__name = name
        self.__parent = parent
        self.__child = None
        if parent: parent._child = self
    def cleanup(self):
        self.__child = self.__parent = None      ● Break any
    def __del__(self):                             cycles.
        print "__del__ called on", self.__name

def test1():
    a = Circle("a", None)
    b = Circle("b", a)

def test2():
    c = Circle("c", None)
    d = Circle("d", c)
    d.cleanup()
```

```
>>> test1()
>>> test2()
__del__ called on c
__del__ called on d
```

❶ **a and b are not removed.**
● **The explicit call to the cleanup method is necessary to avoid this.**

❶ Since they still refer to each other, a and b are not removed when test1 exits. This is a memory leak. That is, each time test1 is called, it will leak two more objects.

The cycle is broken in the cleanup method, not the destructor, and we only had to break it in one place. Python's reference counting mechanism took over from there.

A more robust method of ensuring that our cleanup method is called is to use the try-finally compound statement. It takes the form:

The try-finally statement can be used to ensure actions are performed regardless of how or why a body of code is left.

```
try:
    body
finally:
    cleanupBody
```

It ensures that *cleanupBody* will be executed regardless of how or from where *body* is exited. This can be easily seen by writing and executing another test function for the Circle class we've defined above.

```
def test3(x):
    try:
        c = Circle("c", None)
        d = Circle("d", c)
        if x == 1:
            print "leaving test3 via a return"
            return
        if x == 2:
            print "leaving test3 via an exception"
            raise RuntimeError
        print "leaving test3 off the end"
    finally:
        d.cleanup()

>>> test3(0)
leaving test3 off the end
__del__ called on c
__del__ called on d
>>> test3(1)
leaving test3 via a return
__del__ called on c
__del__ called on d
>>> try:
...        test3(2)
... except RuntimeError:
...        pass
...
leaving test3 via an exception
__del__ called on c
__del__ called on d
```

Here, with the addition of three lines of code, we are able to ensure that our cleanup method is called when our function is left, which in this case can be via an exception, a return statement, or simply returning after its last statement.

16.11 Multiple inheritance

Compiled languages place severe restrictions on the use of multiple inheritance, the ability of objects to inherit data and behavior from more than one parent class. For example, the rules for using multiple inheritance in C++ are so complex that many people avoid using it, and in Java, multiple inheritance is completely disallowed, although Java does have the interface mechanism.

Python places no restrictions on multiple inheritance.

Python places no such restrictions on multiple inheritance. A class can inherit from any number of parent classes, in the same way it can inherit from a single parent class. In the simplest case, none of the involved classes, including those inherited indirectly through a parent class, contains instance variables or methods of the same name. In such a case, the inheriting class behaves like a synthesis of its own definitions and all of its ancestor's definitions. For example, if class A inherits from classes B, C, and D, class B inherits from class E and F, and class D inherits from class G, and none of these classes share method names, then an instance of class A can be used as if it were an instance of any of the classes B-G, as well as A; an instance of class B can be used as if it were an instance of classes E or F, as well as class B; and an instance of class D can be used as if it were an instance of class G, as well as class D. In terms of code, the class definitions would look like this:

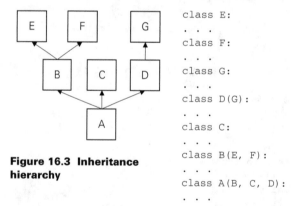

Figure 16.3 Inheritance hierarchy

```
class E:
    . . .
class F:
    . . .
class G:
    . . .
class D(G):
    . . .
class C:
    . . .
class B(E, F):
    . . .
class A(B, C, D):
    . . .
```

The situation is more complex when some of the classes share method names, because Python must then decide which of the identical names is the correct one. For example, assume we wish to resolve a method invocation a.f(), on an instance a of class A, where f is not defined in A but is defined in all of F, C, and G. Which of the various methods will actually be invoked?

Name clashes in multiple inheritances are resolved by a search order on ancestor objects.

The answer lies in the order in which Python searches base classes when looking for a method not defined in the original class on which the method was invoked. Python looks through the base classes of the original class in left-to-right order, but always looks through all of the ancestor classes of a base class before looking in the next base class. In attempting to execute a.f(), the search goes like this:

CHAPTER 16 CLASSES AND OBJECT-ORIENTED PROGRAMMING

1 Python first looks in the class of the invoking object, class A.

2 Since A does not define a method f, Python starts looking in the base classes of A. The first base class of A is B, so Python starts looking in B.

3 Since B does not define a method f, Python continues its search of B by looking in the base classes of B. It starts by looking in the first base class of B, class E.

4 E does not define a method f, and also has no base classes, so there is no more searching to be done in E. Python goes back to class B, and looks in the next base class of B, class F.

Class F does contain a method f, and because it was the first method found with the given name, it is the method used. The methods called f in classes C and G are ignored.

Of course, making use of internal logic like this isn't likely to lead to the most readable or maintainable of programs. In addition, if you do need to resolve name clashes, it might be wiser to do it by either altering some variable/method names to differentiate them, or making names private as appropriate, to avoid name clashes entirely.

However, this is probably a more complex hierarchy than one would expect to see in practice. If you stick to the more standard uses of multiple inheritance, as in the creation of Mixin or Addin classes, keeping things readable and avoiding name clashes can be handled quite easily.

Some people have come to a strong conviction that multiple inheritance is a bad thing. It can certainly be misused and there is nothing in Python forcing one to use it. After being involved with a number of object-oriented project developments in industry since starting with one of the first versions of C++ in 1987, I've concluded that one of the biggest dangers seems to be creating inheritance hierarchies that are too deep. Multiple inheritance can at times be used to help keep this from happening. That issue is beyond the scope of this book. The example we use here illustrates how multiple inheritance works in Python, not a good case (i.e., as in Mixin or Addin classes) where one may want to use it.

16.12 Summary

This chapter has very briefly presented the basics of Python object-oriented programming in a way that will make it easy for any reader familiar with OO to instantly use these features of Python. No attempt was made to make this an introduction to OOP. If you need to learn the basic concepts, refer to OOP books on the market.

In addition to the features described in this chapter, an aspiring Python OO programmer may also wish to make use of the operator overloading features provided by special method attributes, which are described in chapter 20. There may also be times when you want to add type checking. Chapter 19 will introduce the tools necessary for this. A number of the chapters in part 4 also give examples of the creation and use of Python class instances.

As you become more experienced with Python, you'll find you can also do deeper things than have been described here, though in most circumstances there is no need to do so.

CHAPTER 17

Graphical User Interfaces and Tk

This chapter, an introduction to programming GUIs in Python, will attempt to do two things. First, it will provide a look at the best GUI package for use with Python, taking into account things like ease of use, power of the package, crossplatform portability, and so forth. Second, it will give a very broad overview of what else is available for GUI programming with Python, and how to find it.

The Python core language has no built-in support for GUIs. It is a pure programming language, like C, Perl, or Pascal, unlike Java which defines a platform-independent GUI as part of the language. As such, any support for GUIs must come from libraries external to Python, and many such libraries have been developed.

Of all the GUI packages currently available to Python programmers, Tk is the most popular and is of particular interest for several reasons:

- It is very mature.

  The code which drives it is stable, efficient, and well-supported. Until recently, Sun sponsored the team which brings Tk to the rest of the world; that team is now an independent company called Scriptics (http://www.scriptics.com), and it is continually adding features.
- It is extremely powerful.

  Complex GUIs can be coded in a short period of time and with a small amount of code. Few other GUI libraries, Visual Basic included, even remotely approach Tk in power.
- It is a true crossplatform GUI.

  When you learn it on any supported platform, currently Windows, Macintosh, and almost all variants of UNIX, you can transfer all of your knowledge directly to all other supported platforms. Even the look and feel of the native GUI is supported.
- Tk, like Python, is free.

  You can use it widely throughout your organization without worries about cost.

If you decide that Tk is not for you, or you already have enough experience with Tk to know this, look at the section near the end of this chapter, which covers other possible GUI solutions.

!!!   Tk contains a huge number of features. The following sections aren't a lesson on how to use Tk, but more of an introductory overview, primarily aimed at readers who aren't familiar with Tk and want to know if it is worth their while to look further into it. Remember, for every feature I mention, there are dozens more that I don't. The Tk command reference alone is almost 300 pages, and that doesn't cover any of the basic concepts.

17.1 Installing Tk

If you are using IDLE, you will already have Tk installed. On many platforms Tk comes as part of the Python distribution. If you do not have it installed, the Python home page will contain a link to it. There, you should be able to download the latest version for your platform. Don't be confused by the fact that you'll be downloading something probably called Tcl/Tk, followed by some version number. Tcl is a scripting language, and Tk is a GUI extension. Python uses Tcl to access Tk, but in a transparent fashion, so you will never need to worry about the Tcl aspect of the package.

17.2 Starting Tk and using Tkinter

Once you've installed Tcl/Tk on your system, check to make sure everything is working properly. Start up Python and type

```
>>>
```

```
>>> from Tkinter import *
```

Tkinter is the Python library which interfaces to Tk. If you received another Python command prompt >>> and no errors, then everything is working okay, and Tk has been started automatically, by the importation of Tkinter.

If you'd like to see a very brief example of Tkinter in action, type:

```
...
```

```
import sys
win = Tk()
button = Button(win, text = "Goodbye", command = sys.exit)
button.pack()
mainloop()
```

This should create a small window containing one button labeled Goodbye. When you click this button, the `sys.exit` command will be executed, and Python will quit. This window will be only a little larger than the button it contains, and might appear behind another window. But as long as you didn't get any error messages, it should be there.

17.3 Principles of Tk

The Tk GUI package is based upon a small number of basic principles and ideas, and this is the main reason it is relatively easy to learn and use. While it will certainly help if you have some previous knowledge of GUI-based programming, this is not strictly necessary. Tk is probably about the easiest way you can learn GUI and event-driven programming.

17.3.1 Widgets

The first basic idea behind Tk is the concept of a *widget*, which is short for *window gadget*. A widget is a data structure which also has a visible, onscreen representation. When the program changes the internal data structure of the widget, that change will automatically be displayed on the screen. Various user actions on the visible representation of the widget (mouse clicks and so forth) can, in turn, cause internal changes or actions within the widget's data structure.

Tk is basically a collection of widget definitions, together with commands for operating on them, and a few extra commands which do not apply to any specific widget, but which are still relevant to GUI programming. In Python, each different type of widget is represented by a different Python class. A button widget is of the Button class, a label widget is of the Label class, and so forth.

This direct mapping between Tk widget types and Python classes makes using widgets in a Python program extremely simple. For example, a Python program which created and used a Button widget and a Label widget would look something like this:

```
from Tkinter import *
...
myButton = Button(...optional arguments...)
myLabel = Label(...optional arguments...)
...
```

This ease-of-use is in sharp contrast to older GUI environments under traditional compilers, which often require several lines of code to set up a single widget.

17.3.2 Named attributes

The second basic idea behind Tk is the availability and use of *named attributes* to fine-tune widget behavior. To understand why this is necessary, and just how useful it is, let's look at an apparently simple task—creating a button.

The most simple way to do this would be to specify a function, say AButton, as a one-argument object constructor, whose single argument is a string which will become the name displayed on the button. Creating a button would then look like:

```
myButton = AButton(name) # Obvious idea, but it will lead to trouble...
```

However, this provides no way to associate a command with the button; that is, the name of a function that should be executed with the user clicks the button. To do this, make AButton a two-argument constructor, with the command as the second argument:

```
myButton = AButton(name, command)     # ...as we start to need
                                       # more arguments...
```

Sometimes, though, we will want our button to stand out; maybe instead of black text on a gray background, we'll want red text on a green background. This necessitates giving even more arguments to AButton:

```
myButton = Button(name, command, foregroundColor,
          backgroundColor)     # ...things would get messy.
```

Even this isn't enough. We might want to have buttons with thicker borders, or specific heights or widths, or buttons that contain a small picture instead of text. We could easily require an AButton command with twenty different arguments, with the end results being the AButton command would be practically unusable and it wouldn't give us the control we want.

Tk solves this problem by specifying almost all properties of widgets as *named attributes*, values which can optionally be given by name when the widget is created, and which can be accessed or modified by that same name later in the life of the widget. This works well with Python's named parameter passing, making it easy to create widgets with the desired attributes. For example, the name of the attribute which defines the string displayed in a button is text. The Python command to create a button which displays the string "Hello!" is just:

```
myButton = Button(text="Hello!")
```

Most attributes of a widget will have a default value, which is used when no value for that attribute is supplied by the programmer. Generally speaking, these defaults will make sense for the common case, and so most of the time, most named attributes can be ignored. For example, the named attribute which controls the color of the text in a button is called foreground, and its default value is the string "black", which causes the button text to display as black. To override this default, give a specific value for the foreground attribute:

```
myButton = Button(text="Hello!", foreground="red")
```

Named attributes are used extensively throughout the Tk widget set, and many attributes can be used with almost all widgets. The use of named attributes greatly simplifies the process of GUI programming, as well as making code more readable.

17.3.3   Geometry management and widget placement

The final basic aspect of Tk which needs to be understood is the idea of geometry management, meaning how are widgets placed on the screen? It isn't obvious from the above, but typing in a line of Python code like so:

```
myButton = Button(text="Alright!")
```

isn't enough to display the button onscreen. Tk doesn't know where you want the button to show up, and until it is told the desired position, it will keep the button hidden. Deciding where to display the button onscreen is a function of the window hierarchy and associated Tk geometry managers.

To understand the idea of the Tk window hierarchy, you need to know about two special Tk widget classes, called `Toplevel` and `Frame`. A `Toplevel` widget is what Tk uses to represent a complete window in a GUI, complete with title bar, close and zooming buttons, and so forth. A `Frame` can be thought of as a subwindow, or a window in a window, because it is always contained in some other window. Both Toplevel widgets and Frame widgets may contain other Tk widgets (including other frames), and are the basic building blocks for constructing complex GUIs. In many ways, a window hierarchy is similar to a folder hierarchy on a hard drive, with a Toplevel widget corresponding to a single drive, Frame widgets corresponding to folders, and all other widgets corresponding to data files.

The subwidgets contained in any particular frame are arranged for display according to one of Tk's three built-in geometry managers which permit the programmer to specify the arrangement of the subwidgets in various ways, ranging from giving exact coordinates for each widget within a window, to giving only relative placement, leaving the precise sizing of each widget to the geometry manager.

For the purposes of talking about Tk in this chapter, we'll refer to only one geometry manager, the grid manager, which is the most powerful. `grid` works by placing all widgets in an implicit `grid`, similar to a spreadsheet layout. If you start using Tk, you will want to learn the pack and place geometry managers as well, which can be used to specify that widgets should be placed relative to one another (pack), or in absolute locations in a window (place).

17.4   A simple Tkinter application

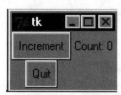

Figure 17.1 A simple application

Let's start with an example which introduces all of the basic Tk concepts: window hierarchies, geometry management, Tk attributes, and a couple of the most basic widgets. The example is a simple one. When run, it produces a window which resembles figure 17.1. It may look different on your machine, because Tk provides a native look and feel for whatever operating system it is running on. This example was produced under the Windows 95 operating system.).

Clicking on the Increment button adds one to the number shown in the Count: field, and clicking the Quit button quits the application.

Here's the code to do this:

```
from Tkinter import *

# Initialize Tk and get a reference to the top-level window it automatically creates.
```

CHAPTER 17   GRAPHICAL USER INTERFACES AND TK

```
mainWindow = Tk()
```

 # Create a label which displays the text "Count: 0", and place it into the top-level window.
```
countLabel = Label(mainWindow, text="Count: 0")
countLabel.grid(row=0, column=1)
```
 # The value of the counter starts at 0.
```
countValue = 0
```

 # This function is called whenever the "Increment" button (defined below) is clicked
```
def incrementCount():
    global countValue, countLabel
```
    # Increment the counter.
```
    countValue = countValue + 1
```
    # Configure the counter label so that the text displayed in it is the string "Count: " followed by
    # the number in the counter.
```
    countLabel.configure(text = 'Count: ' + `countValue`)
```

 # Make a button displaying the text "Increment". Whenever the button is clicked, it executes as a
 # command the function 'incrementCount'.
```
incrButton = Button(mainWindow, text="Increment",
                    command=incrementCount)
```
 # Place the button into its parent window (which is "mainWindow").
```
incrButton.grid(row=0, column=0)
```

 # Make a button displaying the text "Quit":. Whenever it is clicked, it destroys the top level window.
```
quitButton = Button(mainWindow, text="Quit",
                    command=mainWindow.destroy)
```
 # Place the button into its parent window (which is "mainWindow").
```
quitButton.grid(row=1, column=0)
```

 # Enter the Tk event loop
```
mainloop()
```

The example shows the basic principles of Tkinter-based programming:

- Widget creation, accomplished above by the `Label` and `Button` commands. Tkinter lets you create many different types of widgets, such as lists, scroll bars, dialogs, radio and check buttons, and so on.
- Widget placement, accomplished in this case by the `grid` command. Tk provides a great deal of control over how widgets are placed and sized. `grid` will be discussed in more detail in a later section.
- The use of widget attributes, to set and modify the appearance and behavior of widgets. The widget attributes used in the example above are the `text` attribute, which controls the text displayed by a widget, and the `command` attribute, which sets the function a button widget will execute when it is clicked. Widget attributes can be set when a widget is first created, and they can be changed after a widget has been created by using the `configure` widget method.
- A very basic window hierarchy has been created by the above program. The main-Window is the top-level window widget. It, in turn, contains the countLabel, incr-Button, and quitButton widgets.

17.5 Creating widgets

Widgets are created in Python with a single command which is the name of the type of widget being created. Button and Label widgets were created in the example above, but you can also create Menu, Scrollbar, Listbox, Text, and many other types.

The widget creation commands all follow the same general form. They all have one mandatory argument, the parent window (or parent widget) followed by zero or more optional named widget attributes, which determine the precise appearance and behavior of the new widget. Each creation command returns the new widget as a result. You'll usually want to store this new widget somewhere, so that you can modify it later if necessary. So, a line in a Python program which creates a widget will usually look something like this:

```
newWidget = WidgetCreationCommand(parent, attribute1=value1,
        attribute2=value2, . . .)
```

The parent window of a widget called *w* is just the window (or widget) which contains *w*.* It's important to define a parent for several reasons. First, widgets are always displayed inside and relative to their parent window. Second, Tk provides a powerful event mechanism (which we won't have the space to discuss) and a widget might pass events to its parent if it can't handle them itself. Finally, Tk can have widgets which act as windows, in that they themselves are the parent window for (and contain) other widgets, and the widget creation commands need to be able to set up this sort of relationship.

All of the other optional arguments in a widget creation command define widget attributes and control different aspects of the widget. Some widget attributes are common to several different widget types (for example, the `text` attribute applies to all types of simple widgets which can display a label or a line of text of some sort), while other attributes are unique to certain widgets. One characteristic which makes Tk special, compared to other GUI packages, is that it gives you a great deal of control over your widgets. There are a *lot* of attributes for each widget. To give you an idea of this, here is a program which uses just some of the attributes which control the appearance of widgets:

```
from Tkinter import *
mainWindow = Tk()
label = Label(mainWindow, text="Hello", background='white',
        foreground='red', font='Times 20',
        relief='groove', borderwidth=3)
label.grid(row=0, column=0)
mainloop()
```

Figure 17.2 is the resulting window (in black and white, unfortunately).

Figure 17.2 A widget window

---

* This is an oversimplification. The parent window of a widget is generally the widget which contains that widget. But this is not strictly necessary.

17.6 Widget placement

Creating a widget does not automatically draw it on the screen. Before this can be done, Tk needs to know where it should be drawn. The `grid` command was used in the example above and will be discussed in detail.

Tk is more sophisticated in the way it handles widget placement than most GUI packages. Under Windows, the standard way of setting the locations of widgets is to specify an absolute position in their parent window. This can also be done in Tk (using the `place` rather than the `grid` command), but usually isn't, because it's not very flexible. For instance, if you set up a window for use on a monitor which has 640×480 resolution, and a user uses it on a monitor which has 1600×1200 resolution, the window will use only a small amount of the available screen space, and cannot be re-sized (unless you write the code to re-size the window). This is a common problem with many programs.

Instead, Tk usually makes use of the notion of relative placement, where widgets are placed in such a manner that their positions relative to one another are maintained, no matter what size the enclosing window happens to be. This can get quite complex. For example, you can specify that widget *A* should be to the left of widget *B*, and that when the enclosing window is re-sized, widget *A* should grow to take advantage of the extra space, but widget *B* shouldn't. We won't get into all of the possibilities, but will attempt to present enough of the features of Tk widget placement to illustrate the ease and power of the methods it uses.

The `grid` command places widgets in a window by considering a window as an infinite grid of cells. A widget is placed into this grid by specifying `row` and `column` arguments to the grid command, which tell it in which cell to place the widget. The rows and columns will expand as needed to display the widgets they contain, and any rows or columns which do not display any widgets will not be displayed at all.

As a simple example, put two buttons in the corners of a 2×2 grid:

```
from Tkinter import *
win = Tk()

button1 = Button(win, text="one")
button2 = Button(win, text="two")

button1.grid(row=0, column=0)
button2.grid(row=1, column=1)

mainloop()
```

Figure 17.3 A two button window

When run, this program produces a window which looks like figure 17.3.

The cells of the grid are automatically sized so as to be large enough to display what they contain, although this can be overridden constraints placed upon the maximum sizes of the cells.

Text widget	Vertical Scrollbar widget
Horizontal Scrollbar widget	

Figure 17.4 Grid usage

This makes it easy to set up a text window with scroll bars and, with the proper placement (figure 17.4), treat the window as a 2×2 grid into which the Text and Scrollbar widgets will be placed.

The program to do this is

```
from Tkinter import *
main = Tk()
```

 # These commands ensure that any extra space given to the grid as a result of re-sizing
 # the top-level window will be allocated to column 0, row 0, i.e. to the Text widget.
```
main.columnconfigure(0, weight=1)
main.rowconfigure(0, weight=1)

text = Text(main)
text.grid(row=0, column=0, sticky='nesw')

verticalScroller = Scrollbar(main, orient='vertical')
verticalScroller.grid(row=0, column=1, sticky='ns')

horizontalScroller = Scrollbar(main, orient='horizontal')
horizontalScroller.grid(row=1, column=0, sticky='ew')

mainloop()
```

The resulting window is shown in figure 17.4.

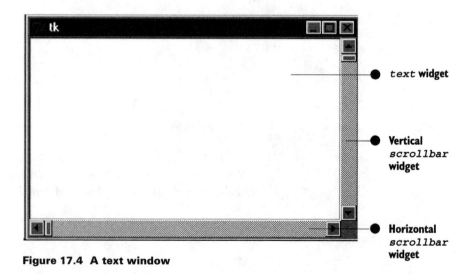

text widget

Vertical scrollbar widget

Horizontal scrollbar widget

Figure 17.4 A text window

CHAPTER 17 GRAPHICAL USER INTERFACES AND TK

In addition to the three `grid` method invocations which place the text box and two scroll bars in their appropriate cells, there are new aspects of Tk revealed by this code, which build upon the fundamentals of Tk to provide further control over the user interface.

- The `orient` attributes of the `Scrollbar` widgets control whether a scroll bar scrolls vertically or horizontally.
- The `sticky` attributes of all three widgets control how they will be placed in their cells. For example, the `Text` widget has a sticky value of `'nesw'` which means that its north (top) side should stick to the north side of the cell it is in, its east (right) side should stick to the east side of its containing cell, and similarly for the south and west sides. In other words, the `Text` widget should completely fill its cell, which means that if its cell grows, the text widget should also grow and automatically re-format the text it contains, to take advantage of the extra space. It's then fairly easy to guess that the sticky value of `'ns'` for the vertical scroll bar means it should always stretch in the vertical direction to fill its cell (and thus always be the same height as the `Text` widget), and analogously for `'ew'` and the horizontal scroll bar.
- The `columnconfigure` command specifies that if the window containing the entire grid of widgets is expanded in the horizontal direction, all of the extra space resulting from the re-sizing should be allocated to column 0, the column containing the `Text` widget. `rowconfigure` specifies similarly in the vertical direction. Together, the `columnconfigure` and `rowconfigure` ensure that if the top-level is re-sized to be larger, then the extra space resulting from that re-sizing should be given to the `Text` widget, which is generally the desired behavior.

That's a lot of GUI detail specification in a small amount of space. But that's exactly the point of Tk—to enable you to rapidly specify your GUI, right down to the details. The fact that settings are accomplished through easy-to-remember keywords, rather than a multitude of binary flags, doesn't hurt either.

17.7 What else can Tkinter do?

The above examples don't come close to exploring the capabilities of Tkinter, but they should give you some idea of what it feels like. There is no way in the space of one chapter to illustrate by example all of the facilities provided by Tk. The next few sections will cover the remainder of Tk's abilities on a much higher level. If you are familiar with GUI programming, you will be at home with most of what is discussed.

If you are not familiar with GUI programming, the examples above are a good starting point for learning by experimentation. They should give you grounding in Tk's basic philosophy and concepts. Further detailed information can be found linked off of the Tkinter page on the Python Web site (particularily Fredrik Lundh's excellent introduction and the Tk man pages at Scriptics). Also be sure to check out John Grayson's comprehensive book *Python and Tkinter Programming*.

17.7.1 Event handling

Event handling—how a GUI library handles user actions such as mouse movements or clicks, or key presses—is a critical part of GUI programming. An awkward event-handling scheme can make your GUI development a real nightmare, while a good event-handling mechanism can make your task far more pleasant. Tk event handling, while not perfect, is up near the top.

One of the big questions with event handling is *event direction*—if I press a key on the keyboard, which text entry box or text widget (or other widget) of the many in my interface is that directed to? Many GUI libraries require a complete specification of how events are to be directed; the programmer must say, If this widget can't handle a mouse click event, it should pass that event over to this other widget, and so on and so forth. You can do this in Tk, but you are not required to. Tk uses the hierarchical structure of your user interface, together with various commonsense rules, to try to automatically direct events towards the appropriate widget. Most of the time, it gets it right.

Tk also provides a very rich set of events to choose from. For example, look at the problem of changing the mouse cursor to a paint brush, as the mouse enters the main paint window of a painting program. One way to do this would be to continually (explicitly) monitor the position of the mouse relative to the main paint window, and manually adjust the cursor as necessary. This would be necessary if only basic mouse-related events, such as movements, were reported by and to Tk. However, Tk provides a higher-level event for all windows, sub-windows, and widgets, called the `<Enter>` event. An `<Enter>` event for a window or widget is generated every time the mouse cursor enters that window or widget (and a corresponding `<Leave>` event is generated when the mouse leaves.) A built-in `bind` command makes it easy to bind `<Enter>` events for a particular window, such as a painting window, to specific functions, such as a function to change the mouse cursor to a paintbrush.

If the built-in set of Tk events isn't enough, you can define or generate your own *virtual events*. These are events defined by the programmer, just as application-specific functions might be defined by the programmer. For example, you might wish to define the virtual event called `<<Copy>>` and set it to be equivalent to the keyboard event generated by pressing CTRL-C. If you ever migrated your program to a platform or language (such as Chinese, say) where CTRL-C was not an appropriate key binding for a `<<Copy>>` event, you could simply re-define `<<Copy>>` in terms of another keystroke—but all references to `<<Copy>>` in your code would remain valid, without needing any changes. Generating virtual events is also a convenient way to distribute events widely throughout your application, without worrying about plumbing details. For example, you could define a button called MyButton, such that pressing said button would generate a `<<MyButtonPressed>>` event. Any other widgets could then be instructed to listen for `<<MyButtonPressed>>` events, without actually referencing the original button, indeed, without knowing or caring that a button was the source of the event.

17.7.2 Canvas and text widgets

Two widgets in the Tk widget set deserve special mention, because they provide abilities reflecting literally years of implementation effort. These are the `Canvas` and `Text` widgets, which respectively provide very high-level manipulation capabilities for object-oriented graphics and for text. Both widget types are an order of magnitude more advanced than analogs found in most other GUI libraries.

The `Text` widget supports all of the basic functionality necessary for a basic WYSI-WYG word processor, including font families, styles, and sizes, a rich set of default key bindings, automatic controllable line wrapping, settable tabs, the ability to embed images or other widgets onto the text drawing surface, and so forth. In addition, text within the widget can be tagged with any number of user-chosen strings, and then manipulated via those tags. You could, for example, define a tag called bold, to be applied to all text in your widget which should be displayed in boldface. A single line of code would then let you change the actual display style for all bold text from Helvetica 10 pt. bold to Times Roman 14 pt. bold, or, if you preferred, to red text on a green background with a two-pixel-wide raised border. In fact, you can easily define sections of text which highlight as the mouse cursor passes over them, and which cause some action when they are clicked, mimicking the effect of buttons or hypertext. Many other abilities also come along with the Text widget.

The Canvas widget is similar, particularly with respect to the use of tags. You can associate arbitrary tags with an object and manipulate as a whole all objects on the canvas which have a given tag. So, for example, it is an easy matter to define a complex shape by drawing a series of lines, curves, and other shapes, all with the same programmer-defined tag, and then to move that shape around the canvas as a unit, by instructing the Canvas widget to move all simple shapes having the given tag. It is also easy to use shapes as buttons, to set various aspects of their appearance (such as foreground and background colors, line width), to define layering of shapes atop one another, and to perform many other advanced tasks which would take months of effort if undertaken from scratch.

17.7.3 Extensions to Tk and Tkinter

Because Tk has been in wide use for quite some time, many people have developed extensions for it, many of which have been made freely available. Notable extensions include extensions providing drag and drop facilities, extremely impressive Graph and Table widgets, and a number of widget collections. Extensions to Tk itself (as opposed to Python extensions to Tkinter) are typically coded directly in C, which makes for very fast execution, but which may mean some difficulty in using these extensions on your system. Scriptics is working toward a more unified release of many of the most useful contributions, but until this is generally available, you may need some talent with a compiler to make use of everything that is out there.

An extension of particular interest to Python users is Python Megawidgets, or Pmw. Although Tkinter includes many basic widgets, it is missing many other useful ones, such as drop-down lists, counters, notebooks, paned widgets, and so forth. Whenever a programmer wants a new widget like these, it must be built out of existing widgets. What is required is a convenient way of building these megawidgets, so that they can be used like the basic widgets.

Pmw provides a comprehensive framework for building high-level compound widgets constructed using others as component parts. Pmw also contains a library of over thirty flexible megawidgets that can be used alongside base Tkinter widgets in your graphical applications.

Here is a complete script which creates a Pmw combo box (or drop-down list):

```
import Pmw

items = ('These', 'are', 'some', 'items', 'for', 'the',
         'combobox',)
```

```
combo = Pmw.ComboBox(
  label_text = 'ComboBox:',
  labelpos = 'w',
  scrolledlist_items = items,
)
combo.pack()
combo.mainloop()
```

More information on Pmw is available from the Pmw home page at http://www.dscpl.com.au/pmw/. Download the latest version from the directory ftp://ftp.dscpl.com.au/pub/pmw/.

17.8 Alternatives to Tk and Tkinter

Tkinter may not satisfy your needs. It is not particularly fast, and so is not a good candidate for games or for image manipulation programs. Its high-level approach means that particularly unusual or specialized user interfaces may be difficult to implement. Or, you may not have the time to learn Tkinter. Fortunately, many alternatives are available.

While every effort has been made to keep this book platform-independent, Microsoft Windows is ubiquitous enough that a particular ability of Python deserves special mention. It is possible to access native Windows libraries from Python, including the Windows GUI libraries. The chapter on using Python, Windows, and COM discusses what is possible in this arena.

Chapter 24 explains how to use Java's quickly evolving and improving GUI capabilities with Python.

Two windowing/GUI libraries for use in the UNIX environment stand out. The first is the Qt package, which forms the basis for the very well-done KDE desktop environment effort, a large project geared toward producing an integrated and comprehensive desktop environment for UNIX and compatible operating systems. Qt is not a fully free package. The originators maintain control of the source code, and Qt may be used freely only for noncommercial software, otherwise a commercial license fee applies. Find out more about Qt at http://www.trolltech.com. http://www.kde.org will give you a chance to browse screenshots of many applications built using KDE.

The major contender to Qt is Gtk. This is the Gnu Toolkit, and is the basis for the Gnome desktop environment project, which is comparable to KDE. Gtk is similar to Qt in scope and capability, and at the moment it is unclear which will emerge as the predominant force in the UNIX GUI environment. Many people prefer Gtk because it is distributed under a true open-source model, without the restrictions imposed by Qt. A good starting point for finding out about Gtk is the Gnome project, at http://www.gnome.org.

There are many cross-platform GUI libraries available. Good descriptions and evaluations are available at www.theoffice.net/guitool.

17.9 Summary

Python ships with a comprehensive and well-thought-out interface (a Python module) called `Tkinter`, which allows access to the freely available and very powerful Tk user interface library. Tk is an ideal scripting-style GUI builder for a scripting-style language, in that it allows very rapid interface development, interactive execution, and run-time control over all aspects of the interface, with very powerful abilities. It suffers some of the same drawbacks of scripting languages, particularly execution overhead that may be too high for graphics-intense applications, and an inflexibility in the UI model it uses.

There are many alternatives. Users programming only for the Windows environment can take advantage of their MS UI library knowledge through direct calls to the Microsoft APIs. Qt and Gtk exist on the UNIX side. Check out all the alternatives at:
www.theoffice.net/guitool.

All of the packages mentioned have Python interfaces available, although the Python interfaces may not come with the package.

Advanced 3
language
features

CHAPTER 18

Packages

18.1 What is a package?

A module is a file containing code. A module defines a group of usually related Python functions or other objects. The name of the module is derived from the name of the file.

A package is a directory of related Python code, used in a manner similar to a module.

Once modules are understood, packages are easy, because a package is a directory containing code and possibly further subdirectories. A package contains a group of usually related code files (modules). The name of the package is derived from the name of the main package directory.

Packages are a natural extension of the module concept, and are designed to handle very large projects. Just as modules group related functions, classes and variables, packages group related modules.

18.2 A first example

To see how this might work in practice, let's sketch a design layout for a type of project that is by nature very large—a generalized mathematics package, along the lines of

211

Mathematica®, Maple®, or Matlab®. Maple®, for example, consists of thousands of files, and some sort of hierarchical structure is vital to keeping such a project ordered. We'll call our project as a whole `mathproj`.

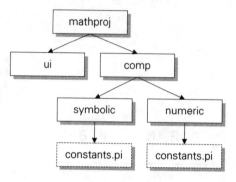

Figure 18.1 Organizing a math package

There are, of course, many ways to organize such a project, but a reasonable design might split the project into two parts; `ui`, consisting of the user interface elements, and `comp`, the computational elements. Within `comp`, it might make sense to further segment the computational aspect into `symbolic` (real and complex symbolic computation, such as high school algebra) and `numeric` (real and complex numerical computation, such as numerical integration). It might then make sense to have a `constants.py` file in both the `symbolic` and `numeric` parts of the project (figure 18.1).

The constants.py file in the numeric part of the project might define pi as:

```
pi = 3.141592
```

while the constants.py file in the symbolic part of the project could define pi as

```
class piClass:
    def __str__(self):
        return "PI"

pi = piClass()
```

In other words, the symbolic constants.py file defines `pi` as an abstract Python object, the sole instance of the piClass class. As the system is developed, various operations can be implemented in this class, which return symbolic rather than numeric results.

There is a natural mapping from this design structure to a directory structure. The top-level directory of the project, called `mathproj` will contain subdirectories `ui` and `comp`; `comp` will in turn contain subdirectories `symbolic` and `numeric`; and each of `symbolic` and `numeric` will contain their own constants.py file.

Given this directory structure, and assuming that the root `mathproj` directory is installed somewhere in the Python search path, Python code both inside and outside the `mathproj` package can access the two variants of `pi` as `mathproj.symbolic.con-stants.pi`, and `mathproj.numeric.constants.pi`. In other words, the Python name for an item in the package is a reflection of the directory path name to the file containing that item.

That is what packages are all about. They are ways of organizing very large collections of Python code into coherent wholes, by allowing the code to be split among different files and directories, and imposing a module/submodule naming scheme based on the directory structure of the package files. Unfortunately, all is not quite this simple in practice, because details intrude to make their use more complex than their theory. The practical aspects of packages are the basis for the remainder of this chapter.

18.3 A concrete example

The rest of this chapter will use a running example to illustrate the inner workings of the package mechanism (figure 18.2). For the purposes of this chapter only, we will present file names and paths in *filename* style, to avoid confusion as to whether we are talking about a file/directory or the module/package defined by that file/directory. Here are the files we'll be using in our example package:

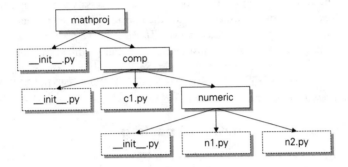

Figure 18.2 Example package

Here are some files used in the examples later in the chapter.

File mathproj/__init__.py

```
print "Hello from mathproj init"
__all__ = ['comp']
version = 1.03
```

File mathproj/comp/__init__.py

```
__all__ = ['c1']
print "Hello from mathproj.comp init"
```

File mathproj/comp/c1.py

```
x = 1.00
```

File mathproj/comp/numeric/__init__.py

```
print "Hello from numeric init"
```

File mathproj/comp/numeric/n1.py

```
from mathproj import version
from mathproj.comp import c1
from n2 import h

def g():
    print "version is",version
    print h()
```

File mathproj/comp/numeric/n2.py

```
def h():
    return "Called function h in module n2"
```

For the purposes of the examples in this chapter, we will assume that you have created these files in a *mathproj* directory which is on the Python search path. (It is sufficient to simply ensure that the current working directory for Python is the directory containing mathproj, when executing these examples.)

!!!

In most of the examples in this book, it is not necessary to start up a new Python shell for each example. You can usually execute them in a Python shell you have used for previous examples, and still get the results shown. *This is not true for the examples in this chapter*, because the Python namespace must be clean (i.e., unmodified by previous `import` statements) for the examples to work properly. So if you do run the examples shown below, please ensure that you run each separate example in its own shell. In IDLE this requires exiting and restarting the program, not just closing and reopening its shell window.

18.3.1   Basic use of the mathproj package

Before getting into the details of packages, let's look at accessing items contained in the `mathproj` package. Start up a new Python shell, and do the following:

```
>>>
```

```
>>> import mathproj
Hello from mathproj init
```

Packages can be imported and used like modules.

If all went well, you should get another input prompt, and no error messages. As well, the message "Hello from mathproj init" should be printed to the screen, by code in the mathproj/__init__.py file. We'll talk more about __init__.py files in a bit; for now, all you need to know is that they are run automatically whenever a package is first loaded.

The mathproj/__init__.py file assigns 1.03 to the variable `version`. `version` is in the scope of the `mathproj` package namespace, and so once created, can be seen via `mathproj`, even from outside the mathproj/__init__.py file:

```
...
```

```
>>> mathproj.version
⇒ 1.03
```

So, in use, packages can look a lot like modules, that is they can provide access to objects defined within them via attributes. This isn't surprising, since packages are really just a generalization of modules.

18.3.2   Loading subpackages and submodules

Now, let's start looking at how the various files defined in the *mathproj* package interact with one another. We will do this by invoking the function g defined in the file mathproj/comp/numeric/n1.py. The first obvious question is, has this module been loaded? Let's see if it is known to Python:

```
⌐ ... ⌐
```

```
>>> mathproj.comp.numeric.n1
Traceback (innermost last):
  File "<interactive input>", line 0, in ?
AttributeError: comp
```

Importing a package does not automatically import its sub-packages.

In other words, simply loading the top-level module of a package is not enough to load all of the submodules. This is in keeping with Python's philosophy that it should not do things behind your back. Clarity is more important than conciseness.

This is simple enough to overcome; just import the module of interest, and then execute the function g in that module:

```
⌐ ... ⌐
```

```
>>> import mathproj.comp.numeric.n1
Hello from mathproj.comp init
Hello from numeric init
>>> mathproj.comp.numeric.n1.g()
version is 1.03
Called function h in module n2
```

Every package directory contains a __init__.py file, giving package initialization code.

Notice, however, that the lines beginning with Hello were printed out as a side effect of loading `mathproj.comp.numeric.n1`. These two lines are printed out by `print` statements in the __init__.py files in *mathproj/comp* and *mathproj/comp/numeric*. In other words, before Python could import `mathproj.comp.numeric.n1`, it first had to import `mathproj.comp`, and then `mathproj.comp.numeric`. Whenever a package is first imported, its associated __init__.py file is executed, resulting in the Hello lines. To confirm that both `mathproj.comp` and `mathproj.comp.numeric` were imported as part of the process of importing `mathproj.comp.numeric.n1`, we can check to see that `mathproj.comp` and `mathproj.comp.numeric` are now known to the Python session:

```
⌐ ... ⌐
```

```
>>> mathproj.comp
⇒   <module 'mathproj.comp'>
>>> mathproj.comp.numeric
⇒   <module 'mathproj.comp.numeric'>
```

18.3.3   Import statements within packages

Files within a package do not automatically have access to objects defined in other files in the same package. Just as in outside modules, `import` statements must be used to explicitly access objects from other package files. To see how this works in practice, look back at the n1 subpackage. The code contained in n1.py is

Package files must use the import statement to gain access to other files in the same package.

```
from mathproj import version
from mathproj.comp import c1
from n2 import h

def g():
    print "version is", version
    print h()
```

g makes use of both `version` from the top-level `mathproj` package, and the function h from the n2 module; hence, the module containing g must import both `version` and h, to make them accessible. We import `version` just as we would in an import statement from outside of the mathproj package, that is by saying `from mathproj import version`. If we were importing h into code outside the mathproj package, we would say `from math-proj.comp.numeric.n2 import h`, and this would also work in the n1.py file. In other words, we could say

```
from mathproj.comp.numeric.n2 import h
```

as the third line in n1.py, and it would work fine.

Package files can refer to sibling files directly, without specifying an absolute package name in import statements.

However, this is a lot of typing, and there is a shorter way. The Python package mechanism makes a special allowance for the common case of one package file importing objects from another file in the same directory, and, in this case only, allows the import statement to refer directly to the file being imported from, rather than specifying the absolute position of that file in the package. In other words, because n1.py and n2.py are in the same directory, in n1.py we can just say

```
from n2 import h
```

This is the *only* time when you can "shortcut" a package name when doing imports within a package. To make this clear, I've also included a statement in n1.py to import c1 from `mathproj.comp`. In this situation, where the comp.py file is not in the same directory as n1.py, attempting to shortcut the package name by saying something like `from comp import c1` would not work. It would cause an error to be raised.

18.3.4 __init__.py files in packages

You will have noticed that all of the directories in our package—mathproj, mathproj/comp, and mathproj/numeric—contain a file called __init__.py. An __init__.py file serves two purposes:

- It is automatically executed by Python the first time a package or subpackage is loaded. This permits whatever package initialization might be desired by the programmer.

Each package or subpackage directory must contain an __init__.py file, even if that file is empty.

- Python requires that a directory contain an __init__.py file before it can be recognized as a package. This prevents directories containing miscellaneous Python code from being accidentally imported as if they defined a package.

The second point is probably the more important. For many packages, you will not need to put anything in the package's __init__.py file—just make sure than an empty __init__.py file is present.

18.4 The __all__ attribute

If you look back at the various __init__.py files defined in mathproj, you will notice that some of them define an attribute called `__all__`. This has to do with execution of statements of the form `from ... import *`, and requires explanation.

Generally speaking, one would hope that if outside code executed the statement `from mathproj import *`, it would import all non-private names from mathproj. In practice,

The __all__
attribute pro-
vides a list of
names which will
be accessed by a
`from ... import *`
statement. This is
necessary because
some operating
systems do not cor-
rectly handle case
in filenames.

life is more difficult. The primary problem is that some operating systems have a very ambiguous definition of case when it comes to filenames. Microsoft Windows 95/98 is particularly bad in this regard, but it is not the only villain. Since objects in packages can be defined by files or directories, this leads to ambiguity as to exactly under what name a sub-package might be imported. If we say `from mathproj import *`, will comp be imported as comp, Comp, or COMP? If we were to rely only on the name as reported by the operating system, the results might be unpredictable.

There is no good solution to this. It is an inherent problem caused by poor OS design. As the best possible fix, the __all__ attribute was introduced. If present in an __init__.py file, __all__ should give a list of strings, defining those names which are to be imported when a `from ... import *` is executed on that particular package. If __all__ is not present, then `from ... import *` on the given package will do nothing. Because case in a text file is always meaningful, the names under which objects are imported is not ambiguous, and if the OS thinks that comp is the same as COMP, that is its problem.

To see this in action, fire up Python again, and try the following:

```
>>>
```

```
>>> from mathproj import *
Hello from mathproj init
Hello from mathproj.comp init
```

The __all__ attribute in mathproj/__init__.py contains a single entry, comp. Thus, the import statement imports just comp. It's easy enough to check that comp is now known to the Python session:

```
...
```

```
>>> comp
⇒   <module 'mathproj.comp'>
```

Note, however, that there is no recursive importing of names with a `from ... import *` statement. The __all__ attribute for the comp package contains c1, but c1 is not magically loaded by our `from mathproj import *` statement:

```
...
```

```
>>> C1
Traceback (innermost last):
  File "<interactive input>", line 0, in ?
NameError: c1
```

To insert names from `mathproj.comp` we must, again, do an explicit import:

```
...
```

```
>>> from mathproj.comp import *
>>> c1
⇒   <module 'mathproj.comp.c1'>
```

18.5 Proper use of packages

Most of your packages should not be as structurally complex as the above examples would imply.

The package mechanism is relatively new to Python, and there are still no clear guidelines as to what constitutes good or bad package design. It is obvious that very complex packages can be built, but it is not obvious that they should be built.

The following rules of thumb are appropriate in most circumstances:

- Packages should not use deeply nested directory structures. Except for absolutely huge collections of code, there should be no need to do so. For most packages, a single top-level directory is all that is needed. A two-level hierarchy should be able to effectively handle all but a very few of the rest.
- See if it works for your situation: hide subpackages from the external user, that is, leave them for use in the package only.
- You can use the __all__ attribute to hide names from `from … import *`, by not listing those names; this is probably *not* a good idea, because it is inconsistent. If you want to hide names, make them private by prefacing them with an underscore.

C H A P T E R   1 9

Data types as objects

By now, you've learned the basic Python types, and also how to create your own data types using classes. For many languages, that would be pretty much it, as far as data types are concerned. However, Python is dynamically typed, meaning that types of things are determined at run time, not at compile time. This is one of the reasons Python is so easy to use. It also makes it possible, and sometimes necessary, to compute with the types of objects (and not just the objects themselves).

19.1 Types are objects, too

Fire up a Python session and try out the following:

```
>>>
```

```
>>> type(5)
⇒   <type 'int'>
>>> type(['hello', 'goodbye'])
⇒   <type 'list'>
```

The type *function returns the type of an object.*

This is the first time we've seen the built-in type function in Python. It can be applied to any Python object, and simply returns the type of that object. In the above

219

example, it told us that 5 is an 'int' (integer), and that `['hello', 'goodbye']` is a list, something you probably already knew.

A type is just another kind of Python object.

Of greater interest is that Python actually returned objects in response to the calls to type; `<type 'int'>` and `<type 'list'>` are the screen representations of the returned objects. What sort of object is returned by a call of `type(5)`? Well, we have any easy way of finding out—just use type on that result:

```
...
```

```
>>> typeResult = type(5)
>>> type(typeResult)
⇒   <type 'type'>
```

In other words, the object returned by type is an object whose type happens to be `<type 'type'>`—we could call it a *type object*. A type object is another kind of Python object whose only outstanding feature is the confusion its name might sometime cause. Saying a 'type' object is of type `<type 'type'>` has about the same degree of clarity as the old Abbot and Costello *Who's on First?* comedy routine.

19.2 Using types

Types can be compared for equality.

Now that we know that data types can be represented as Python type objects, what can we do with them? Well, we can compare them, because any two Python objects can be compared:

```
>>>
```

```
>>> type("Hello") == type("Goodbye")
⇒   1
>>> type("Hello") == type(5)
⇒   0
```

In other words, the types of `"Hello"` and `"Goodbye"` are the same (they are both strings), but the types of `"Hello"` and 5 are different. Among other things, you can use this to provide type checking in your function and method definitions.

19.3 The types module

Constants denoting the different type objects are available through the types module.

Python has a built-in types module, which provides constants for every type known to Python. Rather than listing all of them here, we'll obtain them directly from Python and illustrate a useful trick in the process. First, import the types module:

```
>>>
```

```
>>> import types
```

Now, use dir to get a list of the names defined in this module:

```
...
```

```
>>> dir(types)
⇒   ['BuiltinFunctionType', 'BuiltinMethodType', 'ClassType',
     'CodeType', 'ComplexType', 'DictType', 'DictionaryType',
```

```
'EllipsisType', 'FileType', 'FloatType', 'FrameType',
'FunctionType', 'InstanceType', 'IntType', 'LambdaType',
'ListType', 'LongType', 'MethodType', 'ModuleType', 'NoneType',
'SliceType', 'StringType', 'TracebackType', 'TupleType',
'TypeType', 'UnboundMethodType', 'XRangeType', '__builtins__',
'__doc__', '__file__', '__name__']
```

Names beginning with a double underscore are private to the `types` module, and can be disregarded. The remaining names define all the allowable types in Python and can be used for type testing. `types` is really intended for importation using the `from module import *` statement, so

```
>>>
```

```
>>> from types import *
>>> type(5) == intType
⇒  1
>>> type(5.0) == intType
⇒  0
```

19.4 *Types and user-defined classes*

The type *function does not return class information when applied to a class instance. To obtain such information, use the* __class__*,* __bases__*, and* __name__ *special attributes.*

If you read completely through the list of constants defined in the types module, you'll notice an `InstanceType` constant. This is the type of any class instance in Python, that is if `obj` is a class instance, then `type(obj)` will return `InstanceType`.

The problem is that we usually think of the type of an instance as being defined by the class to which it belongs, and the `type` function does not return this information. To obtain information about the class(es) to which an instance belongs, we must use the instance's special `__class__` attribute, which contains the class object from which the instance directly inherits. Once we've obtained this class object, we can then use its `__bases__` attribute to find any further base classes from which the instance inherits, and with any of the classes we obtain, we can use the classes' `__name__` attributes to obtain the names of the classes.

Of course, an example makes things much clearer. To start, let's define a couple of empty classes, so as to set up a simple inheritance hierarchy.

```
>>>
```

```
>>> class A: pass
...
>>> class B(A): pass
...
```

Now, create an instance of class B:

```
...
```

```
>>> b = B()
```

As expected, applying the `type` function to b just tells us that b is an instance of some class—not terribly informative:

```
…
```

```
>>> type(b)
⇒   <type 'instance'>
```

To find out what class b belongs to, access its special __class__ attribute:

```
…
```

```
>>> b.__class__
⇒   <class __main__.B at 86dec0>
```

We'll be working with that class quite a bit to extract further information, so store it somewhere:

```
…
```

```
>>> bClass = b.__class__
```

Now, to emphasize that everything in Python is an object, the class we obtained from b really is the class we defined under the name B:

```
…
```

```
>>> bClass == B
⇒   1
```

In other words, in this example we didn't need to store the class of b at all—we already had it. When you're analyzing the class of an instance in a program, though, that won't be the case. I want to make clear that a class is just another Python object, and can be stored or passed around like any Python object.

Now, given the class of b, we can find the name of that class using its __name__ attribute:

```
…
```

```
>>> bClass.__name__
⇒   'B'
```

and, we can find out what classes it inherits from by accessing its __bases__ attribute, which contains a tuple of all of its base classes:

```
…
```

```
>>> bClass.__bases__
⇒   (<class __main__.A at 864e50>,)
```

Used together, __class__, __bases__, and __name__ allow a full analysis of the class inheritance structure associated with any instance.

There are, however, two built-in functions that provide a more user friendly way of obtaining most of the information one usually needs: isinstance and issubclass. The isinstance function is what you want to use to determine if, for example, a class passed into a function or method is of the expected type.

```
>>> class C: pass
...
>>> class D: pass
...
>>> class E(D): pass
...
>>> x = 12
>>> c = C()
>>> d = D()
>>> e = E()
>>> isinstance(x, E)
⇒ 0
>>> isinstance(c, E)
⇒ 0
>>> isinstance(e, E)
⇒ 1
>>> isinstance(e, D)
⇒ 1
>>> isinstance(e, E)
⇒ 0
```

Use isinstance to determine if a variable is an instance of a given class.

● **For class types, check against the class.**

● **e is an instance of class D as E inherits from D,**

● **but d is not an instance of class E.**

Or use it to determine if a variable is of a given type.

It isn't restricted to class types.

```
...
```

```
>>> y = 12L
>>> isinstance(y, type(5L))
⇒ 1
>>> from types import *
>>> isinstance(y, LongType)
⇒ 1
```

● **For other types, you can use an example,**

● **or use the type from the types module.**

Use issubclass to determine if a class inherits from another class.

The issubclass function is only for class types.

```
...
```

```
>>> issubclass(C,D)
   0
>>> issubclass(E,D)
⇒ 1
>>> issubclass(D,D)
⇒ 1
>>> issubclass(e.__class__,D)
⇒ 1
```

● **A class is considered a subclass of itself.**

Using assert statements, it's possible to add in type checks for use during development, while also being able to turn them off if desired for production use.

With what we've covered here, you have all the tools necessary to provide type check-ing in the situations where it is necessary for your applications. One technique that some people employ is to use assert statements in these situations. They can leave them in while developing and testing their program. However, any costs (in execution speed) of perform-ing these checks can be eliminated if desired when their program is put into production use (i.e., by setting the PYTHONOPTIMIZE variable).

Special method attributes

Python is unique in its ability to modify fine details of the behavior of user-defined objects in a way that makes them appear to possess features of ones which are built-in. For C++ users, this is somewhat similar to operator overloading, but more comprehensive and easier to use. I know of no other language which provides similar features.

This chapter will focus on this feature of Python. The reference appendix lists all of the special method attributes that Python provides. The use of special method attributes is inherently object-oriented. You'll need to be at least moderately familiar with OO programming to use this feature.

20.1 What is a special method attribute?

A special method attribute is simply an attribute of a Python class with a special meaning to Python. It is defined as a method, but is not intended for use as such. It is not usually directly invoked. Instead, it is called automatically by Python in response to a demand made on an object of that class.

Perhaps the simplest example of this is the __str__ special method attribute. If it is defined in a class, then any time an instance of that class is used where Python requires

A special method attribute is a method definition whose name gives it a special meaning in Python. The __str__ method is a simple example.

a user-readable string representation of that instance, the __str__ method attribute will be invoked, and the value it returns will be used as the required string. To see this, let's define a class representing RGB colors as a triplet of numbers, one each for red, green, and blue intensities. As well as defining the standard __init__ method to initialize instances of the class, we'll also define a __str__ method to return strings representing instances, in a reasonably human-friendly format. Our definition looks something like this:

```
class Color:
    def __init(self, red, green, blue):
        self._red = red
        self._green = green
        self._blue = blue

    def __str__(self):
        return "Color: R=%d, G=%d, B=%d" % (self._red, self._green,
                self._blue)
```

If we now put this definition into a file (say, colorModule.py), we can load it and use it in the normal manner:

```
>>>
```

```
>>> from colorModule import Color
>>> c = Color(15, 35, 3)
```

The presence of the __str__ special method attribute can be seen if we now use print to print out c:

```
...
```

```
>>> print c
Color: R=15, G=35, B=3
```

Even though our __str__ special method attribute has not been explicitly invoked by any of our code, it has nonetheless been used by Python, which knows that the __str__ attribute (if present) defines a method to convert objects into user-readable strings. This is the defining characteristic of special method attributes—they allow you to define functionality which hooks into Python in special ways. Special method attributes can be used to define classes whose objects behave in a fashion which is syntactically and semantically equivalent to lists, or to dictionaries. You could, for example, use this ability to define objects which are used in exactly the same manner as Python lists, but which use balanced trees rather than arrays to store data. To a programmer, they would appear to be lists, but with faster inserts, slower iterations, and certain other performance differences which would presumably be advantageous in the problem at hand.

The rest of this chapter covers longer examples using special method attributes. It doesn't discuss all of Python's available special method attributes, but it does expose you to the concept in enough detail that you can then easily make use of the other special attribute methods, all of which are defined in the reference appendix.

20.2　*Making an object behave like a list*

*Special method
attributes are
often used to
make objects
behave like lists,
or some aspect of
lists.*

This sample problem involved a large text file containing records of people; each record consisted of a single line containing the person's name, age, and place of residence, with a double semicolon (::) between the fields. A few lines from such a file might look like this:

```
    .
    .
    .
John Smith::37::Springfield, Massachusetts
Ellen Nelle::25::Springfield, Connecticut
Dale McGladdery::29::Springfield, Hawaii
    .
    .
    .
```

Basically, I needed to collect information as to the distribution of ages of people in the file.

There were many ways the lines in this file could be processed. Here was one way:

```
fileobject = open(filename, 'r')
lines = fileobject.readlines()
fileobject.close()
for line in lines:
    . . . do whatever . . .
```

That would work in theory, but it read the entire file into memory at once. If the file was too large to be held in memory (and these files potentially were that large), the program wouldn't work.

Another way to attack the problem was this:

```
fileobject = open(filename, 'r')
line = fileobject.readline()
while line != "":
    . . . do whatever . . .
    line = fileobject.readline()
fileobject.close()
```

This got around the problem of too little memory by reading in only one line at a time. It worked fine, but I still wasn't happy. I'd frequently needed to process large files with one record per line in the past, and knew I'd have to do the same thing in the future, and I was getting tired of writing the same five lines of code (open the file, read a line, while the line contains something, etc.) over and over again. I wanted something that could, at least for the purposes of a for loop, treat a text file as a list of lines, but without reading the entire text file in at once.

20.2.1　The __getitem__ special method attribute

A solution would be to use the __getitem__ special method attribute which may be defined in any user-defined class, to enable instances of that class to respond to list access syntax and semantics. In other words, if AClass is a Python class which defines __getitem__, and *obj* is an instance of that class, then saying things like x = *obj*[*n*] and for x in *obj*:... are meaningful—*obj* may be used in much the same way as a list.

The resulting code is below, explanations follow. Parts of particular interest are in bold.

```
class lineReader:
    def __init__(self, filename):
        # Open the given file for reading, and remember the open fileobject.
        self.fileobject = open(filename, 'r')

    def __getitem__(self, index):
        # Try to read in a line.
        line = self.fileobject.readline()
        # If there was no more data to be read...
        if line == "":
            # ...close the fileobject.
            self.fileobject.close()
            # ...and raise an IndexError to break out of any enclosing loop.
            raise IndexError
        # Otherwise, return the line that was just read.
        else:
            return line


for line in lineReader("filename"):
    . . . do whatever . . .
```

At first glance, this might look worse than the previous solution because there's more code, and it is difficult to understand. But most of that code is in a class, which could be put into its own module, say the myutils module. Then the program becomes

```
import myutils
for line in myutils.lineReader("filename"):
    . . . do whatever . . .
```

The lineReader class handles all the details of opening the file, reading in lines one at a time, and closing the file. At the cost of somewhat more initial development time, it provides a tool which makes working with one-record-per-line large text files easier and less error-prone.

20.2.2 How it works

Evaluations of expressions like obj[i] automatically result in an invocation of the __getitem__ method.

LineReader is a class, and the __init__ method opens the named file for reading, and stores the opened fileobject for later access. To understand the use of the __getitem__ method, you need to know the following three points:

- Any object which defines __getitem__ as an instance method can return elements as if it were a list, because all accesses of the form *object*[*i*] are transformed by Python into a method invocation of the form *object*.__getitem__(*i*), which is then handled as a normal method invocation, that is it is ultimately executed as __getitem__(*object*, *i*), using the version of __getitem__ defined in the class.

The first argument of each call of __getitem__ is the object from which data is being extracted, and the second argument is the index of that data.

- Since `for` loops simply access each piece of data in a list, one at a time, a `for arg in sequence :` loop works by calling __getitem__ over and over again, with sequentially increasing indexes. That is, the `for` loop will first set *arg* to `sequence.__getitem__(0)`, then to *sequence.*`__getitem__(1)`, and so on.
- A `for` loop catches `IndexError` exceptions, and handles them by exiting the loop. This is how `for` loops are terminated when used with normal lists or sequences.

The lineReader class is intended for use only with and inside a `for` loop, and the `for` loop will always generate calls with a uniformly increasing index: __getitem__(self, 0), __getitem__(self, 1), __getitem__(self, 2), and so on. The code above takes advantage of this knowledge, and returns lines one after the other, ignoring the index argument.

With this knowledge, understanding how a lineReader object emulates a sequence in a `for` loop is easy. Each iteration of the loop causes the special Python attribute method __getitem__ to be invoked on the object; as a result, the object reads in the next line from its stored fileobject, and examines that line. If the line is non-blank, it is returned. A blank line means the end of the file has been reached, and the object closes the fileobject and raises the `IndexError` exception. `IndexError` is caught by the enclosing `for` loop, which then terminates.

Remember that this example is here for illustrative purposes only. The `fileinput` library module (introduced in chapter 15) provides this functionality along with some nice bells and whistles. Look at its code (use IDLE to find it) to see how it uses the __getitem__ attribute.

20.2.3 Implementing full list functionality

In the example above, an object of the `lineReader` class behaves like a list object only to the extent that it will correctly respond to sequential accesses of the lines in the file it is reading from. You might be wondering how this functionality could be expanded to make lineReader (or other) objects behave more like a list.

First, the __getitem__ method should handle its index argument in some way. Since the whole point of the lineReader class was to avoid reading a large file into memory, it wouldn't make sense to have the entire file in memory and return the appropriate line. Probably the smartest thing to do would be to check that each index in a __getitem__ call is one greater than the index from the previous __getitem__ call (or is 0, for the first call of __getitem__ on a lineReader instance), and to raise an error if this is not the case. This would ensure that lineReader instances are only used in `for` loops as was intended.

Various other special method attributes define other aspects of list behavior. More generally, Python provides a number of special method attributes relating to list behavior. __setitem__ provides a way of defining what should be done when an object is used in the syntactic context of a list assignment, that is *obj*[n] = val. __getslice__ and __setslice__ are similar to __getitem__ and __setitem__, but for slice (as opposed to single-element) access and assignment. Some other special method attributes provide less obvious list functionality, such as the __add__ attribute, which enables objects to respond to the + operator, and hence to perform their version of list concatenation. There are several other special methods which also need to be defined before a class fully emulates a list, but you can achieve this complete list emulation simply by defining the appropriate Python special method attributes. The next section gives an example which goes further towards implementing a full list emulation class.

20.3 Sample problem 2

The use of __getitem__ is just one of many Python special function attributes which may be defined in a class, to permit instances of that class to display special behavior. To see how this can be carried further, effectively integrating new abilities into Python in a seamless manner, we'll look at another, more comprehensive example.

When lists are used, it's common that any particular list will contain elements of only one type such as a list of strings, or a list of numbers. Some languages, such as C++, have the ability to enforce this. In large programs, this ability to declare a list as being a list of a certain type of element can help track down errors. An attempt to add an element of the wrong type to a typed list will result in an error message, potentially identifying a problem at an earlier stage of program development than would otherwise be the case.

Python doesn't have typed lists built in, but special method attributes make it easy to create a class which behaves just like a typed list. Here is the beginning of just such a class (which makes extensive use of the Python built-in type function, which given an object, returns the type of that object):

```
class TypedList:
    def __init__(self, exampleElement, initialList = []):
        # The "example element" argument defines the type of element this list
        # can contain by providing an example of the type of element.
        self.type = type(exampleElement)
        if type(initialList) != type([]):
            raise TypeError("Second argument of TypedList must "
                            "be a list.")
        for element in initialList:
            if type(element) != self.type:
                raise TypeError("Attempted to add an element of "
                                "incorrect type to a typed list.")
        self.elements = initialList[:]
```

The TypedList class, as defined above, gives us the ability to make a call of the form

```
x = TypedList('Hello', ["List", "of", "strings"])
```

The first argument, 'Hello', isn't incorporated into the resulting data structure at all. It is simply used as an example of the type of element the list must contain (strings, in this case). The second argument is an optional list which can be used to give an initial list of values. The __init__ function for the TypedList class checks that any list elements passed in when a TypedList instance is created are of the same type as the example value given. If there are any type mismatches, an exception will be raised.

This version of the TypedList class can't be used as a list, because it doesn't respond to the standard methods for setting or accessing list elements. To fix this, we need to define the __setitem__ and __getitem__ special method attributes. The __setitem__ method will be called automatically by Python any time a statement of the form `typedListInstance[i] = value` is executed, and the `__getitem__` method will be called any time the expression `typedListInstance[i]` is evaluated to return the value in the *i*th slot of `typedListInstance`. Here is this next version of the TypedList class. Because we'll type-checking a lot of new elements, we've abstracted this function out into the new private method `__check`:

```
class TypedList:
    def __init__(self, exampleElement, initialList = []):
        self.type = type(exampleElement)
        if type(initialList) != type([]):
            raise TypeError("Second argument of TypedList must "
                            "be a list.")
        for element in initialList: self.__check(element)
        self.elements = initialList[:]

    def __check(self, element):
        if type(element) != self.type:
            raise TypeError("Attempted to add an element of "
                            "incorrect type to a typed list.")

    def __setitem__(self, i, element):
        self.__check(element)
        self.elements[i] = element

    def __getitem__(self, i):
        return self.elements[i]
```

Now instances of the TypedList class look more like lists. For example, the following code is valid:

```
>>> x = TypedList("", 5 * [""])
>>> x[2] = "Hello"
>>> x[3] = "There"
>>> print x[2] + ' ' + x[3]
Hello There
>>> a,b,c,d = x
>>> a,b,c,d
⇒   ('', '', 'Hello', 'There'
```

The accesses of elements of x in the `print` statement are handled by `__getitem__`, which simply passes them down to the actual list instance stored in the TypedList object. The assignments to `x[2]` and `x[3]` are handled by `__setitem__`, which checks that the element being assigned into the list is of the appropriate type, and then performs the assignment on the list contained in `self.elements`. The last line will use `__getitem__` to unpack the first four items in x and then pack them into the variables a, b, c, and d respectively. The calls to `__getitem__` and `__setitem__` are made automatically by Python.

Full emulation of lists requires a total of eleven method definitions.

Completion of the TypedList class, so that TypedList objects behave in all respects like list objects, requires several more methods. The special method attributes `__setslice__` and `__getslice__` should be defined so that TypedList instances can handle slice notation. `__add__` should be defined so that list addition (concatenation) can be performed, and `__mul__` should be defined so that list multiplication can be performed. `__len__` should be defined so that calls of `len(typedListInstance)` are evaluated correctly.

__delitem__ and __delslice__ should be defined so that the TypedList class can handle del statements correctly. Also, an append method should be defined so that elements can be appended to TypedList instances using the standard list-style append, and similarly for an insert method.

If you are planning to implement your own list-like structure along the lines demonstrated here, look first at the UserList library module. It may save you some time. There is also a UserDict module available for dictionaries.

20.4 *When to use special method attributes*

As a rule, it's a good idea to be somewhat cautious with the use of special method attributes. Other programmers who need to work with your code may wonder why one sequence-type object responds correctly to standard indexing notation, while another does not.

Use special method attributes cautiously and where appropriate.

My general guidelines are to use special method attributes in one of two situations. First, if I have a frequently used class in my own code which behaves in some respects like a Python built-in type, I will define such special method attributes as useful. This occurs most often with objects that behave like sequences in one way or another. Second, if I have a class that behaves identically or almost identically to a built-in class, I might choose to define all of the appropriate special function attributes and distribute the class. An example of the latter might be lists implemented as balanced trees so that access is slower but insertion is faster than with standard lists.

These aren't hard-and-fast rules. For example, it's often a good idea to define the __str__ special function attribute for a class, so that you can say print *instance* in debugging code and get an informative and nice-looking representation of your object printed to the screen.

C H A P T E R   2 1

Regular expressions

In some sense, regular expressions shouldn't be talked about in this book at all. They are implemented by a single Python module, and are advanced enough that they don't even come as part of the standard library in languages like C or Java. But if you're using Python at all, you're probably doing text parsing, and if you're doing that, then regular expressions are just too useful to be ignored. Perl, Tcl, and UNIX users will be familiar with regular expressions, but other readers may not be, so this chapter will go into them in some detail.

21.1 What is a regular expression?

A regular expression is a string which denotes a pattern of text.

A regular expression (RE) is a way of recognizing and often extracting data from certain patterns of text. An RE which recognizes a piece of text or a string is said to *match* that text or string. An RE is defined by a string in which certain of the characters (the so-called *metacharacters*) can have a special meaning, which enables a single RE to match many different specific strings.

*Regular
expressions can be
used for simple
string searches.*

It's easier to understand this through example than through explanation. Here is a program using a regular expression, which counts how many lines in a text file contain the word "hello". A line which contains "hello" more than once will be counted only once.

```
import re
regexp = re.compile("hello")
count = 0
file = open("textfile", 'r')
for line in file.readlines():
    if regexp.search(line):
        count = count + 1
file.close()
print count
```

The program starts by importing the Python regular expression module, called re. It then takes the text string "hello" as a *textual regular expression*, and compiles it into a *compiled regular expression*, using the re.compile function. This is not strictly necessary, but compiled regular expressions can significantly increase a program's speed, so are almost always used in programs which process large amounts of text.

What can the regular expression compiled from "hello" be used for? Basically, it can be used to recognize other instances of the word "hello" within another string; in other words, it can be used to determine if another string contains "hello" as a substring. This is accomplished by the search method above, which returns true if a line contains a string corresponding to regexp, and false otherwise. Actually, search returns None if the regular expression is not found in the string argument, and Python interprets None as false in a Boolean context. If the regular expression is found in the string, than Python returns a special object, which can be used to determine various things about the match (such as where in the string it occurred). This will be discussed later.

21.2 *Regular expressions with metacharacters*

*Metacharacters
are characters
which have special
meaning in the
context of a regu-
lar expression.*

The example above has a small flaw—it will count how many lines contain "hello", but will ignore lines that contain "Hello" because it doesn't take capitalization into account.

One way to solve this would be to use two regular expressions, one for "hello" and one for "Hello", and test each of these REs against every line. A better way is to use the more advanced features of regular expressions. For the second line in the program above, substitute

```
regexp = re.compile("hello|Hello")
```

This regular expression uses the special vertical bar metacharacter |. A metacharacter is a character in a regular expression which isn't interpreted as itself—it has some special meaning. | means "or," so the regular expression will match "hello" *or* "Hello".

Another way of doing this would be to use

```
regexp = re.compile("(h|H)ello")
```

In addition to using |, this regular expression uses the *parentheses* metacharacters to group things, which in this case means that the | only chooses between a small or capital H. The resulting regular expression will match either an "h" or an "H", followed by "ello".

Another way of performing the match would be

```
regexp = re.compile("[hH]ello")
```

The square bracket metacharacters permit a sequence of characters to be given as potential matches to a single character in the searched text.

The metacharacters [and] take a string of characters between them, and match any single character in that string. There's a special shorthand to denote ranges of characters in [and]; [a-z] will match a single character between a and z, [0-9A-Z] will match any digit or any uppercase character, and so forth. Sometimes you might want to include a real hyphen in the [], in which case put it as the first character to avoid defining a range; [-012] will match a hyphen, or a '0' or a '1' or a '2', and nothing else.

There are quite a few metacharacters available in Python regular expressions, and describing all of the subtleties of using them in regular expressions is beyond the scope of this book. However, a complete list of the metacharacters available in Python regular expressions, as well as descriptions of what they mean, is given in the reference section at the end of this book. For the remainder of this chapter, we'll describe the metacharacters we use as they appear.

21.3   *Regular expressions and raw strings*

The functions which compile REs, or search for matches to REs, understand that certain character sequences in strings have special meanings in the context of regular expressions. For example, RE functions understand that \n represents a newline character. However, if you use normal Python strings as regular expressions, the RE functions will typically never see such special sequences, because many of these sequences also possess a special meaning in normal strings. \n, for example, also means newline in the context of a normal Python string, and so Python will automatically replace the string sequence backslash-n with a newline character, before the RE function ever sees that sequence. The RE function, as a result, will compile strings with embedded newline characters—not with embedded backslash-n sequences.

Backslashea special sequences are used in both regular expressions and normal strings. This can cause strange interactions.

In the case of backslash-n, this makes no difference, because RE functions interpret a newline character as exactly that, and do the expected thing—they attempt to match it with another newline character, in the text being searched. However, let's look at another special sequence, "\\", which represents a *single* backslash to REs. Assume that we wish to search some text for an occurrence of the string "\ten". Since we know that we have to represent a backslash as a double backslash, we might try:

```
regexp = re.compile("\\ten")     # wrong!
```

This will compile without complaining, but it is wrong. The problem is that \\ also means a single backslash in Python strings. So, before re.compile is invoked, Python will interpret the string we typed as meaning \ten, which is what will be passed to re.compile. In the context of regular expressions "\t" means tab so our compiled regular expression will actually search for a tab character, followed by the two characters "en".

To fix this while using regular Python strings, we would need four backslashes. Python interprets the first two backslashes as a special sequence representing a single backslash, and likewise for the second pair of backslashes, resulting in two *actual* backslashes in the Python string. That string is then passed in to re.compile, which interprets the two actual backslashes as a RE special sequence representing a single backslash. Our code would look like this:

```
regexp = re.compile("\\\\ten")
```

That seems confusing, and it is why Python has a way of defining strings, called raw strings.

21.3.1   Raw strings to the rescue

A raw string looks very similar to a normal string, except that it has a leading r character immediately preceding the initial quotation mark of the string. Here are some raw strings:

```
r"Hello"
r"""\tTo be\n\tor not to be"""
r'Goodbye'
r'''12345'''
```

As you can see, you can use raw strings with either the single- or double-quotes quotation marks, and with the regular or triple-quoting convention. You can also use a leading R instead of r if you wish. No matter how you do it, raw string notation can be taken as an instruction to Python, saying *Do not process special sequences in this string*. In the examples above, all of the raw strings are equivalent to their normal string counterparts, except for the second example, in which the "\t" and "\n" sequences are *not* interpreted as tabs or newlines, but are left as two-string character sequences beginning with a backslash.

Raw strings aren't a different type of string. They are a different way of *defining* strings. It's easy to see what is happening by running a few examples interactively:

Raw strings turn off the special meanings of backslashed characters in Python strings. This permits the backslashes to go through to the regular expression functions.

```
>>>
```

```
>>> r"Hello" == "Hello"
⇒ 1
>>> r"\the" == "\the"
⇒ 0
>>> r"\the" == "\\the"
⇒ 1
>>> print r"\the"
\the
>>> print "\the"
    he
```

Using raw strings with regular expressions means that we do not need to worry about any funny interactions between string special sequences and regular expression special sequences. We use the regular expression special sequences. The RE example above then becomes:

```
regexp = re.compile(r"\\ten")
```

which works as expected. The compiled RE will look for a single backslash, followed by the letters "ten".

It is recommended that you get into the habit of using raw strings whenever defining REs, and we will do so for the remainder of this chapter.

21.4 *Extracting matched text from strings*

One of the most common uses of regular expressions is to perform simple pattern-based parsing on text. This is something you should know how to do, and it's also a good way to learn more regular expression metacharacters.

Assume, for example, that we have a list of people and phone numbers in a text file. Each line of the file will look like this:

```
surname, firstname middlename: phonenumber
```

That is, a surname, followed by a comma and space, followed by a first name, followed by a space, followed by a middle name, followed by colon-space, followed by a phone number.

However, just to make things complicated, the middle name may or may not exist, and in addition the phone number may or may not have an area code. It might be 800-123-4567, or it might be just 123-4567. Writing code to explicitly parse data out from such a line is straightforward, but tedious and error-prone. Regular expressions provide a simpler answer.

We'll start by coming up with a regular expression which will match lines of the given form. The next few paragraphs will throw quite a few metacharacters at you. Don't worry if you don't get them all on the first read—as long as you understand the gist of things, that's all right.

Let's take advantage of the fact that first names, surnames, and middle names can all be assumed to consist of just letters and, possibly, a hyphen. The [] metacharacters defined in the section above can be used to define a pattern which will define only name characters:

```
[-a-zA-z]
```

This pattern will match a single hyphen, or a single lowercase letter, or a single upper-case letter.

The + metacharacter indicates one or more repetitions.

To match a full name (like McDonald), we need to repeat this pattern. The + metacharacter repeats whatever comes before it one or more times as necessary to match the string being processed. So, the pattern

```
[-a-zA-Z]+
```

will match a single name, like Kenneth or McDonald or Perkin-Elmer. It will also match some strings that aren't names, like --- or -a-b-c-, but that's all right for our purposes.

The regular expression special sequence \d matches a single

Now, what about the phone number? The special sequence \d matches any digit, and a hyphen outside of [] is just a normal hyphen. So, a good pattern to match the phone number is

```
\d\d\d-\d\d\d-\d\d\d\d
```

That is, three digits, followed by a hyphen, followed by three digits, followed by a hyphen, followed by four digits.

Optional elements of a regular expression are indicated with the metacharacter ?.

This will only match phone numbers with an area code, and our list might contain numbers that don't have one. The best solution is to enclose the area code part of the pattern in (), to group it, and then follow that group with a ? metacharacter, which says that the thing coming immediately before the ? is optional:

```
(\d\d\d-)?\d\d\d-\d\d\d\d
```

The pattern will match a phone number which may or may not contain an area code. We can use the same sort of trick to account for the fact that some of the people in our list have their middle name included, and some don't. (To do this, make the middle name optional using grouping and the ? metacharacter).

Commas, colons, and spaces don't have any special meaning in regular expressions (they just mean themselves), so putting everything together, we come up with a pattern that looks like this:

```
[-a-zA-Z]+, [-a-zA-Z]+( [-a-zA-Z]+)?: (\d\d\d-)?\d\d\d-\d\d\d\d
```

A real pattern would probably be a little bit more complex, because we wouldn't assume that there is exactly one space after the comma, exactly one space after the first and middle names, and exactly one space after the colon. But that's easy to add in later.

The problem is that, while the above pattern will let us check if a line has the anticipated format, we can't extract any data yet. All we can do is write a program like this:

```
import re
regexp = re.compile( r"[-a-zA-Z]+,"         # last name and comma
                     r" [-a-zA-Z]+"          # first name
                     r"( [-a-zA-Z]+)?"       # optional middle name
                     r": (\d\d\d-)?\d\d\d-\d\d\d\d" # colon and phone number
                     )
file = open("textfile", 'r')
for line in file.readlines():
    if regexp.search(line):
        print "Yeah, I found a line with a name and number. So what?"
file.close()
```

Notice that we have split up our regular expression pattern using the fact that Python will implicitly concatenate any set of strings separated by whitespace. As one's pattern grows, this can be a great aid in keeping it maintainable and understandable. It also solves the problem with the line length possibly increasing beyond the right edge of the screen.

Parts of a regular expression grouped with () can be given names.

Fortunately, regular expressions can be used to extract data from patterns, as well as to check to see if the patterns exist. The first part of doing this is to group each subpattern corresponding to a piece of data we wish to extract using the () metacharacters, and then give each subpattern a unique name with the special sequence ?P<*name*>, like:

```
(?P<last>[-a-zA-Z]+), (?P<first>[-a-zA-Z]+)( (?P<middle>([-a-zA-Z]+)))?:
(?P<phone>(\d\d\d-)?\d\d\d-\d\d\d\d)
```

(Please note that the above line should be entered as a single line with no line breaks. Due to space constraints, it could not be represented here in that manner.)

There's an obvious point of confusion here: The question marks in ?P<...>, and the question mark metacharacters that say the middle name and area code are optional, have nothing to do with one another. It's an unfortunate semicoincidence that they happen to be the same character.

The group method for match objects can be used to extract named, matched substrings.

Now that the elements of the pattern have been named, they can be extracted as matches are made, by using the **group** method. This is possible because when the search function returns a successful match, it doesn't just return a truth value, it returns a data structure which records what was matched. A simple program to extract names and phone numbers from our list and print them right out again can be written as follows:

```python
import re
regexp = re.compile(r"(?P<last>[-a-zA-Z]+),"      # last name and comma
        r" (?P<first>[-a-zA-Z]+)"                 # first name
        r"( (?P<middle>([-a-zA-Z]+)))?"           # optional middle name
        r": (?P<phone>(\d\d\d-)?\d\d\d-\d\d\d\d)" # colon and phone number
         )
file = open("textfile", 'r')
for line in file.readlines():
    result = regexp.search(line)
    if result == None:
        print "Oops, I don't think this is a record"
    else:
        lastname = result.group('last')
        firstname = result.group('first')
        middlename = result.group('middle')
        if middlename == None:
            middlename = ""
        phonenumber = result.group('phone')
        print 'Name: ' + firstname + ' ' + middlename + ' ' + \
              lastname + '  Number: ' + phonenumber
file.close()
```

There are some points of interest here:

- We can find out if a match succeeded or didn't by checking the value returned by search. If the value is None, the match failed; otherwise, the match succeeded, and we can extract information from the object returned by search.
  group is used to extract whatever data matched with our named subpatterns. We just pass in the name of the subpattern we are interested in.
- Because the middle subpattern was optional, we can't count on it having a value, even if the match as a whole was successful. If the match succeeded, but the match for the middle name didn't, then using group to access the data associated with the middle subpattern will return the value None.
- Part of the phone number was optional, but part wasn't. If the match succeeded, the phone subpattern must have some associated text, so we don't have to worry about it having a value of None.

21.5 Substituting text with regular expressions

The method sub *for compiled regular expressions can be used to perform string substitution.*

In addition to extracting strings from text, as shown above, Python's regular expression module can be used to find strings in text, and substitute other strings in place of those that were found. This is accomplished using the regular substitution method, sub. The following example replaces instances of "the the" (presumably a typo) with single instances of "the":

```
>>>
```

```
>>> import re
```

```
>>> string = "If the the problem is textual, use the the re module"
>>> pattern = r"the the"
>>> regexp.sub("the", string)
⇒ 'If the problem is textual, use the re module'
```

The sub method uses the invoking regular expression (regexp, in this case) to scan its second argument (string, in the example), and produces a new string by replacing all matching substrings with the value of the first argument ("the", in this example.)

sub can take a function (not just a string) as a first argument, making it very powerful.
However, what if we want to replace the matched substrings with new ones that actually reflect the value of those that matched? This is where the elegance of Python comes into play. The first argument to sub—the replacement substring, "the" in the above example—doesn't have to be a string at all. Instead, it can be a function, and if it is a function, Python calls it with the current match object, and lets that function compute and return a replacement string.

To see this in action, we'll build an example which will take a string containing integer values (i.e., no decimal point or decimal part), and return a string with the same numerical values, but as floating numbers (with a trailing decimal point and zero.)

```
>>>
```

```
>>> import re
>>> string = "1 2 3 4 5"
>>> def intMatchToFloat(matchObj):
        return(matchObj.group('num')
...     + ".0")
...
>>> pattern = r"(?P<num>[0-9]+)"
>>> regexp = re.compile(pattern)
>>> regexp.sub(intMatchToFloat, string)
⇒ '1.0 2.0 3.0 4.0 5.0'
```

In this case, the pattern looks for a number consisting of one or more digits (the [0-9]+ part). However, it is also given a name (the ?P<num>… part) so that the replacement string function can extract any matched substring by referring to that name. The sub method then scans down the argument string "1 2 3 4 5", looking for anything that matches [0-9]+. When sub finds a substring that matches, it makes a match object defining exactly which substring has matched the pattern, and calls the intMatchToFloat function with that match object as the sole argument. intMatchToFloat uses group to extract the matching substring from the match object (by referring to the group name num), and produces a new string by concatenating the matched substring with a ".0". The new string is returned and incorporated as a substring into the overall result by sub. Finally, sub starts scanning again just after the place where it found the last matching substring, and keeps going like that until it can't find any more matching substrings.

21.6 What else can regular expressions do?

I wish I could say I have provided a reasonably comprehensive overview of the regular expression abilities of Python. I haven't, not by a long shot. I've attempted to give a good introduction to the topic, and to give a reasonable description of the most important of the regular expression facilities in Python. However, I've skipped many of the regular expression metacharacters but you can find a complete list in the appendix. I've talked about the `search` and `sub` methods, but omitted many other methods which can be used to split strings, extract more information from match objects, look for the positions of substrings in the main argument string, or precisely control the iteration of a regular expression search over an argument string. I've mentioned the `\d` special sequence, which can be used to indicate a digit character, but there are many other special sequences—they are listed in the appendix. And, I've failed to mention regular expression flags, which can be used to control some of the more esoteric aspects of how extremely sophisticated matches are carried out.

If you do a lot of text processing and searching, I'd strongly suggest learning as much about regular expressions as possible. Start by becoming familiar with the features described in this chapter, and delve into the additional features described in the appendix as you become more comfortable with regular expressions. If you need still more power, go to the main Python documentation for *all* of the details on regular expressions.

In addition to the section on them in the *Python Library Reference Manual* there is an excellent tutorial written by Andrew Kuchling that can be found at the Python web site. Also, the Python String SIG reports contain more links and information.

Advanced topics and applications 4

C H A P T E R   2 2

Python, Windows, and COM

BY ANDY ROBINSON

22.1 Introduction

Python is a scripting language, and is frequently used as glue to connect diverse applications. Windows provides many ways for applications to interact; this chapter will show how Python supports them all.

COM is Microsoft's standard for letting objects in different programming languages communicate. It is built into Windows 95, Windows NT 4.0 and Windows 98 at a very fundamental level, and is an essential part of many applications, including Explorer (which manages the Windows desktop). If you are developing for Windows, you can't and shouldn't ignore it. It is also very elegant and fast, and even die-hard Microsoft-bashers tend to look on it with respect. Python has superb support for COM, thanks to Mark Hammond and the PythonWin package.

All the Microsoft Office applications, as well as many parts of the desktop and operating system, and an increasing number of other applications, expose their brains as COM objects. This means that you can use almost any programming language to create and manipulate these objects.

COM is intimately tied up with the Windows Registry. When Windows 95 came along, the Registry was most commonly explained as a place for applications to store configuration data—a replacement for all those INI files. Actually that function is secondary. The primary function of the Registry is to know what objects are available in the system, and to construct them for you on demand.

In this chapter we will deal both with *server side COM*, where you create Python objects for use by other programs and *client side COM*, where you use Python to get at objects other people have created. We will also try to evolve a coherent approach to building simple, robust systems using COM. Finally, we will also take some time out to look at a selection of the other Windows integration tools available to the Python programmer.

22.2 How to use Python with COM

This chapter will outline a philosophy for building Python applications on Windows, one which lets Python do what Python is good at and Microsoft tools do what they are good at.

There are vast numbers of Windows developers using tools like Visual Basic and Delphi. These are good tools that let you paint your interface with great precision, and are great for building database front-ends or fairly simple applications. There are also a lot of third-party components on the market, although most of these cover user interface development (i.e., new widgets) rather than business logic.

Python is great for building the internal logic of any application. It is superb at manipulating lists and objects. You can write code to define your data structures, manipulate them, and load and save them to a file or over a network, with less effort and fewer lines of code than other languages. There are also vast amounts of public-domain or freely reusable code in Python to solve networking and algorithmic problems. However, some people feel that it lacks somewhat for user interface development. By using something like Visual Basic (or Delphi, PowerBuilder, etc.) with Python and COM, you can get the best of both worlds.

So, let's assume you are a developer, or part of a team, that is getting the job done using a set of tools you know well. Sheer love of Python is not a good enough justification to include another tool. When might you want to reach for Python? The rest of this book is full of reasons, but I will mention four:

- *Serialization*
  Any Python object or data structure can be saved to disk in one line, and reloaded in another one, using the cPickle module. Serialization is also the key to sending objects over a network, or storing them in databases. In VB, Delphi, or C++, you would have to write the code to serialize objects yourself, and change this code whenever you change an object. With Python, the same line of code always does the job.

- *Macros*

  When you need to let the user write macros, you need an interpreted scripting language, and there is no way around it. Don't start writing a new macro language yourself.

- *Expression evaluation*

  You may need to evaluate user-specified formulae (for example, 2*H + 4*B + 2*T with certain values of H, B, and T). You can write your own math parser or just pass Python the data and function to evaluate directly. With the latter you can offer a wider range of functions. This can be extended to user-coded business rules, such as a tax calculation formula that varies from country to country.

- *Data manipulation*

  Python works natively with lists, and a set of data from a database is simply a list of lists. You can acquire data via flat files, from ODBC databases, from each database vendors' own database API, or from ftp, http, Word, Excel, or other operating systems. Convert it as needed and output it back to any of these sources. This will need very few lines of code, as you don't need to worry about declaring array sizes or whether each datum is a string or a number. So if you need to grab data from source *A*, perform some operation on it, and send it to destination *B*, Python will be the easiest way to do it and it will support most future data sources you are likely to come across as well.

This chapter will help you with two main scenarios:

- You are building existing software in something like VB, but have come across a problem which can be solved much faster in Python. You need a quick and easy way to integrate Python with the host language.
- You want to build an advanced business application in Python, which could be multi-platform or distributed across a network, but put a totally standard Windows interface on top of it.

Let's imagine we're building an enterprise-wide accounting system. Here's what we can achieve, quite easily, with Python and VB:

- A basic Python class stores the accounting data objects and logic; this could run on any platform. This can be implemented far faster in Python than in other languages.
- A wrapper around this makes it available as a COM server on Windows.
- Whatever the structure of the data manipulated by the program, the same half-a-dozen lines of code will load and save that data.
- Users get a completely Windows-conformat interface to view and manipulate the data.
- Power users can call up a Python prompt and interactively query and manipulate the data on a command line.
- Users can write their own macros to extend the system, for example: custom validation rules for adding and editing transactions, views for analyzing the data, or batch processing rules for ultrarapid input into a grid.
- Python's extensive networking capabilities let us distribute the application across a network.
- We can easily output the data into Word or Excel by scripting them through COM.

- The extensive Python CGI libraries could also be used to easily produce a web site with monthly updates of all the management accounts.

So, that's the vision. On to the details.

22.3 Installation and setup

This section covers setting up Python for use with COM. Rather than having a nonstand-ard version of Python around, one first installs the basic Python language, then installs PythonWin (a bundle of Python extensions for use with Windows) as an extension on top of this.

At http://www.Python.org/windows/, do the following:

- Get Python. Run the EXE install file to install. The default installation directory is `C:\Program Files\Python`. Installation of Python is covered elsewhere in the book.
- Get PythonWin off the same page—the file is `win32all.exe`—and run it. It installs into the Python tree above. Note that it contains useful COM documentation in the `win32com\HTML` subdirectory.
- While you are at it, get the file ftp.Python.org/pub/Python/Pythonwin/oadist.exe and run it. This is a bug fix from Microsoft, also available on its web site. Some parts of COM were broken in the first releases of Windows 95. If you have NT Service Pack 3, Windows 98, or Internet Explorer 4, you probably don't need it. If it asks, don't let it overwrite any newer files, just update older ones.

That should be all you need to do on the Python side. If there is a problem, it will likely become apparent when you run your first COM server; a troubleshooting section comes later in this chapter.

On the client side, you'll need a language. If you have Visual Basic 4 or 5, you are in business. If you have Delphi, you should be able to translate the client code pretty easily. If you have neither, a copy of Microsoft Office will do, as it contains a fully-fledged Visual Basic editor. People have also done lots of work with PowerBuilder and Visual C++, and just about every language vendor has by now added COM support.

If you plan to use Office as a client, I strongly recommend re-running Office Setup and ensuring that the Visual Basic for Applications (VBA) Help files for Excel and Word are installed. These will tell you what objects and methods are available.

22.4 Anatomy of a Python COM server

This section describes a standard template for laying out a simple Python COM server and registering it. This is basically boilerplate code that you can modify for your own applications.

22.4.1 Importing the Python COM Modules

Your module should start with the following `import` statements. You usually need only the first two, which cover utilities and exception handling. `win32com.client.dynamic` handles client-side COM, but we'll want it in testing, so it is included also.

```
from win32com.server.exception import COMException
import win32com.server.util
import win32com.client.dynamic
```

22.4.2 Setting up the Python COM server class

Begin defining the Python COM server class. This is a normal Python class defined within
your module, but with Python attributes which have a special meaning to the COM modules you previously imported. Below is how you might start off defining a Python COM
server class.

```
# ...Previous part of the module comes here—usually just the import statements above...

class DemoServer:
    _reg_clsid_ = "{864C87C0-DCB8-11D0-A30E-444553540000}"
    _reg_desc_ = "PythonComExample DemoServer"
    _reg_progid_ = "PythonComExample.DemoServer"
    _reg_class_spec_ = "ar_com_servers.DemoServer"
    _public_methods_ = ['DoubleIt', 'AskMeAQuestion']
    _readonly_attrs_ = ['author']
```

These special attributes have the following meanings within COM:

- _reg_clsid_ is a globally unique ID used to identify your class in the Windows
  registry. To create one of these IDs, enter the following in a console, and copy the
  resulting GUID into your code. It only needs to be done once (while coding), and
  ensures that your class gets the same ID on every machine it runs on in the world.
  This is important in case you need to connect to a COM server on another machine.

```
>>>

>>> import Pythoncom
>>>print Pythoncom.CreateGuid()
⇒{864C87C0-DCB8-11D0-A30E-444553540000}
```

- _reg_desc_ is a description of the program, that is, a text string that might be read
  by a user or programmer.
- _reg_progid_ is the phrase clients will use to construct your class later, made up of
  an application name and a class name.
- _reg_class_spec_ tells Python how to create the object later on. The first part of
  this string is the name of the Python module containing the server, and the last part is
  the name of the Python class to create, with the two parts of the string separated by a
  period.
- _public_methods_ is a list of names of methods which can be called from Visual
  Basic (or whatever other application might be using COM to access our Python
  server). This is required, and omitting it can actually crash Visual Basic!
- _public_attrs_ is optional (and is not used in the example above). If defined, it is
  a list of attribute names which are accessible (i.e., readable and writable) to COM.
- _readonly_attrs_ is similar to _public_attrs_, but if defined, it contains a list
  of attribute names to which COM should have read-only access.

There are also a few other optional attributes to do with version numbering and unregistering, all covered in the PythonWin documentation.

22.4.3 Writing server class methods

Once the server class has been properly set up, we can define methods for the class, as we would normally do for any other Python application. Continuing on with the class definition above:

```
def __init__(self):
    self.author = 'Andy Robinson'

def DoubleIt(self, num):
    return num * 2

def AskMeAQuestion(self, str):
    return "The answer is 42"
```

COM client applications will be able to call these methods directly later on.

22.4.4 Registering the Python server class with COM

Before using our Python server class, we need to register it with the Windows Registry, which is used by COM to figure out how to respond to calls. A client program wishing to use our class will ask Windows itself to give it an object called a `PythonComExample.DemoServer`. At this point, Windows searches the Registry, finds the class entry, and uses that information to make the appropriate calls. So, no Registry entry, no COM.

Functions to register and unregister a Python server class follow. They can be copied into your own code, changing only the bolded text to reflect the name of your server class. Note that these are top-level functions within the server module, and not class methods. Of course, defining the functions doesn't execute them. We'll see in our script a bit later how they are executed so as to register (or unregister) our Python server.

```
def Register():
    import win32com.server.register
    win32com.server.register.UseCommandLine(DemoServer)

def UnRegister():
    from win32com.server.register import UnregisterServer
    UnregisterServer(DemoServer()._reg_clsid_)
    print "DemoServer Class unregistered."
```

22.4.5 Test code

Following are two test functions we'll include in our demo Python COM module.

```
def TestDirect():
    ds = DemoServer()
    if ds.DoubleIt(2)==4:
        print 'passed direct test'

def TestCOM():
    try:
```

```
        ds = win32com.client.dynamic.Dispatch(
            "PythonComExample.DemoServer")
        print 'DemoServer class created from COM'
    except:
        print "**** - The PythonComExample.DemoServer is not " \
            "available"
        return
    if ds.DoubleIt(2)==4:
        print 'passed COM test'
```

The second test uses client-side COM—exactly the same technique we will use to remote control Excel later on in this chapter—to create and test the server. In other words, it is doing the same thing a Visual Basic client would do. This is a good way of checking that all of the public methods work and are described properly. However, it cannot test whether the module being tested is on the Python path, as you have already imported that module manually. If your module passes the tests, but VB clients fail to create your object, check where you have put your code module.

Including a bit of test code like this isn't a requirement, but is probably a good idea, as an aid to tracking down which of the many things that might go wrong.

22.4.6   Creating a module body

We'll end the Python COM server module with a short bit of executable Python code, that is, code that actually performs some actions if the module is executed, rather than just defining classes or functions. If this were a standard Python module, such code would probably be unnecessary, and even undesirable. This code will *not* be executed when the module is imported, which is the normal method of using a Python module. However, including such code also lets us execute the module to register or unregister it from COM, and to perform a module self-test. As with most of the above, this is basically boilerplate code you can copy to your own module, and modify as desired.

```
if __name__=='__main__':
    import sys
    if "/unreg" in sys.argv:
        UnRegister()
    elif "/test" in sys.argv:
        print "doing direct tests..."
        TestDirect()
        print "testing COM"
        TestCOM()
    else:
        Register()
```

This final script handler gives us three options. With no command-line flags, the script will register the server (so you can just double-click on the file in Explorer to register the server). It also recognizes command-line flags "/unreg" to unregister the server, and "/test" to test the logic of the module.

22.4.7 The Python COM server template as a whole

Now that you know what is in the template code, you can adapt the details easily for new classes without worrying too much about why it works. To save time, we'll repeat the entire template in one place here. Parts of the template you need to change to reflect your own application are shown in bold (but, of course, you can change much more than just the bolded parts, if you wish):

```
# generic Python COM server template

# import statements
from win32com.server.exception import COMException
import win32com.server.util
import win32com.client.dynamic

class DemoServer:
    # COM-specific special attributes.
    _reg_clsid_ = "{864C87C0-DCB8-11D0-A30E-444553540000}"
    _reg_desc_ = "PythonComExample DemoServer"
    _reg_progid_ = "PythonComExample.DemoServer"
    _reg_class_spec_ = "ar_com_servers.DemoServer"
    _public_methods_ = ['DoubleIt', 'AskMeAQuestion']
    # You can use a _public_attrs_ list also.
    _readonly_attrs_ = ['author']

    # Class methods.
    def __init__(self):
        self.author = 'Andy Robinson'

    def DoubleIt(self, num):
        return num * 2

    def AskMeAQuestion(self, str):
        return "The answer is 42"

# Registration and unregistration functions—note that these are not methods!
def Register():
    import win32com.server.register
    win32com.server.register.UseCommandLine(DemoServer)

def UnRegister():
    from win32com.server.register import UnregisterServer
    UnregisterServer(DemoServer()._reg_clsid_)
    print "DemoServer Class unregistered."

# Testing code—these are functions, not methods of the server class.
def TestDirect():
    ds = DemoServer()
    if ds.DoubleIt(2)==4:
        print 'passed direct test'

def TestCOM():
    try:
        ds = win32com.client.dynamic.Dispatch(
            "PythonComExample.DemoServer")
        print 'DemoServer class created from COM'
```

```
    except:
        print "**** - The PythonComExample.DemoServer is not " \
            "available"
        return
    if ds.DoubleIt(2)==4:
        print 'passed COM test'

# This code is executed whenever the module is executed; it can be used to register, unregister,
# or test the module.
if __name__=='__main__':
    import sys
    if "/unreg" in sys.argv:
        UnRegister()
    elif "/test" in sys.argv:
        print "doing direct tests..."
        TestDirect()
        print "testing COM"
        TestCOM()
    else:
        Register()
```

22.5 Creating and using the server from Visual Basic

Now the fun can begin. We'll build a basic client to talk to our server. Then we'll add methods at the back end and show how to use them at the front end. We'll start with simple numbers and strings, and build up to passing complex objects back and forth.

This is all you need in your VB application to create a server:

```
Dim DemoSrv as Variant
Set DemoSrv = CreateObject("PythonComExample.DemoServer")
```

In a production application, you will want to make the variable DemoSrv global, initialize it when the application starts, and put some error-trapping around it. In your first attempt, put the above code under a button; then you can check that the VB application has started satisfactorily before creating the class.

Experience has shown that if you are going to have any trouble at all, it will occur at this point; if so, refer to the troubleshooting section below.

Quite a lot happens behind the scenes when you execute this code. Here is a rough description:

- Windows looks in the Registry for a class called PythonComExample.DemoServer.
- Information in the registry tells it to start PythonCom. To see how this works, search the Registry for keys matching your GUID; it should find this under HKCR\CLSID\{your class id}. You will find keys called 'InProcServer32' and 'LocalServer32' specifying the location of the Pythoncom DLL and executable.
- PythonCom looks at the attribute _reg_class_spec_. The first part of the string in _reg_class_spec_ is the name of the Python module to import (ar_com_servers.py, which must be on the Python path).

- It looks in that module for a class matching the last half of the name in `_reg_class_spec`, and creates an object of that class for you.

This explains why you have to be very careful about spelling and file locations for it to work. However, once it does work, it keeps on working very reliably.

22.5.1 Troubleshooting the server

The most common PythonWin errors occur when the client fails to create an object of the required class, that is, on the `CreateObject` command above. If you get **Run-time error 80004005**, it means that the COM framework cannot create the class you have asked for. There are four common causes of this:

- COM is not properly installed on your machine. Refer back to the installation section above and run OADIST.EXE.
- Some earlier builds of PythonWin had trouble creating COM servers, but from build 105, this was fixed. Make sure you have an up-to-date build. You should also get Python 1.5.1 or later, which fixed some bugs in Python 1.5.
- Your server is not yet registered.
- The Python script containing the server class is not on the Python path.

22.5.2 Using the server

Figure 22.1 is a simple Visual Basic client up and running, using the example server in the previous section.

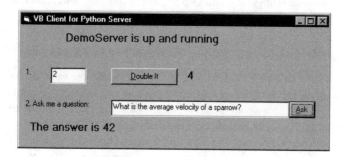

Figure 22.1   A VB client

This is a one-form application painted using Visual Basic's interface design tools. And here is the VB code to implement it (minus error trapping):

```
Option Explicit
Public Server As Object

Private Sub Form_Load()
    Set Server = CreateObject("PythonComExample.DemoServer")
    lblServerStatus.Caption = "DemoServer is up and running"
End Sub
```

```
Private Sub cmdAsk_Click()
    lblAskAnswer.Caption = Server.AskMeAQuestion(txtAsk.Text)
End Sub

Private Sub cmdDoubleIt_Click()
    lblDoubleResult.Caption = \
        Server.DoubleIt(Val(txtDoubleInput.Text))
End Sub
```

As you can see, we can directly call the methods of the server without any trouble.

22.5.3 Server shutdown

The PythonCOM engine and your class will be freed automatically when your client application shuts down. For the sake of tidiness, you can do `Set DemoSrv = Nothing` at the end of the client program if you wish. You can trap this event by providing a standard special Python method called `__del__` in your server class definition to do something useful, like save application data:

```
def __del__(self):
    "do something when freed"
    from time import time, gmtime, asctime
    f = open('C:\\temp\\ServerKilled.txt ','a')
    f.write('DemoServer shut down at' + asctime(gmtime(time())))
    f.write('\n')
    f.close()
```

It is probably a good practice to explicitly control your application's shutdown with a save or shutdown method, which you can call from the client. Don't rely on `__del__` working in the event of a crash.

22.6 *Passing data in and out of the server*

Now we'll add a number of methods to our server, and look at both the client and server-side code needed to manipulate all the basic data types. In each case, the methods must be referred to in the list of `_public_methods_`.

One warning: use a fixed number of arguments for your COM-accessible methods. Python methods with default arguments or variable-length argument lists cannot be called via COM at present.

22.6.1 Numbers

PythonCOM automatically converts numbers between the appropriate types in Visual Basic and Python. You can declare them as `Integer` or `Double` at the Visual Basic end, if you know what you expect to get back, or as `Variant` if you don't.

Visual Basic	Python
Dim x as Integer X = DemoSrv.DoubleIt(2)	Def DoubleIt(self, number): return 2 * number

22.6.2 Strings

Strings are almost as easy.

Visual Basic	Python

Dim S as String
S = DemoSrv.Repeat("Hello")
	def Repeat(self, word):
	    # note use of 'str()'
	    return 2 * str(word)

The only hitch is when passing in a string as an argument. COM uses Unicode strings. These use two bytes per character, and can handle languages like Japanese, with thousands of different characters. A Unicode string will be represented at a Python console with a letter *L* in front, like this: `L'Hello'`. To convert these to ordinary strings, use the Python `str` function on any string arguments to your methods, as above. Calling `str` on an ordinary string returns the same string.

22.6.3 Retrieving lists

If you are creating a server, you'll probably want to retrieve data from it. Here we fetch a list of items, and put it into a VB `ListBox`. Python sends a list, and Visual Basic gets a Variant Array. Unless you are very sure what the server will return, you should loop over this using a `Variant` for each item. As in Python, any element could be a string, integer, or float.

Visual Basic	Python

Dim pyList As Variant, item As Variant
 	
List1.Clear
PyList = Server.GetList
For Each item In pyList
List1.AddItem item
Next item
	def GetList(self):
	    # return mixed strings & numbers
	    return ['heading'] + range(10)

22.6.4 Passing in lists

The `Array` function in VB will create arrays which can be passed as an argument to Python. Again, these can contain any combination of strings, integers, and floating point numbers:

Visual Basic	Python
MyList = Array(1,2,3, "Spam") Server.Reverse(MyList)	def Reverse(self, list): result = list.reverse()

22.6.5 Retrieving tabular data

Now let's imagine that we want to get back a big table with rows and columns of data. This will be a list of tuples in Python with, for example, account names down the side, months across the top, and balances in the various cells. Assume that the table is known to be rectangular (i.e., each tuple has the same number of items), but that we don't know how many rows or columns are present. I have added a method called GetFinancials to the server to create the data you can see on the right (figure 22.2). (GetFinancials simply returns a list of Python tuples. For an abbreviated version of the list used to construct the screenshot below, see "Using Excel as a client" later in this chapter.) As you can see from the VB example code, extracting out the data from the returned Python data structure is a simple affair.

Visual Basic	Python

Dim MyTable As Variant
Dim Rows As Integer, Cols As Integer
Dim x As Integer, y As Integer
 	
MyTable = Server.GetFinancials
Rows = UBound(MyTable, 1) 'the first dimension
Cols = UBound(MyTable, 2) 'the second dimension
MSFlexGrid1.Rows = Rows
MSFlexGrid1.Cols = Cols
 	
For y = 0 To Rows – 1
  For x = 0 To Cols – 1
    MSFlexGrid1.Row = y
    MSFlexGrid1.Col = x
    MSFlexGrid1.Text = MyTable(y, x)
  Next x
Next y
	def GetFinancials(self):
	  # returns a list of tuples of
	  # numbers and strings
	  # eg.:
	  # return [(1, "Hello"), (2, "G'bye"), ...]

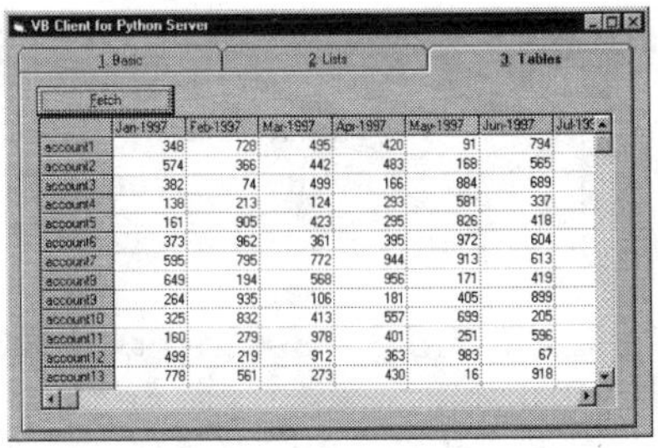

Figure 22.2 Comparing tabular data

22.6.6 More about variant arrays

As we have seen, Python lists and tuples come back to COM and Visual Basic as variant arrays. C programmers will know these as safe arrays, and they are a fundamental part of COM. They are safe because they have extra information to describe their dimensions; ordinary C arrays allow programmers to access the 101st element of a 100-element array. (Note that using this meaning, *all* Python arrays are safe). The file OLEAUTO32.DLL contains lots of functions called SafeArray*X* for manipulating safe arrays.

Some notes are in order on using these from VB. (In *Visual Basic Online Help*, look up VarType to see more on this). The following Visual Basic debug session, done with the Python list ['heading', 0,1,2,3,4,5,6,7,8,9], will illuminate a few things:

```
? pyList(0)
heading
? lbound(pyList), ubound(pyList)
 0        10
```

```
? VarType(pyList), VarType(pyList(0))
 8204     8
```

We have already seen a "for each item in array"-type loop. As you can see from the above, elements in variant arrays can also be accessed by index. The functions `lbound` and `ubound` tell you what dimensions the array has.

The `VarType` function tells you what kind of object it is. `8204` is `vbArray + vbVari-ant`, which means an array of variants. `8` is simply `vbVariant`.

If you have a list of lists, you can ask for two dimensions by calling `ubound(MyTable, 1)`, which gives the size of the outermost list, and `ubound(MyTable, 2)` for the innermost ones (which your code should ensure are all of the same length). Sadly, Visual Basic does not seem to provide a function for finding out how many dimensions are present.

22.6.7   Odd-shaped lists

Safe arrays can represent an array of known dimensions (e.g. 3×4×5 = 60 elements), but are not appropriate for more flexible list structures like `[1,2,3,[4,5,[6]]]`. A detailed description of how these structures are handled would require studying the PythonCom source. What seems to happen in the above case is that you get an array of four elements, and the fourth element is another array, and so on. However, if you started with the list `[[1,2],3]`, it would try to create a two-dimensional array, and get confused.

A useful approach is to loop over each item in a variant array asking for its type. If a list item is type `8204` (array of variants) as above, grab that and loop over it. You can easily write a recursive VariantToString function which builds up a string looking like `[1,2,3,[4,5,6],7]` when the equivalent list is passed in by Python.

22.6.8   Passing objects

We can also pass Python objects around. Imagine a basic employee management system. We need to add, edit, and delete employees. First we'll define and register another server class, in the same module as before. This acts just as a packet of data, but it could be more complex.

```
class Employee:
    _reg_clsid_ = "{DAFFCF40-24A4-11D2-BCC8-0040333B49A4}"
    _reg_desc_ = "PythonComExample Employee"
    _reg_progid_ = "PythonComExample.Employee"
    _reg_class_spec_ = "ar_com_servers.Employee"
    _public_methods_ = []
    _public_attrs_ = ['name','salary']

    def __init__(self):
        self.name = '<new employee>'
        self.salary = 0
```

Now we will add to our server. We'll give it an empty list to hold Employee objects when it is initialized, and provide the following methods to manipulate them:

```
# basic data management
def AddEmployee(self, ComEmp):
    PyEmp = win32com.server.util.unwrap(ComEmp)
    self.employees.append(PyEmp)
```

```
    def GetEmployee(self, idx):
        return win32com.server.util.wrap(self.employees[idx])

    def DeleteEmployee(self, idx):
        del self.employees[idx]

    def CountEmployees(self):
        return len(self.employees)

    def ReportEmployees(self):
        reportList = []
        for emp in self.employees:
            reportList.append(emp.name + ': ' + str(emp.salary))
        return reportList
```

The only difference between this and standard Python object passing is that we need to wrap the object in a COM wrapper when giving it out, and unwrap it when it comes back, as shown by the bits of the code in bold.

Now, in Visual Basic, we can create employees and add them like this:

```
Private Sub cmdAddEmp_Click()
  Dim Emp As Object

  Set Emp = CreateObject("PythonComExample.Employee")
  Emp.Name = txtName.Text
  Emp.Salary = Val(txtSalary.Text)
  Server.AddEmployee Emp
End Sub
```

The only hitch with this ultrasimple example is that the employee's name is in Unicode. This might be appropriate—perhaps you have Japanese employees and want to use the correct characters on Japanese Windows—but otherwise it would be better to put a SetName method in the server, which can then convert the name to an ordinary string by calling str.

22.7 Callbacks

Callbacks provide a way of letting the Python server control elements of the user interface. For example, you might want to draw on a Visual Basic form (figure 22.3). This is not too difficult.

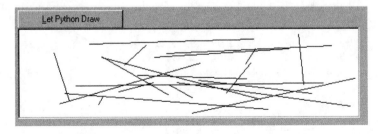

Figure 22.3 Drawing on a VB form

Almost any object in Visual Basic (including forms and the standard controls) is a COM object, so Python can call its methods and set its properties. To achieve the results in figure 22.3, I did the following:

Visual Basic	Python

Public Sub DrawLine(x1, y1, x2, y2)
  Picture1.Line (x1, y1)-(x2, y2)
End Sub
	def DrawOn(self, vbForm):
	  from random import random
	  pyForm = win32com.client.dynamic.Dispatch(vbForm)
	  for i in range(20):
	    x1 = int(random() * 200)

Private Sub cmdLetPythonDraw_Click()
  Server.DrawOn Me
End Sub
	y1 = int(random() * 200)
	    x2 = int(random() * 200)
	    y2 = int(random() * 200)
	    pyForm.DrawLine(x1,y1,x2,y2)

The magic line is `pyForm = win32com.client.dynamic.Dispatch(vbForm)`. When you pass a VB object as an argument to a Python method, Python gets a fairly minimal pointer that cannot do much. `Dispatch` puts a wrapper around it allowing all of its methods to be called, and properties set, from Python

A more useful approach would be to give the Python server an instance variable called `CallBackForm`, and set it up earlier in the program. Python would then have a number of methods with which it could work. It would be easy to redirect Python's standard output to, say, an edit control or list box.

22.8 *Using Excel as a client*

This is an interesting example, as many more people have a copy of Excel handy than have a full copy of Visual Basic. However, and more importantly, Excel is a very good front end for all kinds of applications. If you are working with scientific or engineering data, it is a much more useful output destination than a stack of paper, or a custom application. The same techniques apply equally well to using Word as a client, but naturally you would use it for different types of applications.

Assume our company has lots of financial data available to its managers via a COM server. To simulate this, I have added a function to the DemoServer which generates a table of Python data. By table, I mean a list of tuples, all of the same length, like this:

```
[
('', 'Jan-1997', 'Feb-1997', .....'Dec-1997', 'Total')
('account1', 576, 205, .....547, 5434)
('account2', 902, 365, ....., 678, 7691)
  .
  .
  .
('account20', 611, ....., 151, 4575)
]
```

This is a natural way to organize tabular data in Python, and is the format in which database queries are usually returned. Calling `DemoSrv.GetFinancials()` will return a block of data, by default, 14 columns and 21 rows, which is a reasonable screenful.

22.8.1 Setting up an Excel workbook with a server

Now we want to get this into Excel. First of all, we will create an Excel workbook with a VBA module to create the COM server when the book opens (figure 22.4). Do the following:

- Create an Excel workbook, name it, and save it.
- Choose Tools - Macro - Visual Basic Editor.
- Choose Insert - Module from the menu, name it, and save it (I called mine PythonClient).
- Drop down the right combo box and select Open event, or just copy the code below.

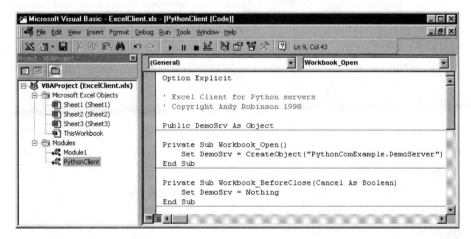

Figure 22.4 Excel's Visual Basic Editor

When you return to Excel and open the spreadsheet, it will automatically start up a COM server which can be accessed through the variable `DemoSrv`. For tidiness's sake, I wrote code to release the variable `DemoSrv` when the workbook is closed, although that should happen automatically.

One more tip when developing in Excel's editor: any time you modify your Excel code, it may reset the program and empty the `DemoSrv` variable. It is worth adding a button on the sheet which can restart the COM server without having to close and reopen the sheet.

22.8.2 Fetching data

Now that we have our server open, let's fetch data. I placed a button near the top of a sheet called Fetch Financials. Double-click in design mode to create an event handler, and enter this code:

```
Private Sub cmdFetchFinancials_Click()
    'push array data out
```

```
    Dim mystuff As Variant
    mystuff = DemoSrv.GetFinancials
    Worksheets("Sheet2").Range("C7:p27").Value = mystuff
End Sub
```

The result will look similar to figure 22.5.

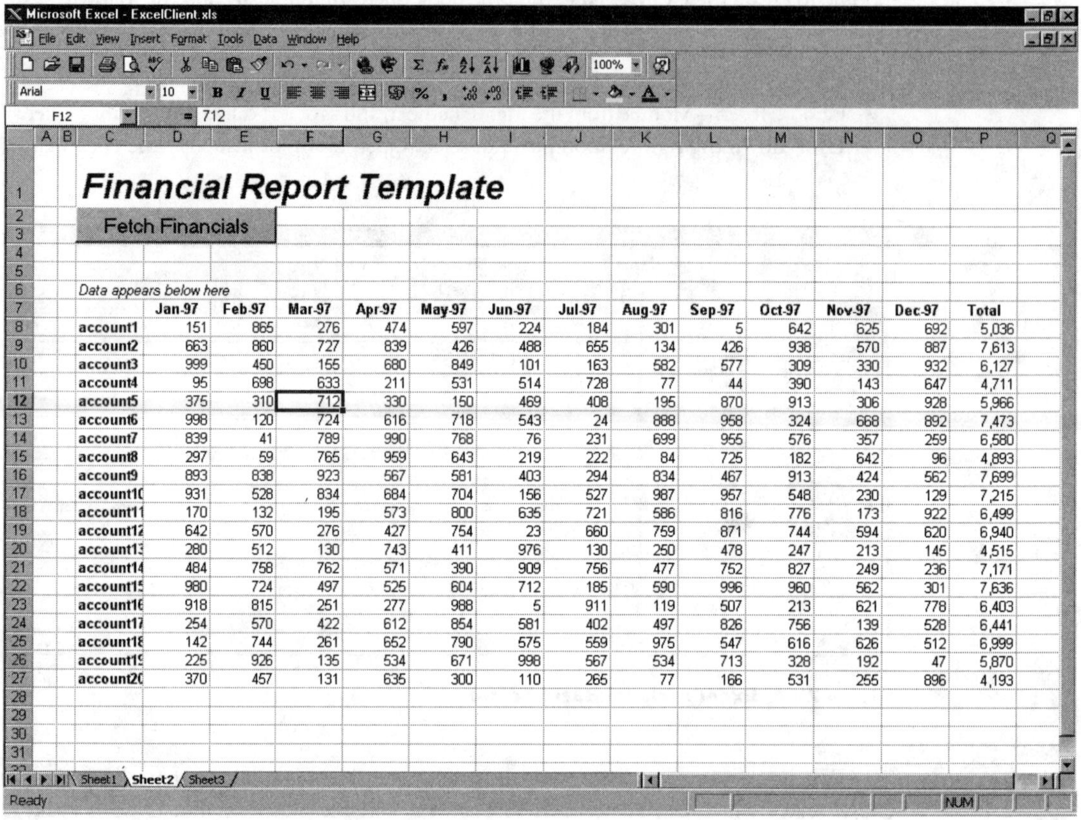

	Jan-97	Feb-97	Mar-97	Apr-97	May-97	Jun-97	Jul-97	Aug-97	Sep-97	Oct-97	Nov-97	Dec-97	Total
account1	151	865	276	474	597	224	184	301	5	642	625	692	5,036
account2	663	860	727	839	426	488	655	134	426	938	570	887	7,613
account3	999	450	155	680	849	101	163	582	577	309	330	932	6,127
account4	95	698	633	211	531	514	728	77	44	390	143	647	4,711
account5	375	310	712	330	150	469	408	195	870	913	306	928	5,966
account6	998	120	724	616	718	543	24	888	958	324	668	892	7,473
account7	839	41	789	990	768	76	231	699	955	576	357	259	6,580
account8	297	59	765	959	643	219	222	84	725	182	642	96	4,893
account9	893	838	923	567	581	403	294	834	467	913	424	562	7,699
account10	931	528	834	684	704	156	527	987	957	548	230	129	7,215
account11	170	132	195	573	800	635	721	586	816	776	173	922	6,499
account12	642	570	276	427	754	23	660	759	871	744	594	620	6,940
account13	280	512	130	743	411	976	130	250	478	247	213	145	4,515
account14	484	758	762	571	390	909	756	477	752	827	249	236	7,171
account15	980	724	497	525	604	712	185	590	996	960	562	301	7,636
account16	918	815	251	277	988	5	911	119	507	213	621	778	6,403
account17	254	570	422	612	854	581	402	497	826	756	139	528	6,441
account18	142	744	261	652	790	575	559	975	547	616	626	512	6,999
account19	225	926	135	534	671	998	567	534	713	328	192	47	5,870
account20	370	457	131	635	300	110	265	77	166	531	255	896	4,193

Figure 22.5 A simple spreadsheet

Yes, it really is that simple. I cheated a bit. I formatted the worksheet first to make the title rows bold, and assumed I knew how much data would come back. I had imagined I would need to loop over the return data poking it into cells, as I did with the VB client; but PythonCOM does it all for you. The PythonCOM framework converts your lists to variant arrays, which happen to be the correct binary format used by Excel arrays.

Performance is always an issue, and I did a spot of benchmarking by rearranging the `GetFinancials` method to return sixty months and 100 accounts. On a Pentium 75, it took 1.002 seconds to generate 6,000 pieces of random data, put them all into a table, and transfer it to Excel. I then separated the code to generate the data from the actual transfer.

It took about one second to generate the random result set, and the transfer into Excel was less than a millisecond, too fast to time using standard VB techniques. In other words, COM is a *very* fast way to shift data around, and Excel is a very fast way to capture it.

22.8.3 What next?

To input data from Excel into a COM server, there are a couple of strategies. Excel has a forms designer which can be used to create modal dialogs. Alternatively, one can designate a number of cells for input data, and add a button to, say, take the data in these cells and push it into the server.

There is a lot more to be done. We would presumably end up with a toolkit of helper functions in VBA to grab Python data of various types and put it into Excel. If we know the size of the output, we can preformat Excel to give us attractive output, and charts based on it. Otherwise we will have a little VBA programming to do.

The key point to remember is to use Excel's strengths rather than trying to do it all in Python. It would be very laborious to write Python scripts to create a spreadsheet, format it, and insert charts in all the right places. Instead, one can design an Excel template that gets the right information across in the right way, and pulls the information it wants into the spreadsheet from a COM server. Changes and improvements to the Excel output can often be made by users without needing any server-side programming.

22.9 *Distributed COM*

So, we have written a server, but all it really does is mix Visual Basic user interface code with a Python engine. By default, the server runs *in process*, which means that Python and your server run in the process space of the Visual Basic executable. This is known as an *in process server*.

COM is capable of doing two rather more clever tricks. Your Python code can be made to run as a *local server* (a separate process on the same machine) or a *remote server* (a different machine anywhere on the Internet) without changing a single line of code.

Space prevents me from covering this here, but it is well covered in the documentation for COM. It is basically a matter of making the right registry entries, so that the client app asks COM to connect to a remote machine and fire up a copy of your Python COM server there. COM takes care of the marshaling, that is, packing up the arguments and sending them over the network.

Although there is little or no programming to do, some configuration is necessary. If you want to pursue this, look up DCOM on http://www.microsoft.com, or read any of the numerous books on DCOM.

22.10 *Client side COM—automating Office*

This section shows the other side of the coin, which is arguably better known: using Python to script Office applications. We'll just show a group of snippets of code which carry out common tasks to get you started.

22.10.1 Fetching data from Access

The following example shows us connecting to an Access database with Python, and fetching a group of records. Executing this script, or typing it in interactively, will produce something similar to the given output, assuming, of course, that you have Access and a suitable database set up.

```
from win32com.client.dynamic import Dispatch
dbEngine = Dispatch('DAO.DBEngine')
db = dbEngine.OpenDatabase('C:\\Database\\Recept.mdb')
db = dbEngine.OpenDatabase('C:\\Database\\Recept.mdb')
MyQueryString = "SELECT MemberID, FirstName, Surname FROM Members " \
                "ORDER BY MemberID"
MyRecordset = db.OpenRecordset(MyQueryString)
MyRecordset.MoveFirst()
FieldCount = MyRecordset.Fields.Count
while not MyRecordset.EOF:
row = []
for i in range(FieldCount):
    MyFieldValue = MyRecordset.Fields(i).Value
    row.append(MyFieldValue)
print row
MyRecordset.MoveNext()    #move to next record
```

On my system, the above code produced the following output:

```
[1, 'Andy', 'ARGUILE']
[2, 'Paul', 'ARGULE']
[3, 'Jon', 'ARGYLL']
```

In this example, we have written a loop over all the rows and fields of the record set. This could be optimized enormously by (a) using makepy and (b) knowing in advance which fields one wants to access and structuring the code accordingly.

The ODBC module provides a more versatile and database-independent way of getting at data from Python that is not specific to access.

22.10.2 Update an Access record

There are two ways to do this. First, we'll use SQL from Python:

```
MyDatabase.Execute("UPDATE Members SET FirstName = 'John' " \
                   "WHERE FirstName = 'Jon'")
```

Working with SQL is very pleasant in Python, as you can use triple-quoted strings, the format operator, and other features to build big SQL strings quickly and easily. Access actually has a full SQL Data Definition Language, so you can easily write long SQL scripts to generate complete databases in Python.

Secondly we can use the DAO library directly, as in the following bit of code:

```
MyRecordset.MoveFirst()
MyRecordset.Edit()
MyRecordset.Fields('Surname').Value = 'Robinson'
MyRecordset.Update()
```

Using the method `AddNew` instead of `Edit` would have created a record. Note also that we can refer to fields by name or by position.

22.10.3 Start Excel from Python, push in some data

As we have seen when using Excel as a client, one can directly assign Python lists to an Excel range to get lots of data in quickly. Even better, you can start Excel automatically before you do this:

```
xlApp = Dispatch("Excel.Application")
xlApp.WorkBooks.Add()
xlApp.Range('A1:C1').Value = ['January','February','March']
```

Everything else is a matter of learning the Excel object model.

22.10.4 Start Word, push in some data

This starts Word 8 (the one in Office 97) from Python, creates a blank document, and inserts text. Previous versions of Office had a very different object model.

```
Word = Dispatch("Word.Application")
Word.Visible = 1
WordDoc = Word.Documents.Add()
WordRange = WordDoc.Range()
WordRange.InsertAfter('Python was here')
```

In the real world, you would probably want to create a document from a template, insert text at specific points or in specific styles, and save or print it. All of these are simple to achieve and involve learning your way around the Word object model, rather than complex programming.

22.11 Type libraries

In the previous examples, we have used the function `win32com.client.dynamic.Dispatch` to create our COM servers. This creates a `Dispatch` object to communicate with the servers. When one calls a method of a `Dispatch` object, it basically sends a string off and tries to find a method of a corresponding name. In the Word example, when we called `WordRange.InsertAfter('Python was here')`, we would only find out if there was a valid method called `InsertAfter` when the method was called. This late binding is slow to run and error-prone.

COM also specifies a format for *type libraries*, which allow you to find out the correct methods at compile time. In a compiled language, this would give you the addresses of the correct functions to call in each interface. This is much faster and can eliminate numerous errors. If you have used the drop-down auto-completion in Visual Basic 5, you'll appreciate how useful type libraries can be.

PythonWin provides the Makepy utility to get at type libraries. This is well-documented and almost totally transparent to users. To access Word with early binding, we would do the following:

On the PythonWin menu, select COM makepy utility. The window in figure 22.6 appears.

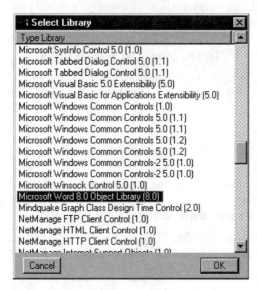

Figure 22.6 Selecting a library

Select the object library you want, and click OK. Pythonwin will build a wrapper using the type library, and save it in a special directory. In the future, whenever you wish to use Word, you simply use

```
win32com.client.Dispatch('Word.Application')
```

...rather than...

```
win32com.client.dynamic.Dispatch('Word.Application')
```

...and you'll get a much faster early-bound wrapper around Word.

Behind the scenes, makepy has actually built the source code for a group of Python classes which wrap up all the functionality in the Word library, and this is what you use.

It is unnecessary for a user, but you can actually look at these files. They live in `C:\Program Files\Python\win32com\gen_py`, although they have somewhat cryptic names. If you don't have the Help files available for your type library, a glance through these will tell you what objects and methods are available.

22.12 *Guidelines*

Writing the kind of code discussed in this chapter has a lot to do with learning the object model of each relevant application. It also soon becomes obvious that you are repeating yourself a great deal. You will probably want to write some helper modules to wrap up this functionality. For example, I wrote a crude module to wrap up Access which went like this:

```
Import axsaxs    #"Access Access"– get it?
Db = axsaxs.Accessor('c:\data\pubs.mdb')
```

```
# Dataset is a list of tuples
Dataset = Db.fetch('SELECT ISBN, Title FROM Titles')
```

If you are using Excel or Word, it is probably because you want their output capabilities. Your best approach is to write a reusable Python object to represent the kind of document you are working on, and give it methods for common tasks; for example, adding a paragraph to Word with a named style.

It is tempting to try to do everything in Python, but this neglects the full power of Office. You should get as far as you can by designing document or spreadsheet templates with most of the design elements you want, and then use the minimum code you can get away with to pump in your data.

There are stability concerns with both Excel and Word. Several people have been using client-side Python to create huge reports, with many thousands of COM calls in quick succession, or passing in 1 MB RTF strings, and they report that the applications tend to hang. These applications were designed for interactive use rather than remote control, so keep it simple.

For reporting, one can also easily adopt a pull model, where a Word or Excel template contains formatting and the VB code to start a Python COM server and pull in the data.

22.13   Other goodies

Here we present a small sample of the many other things Python can do on Windows.

22.13.1   Windows Scripting Host

You can find out about this at http://msdn.microsoft.com/scripting.

If you have Win98, it is installed already; otherwise, it is a small free download. The Windows Scripting Host lets you run scripts in any language including Python. It also provides some very handy COM objects to do things like attach network drives, find out who the current user is, create desktop icons, and so on.

Assuming you have installed both PythonWin and Windows Scripting Host, go to Explorer and double-click on the script

```
C:\Program Files\Python\win32comext\client\pyscript.py
```

This registers everthing necessary. Then go to

```
C:\Program Files\Python\win32comext\client\demos\client\wsh
```

and double-click on any file ending in .pys. Associate it with the application wscript.exe, the Microsoft application that runs scripts.

You can now write any Python script you want, save it ending in PYS, and it will have access to the magical WScript object.

The following example uses Python to create shortcuts to Notepad on the Desktop and Start Menu:

```
# Get at the Shell object, which knows how to make shortcuts.
WSHShell = WScript.CreateObject("WScript.Shell")

# Put a shortcut to Notepad on the desktop.
```

```
DesktopPath = WSHShell.SpecialFolders("Desktop")
MyShortcut = WSHShell.CreateShortcut(
    DesktopPath + "\\A shortcut to notepad.lnk")
MyShortcut.TargetPath =
WSHShell.ExpandEnvironmentStrings("%windir%\\notepad.exe")
MyShortcut.WorkingDirectory =
WSHShell.ExpandEnvironmentStrings("%windir%")
MyShortcut.WindowStyle = 4
MyShortcut.IconLocation =
WSHShell.ExpandEnvironmentStrings("%windir%\\notepad.exe, 0")
MyShortcut.Save()

# Now put a shortcut to Notepad in the start menu.
StartMenuPath = WSHShell.SpecialFolders("StartMenu")
MyShortcut = WSHShell.CreateShortcut(
    StartMenuPath + "\\Another
    shortcut to notepad.lnk")
MyShortcut.TargetPath =
WSHShell.ExpandEnvironmentStrings("%windir%\\notepad.exe")
MyShortcut.WorkingDirectory =
WSHShell.ExpandEnvironmentStrings("%windir%")
MyShortcut.WindowStyle = 4
MyShortcut.IconLocation =
WSHShell.ExpandEnvironmentStrings("%windir%\\notepad.exe, 0")
MyShortcut.Save()

WScript.Echo("Shortcuts created")
```

The `WScript` object lets you get at lots of other useful objects such as network drives, users, groups, and security information.

22.13.2 ODBC

Open Database Connectivity is a Microsoft standard API for database access. It allows you to connect to virtually any database in the world, as long as the correct drivers are available on your system.

It is quite easy to write Python extension modules which wrap up DLLs and allow Python to access them, and the extension which handles ODBC is part of the standard PythonWin distribution. Data comes back as a list of tuples. This little script

```
import dbi, odbc
MyConnection = odbc.odbc('RECEPT')
MyCursor = MyConnection.cursor()
MyCursor.execute('SELECT FirstName, Surname FROM Members')
print MyCursor.fetchall()
```

produces (on my system)

```
[('Andy', 'ARGUILE'), ('Paul', 'ARGULE'), ('John', 'ARGYLL')]
```

Note that in line one we first imported the `dbi` module. This is something worked out by the Python database special interest group to provide a standard Python API for database access. odbc.py uses `dbi`, but it is not alone.

22.13.3 MFC wrappers

PythonWin itself contains modules which wrap up Microsoft Foundation Classes (MFCs). You can write a complete Windows application in Python, and the PythonWin GUI is one such example. If you know MFC well, you should have few problems.

22.13.4 Other Windows API wrappers

Mark Hammond has been steadily wrapping up just about every Windows API you could imagine. These are documented in the PythonWin help files. A quick glance through the directory `C:\program files\Python\win3`' reveals the following modules (as of Build 109):

```
dbi, dde, mapi, mmapfile, odbc, perfmon, timer, win32api,
win32event, win32evtlog, win32file, win32lz, win32net, win32pdh,
win32pipe, win32print, win32ras, win32security, win32service,
win32trace
```

Anyone accustomed to calling Windows API functions should have a good idea what areas the above items cover.

22.13.5 Call any DLL

Sam Rushing's `calldll` is an extension module which lets you import *any* Windows DLL and call the functions it exports, from within Python. `calldll` also provides a few basic tools to help handle things like pointers and string buffers.

Sam has now written complete Windows applications with callbacks and event loops in Python, proving that there are no limitations to what Python can do on this platform.

22.14 *Sources of information*

Microsoft's COM documentation can be found at http://www.microsoft.com/com/. The full COM specification is available to download, and is far more readable than many of the doorstoppers available from bookshops.

For examples of client-side COM scripts, look in `C:\Program Files\Python\win32com\test`. This has test functions for each office application, Exchange, Outlook, Netscape, marshaling, OLE Structured Storage, and many other useful examples.

Python for Windows, and PythonWin, are available at
http://www.Python.org/windows/.

Examples for much of the material covered in this chapter, with examples for other languages as well, are available from the author's web site at http://www.roba-nal.demon.co.uk/, and there is also a link from the Python for Windows page above. The site also includes examples of other client languages such as Delphi and PowerBuilder.

Mark Hammond's Starship page has the very latest builds of PythonWin and a lot more useful information: http://www.Python.org/crew/mhammond/.

Sam Rushing's site at http://www.nightmare.com covers low-level Windows magic in Python. If you are used to programming Windows applications in C, this should be right up your alley and shows that there are no limits at all.

There is a web site devoted to Windows Scripting, at http://cwashington.netreach.net/. This includes WSH, VBScript, and Python, and has plenty of scripts for system administration. VB and Javascript scripts are easily translatable to Python, since they use exactly the same COM objects and methods.

The PDF Library is at http://www.ifconnection.de/~tm/software/pdflib/index.html. The latest version includes sample Python client software. At the time of this writing it is necessary to compile it for each platform, but a compiled Python DLL will probably be out before this is in print.

Finally, DejaNews (http://www.dejanews.com) archives the comp.lang.Python discussion group. Most issues that you come across have been discussed (and often solved) there already.

C H A P T E R   2 3

Extending Python with C and C++

Python is easily extended with C or C++, which is one of the things that makes the language suitable for large projects. You can implement a project using Python and then simply rewrite computationally intensive parts of the application as a C or C++ extension to Python. You can also take existing C/C++ code libraries you already have, and put them in a Python wrapper to make them available as an extension. Typically, this will not involve a great deal of work.

23.1 Using this chapter

The intent in this chapter is to get you to the point where you are able to write and compile extremely simple Python extensions, so that you have a solid starting point. Then, it will be up to you to read the Python documentation on the subject, experiment, and when necessary, ask questions of the Python newsgroup.

This approach is based on my own experience, which has indicated to me that the hard part of being a Python extension writer is simply getting started. While I'm quite comfortable with C and C++, Python does some things with function pointers which puzzled me for a while. Also, extensions are usually dynamically loadable modules, and while many programmers are familiar with the details of these, many others are not. When I first approached extensions, I started learning a lot more about compilation and linkage than I needed to, because I thought I had to do all this by hand. As it turns out, scripts included with the Python distribution make this entirely unnecessary. You can write Python extensions without learning *anything* exotic, which means that if you are comfortable with C or C++, you are already most of the way to being a proficient Python extension writer.

23.2 Compilation details

This section gives an overview of some of the issues you will face when you begin to compile your C code. Details vary by platform, and, accordingly, the final reference for the compilation process has to be the example extension and accompanying source code that comes with the Python source distribution.

23.2.1 Which compiler?

Standard compilers (gcc on UNIX—MS C on Windows) work fine.

Python extensions are typically compiled with GNU C on UNIX systems, and with Microsoft C on Windows systems. GNU C is available for the Windows environment, but I have been told that one can run into trouble using it to compile DLLs (Python extensions are on Windows) due to some low-level binary code format issues. The general advice seems to be to stick with Windows-specific compilers when compiling under Windows.

23.2.2 Shared versus static extensions

You can implement Python extensions as either static or shared extensions. A *static* extension is one which is statically linked to the Python executable; in order to get it working, you need to recompile the entire Python core system, with your code included. A *shared* extension is one which can be dynamically loaded by Python as needed; its object code exists as a separate file (in UNIX, as a shared library; in Windows as a DLL file), and the use of a shared extension does not require any recompilation of the Python core.

Extensions are normally compiled as shared (dynamically loadable) object files.

Clearly, shared extensions are preferable in almost all cases, except a specialized Python binary you might wish to distribute as a single unit. In the past, some systems did not support shared object files, but such systems are exceedingly rare these days. Accordingly, we will assume for this chapter that you are compiling a shared, dynamically loadable extension. The material covered in this chapter is, for the most part, correct regardless of whether you are compiling a static or shared extension, the differences being in the compilation process and *not* in the code you write.

23.2.3 Compilation details for your system

In order to compile extensions for Python under your system, you will need the Python source distribution as well as the binary distribution. This is available on the Python home page. You will also receive an extension module example, a small demonstration C exten-

*Compiling exten-
sions requires the
source (not just
the binary)
Python
distribution.*

sion, along with supporting files and documentation. This is your primary reference for the details of how to compile extensions on your platform. Using the compilation tools Python has provided will make your life much simpler.

- If you are working on a Microsoft Windows system, then everything is together in the same directory for you. As of the current Python distribution, the directory is Python-1.5.2/Pc/example_nt, which contains documentation files and configuration and code files.
- If you are working on a UNIX system, the directory is Python-1.5.2/Demo/extend. This contains a short readme file, and various UNIX scripts which can be used to make static or shared extensions, or to clean up after making an extension. These scripts are written assuming the name of the module you are creating is "xx". You will need to change names in the scripts to suit the name of your module, a simple modification. The Python-1.5.1/Demo/extend directory does not contain a sample C extension; copy the example from the Python-1.5.1/Pc/example_nt directory if you wish to test the scripts out on known good code.

You probably won't be comfortable using the UNIX compilation scripts unless you have at least a passing familiarity with UNIX shell scripting and the *make* utility, something beyond the scope of this book. If you know how to program C on UNIX, you almost certainly have all the requisite knowledge.

23.3 A first example

We'll start off with a module called `example1` which does nothing more than reimplement two integer arithmetic operations, addition and multiplication. In spite of its simplicity, this module will illustrate almost everything you need to know to begin writing your own Python extension modules.

First, here is the C code for this extension:

```
#include "Python.h"
```

/* The following C function 'example1_add' will implement the Python function 'example1.add', i.e. the 'add' function in our 'example1' extension module. */

```
static PyObject * example1_add(PyObject *self, PyObject *args) {
```

```
    int m, n;        /* Variables to hold the two numbers to be added. */
```

/* Attempt to parse the tuple containing the argument list as two integers; if parsed successfully, the values of these integers will be placed into the C integer variables referenced by '&m' and '&n'. The standard Python-in-C function 'PyArg_ParseTuple' is used to attempt the parse; the string "ii" tells it to attempt to parse the argument tuple as two integers (each 'i' indicates a single integer.)

If the parse is unsuccessful, PyArg_ParseTuple will place an exception message into a standard global variable xxx, and return NULL to indicate failure. */

```
    if (!PyArg_ParseTuple(args, "ii", &m, &n)) {
        return NULL;
    }
```

```
/* Now, add the two integers, build them into a Python integer object, and return that object.
The string "i" indicates the type of the Python object being built. */

    return Py_BuildValue("i", m+n);
}
```

/* The comments for example1_add also apply to example1_multiply, for the most part, except that, of course, 'example1_multiply' implements the 'multiply' function in the 'example1' extension. */

```
static PyObject * example1_multiply(PyObject *self, PyObject *args) {
    int m, n;
    if (!PyArg_ParseTuple(args, "ii", &m, &n)) {
        return NULL;
    }
    return Py_BuildValue("i", m*n);
}
```

/* Every Python extension module will have a single static array of 'PythonMethdDef' records, as below. The name of this array is formed by concatenating the name of the module ('example1' in this case), with the string '_methods'. There will be one element in the array for each Python method or function defined in the extension module. This array is how Python knows which of your C functions to call, in response to an invocation of a Python function or method. */

```
static PyMethodDef example1_methods[] = {
```

/* The array entry for 'example1.add' contains the name by which this function or method is known within its module ("add"); a (pointer to) the C function 'example1_add'; the integer 1, which Python understands as indicating a more recent version of argument passing (this third element will always be 1 in your extensions); and finally, a human-readable string giving a one-line description of the function or method.*/

```
    {"add", example1_add, 1,
        "This function adds two integers and returns an integer."},
```

/* The array entry for 'example1.multiply' is similar to that for 'example1.add'. */

```
    {"multiply", example1_multiply, 1,
        "This function multiplies two integers and returns an integer."},
```

/* The last record in this array should always be a pair of NULL values. Python needs this as an end-of-array indicator. */

```
    {NULL, NULL}
};
```

/* Finally, the extension needs a single nonstatic initialization function to be executed when the module is loaded into Python. This initialization function simply calls the 'Py_InitModule' function, with the name of the module and the list of functions and methods contained in the module, as arguments. */

```
void example1_init() {
    Py_InitModule("example1", example1_methods);
}
```

Each Python function or method defined in the module is implemented as a C function, which starts out with a declaration of the form:

```
static PyObject * function_C_name(PyObject *self, PyObject *args) {
```

function_C_name is the name of this function as it is known in the C code, and *not* as it is known in the Python code. The common convention is that if the module is called `modulename` and the Python function/method is called *methodname*, then the C function implementing the Python function/method will be called *modulename_methodname*. Each function/method implementation in C takes two arguments, `self` and `args`.

`self` is used only with C functions which implement Python built-in methods, for example operations such as `has_key` which are invoked via a method invocation syntax such as `obj.has_key(x)`. `self` is not used in the example since in Python, `add` and `multiply` operate as Python functions and not as methods. `args` contains the Python arguments passed in to the Python method or function.

Arguments to the C implementation of the function or method are parsed out of the `args` argument by the function `PyArg_ParseTuple`. `PyArg_ParseTuple` takes two initial arguments, the first being the `args` argument, and the second being a string defining the number and types of arguments expected. If *n* argument is expected, then the string argument contains *n* characters, and each character defines what type of argument is expected at the corresponding position in the `args` tuple. In the example, `'i'` indicates an integer is expected.

If `PyArg_ParseTuple` finds that `args` consists of the desired number and types of arguments, as indicated by the string argument, then it will return a true value, to indicate that the arguments have successfully been parsed; otherwise, it will return a false value.

Your function/method implementation should check the return value from `PyArg_ParseTuple`, and if necessary, return a `NULL` value to indicate a failure in the argument parsing. No further action is required from you in case of a parse failure. The proper mechanisms for generating an exception to report the error are built into the Python libraries.

Assuming that `PyArg_ParseTuple` successfully parses out the values from the `args` argument, the C representations of these values are deposited in the remaining arguments to `PyArg_ParseTuple`. There is one of these remaining arguments for each expected Python argument in `args`, and each of these remaining arguments is a C variable which is passed in by reference so that `PyArg_ParseTuple` may write a value into that variable.

For Python objects which have a direct C representation (such as integers), the value written to the variable will be the C representation of the Python value. For Python objects which have no direct C representations, such as Python lists or long integers, the value written to the variable will be a pointer to the Python object.

Within the C implementation of a Python method/function, the `Py_BuildValue` function can be used to construct a Python object to be returned by your function. `Py_BuildValue` is the converse of `PyArg_ParseTuple`, and its usage is similar to what you might expect. Between using `PyArg_ParseTuple` to parse out the argument, and returning the value constructed by `Py_BuildValue`, your C function can perform whatever C computations it desires.

Each C implementation of a Python function/method must be listed in a single `PyMethodDef` static array:

```
static PyMethodDef modulename_methods[] = {
    {"Python_method_name", function_C_name, 1,
        "documentation string."},
    …more function/method entries…
```

```
        {NULL, NULL}
    }
```

This `PyMethodDef` array is effectively a table of the Python functions and methods the C extension module defines. If you don't list your function/method here, Python won't know about it. A good name for the table is *modulename*`_methods`, where *modulename* is the Python name for your module. Each element of the array defines a Python function or method as a four-element record, with the elements of the record being:

- a string giving the Python name for this function or method
- the pointer to the C implementation of this function/method
- the value 1 which indicates, basically, that you are using a modern version of Python
- a string which will be presented to the user as the one-line description for this Python function or method.

The final element of the `PyMethodDef` array should be a record consisting of {NULL, NULL}, which serves as a delimiter indicating the end of the array.

Your C extension module must contain a single *nonstatic* C function definition, which serves as the module initialization function. This is the *only* nonstatic definition in the module code, and is the function that Python will execute when it loads your C extension, to initialize the module. It should be of the form

```
void modulename_init() {
    Py_InitModule("modulename", modulename_methods);
}
```

All that this function does is call the provided `Py_InitModule` function, which takes the module name and table of module methods, and uses that information to set up the module for use by Python.

Those are the basics of writing C extensions for Python. There are, of course, further points and subtleties, but basically, as the above example illustrates, the structure to follow is largely a matter of starting out with a correct C code template and filling in the blanks.

23.3.1 Putting it into a template

It's easy to construct a template file for use as a standard starting point, when writing C extensions to Python.

You've probably realized that all Python extension modules will start from pretty much the same template. In fact, having an extension template around makes starting a new module a lot easier. Here is a small template you can enter and reuse again and again. Just replace the italicized parts with your own names or strings, and fill in the function and datastructure bodies as needed.

```
#include "Python.h"

/* Define your first Python function/method implementation. */
static PyObject * modulename_method1(PyObject *self, PyObject *args)
{
    /* Define variables to hold C versions of the arguments passed in. */
    sometype carg1, carg2, . . .
    /* Parse out the arguments, using the second string arg of PyArg_ParseTuple to indicate their
    number and type. */
```

```
    if (!PyArg_ParseTuple(args, "??…", &carg1, &carg2, . . .)) {
        return NULL; }
    …Perform your own computations here…

    /* If necessary, build and return an appropriate value.
    return Py_BuildValue("?", var);
}

/* Define your second Python function/method implementation. */
static PyObject * modulename_method1(PyObject *self, PyObject *args)
{
    . . .
}

/* Define more function/method implementations. */
    .
    .
    .

/* Define the required listing of methods. */
static PyMethodDef modulename_methods[] = {
    {"method1", modulename_method1, 1,
        "This function blah blah blah…"},
    {"method2", modulename_method2, 1,
        "This function yada yada yads…"},
    .
    .

    /* The last record in this array should always be a pair of NULL values. */
    {NULL, NULL}
};

/* Finally, define the module initialization function. */
void modulename_init() {
    Py_InitModule("modulename", modulename_methods);
}
```

23.4 *Memory management*

The obvious place to start in learning how to manage memory in Python extensions is *Extending and Embedding the Python Interpreter*, by Guido van Rossum, available on http://www.python.org. Guido wrote this as a concise introduction to writing and using C with Python, and gives a more comprehensive treatment of memory management than I do here. However, for both treatments, you'll want to be at least somewhat familiar with what the idea of garbage-collecting memory management actually is.

23.4.1 The need for memory management

There are some points to writing C extensions that were not discussed in the example above. The most important of these is the issue of memory management, correctly allocating and de-allocating blocks of memory to meet the needs of your code.

When you are coding in Python, memory management is not an issue, because Python itself takes care of all memory allocation and de-allocation needs. Like Perl and many other scripting languages, Python does this through a reference-counting garbage collection scheme where each object occupying memory contains a "counter" which holds the number of times that the object is referenced by other data structures. When the counter drops to zero, it means that the object is no longer referenced by any other data structures, and hence can never again be accessed or used by your program. At that point the object can safely be deleted, and the memory it occupied will be freed for reuse. As a Python programmer, you needn't worry about any of this, because the updating and monitoring of the reference counters for objects, and the allocation and de-allocation of memory, are all done automatically by Python.

This scenario is different when you are writing a C extension to Python. In addition to performing standard memory allocation/de-allocation as required by your own internal computations, you must also help out Python's memory management by correctly modifying the reference counts of Python objects you deal with. The Python C library provides functions to help you with managing reference counts, but your own code must call them when references to Python objects are created or destroyed. If you do not call these helper functions appropriately, your extensions may suffer from memory leaks. More rarely, it may suffer from premature de-allocation of memory, which is likely to cause unpredictable crashes.

You are not responsible for explicit calls to allocate and de-allocate memory used by Python objects; this is still handled by the Python routines. As a C extension programmer, your job is simply to see that object reference counts are incremented and decremented as necessary.

23.4.2   A basic example

We will illustrate the basics of memory management with another small Python extension module called `double`. It will contain a single function, `makelist`. `double.makelist` takes a single Python object as argument, and returns a two-element Python list, with each consisting of a reference to the object passed in as an argument. As a result, the number of references to the argument object is greater after `double.makelist` executes (there are two new references to the argument object in the list we return), and our C code must increment the reference counter for the argument object to reflect this. Here is the code:

```
#include "Python.h"

static PyObject * double_makelist(PyObject *self, PyObject *args) {
    PyObject *argument, *list;
    /* Parse out the single argument as a (C pointer to) a Python object. */
    if (!PyArg_ParseTuple(args, "O", &argument)) {
        return NULL;
    }
    /* Create a new two-element list. */
    list = PyList_New(2);
    /* Set the first element of the new list to point to the argument passed to this function.
    This means a new (nontemporary) reference to the argument has been created,
     so increment its reference count. */
    PyList_SetItem(list, 0, argument);
```

```
        Py_INCREF(argument);
        /* Set the second element of the new list to point to the function argument,
        and increment the reference count of the argument again. */
        PyList_SetItem(list, 1, argument);
        Py_INCREF(argument)
        /* Build and return the new list. */
        return Py_BuildValue("O", list);
}

static PyMethodDef double_methods[] = {
    {"makelist", double_makelist, 1,
        "Returns a list of two references to the argument."},
    {NULL, NULL}
};

void double_init() {
    Py_InitModule("double", double_methods);
}
```

This C extension follows the structure of the previous example, though it is simpler because it defines only one function. The highlighted lines illustrate where it becomes necessary to perform some explicit reference count management. As references to the argument object are inserted into the new Python list object, the reference count for the `argument` object must be incremented, to reflect the fact that another Python data structure now holds references to that `argument` object. Reference counts are usually incremented through use of the `Py_INCREF` C macro, as in the code above.

An object's reference count needs to be incremented whenever your code creates a persistent reference to the object.

Note that the reference count for an object needs to be manipulated only to reflect references which are nontemporary, in that the effect of the reference change is visible outside of our own C function body. For example, `argument` itself is a new reference to the object it points to. But we do not call `Py_INCREF` after using `PyArg_ParseTuple` to obtain the value in `argument` because the `argument` variable is purely local to our `double_makelist` function, and will disappear as soon as the function terminates. Thus, `argument` is a temporary reference to the argument object and rather than putting a `Py_INCREF(argument)` at the beginning of `double_makelist` and then a complementary `Py_DECREF(argument)` right at the end, to decrement the reference count reflecting the loss of a reference to the object, we simply omit both of these calls.

Putting them in wouldn't cause any problems but your function would simply run a little slower.

You'll note that we don't call `Py_INCREF` on objects built with `Py_BuildValue`, in the examples above. That is simply because `Py_BuildValue` assumes that we wouldn't want to build an object unless we were going to have a reference to it, so the reference count of the newly constructed object is automatically set to 1. If, at some point in the future an invocation of `Py_DECREF` causes the reference count of that object to fall to zero, that object will be garbage-collected, and the memory it occupies will be freed for reuse. For the same reason, the list created in the previous example by `PyList_New` does not have an explicitly associated `Py_INCREF`.

23.4.3 When are reference counts decremented?

Just as a reference count should be incremented whenever your program creates a reference to an object, your code should also ensure that it decrements the appropriate reference whenever it removes a reference to an object.

23.4.4 Reference counting is a tricky business

Managing reference counts is by far the most difficult part of writing Python extensions in C. The concepts aren't difficult, but you can run into some very subtle problems. The best advice is to keep your code simple and obvious. Don't worry about making it compact at the expense of simplicity, at least not until you have a good deal of experience with the details of memory management in Python extensions.

23.5 Writing extensions in C++

Even though this chapter is all about writing Python extensions in C or C++, we haven't yet said anything about C++. The truth is, there's not a lot to say at the moment.

Python is written in C, and is very comfortable with C. It wasn't written with C++ in mind, and doesn't function well with pure C++ files. If you prefer C++ for all of your coding, the simple solution is to use the extern C directive around your C++ code, to make it look like C code. Guido Van Rossum, the originator of Python, has produced a booklet, *Extending and Embedding the Python Interpreter*, available on the Python website, which covers this.

The bright horizon to this is CXX, which is being developed to use the power of C++ with Python. *CXX* developers also intend it to use the constructor/destructor facilities of C++ to automatically handle much or most of the reference count management which must be done by hand in C extensions to Python.

23.6 Where to go from here

Now that you have a couple of simple toy extension modules up and running, the next step is to go to the Python home site and download *Extending and Embedding the Python Interpreter* and *the Python/C API Reference Manual*. These will give you what you need to begin writing real extension modules. After that, it is a matter of experimentation and asking questions on the Python newsgroup if something doesn't work the way you thought it would.

C H A P T E R   2 4

Integration with the Java Virtual Machine: JPython

BY GUIDO VAN ROSSUM AND KIRBY W. ANGELL

24.1 What is JPython?

JPython is a version of Python which compiles to Java Virtual Machine Code.

JPython code can be mixed freely with Java code, to produce a single compiled executable.

JPython is a version of Python which works with and in Java. It is not merely a Python interface which calls Java; rather it is a Python compiler which, instead of compiling Python code to Python-bytecode, compiles Python code to Java-bytecode, or, more correctly, to Java Virtual Machine (JVM) bytecode.

To you, the programmer, this means you can freely mix Python and Java code in your program, obtaining the benefits of the rapid development of Python, and the higher speed and access to powerful user-interface libraries of Java. Your program will compile to standard JVM code, and will execute on any machine with a Java run time environment. No special setup or libraries are necessary on the target machine.

24.2 Prologue: the false hope for a single language

Every once in a while a new, general programming language receives broad acceptance. A natural response, especially when the language receives as much media attention as Java, is to hope that in the future, all programs will be written in this one language.

This has never happened. Remember PL/1? Or C++? But we keep hoping, in the belief that there's progress in the field of programming language design. The high cost of learning several different languages, each useful for only a fraction of the spectrum of programming tasks, makes managers and programmers alike hope that this next language is The One.

Maybe we're wrong. Maybe there will never be a single language covering the whole programming spectrum. After all, that spectrum covers such diverse activities as finding cheap airline tickets, predicting the weather, and producing 3-D animations of giant lizards, not to mention more mundane activities, such as formatting expense reports or spell checking documents.

We may modify our expectations, hoping that in the future a single programmer will never have to learn more than one language. In our world of super specialists, the task areas are likely to be disjointed anyway. If you're a game programmer in the future, you will use the 3-D real-time language. If you're drilling for oil, you'll use the geological analysis language. If you're writing a data-entry tool, the GUI definition language will be all you ever need

I have a different vision. I'm not so naïve as to believe that we could all be renaissance programmers, capable of writing any kind of program. But I believe strongly that the tasks of most programmers are so diverse that a single language doesn't cut it.

The designers of UNIX knew this. They built two languages into their system right from the start; C as the system programming language to write applications and tools, and the shell for scripting. Lately, more powerful languages like Python, Tcl, and Perl are replacing the shell, but the principle remains the same.

Microsoft knows it. It offers developers C++ and Visual Basic, and many applications are written in a mixture of the two. For example, VB programs have easy access to controls written in C++.

John Ousterhout, the father of the scripting language Tcl, knows it. Several ideas here are taken from his paper *Scripting: Higher Level Programming for the 21st Century*.

In general, we see more and more successful applications written in a combination of system programming and scripting languages. The two complement each other nicely, so that for a typical subtask, it will be clear which language to use. Adding a scripting language also makes it possible to provide much more flexible customization of an application.

The most commonly used general scripting languages are Visual Basic, Perl, Tcl, and Python. So far JavaScript has found few applications outside Web browsers. It is interesting to see which scripting languages are used the most in conjunction with which system programming languages and on which platforms. VB is clearly the scripting language of choice for C++ on Windows; it is platform-specific and cannot easily fulfill the same role on other platforms. Perl and Tcl are used most often with C on UNIX platforms.

Python is traditionally used with C and C++, but is less focused on UNIX than Perl or Tcl. Python has a large following on Windows, and is exceptionally well integrated with COM and the Microsoft Scripting Host architecture on that platform. (It is said to be sec-

24.2.1 So, what about Java?

Java has the elements (and productivity) of a traditional systems language.

I classify Java as a system programming language, not a scripting language. While it is interpreted, much of the JVM's architecture is very similar to a typical modern CPU, a stack containing untyped 32-bit words, pointers, the works.

Java is mostly statically typed, requiring declarations of all variables. The highest-level data type supported directly by the language is a string. While this is an improvement over C++, it's a far cry from the built-in hash tables and flex arrays that make scripting languages so pleasant to use.

Java does not offer the productivity of good scripting languages.

A typical Java program will be a bit shorter than a C++ program that solves the same problem. This has relevance for development time: At best, a Java programmer is perhaps twice as productive as a C++ programmer, a far cry from the productivity factors of 5 to 10 observed over and over for real scripting languages.

If Java is a system programming language, it needs a companion scripting language. My argument here is that Python is an ideal choice as Java's scripting companion.

24.3 JPython, the killer scripting language

Python is a good match for Java because it's object-oriented from the ground up. Contrast this with Perl, where OO was grafted in version 5, or Tcl, where OO is only available as an extension iTcl.

JPython is a great complement to Java.

But it's more than just a good match. The killer reason for choosing Python as Java's scripting companion is JPython, a Python interpreter written in 100 percent pure Java. Using JPython, you can write applets in Python that will run in any JDK-1.1 compliant Web browser. JPython executes Python code at a reasonable speed, about half the speed of "regular" Python, which is still quite fast enough for many, and since JVMs are becoming faster still, there's even hope that JPython will eventually overtake standard Python in speed.

Other scripting complements to Java do not compile to JVM code.

JPython obtains its remarkable speed by translating Python source code directly into Java bytecode. This is in contrast to Jacl, a 100 percent Java reimplementation of Tcl. Jacl is an actual interpreter written in Java, and as such, is much slower. Other Java scripting solutions, available for Tcl (Tcl Blend) and Perl (JPL), are not 100 percent pure Java: they attach a JVM to the C implementation of Tcl or Perl. This obviously creates portability problems; in order to use either Tcl Blend or JPL on a particular platform, you need to find a Tcl or Perl implementation and a JVM that will talk to each other. JPython, on the other hand, needs only a JVM.

Calling Java code from JPython code, or JPython code from Java code, is easy.

JPython's integration between Java and Python is remarkably seamless. A Python script can import any Java class that's accessible on the class path. Python can call static and instance methods of Java classes, create instances, and even create subclasses of Java classes. Instances of those subclasses can be passed back to Java, and their methods implemented in Python can be called by Java code.

Here's a JPython applet displaying the string "Hello world":

```
from java.applet import Applet
```

```
class HelloWorld(Applet);
  def paint(self, gc);
    gc.drawString("Hello world", 02, 30)

if __name__== '__main__';
  import pawt
  Pawt.test(HelloWorld())
```

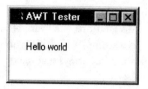

This tiny program (figure 24.1) demonstrates many of JPython's key features: it runs in any (JDK-1.1-compliant) browser, it imports a Java class and creates a subclass of it, and its `paint` method will be invoked by the Java code of the AWT event loop.

Figure 24.1 JPython's Hello world

Here's a somewhat larger example; an applet that implements a simple but functional calculator (figure 24.2).

Figure 24.2 A calculator

```
from java import awt
from pawt import swing

labels = ['7', '8', '9', '+',
    '4', '5', '6', '-',
    '1', '2', '3', '*',
    '0', '.', '=', '/' ]
keys = swing.JPanel(awt.GridLayout(4, 4))
display = swing.JTextField()

# Callback for regular keys
def push(event):
    display.replaceSelection(event.actionCommand)

# Callback for '=' key
def enter(event):
    display.text = str(eval(display.text))
    display.selectAll()

for label in labels:
    key = swing.JButton(label)
    if label == '=':
        key.actionPerformed = enter
    else:
```

```
        key.actionPerformed = push
    keys.add(key)

panel = swing.JPanel(awt.BorderLayout())
panel.add("North", display)
panel.add("Center", keys)
swing.test(panel)
```

Readers familiar with Java code will appreciate the conciseness of these examples, compared to code that accomplishes the equivalent in Java.

Notice in particular the use of `eval` in the `enter` callback. The built-in Python function `eval` takes a string representing an arbitrary Python expression, compiles it into Java bytecode, executes it, and returns the resulting value. This is a standard feature of scripting languages, which is absent in typical system programming languages, including Java; the Java run time doesn't typically have the Java compiler around.

24.4 *Downloading and installing JPython*

If you have the Java run-time environment installed, installing JPython is a snap. In fact, the only real requirement to run JPython is that you have an acceptable JVM. You can download JPython from http://www.jpython.org. JPython is distributed as a single Java class file. Once you have downloaded it, `java -cp . JPython1` should begin the InstallShield wizard for JPython.

This should work 99 percent of the time; there are of course always exceptions. If you are using the Microsoft Java Virtual machine, `jview -cp . JPython11` may work instead. If using `jview`, you may also have to type clspack -auto to an MS-DOS command prompt after installation before you can use JPython.

Most flavors of UNIX will have the Sun Java Virtual Machine and should install normally. If you are running Linux, there are two common Java implementations. The Kaffe implementation that ships with RedHat implements the Personal Java specification that is a subset of the standard Java implementation. JPython is an advanced Java application and requires everything Java has to give; the Kaffe implementation won't run JPython. On Linux, JPython runs best with the Blackdown http://www.blackdown.org Java port.

After JPython is installed you still have a bit of work to do to make sure you can use this tool effectively. Being a Java application itself, JPython is composed of a bunch of Java class files wrapped up in a JAR file. You should add the JAR file to your classpath environment variable. Here is the CLASSPATH variable running on my Windows-based computer:

```
CLASSPATH=.; C:\Progra~1\jdk1.2.1\classes;C:\Progra~1\
    JPython-1.1\jpython.jar
```

You should also add the path to the directory where you installed JPython to your shell's path. Again, the path looks like this on my Windows computer, but yours may be different:

```
PATH=%PATH%;C:\Progra~1\jdk1.2.1\jre\bin;C:\
    Progra~1\jdk1.2.1\bin;C:\Progra~1\JPython-1.1
```

The regular JPython distribution does not include many of the standard Python library modules that you have spent the rest of this book learning and using. You can however, download a JAR file containing the equivalent JPython modules from the JPython web site.

After you have installed JPython you should have the following directory structure:

..\demo	Several sample applications showing how to use JPython.
..\docs	Rudimentary JPython documentation. There is enough documentation to get you started, but consider signing up to the JPython mailing list for more detailed information.
..\Lib	JPython modules available to any JPython script. The modules that come with the base distribution of JPython are only a small subset. You can download the full set of modules from the JPython website.
..\src	The complete source code to JPython.
..\Tools	Mainly contains jpythonc, the JPython equivalent of the standard Python freeze program. Turns a JPython application into a standalone Java application.
..\util	Scripts used in building JPython from scratch.

24.4.1 Test driving JPython

Once you have rebooted a few times (or you lucky UNIX users have just logged out and in) you will have these paths and environment variables correctly configured and are ready to start JPython. It is somewhat anticlimactic at this point, but to start JPython enter jpython at a command prompt. On a Windows computer using the Sun Java SDK, JPython displays the following message:

```
C:\>jpython
JPython 1.1 on java1.2.1
Copyright 1997-1999 Corporation for National Research Initiatives
>>>
```

Bookmark this page then refer to the *Quick python overview* in chapter 4 of this book. One of the beautiful things about JPython and CPython, the implementation of Python that is built on top of the C on language which we've been focusing in the rest of this book, is how interchangeable code is between the two implementations. Most of the examples in chapter 4 for CPython will also work in JPython. A notable exception in the examples of chapter 4 is the os.chdir method called in the section on file objects. Java has no notion of current directories, wherever the JVM is started is the current directory and there isn't a standard Java call to change it. This is notable, because it does not happen very often. Jim Hugunin, the original developer of JPython, went to extraordinary lengths to ensure that JPython was as compatible with CPython as the JVM would allow.

The JPython web site contains an updated list of discrepancies between the Python reference platform and JPython.

24.5 *Using Java from JPython*

Let's get busy and start using JPython for what it was intended: scripting Java classes. Fire up JPython by entering jpython at a command prompt. To use a Java class just import it like you might do a Python module:

```
>>> from javamath import BigInteger
>>> bi = BigInteger("10"
>>> bi
10
```

JPython automatically provides access to any classes that are available in your CLASS-PATH environment variable, just like Java does. JPython also goes to great lengths to make Java classes look and work like regular Python classes and objects. For instance, if you want to find out the services a BigInteger provides:

```
>>> dir(BigInteger)
['getLowestSetBit', 'shiftRight', '__init__', 'and', 'bitLength',
'bitCount', 'valueOf', '__module__', 'remainder', lowestSetBit',
'min', 'divide', 'toByteArray', 'mod', 'divideAndRemainder',
'not', 'subtract', 'ONE', 'signum', 'abs', 'xor', 'modInverse',
'toString', 'clearBit', 'andNot', 'flipBit', 'shiftLeft',
'setBit', 'testBit', 'gcd', 'negate', 'isProbablePrime', 'ZERO',
'add', 'modPow', 'max', 'or', 'compareTo', 'multiply', 'pow']
```

You can also see how JPython makes Java look like Python by studying the first example above. In the last command, JPython had to decide how to output the value of the bi object. Normally, Python calls the hidden class method __repr__ to allow the object to decide how it should be displayed. JPython does this as well, but the default __repr__ for Java classes calls the object method *toString*. You are probably thinking to yourself that the BigInteger object you know does not have a __repr__ method and therefore this chapter is leading you astray. To accomplish the magic of making Java objects look and feel like Python objects, JPython wraps each Java class in a proxy which provides some of the standard and internal methods that Python programmers expect, but that are not part of Java, as most Java programmers know it.

Let's look at another way that JPython goes the extra mile to make Python programmers feel at home with Java.

```
>>> from java.util import Date
>>> d = Date()
Sat May 08 16:17:18 CDT 1999
>>> d.minutes
17
>>> d.seconds
18
>>> d.month
4
```

Ignoring the fact that the Date class has been deprecated (Sun recommends using the Calendar class instead), the Date class does not contain properties that would allow you to get the minutes, seconds, or months from a Date. Instead, in Java you would have to use the `getMinutes()`, `getSeconds()`, and `getMonths()` methods of the Date class. These are really just simple Java beans properties, and JPython maps those methods to Python style properties when it can. JPython accomplishes this in one of two ways. If there is bean info to be found for the class, JPython can use that information to generate the Python style properties. Otherwise, JPython looks for methods that start with the standard get and set prefixes used for such methods and generates properties for them. You can still use the get and set methods instead of the JPython generated properties if you want. When using JPython to test your Java classes, it is probably in your best interests to use the Java methods instead of the generated properties.

Consider the following Java class whose purpose is to encapsulate a single transaction within a general ledger application:

```java
package qp.samples.JPython;

import java.lang.StringBuffer;

public class Transaction {

    String Account;
    double Amount;
    char Type;

    public Transaction() {

        this.Account = "";
        this.Amount = 0.0;
        this.Type = 'D';

    } // default constructor

    public Transaction( String Account, double Amount, char Type ) {

        this.Account = Account;
        this.Amount = Amount;
        this.Type = Type;

    } // constructor

    public String getAccount() { return Account; }
    public void setAccount( String Account )
        { this.Account = Account; }

    public double getAmount() { return Amount; }
    public void setAmount( double Amount ) { this.Amount = Amount; }

    public char getType() { return Type; }
    public void setType( char Type ) { this.Type = Type; }

    public String toString() {
        StringBuffer sb = new StringBuffer();
        sb.append( Account + " " );
        sb.append( Amount );
        sb.append( " " );
        sb.append( Type );

        return sb.toString();
    } // toString
```

```
} // Transaction
```

If you did not have JPython in your arsenal you would have to create another Java class that could perform unit testing on our new Transaction class. But using JPython you can test your class as you write and refine it.

```
>>> from qp.samples.JPython import Transaction
>>> t = Transaction()
>>> t.account = "867-5309"
>>> t.amount = 90210.0
>>> t.type = 'C'
>>> t.account
'867-5309'
>>> t.amount
90210.0
>>> t.type
'C'
>>> t
867-5309 90210.0 C
```

It is quicker and easier to test your Java classes using JPython this way, but there are side benefits from having a separate class perform the unit test. First, you could repeat the test as often as you want. Second, the unit test class could serve as an example to other programmers on how to use your amazing new widget. If you packaged up the code above into a JPython module, you could execute it as often as you like. Unfortunately, for your script to prove a useful tool for showing developers how to use your class, you would have to make some changes. Using the special methods and properties that JPython provides for your class makes writing the test script easier, but doesn't serve as a very good example for other Java developers. To make the script above more instructive to users of your class, stay away from the JPython generated helpers.

```
>>> t = Transaction()
>>> t.setAccount( "867-5309")
>>> t.setAmount( 90210.0 )
>>> t.setType( 'C' )
>>> t.getAccount()
'867-5309'
>>> t.getAmount()
90210.0
>>> t.getType()
'C'
>>> t.toString()
'867-5309 90210.0 C'
```

24.5.1 Extending Java classes

Of course, all of this Java integration is handy as it is, but JPython has much more to offer than that. Among its many talents, JPython allows you to extend Java classes.

```
from qp.samples.JPython import Transaction

class PyTransaction(Transaction):
```

```
        def __init__( self, Account = "", Amount = 0.0, Type = 'D',
            Reference = "" ):
            Transaction.__init__( self, Account, Amount, Type )

            self.reference = Reference

        def __repr__( self ):
            return "%s %s %s %s" % (self.account, self.amount,
                self.type, self.reference)
    if __name__ == '__main__':

        t = PyTransaction ()
        t.amount = 100
        print t
```

In this example, a new Python class (appropriately named PyTransaction) is derived from our venerable Transaction class. PyTransaction adds a new parameter to the constructor and class called `Reference`. Most general ledger transactions allow you to store the source of the transaction, but due to lack of planning, such a field was not added to the Java Transaction class. We've used JPython's ability to subclass Java classes to add this needed functionality. Notice that the first line of PyTransaction's constructor calls Transaction's constructor. Of course, this is JPython, not Java, so we use the Python syntax to call the constructor. JPython can handle overloaded constructors in Java classes, so we could have coded PyTransaction this way:

```
    def __init__( self, Account = "", Amount = 0.0, Type = 'D',
        Reference = "" ):
      Transaction.__init__( self )

      self.account = Account
      self.amount = Amount
      self.type = Type

      self.reference = Reference
```

We also need to override the default `toString` method provided by Transaction. The easiest way to do this is the same way you would provide a string representation in a normal Python object, by providing a `__repr__` method. Here is an interactive session with JPython that shows PyTransaction in action:

```
>>> from pytran import PyTransaction
>>> pt = PyTransaction
>>> pt
0.0 D
>>> pt = PyTransaction( "100-SPAM", 300.25, "D", "CK 2001")
>>> pt
100-SPAM 300.25 D CK 2001
>>> pt.amount = 520.03
>>> pt.amount
520.03
>>> pt.reference
'CK 2001'
```

Notice how our new __repr__ method leaps into action when called upon to display the contents of the pt object?

24.6 *Using JPython from Java*

Due to implementation details of JPython, it is not practical with the current version to directly use JPython classes from a Java application. However, remember that JPython is itself a collection of Java classes and as such they can be used from Java. In this section we will cover loading and executing JPython modules from within a Java class. The standard example for doing this is shown below. For actually executing JPython code from within Java, JPython provides the PythonInterpreter class.

```
import org.python.util.PythonInterpreter;
import org.python.core.*;
public class SimpleEmbedded {
    public static void main(String []args) throws PyException {
        PythonInterpreter interp = new PythonInterpreter();

        System.out.println("Hello, brave new world");
        interp.exec("import sys");
        interp.exec("print sys");

        interp.set("a", new PyInteger(42));
        interp.exec("print a");
        interp.exec("x = 2+2");
        PyObject x = interp.get("x");

        System.out.println("x: "+x);
        System.out.println("Goodbye, cruel world");
    }
}
```

● **Instantiate a PythonInterpreter to execute Python code.**

● **Execute Python code.**

● **Create a variable and put it into JPython. Get a JPython variable out.**

The PythonInterpreter class is your window into the JPython run-time environment. Once you have an object of this class, you have access to an entire compiler and execution environment from within your Java application. The PythonInterpreter class's methods can be divided up into three categories; putting objects into JPython, getting objects out of JPython, and executing JPython code. Being able to populate the JPython namespace allows you to provide an object model to your scripts while they execute. Executing JPython scripts on the fly would not be very useful if you could not provide your own objects to the scripts.

As you can see from the above example, JPython provides wrapper classes for common variable types that you can create from Java and then make available to the interpreter. The PyInteger class allows you to pass integer values into JPython. Table 24.1 shows some of the objects provided by JPython as well as notes on using the objects from your Java applications.

Table 24.1 JPython objects and usage

Object (org.python.core)	Usage
PyDictionary	Implements Python dictionaries. Use anywhere you need to get or retrieve a dictionary in JPython.

Table 24.1　JPython objects and usage (continued)

Object (org.python.core)	Usage
PyList	Implements Python lists. Use anywhere you need to get or retrieve a list in JPython.
PyLong	Long integers.
PyObject	Very important class when creating objects to pass to JPython. PyObject is to JPython as Object is to Java.
PySequence	Base class to PyList. Can be used to derive your own specialized list classes.
PyString	Strings.
PyTuple	Implements immutable sequences.

Most of these classes, especially PyDictionary and PyList, do not usually make for good base classes. They are usually very specialized and it is easier to derive your classes from PyObject. PyObject is at the root of all JPython-based objects and provides default implementations for most of the methods that JPython uses behind the scenes. For instance, when you enter:

```
x = MyObject()
y = MyObject()
if x == y:
    print x
```

JPython translates it into a call to the `PyObject __cmp__` method, like so:

```
If x.__cmp__(y):
```

If you review the "Special method attributes" section in the appendix, you will see a list of special methods that Python objects can implement to provide Python-like behavior. You will find each of these methods already in PyObject, waiting for you to override their behavior in your classes. Of course, JPython already knows how to use Java classes without any special intervention.

The Py class of the `org.python.core` package contains several helper functions that the JPython interpreter uses to execute Python code. You can use them from your Java applications as well. Remember from our discussion that JPython uses a proxy class to wrap normal Java classes so they can be used from within JPython scripts. The `java2py` method of the Py object can create this wrapper for you. The following code passes a Transaction object to the JPython interpreter and executes a script.

```
import org.python.util.PythonInterpreter;
import org.python.core.*;
import qp.samples.JPython.Transaction;

public class TranProcessor {
    public static void main(String []args) throws PyException {
        PythonInterpreter interp = new PythonInterpreter();

        System.out.println("Processing transaction...");
```

```
                Transaction tran = new Transaction();
                interp.set( "tran", Py.java2py(tran) );
                interp.execfile( "proctran.py" );

                System.out.println( tran.toString() );
            System.out.println("Done!");
        } // main
    } // TranProcessor
```

proctran.py:

```
tran.account = "200-SPAMEGGSSAPM"
tran.amount = 100.0
tran.type = 'C'
```

Running TranProcessor results in the following output:

```
C:\ ActivePython>java TranProcessor
Processing transaction...
200-SPAMEGGSSAPM 100.0 C
Done!
```

This is a fine way to execute a JPython script one time, but each time any of the exec methods (exec, eval, and execfile) are called, they have to parse and compile the script before executing. The __builtin__ class also contains many helpful functions; in this case it contains a hook into JPython's compiler. The following section of code creates a list of Transaction objects and then calls proctran.py for each one.

```
import java.io.*;
import org.python.util.PythonInterpreter;
import org.python.core.*;
import qp.samples.JPython.Transaction;

public class TranProcessor {
    public static void main(String []args)
            throws Exception, PyException {
        PythonInterpreter interp = new PythonInterpreter();

        System.out.println("Processing transaction...");

        StringBuffer contents = new StringBuffer();
        BufferedReader in =
            new BufferedReader( new FileReader( "proctran.py" ) );
        String line = null;

        do {                                              ● Reads the
                                                            contents of
            line = in.readLine();                           proctran.py
            if ( line != null )                             into a string
                contents.append( line + "\n" );             variable.

        } while ( line != null );

        PyCode proctran = __builtin__.compile(            ● Compiles the
            contents.toString(),                            proctran.py
            "proctran.py", "exec" );                        string into Java
                                                            bytecodes.
```

```
        Transaction tran = null;
        for( int n = 0; n < 10; n++ ) {
          tran = new Transaction();

          interp.set( "tran", Py.java2py( tran ) );
          Py.exec( proctran, interp.getLocals(),
             interp.getLocals() );
          System.out.println( tran.toString() );

        } // for

      System.out.println("Done!");
    }
  }
}
```

● Executes the compiled Java bytecodes for each Transaction object.

proctran.py:

```
from whrandom import randint

tran.account = "200-SPAMEGGSSAPM"
tran.amount = float( randint(1, 500) )
tran.type = 'C'
```

● A small refinement to make each Transaction object different.

OUTPUT

```
C:\ ActivePython>java TranProcessor
Processing transaction...
200-SPAMEGGSSAPM 278.0 C
200-SPAMEGGSSAPM 296.0 C
200-SPAMEGGSSAPM 158.0 C
200-SPAMEGGSSAPM 89.0 C
200-SPAMEGGSSAPM 69.0 C
200-SPAMEGGSSAPM 236.0 C
200-SPAMEGGSSAPM 487.0 C
200-SPAMEGGSSAPM 182.0 C
200-SPAMEGGSSAPM 147.0 C
200-SPAMEGGSSAPM 484.0 C
Done!
```

Things got a bit more complicated this time around, mostly due to the code to read proctran.py into a string variable for compilation. If you exclude that code, things are back to being fairly simple. The `compile` method of the __builtin__ class returns a PyCode object that contains the Java bytecode version of the Python script. Once you have the bytecodes you can execute the code as often as you want however, we must bypass the PythonInterpreter's version of `exec` since it only accepts strings, not PyCode objects.

The Py class `exec` method can handle PyCode objects, but does require a couple of extra parameters. Most of what PythonInterpreter does is maintain the state of the interpreter when other methods of JPython objects are called. When calling Py's `exec` method, you must pass the global and local variables that should be available to the executing script. Although you can certainly create or maintain your own PyDictionary objects for the global and local namespaces, PythonInterpreter provides methods, `getLocals` and `setLocals`, to access its namespaces. This is what TranProcessor does when calling the `exec` method.

In this overview of embedding JPython in a Java application we have not covered all of the issues involved or the capabilities provided by JPython to Java applications. To further your usage of JPython in your Java applications, I have found the PythonInterpreter, __builtin__, and Py classes to be immensely valuable. In addition, since the source code for JPython (like the source for CPython) is freely available, reviewing the implementation of these and other classes can help with your integration.

24.7 *Compiling JPython classes*

We know that JPython compiles JPython scripts into Java bytecodes. The JVM then executes the Java bytecodes. If you look at the directory where you execute your scripts, you will find the compiled versions of your scripts in files with names like `pytran$py.class`. It might seem that you could just reference these files from your Java applications. You can probably guess that since there is a special section in this chapter, it is not quite as easy as all that.

Python is an extremely flexible scripting language while Java is a typesafe, statically compiled, system language. Consider some of the flexibility that Python classes have:

- Object attributes are not determined by the class definition. You can add new attributes to Python classes on a whim.
- By overriding the `__call__`, `__getattr__`, `__setattr__`, and other methods, you can control how the attributes and methods of your objects are accessed.
- Python classes can have more than one base class.

These are all things that work great in the Python world, but don't fly in the structured world of Java. Much like the CPython `freeze` utility, JPython provides a set of scripts called `jpythonc` that performs the magic of transmuting a flexible script into the static world of Java.

The CPython `freeze` utility works by taking the bytecodes from the CPython compiler, putting them in a set of static arrays, and wrapping the whole thing up with a `main` function that feeds the bytecodes to the CPython interpreter. JPython's `jpythonc` works just like this, only totally differently. `jpythonc` is much closer to a code generator than `freeze` is. There is of course a generous dollop of proxy code and overhead that is necessary to convert a scripting language to a system environment. Mostly, however, `jpythonc` generates Java classes and methods to implement your Python application.

At this point, how it works is probably less important than getting it to work.

```
jpythonc  [ options] module1, module2, …
```

The `jpythonc` script has a fairly complex number of command line options as you can see in table 24.2 below, which gives the options as of the time of this writing. Note that, as JPython is still evolving, there may be some changes. So, if you are working with a newer release than 1.1 , check its documentation for any additions.

Table 24.2 jpythonc command line options

Option	Description
-package *packageName*	Places the compiled code into a Java package named *packageName*.
-jar *jarFile*	Places the compiled code into a JAR file with name jarFile (implies the -deep option).
-deep	Compiles all code that modules depend on.
-core	Includes the core Python libraries (implies the -deep option).
-all	Includes all of the Python libraries (implies the -deep option).
-bean *jarfile*	Same as for -jar but includes creation of the manifest for a bean.
-addpackages *packages*	Includes Java dependencies from the given list of packages.
-workdir *directory*	The working directory for the compiler (defaults to ./jpyworks).
-skip *modules*	Modules not to include in the compilation.
-compiler *compiler*	Uses compiler rather than the standard javac.
-falsenames *names*	Sets the comma separated list of names to false.

In this introduction, there is not space to exhaustively cover all of these options, but let's look at a brief example using the Calc.py applet from the first part of the chapter.

```
C:\ActivePython>jpythonc -jar calc.jar -core Calc.py
processing Calc
processing pawt.swing
processing com.__init__
processing pawt.__init__

Required packages:
  com.sun.java.swing
  java.awt
  javax.swing

Creating adapters:
  java.awt.event.WindowListener used in __init__
  java.awt.event.ActionListener used in Calc

Creating .java files:
  __init__ module
  __init__ module
  swing module
  Calc module

Compiling .java to .class...
['C:\\PROGRAM FILES\\JDK1.2.1\\JRE\\bin\\javac', '-classpath',
   'C:\\Program Files\\JPython-1.1\\jpython.jar;.;
   C:\\Progra~1\\jdk1.2.1\\classes;C:\\Progra~1\\JPython-1.1\\
       jpython.jar '.\\jpywork\\pawt\\__init__.java', '.\\
       jpywork\\com\\__init__.java', '.\\
       jpywork\\pawt\\swing.java', '.\\jpywork\\Calc.java']
0
Building archive: calc.jar
```

```
Tracking java dependencies:
```

Using the following command we can run the generated `Calc` applet using the standard java run command:

```
C:\ ActivePython>java -cp calc.jar Calc
```

Notice that calc.jar stands on it's own, because we used the `-deep` and `-core` options, jpythonc included all of the library modules used by `Calc` and most of the JPython classes from jpython.jar. It is notable that the `-core` option does not include all of JPython, specifically the compiler and parser are left out. These are considerable chunks of code that your application may not be using. If your application uses the `exec`, `execfile`, or `eval` built-in functions you will need to use the `-all` option instead of `-core`. There is a danger here, however. The Java security restrictions on applets do not normally allow for the spontaneous loading of Java bytecodes.

24.7.1 Notes on using jpythonc

While preparing this chapter I installed jfk1.2.1, the latest Java Development Kit from Sun. The directory structure separated the Java compiler (javac) and related tools from the run-time environment (Java). The jpythonc script expects to execute the compiler from the same directory that contains the run time (see the sample execution of jpythonc above). To get the script to work I had to copy javac to the ..\jre\bin directory. But then, to get javac to work, the library files from \jdk1.2.1\lib had to be copied to \jdk1.2.1\jre\lib. I am sure there must have been a better way, but I could not find it at the time.

24.8 Using Java and JPython together

There are a number of ways to use Java and JPython together.

One option is to prototype the entire application in JPython, do several test/redesign/reimplementation cycles, and finally rewrite the whole application in Java. This leverages the increased flexibility and development speed of a scripting language during the early project phases. With a much faster redesign cycle, design experiments are significantly less costly, and design mistakes are easier to fix. The final design to be implemented in Java will be far more thorough than had programming started in Java. Since JPython has access to the same user interface libraries (AWT, Swing) as Java, the Java rewrite will encounter few surprises.

If you try this approach to building a large system, you'll find that its different components or layers often have independent development cycles. Typically, the top-level components keeps evolving while the lower layers are already frozen. This suggests a variant of the rewrite-in-Java approach: rewrite individual components in Java as their design stabilizes. Now JPython's seamless Java integration is essential; interfaces can remain the same while the implementation changes from JPython to Java. Of course, there is no reason why some components can't be written in Java from the start; JPython makes reuse of existing Java code very easy.

The next time-saving option is only to rewrite those components in Java for which performance is critical. The high-level components can generally remain written in JPython.

For many applications, this may mean that only a few low-level parts ever need to be recoded in Java. Sometimes the whole application can remain in JPython. When using good judgment, time-to-market can be reduced drastically in this way.

Once parts of the released version of a system are coded in JPython, the road is open for end-user customization through JPython scripts. Python is an easy language to learn for end users, and the application can easily invoke user scripts at critical points during initialization or execution. JPython programs can be distributed as Java bytecode, so there's little danger that adventurous end users will rewrite components they aren't supposed to touch. Standard precautions against decompilation or reverse engineering can also be taken.

This approach has already been shown to be very successful in the regular Python world. For example, Infoseek's Ultraseek site search product is a Python application built on top of a search engine coded in C; it can be customized via user-supplied Python scripts. Version 1.0 of the product was designed and built in a few weeks by a single programmer who had to learn Python first, and it had more features than any of its competitors. As another example, in 1995-1996 eShop built a Web-based electronic shopping server in Python. It was so successful that the company was bought by Microsoft based on this one product. The short development time made possible by the use of Python was key to their success relative to competitors. The product is now called Merchant Server 3.0 and has been gradually rewritten in C++.

24.9 Conclusion

Many implementation efforts benefit from the combination of a system programming language and a scripting language. The system programming language, Java, needs a scripting companion. JPython, a dialect of the general-purpose scripting language Python, is the ideal candidate; object-oriented from the start, seamlessly integrated, and 100 percent pure Java.

One that has already emerged is the Python Server Pages (PSP). This is a freely available JPython application that implements a server-side scripting engine. PSP, a Java servlet, processes web pages with embedded Python statements. This application goes to great lengths to emulate the active server pages programming model with which Microsoft programmers are familiar. PSP was originally developed on Windows NT, but due to the portable nature of Java and JPython, PSP has been deployed in UNIX environments in support of several intranet applications.

This is only one of many anecdotal stories of JPython's success and usefulness as a scripting language for Java. We expect that the success stores common among Python users will become common in JPython circles as well.

C H A P T E R   2 5

HTML and Python— the HTMLgen package

BY ROBIN FRIEDRICH

HTMLgen is a free Python package used to generate HTML for use in web pages. It does this by providing Python classes corresponding to each HTML element tag, and then using Python object attributes to denote the corresponding HTML tag attributes. This is a natural mapping, and Python scripts can easily assemble these object-oriented data structures into pleasing web pages, which take full responsibility for rendering themselves in HTML. In other words, HTMLgen permits you to deal with HTML at a much higher level than would otherwise be the case. You do not need to manually write HTML, nor do your programs need to assemble strings into HTML.

297

This chapter gives a tour of the more notable classes and shows by example how they are used to emit standards compliant with HTML. The current version of HTMLgen as of this writing is 2.1 and is meant to be a reflection of the HTML 3.2 standard. It retains compatibility with both Python 1.4 and 1.5, but in the near future this may change to a 1.5+ only implementation. You can obtain the most recent release of HTMLgen at http://starship.skyport.net/lib.html.

25.1 Uses for HTMLgen

Today people use HTMLgen in three principle roles:

- Generating web pages programmatically and in bulk
  HTMLgen makes it easy to construct datasets which can emit themselves as consistent, correct HTML markup code, regardless of complexity. For example, a Python script can pull together large amounts of related information and populate Python HTMLgen objects to represent that information as a dataset of web pages. This was the original intended use behind HTMLgen.
- Providing document object rendering for HTML
  Python is naturally adept at dealing with object models such as those used to represent a hierarchically structured document, which can mean just about any hierarchically structured data object on which you wish to see some sort of textual representation. HTML is a natural crossplatform standard for documents these days, and so of course HTMLgen can be used to render such abstract documents into standard HTML, suitable for viewing with any Web browser. An example of a program which uses HTMLgen in this role is gendoc, a Python tool which looks at the structure and documentation strings of a Python module, and automatically generate documentation for that module. gendoc can provide its output in various formats, and to provide HTML output, it uses HTMLgen.
- CGI scripts
  Of course, HTMLgen classes can come in very handy for anyone writing their own Common Gateway Interface (CGI) programs in Python. HTMLgen has full forms support and comes bundled with contributed enhancements for persistent forms as well.

25.1.1 An HTMLgen example

Say you need to whip out some web pages for your college catalog. You have access to a database with schedule and instructor data, text files with course description data, and other files containing feedback from former students. For simplicity we'll assume there are only about a hundred different classes offered at this college, and we want to generate a collection of HTML files linked by some kind of index. Writing a Python program to accomplish this wouldn't be difficult but, for brevity, we'll address only the HTML related bits.

Using HTMLgen to generate pages reduces the problem to simply instantiating Python instances of document classes, and populating them with objects which correspond to the HTML content. HTMLgen provides classes for every HTML 3.2 tag and attribute. Classes are named for easy recall and aliases are provided which correspond exactly to the HTML tag names. For example, there is a BulletList class which generates lists using the UL tag, but a UL Python class alias is also available for those who think in HTML.

We will assume that the home web page for our college provides links to the various colleges, as shown in figure 25.1.

Since this is a small page, we'll assume for the example that it was constructed by hand. The real work is in the pages pointed to by the various "School of" links, the school top pages, which is what HTMLgen will be used to generate.

HTMLgen provides several classes representing HTML documents, depending on your needs. For each of the five school top pages we will use the SimpleDocument class to represent that page. The SimpleDocument class supports the notion of a *resource file*, which can be used to specify several document properties, such as background color, text color, vlink color, and so forth. Resource files make it easy to separate such document properties from your code, and can be reused to provide a consistent look for the web pages.

The school top pages will contain hyperlinks to detailed course description pages, which will be generated using the SeriesDocument class. This class inherits from the SimpleDocument class and adds a predefined page layout to streamline the creation of linear page collections (i.e., page collections which wish to present the pages in a linear order). The primary difference between a SimpleDocument and a SeriesDocument is that the latter provides defined attributes to specify a banner and navigation buttons. Each page in a SeriesDocument will have up to four buttons which take the user to the previous page, the next page, a section top page, and a home page respectively. If attributes are not defined for any of these four links, the corresponding button will be left out. In our case we will use all of them and define the top button to point to the school index page and the home button to point to the main college course page.

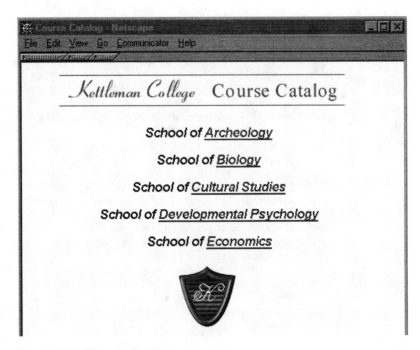

Figure 25.1 The catalog home page

Below is the Python script which generates the first cut for the catalog site. Functions, classes, and attributes known to HTMLgen are presented in bold. Note that many HTMLgen classes (such as SimpleDocument) define standard Python operations such as append, which they use for their own (intuitively obvious) purposes. The details are explained in the comments.

```python
from HTMLgen import *

# kcdb module is assumed to provide course information, and the opinions module provides the
# student feedback text, via an interface which should be obvious ( J ) from the code.
import kcdb
import opinions

schools = ['Archeology', 'Biology', 'Cultural Studies',
           'Developmental Psychology', 'Economics']

term = 'Fall Semester 1999'

# Create an image as a hyperlink to the home page.
# First arg to Href class is the URL, and the second arg is an object to be sensitized.
homelink = Href('index.html', Image('image/logo.gif', align='right',
                border=0))

# Cycle through each of the respective schools.
for school in schools:
    pagetitle = 'School of %s' % school
    schoolurl = school[:4] + '.html'  # Name the page for this school.
    classes = kcdb.allclasses[school[0]]  # Fetch all classes for this school.

    # Create a document object for the school.
    topdoc = SimpleDocument('kc.rc', title = pagetitle)  # kc.rc is the
                                                         # resource file
    topdoc.append(Heading(2, pagetitle))  # put a <H2> heading
    topdoc.append(homelink)  # Add the link back the homepage.
    topdoc.append(Heading(3, term))  # Show which semester it is.
    topdoc.append(HR())  # Add a horizontal rule.
    # A definition list takes (term, definition) pairs. This object will behave like any list object.
    classlist = DefinitionList()
    for cls in classes:  # Populate the list.
        url = '%s.html' % cls
        entry = Href(url, cls)  # This will be the left side of the definition list.
        classlist.append( (entry, kcdb.get_title(cls)) )
    topdoc.append(classlist)  #Remember to attach the list to the document.
    topdoc.append(HR())
    topdoc.write(schoolurl)  # Generate the HTML file for this document.
    # Now we generate the detail file for each course in this school.
    lc = len(classes)
    for i in range(lc):  # Loop through each class.
        cls = classes[i]
        if i != 0:  # Set the reference to the previous HTML file.
          prev = '%s.html' % classes[i-1]
        else:
          prev = None
        if i < lc - 1:  # Set the reference to the next HTML file.
```

```
                    next = '%s.html' % classes[i+1]
                else:
                    next = None
                url = '%s.html' % cls
                pagetitle = '%s: %s' % (school, cls)
                # Now that we have a little context, we create a SeriesDocument.
                doc = SeriesDocument('kc.rc',
                    title = pagetitle,
                    goprev = prev,
                    gonext = next,
                    gotop = schoolurl,
                    gohome = 'index.html')
                # use an <H3> for the class title
                doc.append(H(3, kcdb.get_title(cls)))
                # Now we create a small table to display the course info.
                table = TableLite(border=0, cell_spacing=0)  # This table won't be
                                                             # visible.
                # Load up a list or tuple with info for the table.
                coursedata = ( ('Description', kcdb.get_description(cls)),
                        ('Schedule', kcdb.get_schedule(cls)),
                        ('Prerequisites', kcdb.get_prereq(cls)),
                        ('Instructor', kcdb.get_instructor(cls)),
                        ('Student Comments', opinions.get_comment(cls))
                    )
                for entry, text in coursedata:
                    row = TR()  # Add a row for each entry in coursedata.
                    # Specify the flavor of table cell with TD instances.
                    # Note that the append methods in HTMLgen support adding
                    # more than one thing at a time
                    row.append(TD(entry, bgcolor="#9999cc", valign="TOP"),
                            TD(text))
                    table.append(row)
                # Don't forget to add the table to the document.
                doc.append(table)
                # Generate each course file. Done!
                doc.write(url)
```

Of course, understanding the details of this example requires knowing how HTML functions in principle. Note, however, that you do not need to write any actual HTML. No more trying to match up angle brackets!

For the convenience of specifying appearance aspects of the document separately from the script, we use a resource file. The resource file (kc.rc) used by the above script looks like this:

File kc.rc

```
# This is actually a Python module supporting all the regular syntax.
# The HTMLcolors module provides some web-safe color definitions for those who don't
# think in hex-triplets.
from HTMLcolors import *

# Just set the constant attributes of the document classes here.
```

```
author = 'Dean Nosuchperson'
email = 'dean@kettleman.edu'
bgcolor = WHITE
textcolor = BLACK
linkcolor = RED
vlinkcolor = PURPLE
# Images can be specified as just the file names or as a tuple
# containing the width and height in pixels.
banner = 'image/kc-banner.gif'
# If you don't specify dimensions, HTMLgen will attempt to read the file
# and determine them.
logo = 'image/logo.gif'
blank = ('image/blank.gif', 90, 30)
prev = ('image/back.gif', 90, 30)
next = ('image/next.gif', 90, 30)
top = ('image/school.gif', 90, 30)
home = ('image/college.gif', 90, 30)
```

Figure 25.2 shows a web page that might have been generated by the topdoc script.

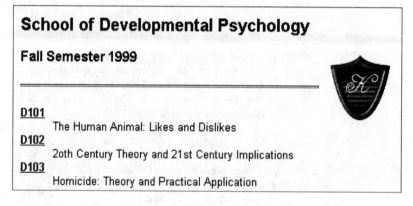

Figure 25.2 Course summary for a school, generated by the HTMLgen script topscript.

Clicking on one of the courses in the school's course list brings up the detailed course page, (generated by the doc instance of SeriesDocument in the script). Figure 25.3 shows the header and body portion of one of these course pages. Note that the Previous button is missing since this was the first page of the series. An equally sized blank GIF is used in its place to provide even spacing. Figure 25.4 shows the footer portion of the same page. The content and style of the footer is customizable by overriding the footer method.

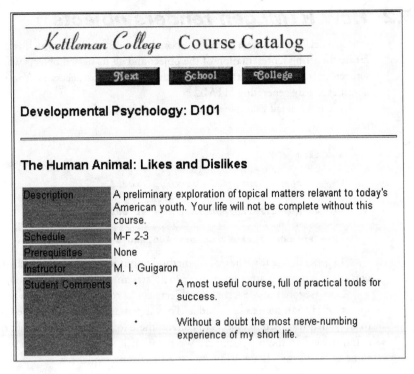

Figure 25.3 Header and body portion of course details page

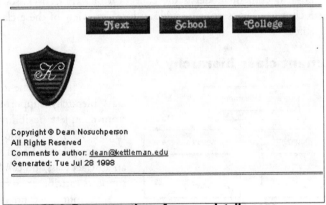

Figure 25.4 Footer portion of course details page

25.2 How HTMLgen renders objects

HTMLgen classes all have a __str__ special method attribute, which is used by Python to create the string representation of the object and all its nested objects when it is printed or written to a file. This method is called automatically as necessary. You need never worry about explicitly generating HTML.

Here is a small example so you can see this in action:

```
>>>
>>> from HTMLgen import *
>>> p = Paragraph("A splash of ")
>>> p.append(Font("color",color="#dd2280"))
>>> p
⇒  <HTMLgen.Paragraph instance at 866870>
>>> print p
<P>A splash of <FONT color="#dd2280">color</FONT></P>
```

In general, one uses the write method to output HTMLgen-generated documents, but you can use the str function or the print statement with HTMLgen objects as well.

Strings stored inside HTMLgen objects could contain characters which are considered special to HTML such as <, >, and &. To compensate for this an escape function is applied to all regular text used in objects to convert these to <, >, and &amp, respectively. This is transparent to the programmer. We mention it simply so that you won't wonder why some of your symbols are being converted to funny sequences.

25.3 Document model

The HTMLgen document model is the collection of HTMLgen classes used to model an HTML document. This section provides a brief overview of these classes and how they work together.

25.3.1 Document class hierarchy

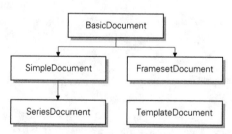

Figure 25.5 Document class inheritance

HTMLgen is implemented with a simple class hierarchy supporting various needs, from complete flexibility to formal layout (figure 25.5). The most basic HTMLgen document class is BasicDocument. It is not an abstract class and can be used directly. It supports attributes such as title and colors but does not support cascading style sheet (CSS) specifications. Likewise, it does not support the use of a resource file to specify attributes. In the BasicDocument constructor, the non-keyword arguments are assumed to be objects to place in the generated HTML document as its initial contents. BasicDocument is typically used when you want to customize everything with your own inheritance or just need something quick for a CGI script.

SimpleDocument inherits from BasicDocument and adds attributes which specify embedded scripts, cascading style sheets, and HTMLgen resource files. For an example of the use of resource files, see the topdoc script above.

SeriesDocument specializes on the SimpleDocument class by adding many attributes to support a particular document structure. This structure was originally patterned after work done at the Yale Center for Advanced Instructional Media* by Patrick Lynch and others. The positioning of titles, subtitles, navigation buttons, banners, logos, copyright notices, email addresses, and date stamps are all defined in this class accordingly.† Some of the features may be modified by overriding methods through a subclass. For example, the make up of the footer is done by the footer method, so writing your own style of page footer is easy via subclassing. The same remark applies to header and nav_buttons. For example, here is a class with a redefinition of footer:

```
class MyDoc(SeriesDocument):
    def footer(self):
        return "Author: Anonymous"
```

The navigation buttons are the most obvious distinction between SimpleDocument and SeriesDocument documents. As the name implies, a SeriesDocument is designed to represent a web page which is part of a series of adjacent pages. As we saw in the quick start to this chapter, it is common to organize pages this way, with appropriate hyperlinks upwards in the web hierarchy. The SeriesDocument class uses the attributes goprev, gonext, gotop, and gohome to provide the relative address information for the previous page, next page in sequence, the top of this section, and the site home page, respectively. The images used for the actual buttons are specified by the prev, next, top, and home attributes accordingly. If any of the various gowherever attributes are set to None, the corresponding buttons will not be rendered, and a blank image will be used as a spacer.

FramesetDocument objects exist just to contain other Frameset objects. See the section on Frames and Framesets for further information.

The TemplateDocument class is not part of the inheritance tree of the other document classes, as its design and use is entirely different. Whereas all the document classes up to this point have been containers which are populated with other HTMLgen objects by hand-coded logic in a Python script, the TemplateDocument supports a simple static substitution approach. This requires that a template HTML file be created in some fashion containing symbols delimited by braces. For example, you might draft up a web page with an elaborate layout using a WYSIWYG tool that you want to use as a template for many pages. By placing names in braces, such as {town}, into the file, they will act as substitution points for variable data. The TemplateDocument class then uses this file as a source to insert content from a substitutions dictionary to generate final web pages. For example, say we saved a template file from a tool such as PageMill™ to a file Xfile and then did the following:

```
T = TemplateDocument('Xfile')
T.substitutions = {'month': ObjectY, 'town': 'Scarborough'}
T.write('Maine.html')
```

---

* See http://info.med.yale.edu/caim/manual/contents.html.

† If this layout doesn't suit your needs, it can be used as an example for writing your own subclass of SimpleDocument.

This would substitute each occurrence of {month} with the string representation of *ObjectY* and each occurrence of {town} with the string 'Scarborough' and write it to the file `Maine.html`. Names in braces can be any string valid as a Python variable name and are case sensitive. {location_A43} is fine but {$temperature} and {place here} are not. Only alphanumeric characters and underscores are allowed between the braces.

This is a simple yet powerful facility. The substitutions dictionary can contain references to any Python object which responds to a `str` call, such as any other simple or compound `HTMLgen` object. *ObjectY* above could have been a prebuilt `Table` object, for example. Moreover, the substitutions attribute itself can refer to any object providing the methods necessary to emulate Python dictionaries. Subclassing from `UserDict` and defining elaborate `get` semantics is perfectly feasible. `TemplateDocument` simply calls the `get` method of the substitutions object. If the name (the string between the braces) is not found as one of the keys in the mapping, the original text, including the braces, is left unchanged. Subsequent calls to the `write` method using different mappings naturally result in different web pages. By the same token, several `TemplateDocument` objects can use the same substitutions mapping making use of differing sets of names to generate their pages.

This class is most useful when you have need to create many similar yet intricately designed HTML documents. Writing `HTMLgen` code to synthesize all the various nonchanging parts of a complicated page can quickly become tedious, though not as tedious as writing the HTML code by hand. TemplateDocument allows you to use your favorite WYSIWYG web page tool to create just the look you need, while inserting symbols for later substitution. Later in this book the DocumentTemplate class bundled with Zope is discussed and takes a similar approach but to a much more feature-full end. Essentially TemplateDocument is a greatly simplified version of the DocumentTemplate concept.

25.4 Tables

There are actually two separate table implementations in `HTMLgen`. The first was historically taken from the old `HTMLsupport.py` function library. It was designed to take a list of lists and construct a table correctly sized to contain the data, and allowed for some limited customization. For general table display this class works fine and is named Table.

The newer table implementation was a result of feedback I received during the 1.2 beta release. It is a collection of classes for the lower level table primitives, TD, TR, TH, and Caption, along with a simple container class called TableLite. I call it TableLite because it does very little for you, but it is easy to use. The user is thus responsible for structuring the contents of each row of the table as well as all other heading and border specifications with the appropriate mix of these classes. Although this requires more coding work on the user's part it does provide complete flexibility and control over the table construction. For those with special table needs, building custom classes on top of TableLite and friends may be the favored approach.

25.4.1 Quick and dirty tables

The Table class assumes you have some data already structured in uniform lists. The `body` attribute should be set to a list of lists. Each sublist will represent a row of the table and should have the same number of elements as all the other sublists. A list is then provided for the heading attribute which provides the column heading text. A minimal example goes like this:

```
>>>
>>> from HTMLgen import *
>>> T = HTMLgen.Table('Caption goes here.')
>>> T.heding = ['A','B','C')
>>> L = [7,8,9]
>>> T.body = [L]
>>> print T
<A NAME="Caption goes here."></A>
<P><TABLE border=2 cellpadding=4 cellspacing=1 width="100%">
<CAPTION align=top><STRONG>Caption goes here.</STRONG></CAPTION>
<TR Align=center> <TH ColSpan=1>A</TH><TH ColSpan=1>B</TH><TH
ColSpan=1>C</TH></TR>
<TR><TD Align=left >7</TD>
<TD Align=left >8</TD>
<TD Align=left >9</TD>
</TR>
</TABLE><P>
```

Note that the Table class takes the liberty of adding an anchor reference at the beginning of the table output.

The Table class provides a limited set of customization options. The expected `<table>` attributes such as `border`, `width`, `cell_spacing`, and `cell_padding` are supported. Color coding the columns of the table body is accomplished with the `body_color` attribute (a list of colors, one for each column). Similarly colors for the headings come from the `heading_color` attribute (a list of color for each column heading). You can control column spanning with the `colspan` attribute. It is set to a list specifying how many columns should be spanned by each heading entry. For example, a five column table might have three headings and setting `colspan = [1,2,2]` results in the first heading spanning one column, the second spanning two columns, and so on.

25.4.2 Full table component version

For a much more direct approach to table construction, HTMLgen provides a family of classes which are instantiated for each cell in the containing table object, a TableLite instance. We saw this used in the course description example at the beginning of this chapter. The TR class is instantiated for each row; the TH class is instantiated for each heading cell; and the TD class is instantiated for each body cell. A supporting Caption class for the caption is provided as well. Each component of the table is appended to the next higher containing object. TD and TH objects are appended to TR objects. TR and Caption objects are appended to a TableLite object. All attributes of these tags as defined by the HTML 3.2 specification are supported, as well as some Internet Explorer™ extensions.

These classes, as well as all classes which inherit from AbstractTag, can control whether text contained in the objects is processed to escape special HTML characters such as < > and &. The `html_escape` attribute can be set to `off`, (or anything not equal to `ON`), to inhibit the default behavior, which is to run all contained strings through the escape function when generating HTML. Controlling this is necessary when you place a string which already is HTML formatted into a container class such as TD. For example,

```
>>> from HTMLgen import *
>>> print TD("<B>Wow!</B>",html_escape="OFF")
<TD><B>Wow!</B></TD>
>>> print TD("<B>Wow!</B>", html_escape="ON")
<TD>&lt;B&gt;Wow!&lt;/B&gt;</TD>
```

25.5 Lists

Defining lists in HTMLgen is essentially the same as in the rest of Python. Any Python list can be given to the HTMLgen.List class and rendered as a conventional bullet list. The List class (and its children) inherit from the UserList.UserList class in the standard Python distribution, so all normal list semantics are supported.

Nested lists are supported by recursing through the list renderer for each embedded sublist. Each time a list is encountered inside a list, it will indent those contents with respect to the prior list entry. This can continue indefinitely through all nested lists. For example, the following illustrates a two-level list.

```
>>> from HTMLgen import *
>>> PL = ['Canada',['Nova Scotia',
    'New Brunswick'],'USA',['Maine','New Hampshire','Vermont']]
>>> print List(PL)
<UL>
<LI>Canada
    <UL>
    <LI>Nova Scotia
    <LI>New Brunswick
    </UL>
<LI>USA
    <UL>
    <LI>Maine
    <LI>New Hampshire
    <LI>Vermont
    </UL>
</UL>
```

As the List class defaults to a bullet list (<UL>), it is also aliased to BulletList. List is also used as a base class for other varieties of lists. For numbered lists use the NumberedList or OrderedList class. It has the same interface but uses the <OL> tag element instead of <UL>.

Other features of the HTMLgen List family include the indent, columns, and bgcolor attributes. A true or false value for indent indicates whether you want the list to start indented with respect to the preceding text or not. The columns value controls the number of columns to render the list into. This can be very helpful in presenting long lists of narrow data. The bgcolor attribute provides a background color for the list area. The multicolumn and background color features are implemented with a table, as can be seen in the following example.

```
...
```

```
>>> print List(PL, indent=0, columns=2, bgcolor="#99CCCC")
<TABLE border="0" cellpadding="3" bgcolor="#99CCCC">
<TD valign="top"><LI>Canada
    <UL>
    <LI>Nova Scotia
    <LI>New Brunswick
    </UL>
</TD><TD valign="top"><LI>USA
    <UL>
    <LI>Maine
    <LI>New Hampshire
    <LI>Vermont
    </UL>
</TD></TABLE>
```

Three other classes inherit from the List class: NonBulletList, DefinitionList, and ImageBulletList. NonBulletList presents the list as a series of items. DefinitionList and ImageBulletList use tuple pairs for each list item. The DefinitionList class takes the tuple to be (*word, definition*) pairs and renders them using the <DL> element tag. The ImageBulletList class uses (*Image, Text*) pairs as items for a bulleted list, with *Image* being an arbitrary Image object which will be displayed as the bullet. This can be useful for color-coding the list items; a green bullet for some items, a red bullet for others, and so on.

25.6 Frames

The FramesetDocument, as mentioned previously, is merely a container for Frameset objects. It inherits from BasicDocument to provide a minimum of functionality. The real action in framed documents comes in specifying the framesets and frame properties to achieve the desired layout. Frameset objects can contain Frame objects or other Frameset objects or both.

In figure 25.6 we have a FramesetDocument containing Frameset A which in turn is composed of Frame 1 and Frameset B. Frameset B is further divided into Frame 2 and Frame 3. Frameset objects use either a cols attribute or a rows attribute to specify how the set of objects they contain is divided. For example, setting rows="20%,*, 10%" results in three rows occupying 20 percent, 70 percent, and 10 percent of the total window height respectively. It would then be necessary to attach three Frame or Frameset objects to this containing Frameset. Below we show how to create the necessary objects to construct a rough approximation of the layout depicted in figure 6.

```
>>>
```

```
>>> from HTMLgen import *
>>> frame1 = Frame(name='top', src='banner.html')
>>> frame2 = Frame(name='left', src='nav.html')
```

```
>>> frame3 = Frame(name='right', src='body.html')
>>> FSB = Frameset(frame2, frame3, cols="30%, *")
>>> FSA = Frameset(frame1, FSB, rows="120, *")
>>> print FramesetDocument(FSA)
<!DOCTYPE HTML PUBLIC "-//W3C//DTD HTML 3.2//EN">
<HTML>
<!-- This file generated using Python HTMLgen module. -->
<HEAD>
 <META NAME="GENERATOR" CONTENT="HTMLgen 2.1">
    <TITLE></TITLE> </HEAD>
<FRAMESET rows="120, *"><FRAME name="top" src="banner.html"></FRAME>
<FRAMESET cols="30%, *"><FRAME name="left" src="nav.html"></FRAME>
<FRAME name="right" src="body.html"></FRAME>
</FRAMESET>
</FRAMESET>
</HTML>
```

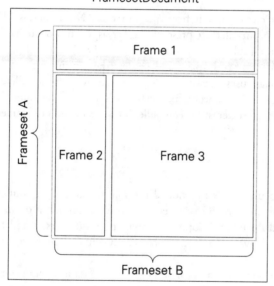

FramesetDocument

Figure 25.6 Frameset/ Frame nesting

The complete objects are typically created from the innermost outward, as the smaller elements must be instantiated before they can be added to containing objects.

25.7 Images

Images are a central part of many web pages. The Image class in HTMLgen supports all the HTML image tag's attributes such as width, height, border, align, and alt. Newer attributes such as hspace and vspace are available as well.

The first argument to the Image class can either be the file name of an image or a tuple containing a file name along with the image pixel width and height, respectively.

```
>>> buzz = Image('Buzz.gif')
>>> print buzz
<IMG src="Buzz.gif" height="51" width="56" alt="Buzz.gif">
>>> buzz = Image(('Buzz.gif', 56,51))
>>> print buzz
<IMG src="Buzz.gif" height="51" width="56" alt="Buzz.gif">
>>> buzz = Image('Buzz.gif', width=56, height=51)
>>> print buzz
<IMG src="Buzz.gif" height="51" width="56" alt="Buzz.gif">
```

All three styles of constructing the image object are equivalent in this case. Notice that when only a file name is given, the constructor will attempt to open the file and read the width and height information automatically. HTMLgen bundles part of the still developing Python Imaging Library (PIL) written by Fredrik Lundh, and uses it for this purpose. All major file formats used for web pages are supported: GIF, JPEG, and PNG. Automatic reading of image sizes will (of course) only work if the file name used is a valid path on the system at the time the script is run. File paths used for Image objects are those valid when taken relative from the final HTML file location, or the document root of the web server.

Depending on how you generate your web pages, it's possible that the image path as seen by your web server may not correspond to the image path when the HTML generation script is being run. In those cases HTMLgen must rely on either the tuple form or the keyword argument to specify the height and width attributes of the image. Browsers use image height and width information to lay out the page correctly as it is being loaded, so it is always good to have these attributes generated one way or the other.

25.8 Image maps

Both client and server-side image maps are supported. One starts with an image and identifies the areas which are to be linked to URLs. This is done with Area class instances which are then assigned to a Map object. That Map object is then grouped with the image via a normal Image class. A minimal example:

```
a1 = Area(coords='0,0,50,50', href='a1.html')
a2 = Area(coords='0,50,50,100', href='a2.html')
csmap = Map(name='rect', areas=(a1,a2))
csimage = Image('../image/csmap_rect.gif', usemap='#rect')
```

Note that the name tag must be referenced with the #namevalue syntax for this to work. In the above example, the name tag of the Map object has the value 'rect', and is referenced by the Image object with '#rect'. Also, both the Map object and the Image object must be written to the document file for client-side maps to work.

The Area instances are constructed with coordinates according to the shape of the area. The default shape is rectangular, (shape='rect'), and the coords attribute is a comma separated string of pixel coordinates—*left*, *top*, *right*, *bottom*—with the origin taken as the upper left corner of the image. If the area is circular, (shape='circle'), the coords attribute is a string consisting of three values, x, y, r, with x, y being the center coordinate and r being the radius of the circle. The area can be an enclosed polygon, (shape='polygon'), with the coords attribute set to a comma separated series of x, y vertex coordinates. For example, coords='33,11,65,90,35,80', would be three vertices of a triangular area. Normally an href attribute is given to associate a hyperlink with the area. If none is given, this will be taken to mean an exclusion area and a NOHREF flag will be generated. Typically, this feature is used when you wish to exclude an area from being active, when that area is contained in or overlaps a larger active area.

25.9 The <A> tag

The <A> or anchor tag is a fundamental element of HTML. It's used to declare both a hyperlink target anchor and a hyperlink jump reference. To make things easier, HTMLgen has an Href class (with an alias to the class name A) to implement the hyperlink reference use of this HTML element. The first argument for Href is the URL referred to, the next is the visible text (or image) of the link, and keyword arguments are supported to specify OnMouseOver and OnClick attributes. For example:

```
>>>
from HTMLgen import *
>>> print Href('www.Python.org','PPython HQ')
<A HREF="www.Python.org">Python HQ</A>
```

To define a named fragment point, the Name class is used. Named fragment points act as precise jump targets within a larger document.

```
...
>>> print Name('tropical')
<A NAME="tropical"></A>
```

To jump to this point in the document one uses the *URL#frag* notation in an Href such as:

```
...
>>> print Href('./plants.html#tropical','Tropical Plants')
<A HREF="./plants.html#tropical">Tropical Plants</A>
```

Another use of the <A> tag, the MailTo class, provides a handy object for adding an email hyperlink to a document. It encapsulates some nice tricks of which most people are not aware, such as the ability to specify an initial subject for the email and an antispam feature to keep the email address from being captured by most Web spiders. The first argument to the MailTo class is the email address, the optional second argument is the text or Image object to be shown in the browser (defaults to the email address if not specified), and the optional third argument is the initial subject which will appear in the mail composition window opened by the browser. (In the generated HTML, the subject is placed as a CGI parameter after the address). Both major browsers support this mechanism, and even though it's not part of the HTML standard it can be very handy. Here's an example:

```
...
```

```
>>> print MailTo('friedrich@Pythonpros.com','Me',
    'Loved HTMLgen but...')
<A
HREF="mailto:&#102;rie&#100;ric&#104;@py&#116;hon&#112;ros&#46;com&#63;sub&#106;ect&#61;Lov&#101;d H&#84;MLg&#101;n
b&#117;t..&#46;">Me</A>
```

The antispam feature is obvious here. In this case every fourth character is replaced with its HTML encoding. MailTo randomly selects what frequency of character replacement to use each time it renders itself. The browser will correctly display this string and moreover insert the subject properly in the mail compose window. This technique shields the email address from the dumber email collection spiders used by spammers.

25.10 Call protocol

Many HTMLgen classes, specifically those which inherit from AbstractTag, support Python's call protocol.* This allows instances of these classes to act as functions. This may be convenient when you have many instances of a particular markup object to be created and wish to avoid the performance penalty of class instantiation for each of them. For example, if you need to generate many text passages with the <sample> tag, you can make one instance of the Sample class and reuse it frequently as a function.

```
>>>
```

```
from HTMLgen import *
>>> samp = Sample()
>>> samp('Some sample text.')
'<SAMP>Some sample text.</SAMP>\012'
>>> samp('Some more sample text.')
'<SAMP>Some more sample text.</SAMP>\012'
```

Using this function-based programming style is not conducive to embedded objects, but it's good to have this option to generate HTML text at high speed when necessary.

25.11 CSS1 support

Cascading style sheets are used to apply consistent typographic style to collections of documents. CSS1 is the first standard issued by the W3C on the use of style sheets. We don't have space here to discuss the many features of cascading style sheets, so we'll assume that the reader already understands the concept and wishes to use them when creating web pages with HTMLgen.

---

* Defined for any class using the __call__ special method attribute.

There are three forms of style specification, all supported by HTMLgen. *In-line* style specification applies to just a single tagged element. The `style` attribute of an HTMLgen class can be assigned a string containing CSS syntax applicable to that instance only. *Document-level* style sheets are embedded in the `<head>` portion of the page and apply to all tags in that page. *External* style sheets are files which may be referenced by many HTML documents to yield a consistent look.

In-line style usage looks like this in HTML:

```
<h1 style="color: blue; font-style: italic">Blue Sky Realty</h1>
```

Calling HTMLgen to generate the same thing would look like this:

```
Heading(1, 'Blue Sky Realty', style="color: blue;
        font-style: italic")
```

All the markup classes in HTMLgen provide the `style` attribute for this purpose. In practice the in-line style approach is rarely the best choice. The purpose of CSS is to allow easy global specification and maintenance of styles across a large collection of documents. Using in-line styles doesn't accomplish this, as maintenance of these point specifications could be a nasty chore.

Document-level style sheets place style specifications in the head of the document, where they can be easily adjusted as the document evolves. This style technique applies only to an individual HTML document, but since we are generating HTML with our scripts, managing these embedded style sheets is not impractical. To specify style settings for a document, set the `style` attribute of a SimpleDocument or SeriesDocument instance to a string containing the desired CSS properties. For example:

```
# All headings should be green with yellow background.
style1 = "H1, H2, H3, H4, H5, H6 {color:green;
                        background-color:yellow}"
doc = SimpleDocument('a1.rc', style=style1)
doc.append(…etc…
```

When the doc object is written it will look something like this:

```
<!DOCTYPE HTML PUBLIC "-//W3C//DTD HTML 3.2//EN">
<HTML>
<!-- This file generated using Python HTMLgen module. -->
<HEAD>
 <META NAME="GENERATOR" CONTENT="HTMLgen 2.1">
    <TITLE></TITLE>
<STYLE type="text/css">
<!--
H1, H2, H3, H4, H5, H6 {color:green; background-color:yellow}
-->
</style>
</HEAD>
```

The style string is placed in an HTML STYLE element in the HEAD of the HTML document, with a MIME type set to `text/css`. To protect browsers unable to recognize styles, HTML comments enclose the actual style specification. The `style` attribute could have been set in the resource file a1.rc if it were constant for the script. Using various CSS settings, some interesting schemes can be implemented in the Python logic, such as differing color schemes for different levels in the documentation hierarchy.

Probably the most commonly used mode of specifying CSS properties is through an external style sheet. An HTML document can link to a CSS file via URL or document relative reference. Placing the style properties in a separate file has the advantage of simplified central management with only a small performance penalty. For HTMLgen document objects we use the `stylesheet` attribute to specify this filename or URL. For example, if the previously defined heading styles were placed in a file green.css in a styles directory off the web server document root, one could refer to it as `/styles/green.css` and the example would then look like:

```
doc = SimpleDocument('a1.rc', stylesheet="/styles/green.css")
```

and would generate HTML as:

```
<HEAD>
 <META NAME="GENERATOR" CONTENT="HTMLgen 2.1">
    <TITLE></TITLE>
 <LINK rel=stylesheet href="/styles/green.css" type="text/css"
 title="/styles/green.css">
 </HEAD>
```

25.11.1 Advanced style features

So far in this section we have only seen the simplest CSS syntax. CSS1 provides for more specific targeting of tagged regions through the use of so-called classes. Any HTML element tag can specify a class attribute to further identify that style of tag. For example, the HTML markup `<P class="abstract">` can be used to mark the abstract of a technical document. In the style sheet a specification such as `P.abstract {font-style: italic; left-margin: 1.1cm; right-margin: 1.1cm}` will apply just to that class of paragraph. To support this, HTMLgen objects have a Class attribute.

Since class is a reserved word in Python, I chose the upper case spelling of the attribute for use as a keyword argument in HTMLgen—class and Class are different! The following object can be used as the abstract text markup:

```
A = Paragraph(abstract_text, Class='abstract')
```

The generic HTML element `<SPAN>` is often used to tag text for style treatments. This will have a similar effect as Paragraph above but without any semantic extras such as paragraph breaks.

```
A = Span(abstract_text, Class='abstract')
```

Span markup applies only the rendering effect defined in the cascading style sheet.

25.12 CGI and forms

HTTP defines the CGI mechanism for server-side programs, as a method to fetch data from the user. An HTMLgen web page typically uses the Form element to package CGI variable names and values for posting to the HTTP server. CGI programs written in Python generally use the standard library's cgi.py module and its FieldStorage class to retrieve this form data and present it as a Python object, which can then be used as desired. See the cgi.py doc string for a good explanation of using the CGI interface. We'll focus here on the HTMLgen aspects.

HTMLgen document objects used within a Python CGI script which generates HTML documents on demand should set their cgi attribute to a true value. This will tell the document class to issue to the requesting browser the appropriate HTTP MIME header indicating a web page, such as "Content-type: text/html". This is necessary since the HTTP server is receiving this document from a standard output stream (the stream the Python CGI script is writing to) rather than a file, hence the server's filename suffix to MIME type mapping doesn't apply. It is always the responsibility of the CGI program to properly type the data it is sending out.

On the other hand, if you are generating web pages normally, that is, saving them to files and *not* generating them on the fly in response to browser requests, the cgi attribute should *not* be used, even if forms are included in the pages. The HTTP server delivering the pages will affix the content type properly.

The Form class in HTMLgen is a container object for defining HTML forms, and can be populated with Input objects, as well as any other HTMLgen constructs useful in designing the layout. The Input class supports all the input element types, text, password, checkbox, radio, file, submit, reset, and hidden. Two other objects are frequently used as well: the Select class for presenting a list of items to choose from, and the TextArea class for multiline text typing areas.

Below is a very simple HTMLgen script, illustrated by figure 25.7.

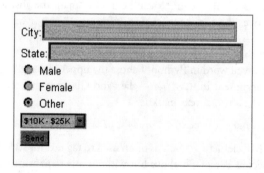

Figure 25.7 Raw form presentation

```
from HTMLgen import *
from HTMLcolors import *
doc = SimpleDocument(title='Income Survey', bgcolor=WHITE)
                                    # If this is in a CGI prog, use cgi=1.
F = Form('http://www.kettleman.edu/cgi-bin/income-survey.py')
                                    # the URL of the CGI program
F.append( Input(type='text', name='city', llabel='City:', size=30),
        BR() )
```

```
F.append( Input(type='text', name='state', llabel='State:',
        size=30), BR() )
for sex in ('Male', 'Female', 'Other'):
    F.append(Input(type='radio', name='sex', rlabel=sex), BR())
incomes = [('$0 - $10K', 0), ('$10K - $25K', 1), ('$25K - $40K', 2),
        ('$40K +', 3)]
F.append( Select(incomes, name='income',size=1), BR() )
doc.append(F)
doc.write('survey.html')
```

As we can see, the raw layout provided by simply placing items into a Form container leaves something to be desired. Much better results come from laying out the input widgets in a table. Here are the results of using some simple convenience classes. The code for these classes is shown below.

In figure 25.8, the InputTable class provides a three-column table layout to help with aesthetics. The RadioButtons class helps automate the creation of a radio button group. (These classes are not part of HTMLgen. They are defined in the code below, which is a fairly nice demonstration of just how easy it is to use HTMLgen and Python to automate desired HTML construction.) Here is the code which does this.

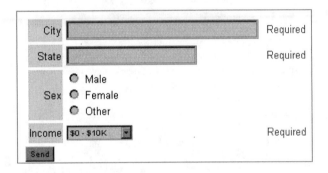

Figure 25.8 Using a table to lay out a form.

```
from HTMLgen import *
from HTMLcolors import *
import string

class InputTable:
    """InputTable(entries, [keyword=value]...)
    Entries is a list of 3-element tuples (name, input_object, note)
    where
    name will label the input object on the left column, the
    input_object can be anything, and the note is a string to provide
    optional notations to the right of the input widgets.
    """

    def __init__(self, entries, **kw):
        self.entries = entries
        self.leftcolor = GREY2        # color used for left label column
```

```python
            self.centercolor = WHITE        # color used for center input column
            self.rightcolor = WHITE         # color used for right label column
            self.notecolor = RED            # color used for notation text
            self.leftalign = 'right'        # text alignment for left label column
            for (item, value) in kw.items():
                setattr(self, item, value)

        def __str__(self):
            table = TableLite(border=0, cellspacing=4)
            for (label, input, note) in self.entries:    #assume a 3-tuple
                row = TR()
                row.append(TD(label, align=self.leftalign,
                        bgcolor=self.leftcolor))
                row.append(TD(input, bgcolor=self.centercolor))
                if note:
                    row.append(TD(Font(note, color=self.notecolor),
                            bgcolor=self.rightcolor))
                table.append(row)
            return str(table)

class RadioButtons:
    widgettype = 'radio'
    def __init__(self, items, **kw):
        self.items = items
        self.name = 'radiochoice'
        self.orient = 'vertical'
        self.selected = []
        for (item, value) in kw.items():
            setattr(self, item, value)
    def __str__(self):
        if self.orient[0] == 'v':
            sep = '<BR>\n'
        else:
            sep = ', \n'
        if type(self.selected) is type(""):
            self.selected = [self.selected]
        s = []
        for item in self.items:
            if item in self.selected:
                s.append(str(Input(type=self.widgettype, name=self.name,
                        checked=1)))
            else:
                s.append(str(Input(type=self.widgettype,
                        name=self.name)))
                s.append(str(item))
                s.append(sep)
        return string.join(s[:-1], "")

class CheckBoxes(RadioButtons):
    widgettype = 'checkbox'

def make_survey_page():
    doc = SimpleDocument(title='Income Survey', bgcolor=WHITE)
```

```
                                          # If this is in a CGI prog, use cgi=1.
          F = Form('http://www.kettleman.edu/cgi-bin/income-survey.py')
                                          # the URL of the CGI program

          survey = []
          survey.append(['City', Input(name='city', size=30), 'Required'])
          survey.append(['State', Input(name='state', size=20),
                      'Required'])
          survey.append(['Sex', RadioButtons(['Male', 'Female',
                      'Other']), ''] )
          incomes = [('$0 - $10K', 0), ('$10K - $25K', 1),
                      ('$25K - $40K', 2), ('$40K +', 3)]
          survey.append(['Income', Select(incomes, name='income', size=1),
                      'Required'] )

          F.append(InputTable(survey))
          doc.append(F)
          doc.write('survey.html')
```

25.12.1 CGI with the StickyForm class

The Form class in HTMLgen is a simple analog of the FORM element in HTML. To enhance it for CGI applications requiring persistence, Amos Latteier wrote StickyForm.py and contributed it to the HTMLgen distribution. It provides a convenient tool to store form contents between CGI script invocations. The StickyForm class inherits from Form and adds an interface to cgi.FieldStorage for accessing the input values from the browser. It stores this structure to a file using cPickle so that the form can be reconstituted easily the next time the page is accessed. Very handy indeed.

25.12.2 CGI with Zope

CGI programming can become very cumbersome, especially for applications which desire a high level of user interaction. Digital Creation's Zope is a very powerful abstraction layer which dramatically reduces the complexity of web-based interactive Python applications. Chapter 26 discusses the Zope system, and I highly recommend it for applications requiring interactive presentation and manipulation of data on the web. HTMLgen is best used for automated generation of static pages and simple CGI.

25.13 Auxiliary modules

Several modules accompany HTMLgen.py in the distribution. HTMLtest.py provides the regression testing as well as a sampling of how to use the HTMLgen classes to construct web pages. HTMLcolors.py simply provides some hex-triplet strings as named colors. The colorcube module uses the table classes to generate a sample display (html/color-cube.html) of all the web-safe colors and their hex-triplet values.

The barchart module provides a couple of classes useful for creating regular color coded and stacked bar charts. A DataList class stores and manipulates the data to be displayed by the BarChart class. These classes are not commercial grade, to say the least, but they do work. This module is included mostly as an example of what can be done with the right mix of HTMLgen objects and Python data handling.

HTMLcalendar.py provides a little tool to generate monthly calendars as linked web pages. It reads a text appointments file and uses TableLite to create the calendar.

The HTMLutil module is very old and is not critical to the operations of HTMLgen. It's mostly a catch-all for various experiments over the years. In particular. the Python source colorizer has been superceded by the excellent PyFontify tool by Guido van Rossum.

25.14 *The future*

HTMLgen continues to be maintained, and by the time you read this it is likely that I will have upgraded it to support the HTML 4.0 specification. XML is the next generation of document markup and Python is at the forefront of tools development to support this new technology. A class library to synthesize XML is a natural, but I'm sure someone will beat me to it.

C H A P T E R   2 6

Using 'Zope'

BY AMOS LATTEIER AND BRIAN LLOYD

26.1 Introduction

Zope is an open source application server and portal toolkit used for building high-performance, dynamic web sites.

Zope can be used to build web applications completely through the web. You don't need to know any Python programming to use Zope. To find out more about Zope visit the Zope website at http://www.zope.org/.

While using Zope doesn't require knowledge of Python, Zope is written in Python and can be extended in Python. This chapter will introduce Zope's low-level object publishing facilities from the perspective of a Python programmer. You will learn how to write and publish your own objects in Python.

Zope consists of a number of components and comes with many publishable objects and a management framework. This introduction covers only three Zope components—the Zope Object Request Broker (ORB), HTML Templates, and the Object Database. These are the basic Zope components, and understanding them is essential to all Zope programming. This introduction does not cover the Zope management framework or the Zope product API.

While the standard Zope distribution comes as an integrated whole, you can mix and match the ORB and other Zope components in your own Python programs. This chapter will demonstrate this kind of use. If you are interested in writing publishable objects which operate within the complete Zope framework, read this introduction, and then investigate the developer documentation at the Zope website.

26.2 Object publishing

Publishing dynamic data on the Web can be unnecessarily difficult. Even with excellent tools like Python's CGI module, a web developer must be familiar with the many technical details of HTTP, CGI, and other Web protocols. Worse, these details often end up in code, reducing clarity and code reuse.

As web applications become more complex, problems due to the non-object-oriented nature of CGI become apparent. Typical web applications consist of a number of single-purpose CGI scripts which have no standard way to share information or specify other objects in the system. Manageability becomes a problem very quickly, and many of Python's object-oriented benefits are lost in such a system.

Zope is a collection of technologies for developing powerful, coherent, and maintainable web applications with Python. It allows collections of Python objects to be published as World Wide Web resources without CGI or HTTP specific code.

Zope allows you to write a web application in the same way that you write any normal Python program. You write classes that model the problem domain, and create objects to actually do the work. Zope does the work of handling incoming web requests, finding and calling your objects, and returning the results. Because they contain no CGI-specific code, these applications can be easily moved from one publishing mechanism, such as CGI, to other mechanisms such as FastCGI or CORBA without change.

Creating a Zope application is simply a matter of creating a regular Python module containing the objects to be published, and placing this module along with Zope-provided support files in the appropriate place on a web server. (The details of this process are covered in the Zope documentation.)

26.2.1 What is object publishing?

Using Zope, normal Python objects are published to the web. The web server calls the objects in much the same way that other Python objects would. Zope works by wrapping a Python module and providing all of the plumbing necessary to turn HTTP requests into object calls. When an incoming HTTP request is received, Zope handles the mapping between HTTP data and Python objects and:

- searches the object space for the object referenced in the incoming request URL
- marshals incoming form data, cookies, and request data to object parameters
- performs authorization and authentication of the incoming request based on authorization data gathered while searching for the object
- invokes the object
- converts the invocation return value or exception value to an HTTP response and returns this to the web server.

Zope does all of the HTTP and CGI drudgery, allowing the developer to write simpler code. In many ways, Zope functions as an ORB. In fact a core component of Zope is called the Zope ORB. Published modules do not need to handle receiving and decoding the HTTP request, nor formatting and sending the HTTP response.

26.2.2 Object traversal: from URLs to object calls

The Zope ORB effectively joins the namespace of the web with the namespace of a Python module.

Take the following example module:

File Hello.py

```
"""A simple Zope application"""
def sayHello(name='World'):
"""Display a greeting"""
 return "Hello %s!" % name
```

From the interactive Python interpreter, you can access this module and call the say-Hello function:

```
>>> import Hello
>>> Hello.sayHello()
⇒   'Hello World!'
>>> Hello.sayHello("Billy")
⇒   'Hello Billy!'
```

Publishing the module with Zope allows you to perform the same interaction via the Web. Simply place this module on a web server with the appropriate Zope support files, and it becomes a fully functional web application. Zope allows you to call the sayHello function with a URL that the Zope ORB maps into the Hello module's namespace.

For example, sending your web browser to
http://www.mydomain.com/cgi-bin/Hello/sayHello is equivalent to

```
>>> import Hello
>>> Hello.sayHello()
```

Both Zope and the interactive interpreter return the text:

⇒   'Hello World!'

Sending your Web browser to
http://www.mydomain.com/cgi-bin/Hello/sayHello?name=Billy is equivalent to

```
>>> import Hello
>>> Hello.sayHello(name="Billy")
```

Both Zope and the interactive interpreter return the text:

⇒   'Hello Billy!'

Once you set up the Zope ORB to publish the Hello module, sending your browser to URLs is just like calling objects in the published module's namespace. The URL is used by Zope to determine which object to call within the module and what arguments to pass to the called object. In other words,

http://www.mydomain.com/cgi-bin/published_module/object1/object2/
meth?arg1=value1&arg2=value2

is equivalent to

```
>>> published_module.object1.object2.meth(arg1="value1",arg2="value2")
```

The Zope ORB performs object traversal by converting steps in the URL path to `getattr` or `getitem` calls. Zope publishes the object that it comes to at the end of the URL.

So object publishing with Zope is really pretty simple.

How about what happens when you POST to Zope with web form? Exactly the same thing happens. Suppose you have this form:

```
<form action="http://www.mydomain.com/cgi-bin/published_module/
object1/object2/meth" method="post">
Arg1: <input type="text" name="arg1">
Arg2: <input type="text" name="arg2">
<input type="submit">
</form>
```

Submitting the form will call the published module in exactly the same way as the previous example. So using this form with Zope is also equivalent to

```
>>> import published_module
>>> published_module.object1.object2.meth(arg1="value1",arg2="value2")
```

However, in the case of the Web form, *value1* and *value2* are determined by what you type into the form inputs.

26.2.3 Object publishing details

The Zope ORB converts URLs to object calls in a controllable way. Zope enforces rules that allow you to control which objects are accessible from the Web. Objects that are accessible from the Web via Zope are known as published objects. The objects defined in a module are published if they

- can be found in the module's global name space
- do not have names starting with an underscore
- have nonempty documentation strings
- are not modules.

Subobjects (or sub-subobjects, ...) of published objects may also be callable from the Web. Applications can publish whole hierarchies of objects that provide a much richer set of services than common CGI scripts, and are far easier to maintain. Subobjects are published if they

- have nonempty documentation strings
- have names that do not begin with an underscore
- are not modules.

Object methods are considered to be subobjects, and may be published as well. When Zope publishes a function or method, it figures out what arguments are expected, and attempts to find values to pass based on argument names in the function or method's signature. Argument values may come from

- form input fields
- HTTP headers
- HTTP cookies
- CGI environment variables
- special values defined by Zope.

The REQUEST and RESPONSE objects provided by Zope allow you the same level of control over request processing as a raw CGI script, but they present a much nicer object interface.

The return value of an object invocation is returned as the HTTP response. When developing Web applications, output to browsers is nearly always in the form of text, especially HTML. By default, Zope assumes that output is in text format. It will automatically detect whether output is plain text or HTML, though an application may also set the returned content type explicitly.

Zope also provides a number of facilities to aid in debugging applications. Here's how Zope deals with any unhandled exceptions that may be raised by an application:

- Prevents traceback listings from being directly displayed and from causing server errors.
- Minimally attempts to convert Python exceptions to HTTP exceptions and automatically sets exception status codes.
- Automatically generates error pages using exception type and value information, including traceback information in HTML comments.

The most basic debugging tool is traceback information provided in error outputs. For example, suppose we introduce an error in a published method. Instead of the inscrutable "Server Error" you would get with normal CGI, Zope will return HTML containing an embedded Python traceback that allows you to pinpoint the error:

```
<html>
<head>
<title>AttributeError</title>
</head>
<body>
Sorry, an error occurred.<p>
<!--
Traceback (innermost last):
File ads.py, line 15 in image_type
AttributeError: spam
-->
</body>
</html>
```

26.2.4 A simple example

A common type of Web application is the feedback form. Usually, the web user is presented with a form that is filled out and then submitted to a CGI script on the server. The

CGI script generally collects the data submitted in the form into some sort of report which is either stored or emailed to a web site administrator.

Let's look at a Zope implementation of the feedback application. First, we need an HTML file for our feedback form:

```
<HTML>
<HEAD><TITLE>Feedback Form</TITLE></HEAD>
<BODY>
<P>
<FORM ACTION="/cgi-bin/feedback/save_feedback" METHOD="POST">
Type of feedback:
<SELECT NAME="feedback_type">
<OPTION> Compliment
<OPTION> Criticism
</SELECT>
</P>
<P>
Your comments:
<TEXTAREA NAME="comments"></TEXTAREA>
</P>
<INPUT TYPE="SUBMIT" VALUE="Submit Feedback">
</FORM>
</BODY>
</HTML>
```

Next, we create our feedback application:

File feedback.py

```
"""feedback.py: A simple feedback form application"""
def save_feedback(feedback_type, comments):
    """A function to handle submitted feedback form data"""
    # Open a file for appending to save the feedback,
    # creating the file if necessary.
    try: file=open("feedback_data", "a")
    except IOError:
        file=open("feedback_data", "w")
    # Save the data
    file.write("Feedback type: %s\n" % feedback_type)
    file.write("Comments: %s\n\n" % comments)
    file.close()
    return "Thank you for your feedback!"
```

That's it. When a web user submits the feedback form, the Zope ORB finds the target of the request, our save_feedback function. It finds that save_feedback takes two arguments, feedback_type and comments. These two values are found in the form data submitted in the request, and passed as the arguments to save_feedback when Zope calls the function. The save_feedback function simply appends the data to a file, and the return value is then sent back to the web user.

Perhaps you later decide that you also want a version of the feedback application that emails the web user's comments to a site administrator. To do this, you would simply add another function to feedback.py:

```python
def mail_feedback(feedback_type, comments):
    """A function to email submitted feedback form data"""
    recipients=['admin@mydomain.com']
    import smtplib
    s=smtplib.SMTP("mail.mydomain.com")

    msg="""
From: webuser@mydomain.com
Subject: Feedback
%s""" % comments

    s.sendmail("webuser@mydomain.com", recipients, msg)
    s.close()
    return "Thank you for your feedback!"
```

26.2.5 Guest books and ad generators

Zope can do everything normal CGI scripts can do, only better.

One of the nice things about using Zope is that you can provide a lot of functionality without having to deal with an ever-growing number of separate CGI scripts. If you need new functionality in your Zope application, you simply add new objects. This program demonstrates a simple Web-based guestbook, which generates a form for web user, handles submissions of that form, and acknowledges successful submissions.

File guestbook.py

```python
"""Module guestbook: a simple guestbook application"""

class GuestBook:
    """A guestbook object that provides both the forms
       and the handling of submitted form data."""

    def __init__(self, title, filename):
        self.title=title
        self.filename=filename

    def guestbookForm(self):
        """Return the guestbook form to the user"""
        return """<HTML>
                <HEAD><TITLE>%s</TITLE></HEAD>
                <BODY>
                <H2>%s</H2>
                Please sign our guestbook!
                <P>
                <FORM ACTION="signGuestBook" METHOD="POST">
                Name: <INPUT TYPE="TEXT" NAME="name"><BR>
                Email: <INPUT TYPE="TEXT" NAME="email"><BR>
                <INPUT TYPE="SUBMIT" VALUE="Sign Guestbook">
                </FORM>
                </BODY>
                </HTML>""" % (self.title, self.title)

    def successPage(self):
        """Return a page to thank the user on success"""
```

```
        return """<HTML>
                <HEAD><TITLE>%s</TITLE></HEAD>
                <BODY>
                <H2>Thank you!</H2>
                Thank you for signing %s!
                </BODY>
                </HTML>""" % (self.title, self.title)

    def signGuestBook(self, name, email='not specified'):
        """Handle a submitted guestbook form"""

        # Open a file to save the Guestbook entry.
        try: file=open(self.filename, 'a')
        except IOError:
            file=open(self.filename, 'w')
        entry='Guestbook entry: %s %s\n' % (name, email)
        file.write(entry)
        file.close()
        return self.successPage()

# Create an instance of a GuestBook.
myGuestBook=GuestBook('My GuestBook', 'guestbookdata.txt')
```

Notice in the GuestBook example that the GuestBook method that handles form submissions (`signGuestBook`) defines `email` as a keyword argument. If the user does not enter an email address in the form, the method will simply use the default value for `email` defined in the method signature. The `name` argument, however, is a required argument. If Zope fails to find a name field in the submitted form data (or elsewhere in the HTTP request), an HTML error message will *automatically* be returned to the user informing him that he forgot to fill in the `name` field. A normal CGI script would have to manually verify that all expected form fields were submitted and handle the chore of returning a meaningful error message to the Web user.

Normally, Zope copies values from form fields as strings, but Zope can be told to perform type conversions automatically by including type information in HTML form variable names.

Let's look at a version of the GuestBook application that makes use of automatic type conversion. Notice that the HTML returned by the `guestbookForm` method contains a few extra form fields whose name attributes now contain Zope type conversion information.

File guestbook2.py

```
"""guestbook2: a simple guestbook application"""

class GuestBook:
    """A guestbook object that uses automatic Zope
        type conversion in its Web form"""

    def __init__(self, title, filename):
        self.title=title
        self.filename=filename

    def guestbookForm(self):
        """Return the guestbook form to the user"""
```

```
            return """<HTML>
                <HEAD><TITLE>%s</TITLE></HEAD>
                <BODY>
                <H2>%s</H2>
                Please sign the guestbook!
                <P>
                <FORM ACTION="signGuestBook" METHOD="POST">
                Name: <INPUT TYPE="TEXT" NAME="name:required"><BR>
                Age: <INPUT TYPE="TEXT" NAME="age:int"><BR>
                Email: <INPUT TYPE="TEXT" NAME="email:required"><BR>
                Which sports do you like? Check all that apply:
                <INPUT TYPE="CHECKBOX" NAME="sports:list"
                   VALUE="baseball"> Baseball <BR>
                <INPUT TYPE="CHECKBOX" NAME="sports:list"
                   VALUE="football"> Football <BR>
                <INPUT TYPE="CHECKBOX" NAME="sports:list"
                   VALUE="basketball"> Basketball <BR>
                <INPUT TYPE="CHECKBOX" NAME="sports:list"
                   VALUE="golf"> Golf <BR>
                <INPUT TYPE="SUBMIT" VALUE="Sign Guestbook">
                </FORM>
                </BODY>
                </HTML>""" % (self.title, self.title)

    def successPage(self):
        """Return a page to thank the user on success"""
        return """<HTML>
                <HEAD><TITLE>%s</TITLE></HEAD>
                <BODY>
                <H2>%s</H2>
                Thank you for signing!
                </BODY>
                </HTML>""" % (self.title, self.title)

    def signGuestBook(self, name, age, email, sports):
        """Handle a submitted guestbook form"""

        # Open a file to save the guestbook entry.
        try: file=open(self.filename, 'a')
        except IOError:
            file=open(self.filename, 'w')

        # Sports will be passed as a list.
        num=len(sports)

        entry='Guestbook entry: %s %s age %d, likes %d sports.\n' \
            % (name, email, age, num)
        file.write(entry)
        file.close()
        return self.successPage()

# Create an instance of a GuestBook.
myGuestBook=GuestBook('My GuestBook', 'guestbookdata.txt')
```

In the form generated by the guestbookForm method, the input tag for the age field is named "age:int". The :int part of the name indicates to Zope that the field should be converted to an integer before passing it to the published method. The guestbookForm HTML now contains a sequence of CHECKBOX fields which allow the user to select his favorite sports. By specifying the name of these fields as "sports:list", Zope can automatically convert the form data relating to the sports fields into a list containing all of the values selected by the user. Finally, we specified :required for both the name and email fields. This lets Zope know that these fields must be nonempty strings.

Other type conversions supported by Zope are float, long, date, tuple, tokens, lines, text, and boolean. If a value entered in a form does not match a type specification, or if a required form value is omitted, Zope automatically generates an error response.

All of this automation is great, but what if you need to do more advanced things like set HTTP cookies or return data of a type other than text or HTML? For every request handled, Zope creates a REQUEST and a RESPONSE object that provide a nice object interface for performing these kinds of tasks. The REQUEST and RESPONSE objects can be used by an application simply by including them in the method signature of a published method.

This program demonstrates the use of the REQUEST and RESPONSE objects. It is a simple random web ad generator whose URL can be called from HTML pages (or Zope-generated HTML) to insert an ad into the page.

File ads.py

```
"""ads: a simple random ad generator"""

class AdGenerator:
    """A random ad generator object. It is passed the name
       of a directory containing ads - files in .gif format"""

    def __init__(self, ad_dir):
        self.ads_dir=ad_dir

    def random_ad(self, RESPONSE):
        """Return a random ad"""
        import os, whrandom

        # Select a random ad file.
        ad_list=os.listdir(self.ad_dir)
        ad_name=whrandom.choice(ad_list)
        ad_name=os.path.join(self.ad_dir, ad_name)

        # Open ad file, using 'rb' to open it in binary mode!
        ad_file=open(ad_name, 'rb')
        ad_data=ad_file.read()
        ad_file.close()

        # Set the content-type of the response.
        RESPONSE.setHeader('content-type', 'image/gif')
        return ad_data

# Create an instance of the ad generator,
# passing the directory where ads are kept.

generator=AdGenerator('/www/ads/gifs')
```

Returning nontext data is as simple as including the RESPONSE object in the method signature and setting the correct content-type. A variation on the random ad generator demonstrates using both the REQUEST and RESPONSE objects. This new version uses HTTP cookies to avoid showing a client the same ad twice in a row, and keeps a log of the names of remote computers that access ads. It can also return ads in both .gif and .jpg format.

File ads2.py

```
"""ads2: a fancier random ad generator"""

class AdGenerator:
    """A random ad generator object. It is passed the name
       of a directory containing ads - files in .gif format"""

    def __init__(self, ad_dir):
        self.ads_dir=ad_dir

    def image_type(self, filename):
        # This method is not published.

        typemap={'.gif' : 'image/gif', '.jpg' : 'image/jpeg'}
        ext=filename[-4:]
        return typemap[ext]

    def log_info(self, remote_host, user_agent)
        # This method is not published.

        try: log=open('log.txt', 'a')
        except IOError:
          log=open('log.txt', 'w')
        line='Host: %s, Browser: %s\n' % (remote_host, user_agent)
        log.write(line)
        log.close()

    def random_ad(self, REQUEST, RESPONSE, last_ad_cookie=''):
        """Return a random ad"""
        import os, whrandom

        # Log some info about this request.
        self.log_info(REQUEST['REMOTE_HOST'],
                      REQUEST['HTTP_USER_AGENT'])

        # Select a random ad file.
        ad_list=os.listdir(self.ad_dir)
        ad_name=whrandom.choice(ad_list)
        ad_name=os.path.join(self.ad_dir, ad_name)

        # Make sure we don't send the same ad twice in a row.
        if last_ad_cookie:
          while (last_ad_cookie == ad_name)
            ad_name=whrandom.choice(ad_list)
            ad_name=os.path.join(self.ad_dir, ad_name)

        # Determine the ad type.
        ad_type=self.image_type(ad_name)

        # Open ad file, using 'rb' to open it in binary mode!
```

```
ad_file=open(ad_name, 'rb')
ad_data=ad_file.read()
ad_file.close()
```

 # Set a cookie containing the name of the ad served this time.
RESPONSE.setCookie('last_ad_cookie', ad_name)

 # Set the content-type of the response.
RESPONSE.setHeader('content-type', ad_type)
```
return ad_data
```

 # Create an instance of the ad generator,
 # passing the directory where ads are kept.

```
generator=AdGenerator('/www/ads/gifs')
```

26.3 Advanced Zope

As we've seen it's quite easy to get started programming with Zope. But what happens when your project grows? Zope provides many advanced features that help you in significant Web application projects. Perhaps, more importantly, Zope gets out of your way, and frees you to write good clean object-oriented code, which can significantly improve your development process on large projects. Zope allows you to get started simply, but provides facilities for advanced work when you are ready for them. Large CGI applications are notoriously fragile, but Zope allows you to avoid these clumsy structures.

Let's explore a couple of Zope's advanced features.

26.3.1 HTML generation with DocumentTemplate

One common problem when writing web applications is the mutual dependence of code and HTML. This interdependence makes it difficult to change the look and feel of a web application without mucking around in the code. This problem frustrates both programmers and designers. Zope's DocumentTemplate package helps solve this problem by allowing an object's HTML representation to be defined outside the code. Using DocumentTemplate, HTML templates may be edited by people who know HTML and don't know Python, while associated Python code may be edited by people who know Python but not HTML.

DocumentTemplates provide for the creation of textual documents, such as HTML pages, from template sources by inserting data from Python objects and namespaces. However, there is nothing web-specific about DocumentTemplate; it can be used for any Python text generation project. Here's a simple DocumentTemplate:

File my_template.dtml

```
My name is <!--#var name--> and I am <!--#var age--> years old.
```

Here's a simple program that uses this template:

 # Create a template from a text file.
#
```
template=DocumentTemplate.HTMLFile("my_template.dtml")
```

```
# Render the template.
#
print template(name="Billy", age=77)
```

When you run the program it will print

⇒ **My name is Billy and I am 77 years old.**

As you can see, DocumentTemplate tag syntax is similar to that of server-side include (SSI) tags commonly used by web servers. There are many special DocumentTemplate tags, but the most basic one is the var tag. A var tag searches for a variable and inserts its value into the template text. In the case of our example we specified the variables name and age as key word arguments when we called the template instance. DocumentTemplates can also locate variables in objects by searching for object attributes and calling object methods. An example:

```
class Person:
    "A simple person"
    def __init__(self,name,age):
        self.name=name
        self.age=age
```

```
# Create a Person instance.
#
bill=Person("Billy",77)
```

```
# Create a template from a text file.
#
template=DocumentTemplate.HTMLFile("my_template.dtml")
```

```
# Render the template.
#
print template(bill)
```

When you run the program it will print

⇒ **My name is Billy and I am 77 years old.**

This is all fine and good, but what does this have to do with Zope, and object publishing? Well, one important thing about DocumentTemplates is that they masquerade as functions, so the Zope ORB will call templates that are stored as attributes of published objects. When publishing the DocumentTemplate, Zope will pass the object in which the template was found and the HTTP request object as arguments.

Let's update our example one more time to demonstrate this principle:

```
class Person:
    "A simple person"
    def __init__(self,name,age):
        self.name=name
        self.age=age

    # document template class attribute
    # which masquerades as a method
    index_html=DocumentTemplate.HTMLFile("my_template.dtml")

bill=Person("Billy",77)
```

Now when Zope publishes the `index_html` method of the `bill` object it will return:

⇒ **My name is Billy and I am 77 years old.**

This is because Zope calls `bill`'s `DocumentTemplate` with the `bill` object and the request as arguments:

```
>>> bill.index_html(bill,REQUEST)
```

Note that the DocumentTemplate is a class attribute, which is shared by all `Person` instances. If you change the template file (`my_template.dtml`), then the rendering of all `Person` instances will change accordingly, and you don't need to change any Python code. So using DocumentTemplates with published objects gives you a simple way to control the look and feel of the published object.

Another thing to note is that when Zope calls a DocumentTemplate, it passes a `REQUEST` object to the template that encapsulates the HTTP request information. This means that your templates can reference HTTP request information like this:

```
You just came from this URL: <!--#var HTTP_REFERER-->
And this is the web browser you are using: <!--#var HTTP_USER_AGENT-->
```

So not only can you use a DocumentTemplate to represent your object in HTML, you can also use it to tune the look and feel of your published object to match the HTTP request.

26.3.2 Conditionals, sequences, and expressions

DocumentTemplate supports the conditional insertion of text. This means you can perform if-then types of comparisons within your templates. Here's a simple example:

```
<!--#if old-->I am old.<!--#/if-->
```

If this template is passed a variable named `old` with a `true` (not `0`, `""` or `None`) value, then the template will display:

⇒ *I am old.*

You can also add an else tag to provide for more powerful condition testing:

```
<!--#if HTTP_REFERER-->
You came to this page from <!--#var HTTP_REFERER-->.
<!--#else-->
You came to this page directly.
<!--#/if-->
```

This template looks for an `HTTP_REFERER` variable in its namespace, and returns an appropriate message.

Another feature of `DocumentTemplate` is to loop over sequences.

File people_template.dtml

```
<!--#in people-->
name: <!--#var name--> age: <!--#var age-->
<!--#/in-->
```

This template will loop over a sequence of objects and print the name and age of each object. Here's an example of how we might use this template:

```
class Person:
    "A simple person"
    def __init__(self,name,age):
        self.name=name
        self.age=age
```

```
# Define a sequence.
#
my_family=[Person("Billy",77),Person("Pearl", 68),
            Person("Willard",72)]
```

```
# Define a template.
#
people_template=DocumentTemplate.HTMLFile("people_template.dtml")
```

```
# Render the template.
#
print people_template(people=my_family)
```

This program will print:

⇒ **name: Billy age: 77**
⇒ **name: Pearl age: 68**
⇒ **name: Willard age: 72**

DocumentTemplate supports many advanced features of sequence insertion including displaying large sequences in batches.

The last feature of DocumentTemplate that we will look at here is the ability to insert snippets of Python code in templates. This trick is performed with variable expressions.

```
I am <!--#var expr="age*7"--> years old in dog years.
```

This template uses the expr feature of the var tag to multiply the variable age by 7 and display the results. This is a very powerful feature of DocumentTemplate and should be used with care. If you find yourself writing very complex expr code, you should probably write a method or function to perform the calculation and call the method or function from your template using a normal var tag instead. Here's a more complex example of how to create an HTML select tag with expr:

```
import DocumentTemplate
```

```
# Define the template.
#
select_template=DocumentTemplate.HTML("""\
<select>
<!--#in choices-->
<option><!--#if expr="_['sequence-item']==chosen"-->
    selected<!--#/if-->><!--#var sequence-item-->
<!--#/in-->
</select>""")
```

```
# Render the template.
```

```
#
print select_template(choices=[1,23,55,65,78,99],chosen=55)
```

When you run the program it prints:

```
⇒   <select>
⇒   <option>1
⇒   <option>23
⇒   <option selected>55
⇒   <option>65
⇒   <option>78
⇒   <option>99
⇒   </select>
```

In this example the DocumentTemplate builds an HTML `select` tag by looping through the sequence variable `choices`. For each item, it compares the current item (a special variable named `sequence-item`) to the variable `chosen` if they are equal, then `selected` is printed.

26.3.3 Object persistence with BoboPOS

After publishing collections of objects with Zope, you will soon want a system for saving your objects and restoring them between requests. The Zope object database `BoboPOS`* provides a solution to this problem. `BoboPOS` is a persistent-object system that provides transparent transactional object persistence to Python applications. `BoboPOS`, like DocumentTemplate is not just applicable to web applications. `BoboPOS` is based on Python's standard object serialization functionality provided by the pickle module. `BoboPOS` takes this basic functionality several steps further by allowing for such advanced features as transactions, lazy object activation, object versioning, and object reference management. Luckily you don't need to understand any of the gory details to make your objects persistent, and have them work with Zope.

To get started with `BoboPOS` you simply create a `PickleDictionary` to act as an object store and place your objects in it. Also, you must make sure your objects inherit from the mix-in Persistent class, and obey some simple conventions. Using `BoboPOS` is similar to using `shelve` for object persistence. Here's a complete example of creating and storing a persistent object with `BoboPOS`:

```
import BoboPOS

class Person(BoboPOS.Persistent):
    "A persistent person"
    def __init__(self,name,age):
        self.name=name
        self.age=age
```

---

* At the time of this writing, Zope's next generation object persistence package, ZODB 3, has just entered alpha testing. ZODB 3 considerably improves Zope's persistence ability by offering concurrency and greater options for object storage. While ZODB 3 adds many new features, the fundamentals of object persistence with BoboPOS covered in this chapter are almost entirely applicable to ZODB 3.

```
# Define the object store.
#
object_store=BoboPOS.PickleDictionary("people_store.db")

# Retrieve billy from the object store.
#
if object_store.has_key("billy"):
    # If billy is in the object store, then
    # load it from the object store.
    #
    billy=object_store["billy"]
else:
    # Since billy isn't already in the object
    # store, we must create the object and
    # place it in the object store.
    #
    billy=object_store["billy"]=Person("Billy",77)

    # Normally Zope will handle transactions,
    # but in this special case, we need to
    # commit the transaction to save the new
    # persistent object.
    #
    get_transaction().commit()

# Display the object that we retrieved
# from the object store.
#
print billy.name, billy.age
```

First we have the definition of a persistent Person class which inherits from Persistent. Then we define the object store, which is a `PickleDictionary` object. Note that a `PickleDictionary` works just like a normal dictionary—you put and get items with the same syntax you would use for putting and getting items from a normal dictionary. Next comes the tricky part of the program where it not only loads an object from the database, but it also checks to see if the object exists, and creates it if necessary. The first time you run the program the object store will be created and the `billy` object will be stored in it. On later executions, the database will already exist, and it will already contain the `billy` object, so the program will merely load `billy` from the object store.

After creating the `PickleDictionary` and placing objects in it, object persistence becomes almost totally transparent. Zope will handle transactions for you when your persistent objects change. If the name or age attributes of the `billy` object are changed in the course of a web request, the new state of the `billy` object will automatically be saved. Another important feature is that subobjects of persistent objects may be created or changed and they are automatically saved by BoboPOS. So for example if `billy` gets a son

```
Billy.son=Person("Dan",55)
```

the subobject will automatically be persistent. In fact, `billy.son` could contain more subobjects, all of which would automatically be saved and restored as needed by BoboPOS.

Zope acts as the transaction manager and automatically starts and commits the transaction at the start and end of an HTTP request. If an error occurs during the request Zope, aborts the transaction, so your persistent objects are never left stranded in an inconsistent state.

Because of the ease of creating persistent object hierarchies, a common Zope practice is to create a `PickleDictionary` with only a few root objects. The rest of the published objects are created as subobjects of the root persistent objects. Not only is this arrangement convenient for `BoboPOS`, but Zope itself excels at traversing objects by mapping URLs to object hierarchies.

To recap, here's a recipe for using `BoboPOS`:

- Create persistent objects by subclassing `BoboPOS.Persistent`
- Create a `PickleDictionary` and store all your persistent objects directly or indirectly, in it as subobjects.
- Create subobjects of persistent objects which are themselves persistent or are used immutably.

Zope will automatically handle transactions and save and restore your persistent objects as needed.

26.3.4 More features

Zope is a powerful collection of tools and techniques for web application development in Python. In this chapter we have only scratched the surface of major Zope components. Though you don't need to know about and understand all aspects of Zope to use it effectively, it is tremendously scalable. As you begin to do more advanced things, it is likely that Zope will already have features to help you.

Zope can provide access control for your published objects by performing automated authentication and authorization. Zope access control works with hierarchies of web objects to provide a flexible way of controlling access to your resources. You can assign access roles to published objects and construct user databases to map web users to access roles.

Zope remote procedure call (`ZPublisher.Client`) is a utility which allows remote procedure calls (RPC) over HTTP with objects published by Zope. Zope RPC allows you to write Python programs that access Web objects as if they were local functions or objects with methods. Not only can you call remote objects, but you can receive the results of the call as real Python objects.

One of the great things about Zope is that it hides the publishing plumbing. Because of this, it is easy to switch publishing protocols easily without changing your published module. One of the most popular reasons to switch plumbing is to go from CGI to a form of *long running process*. A long running process is a server application that doesn't launch and exit with each HTTP request like a CGI program, but instead starts once and services many requests. A long running process in general performs much more efficiently and quickly than a process that starts and stops with every request. There are a number of ways to use long running processes with Zope, including two Python web servers written just for Zope, ZopeHTTPServer and Zserver, and FastCGI, Persistent CGI, and web server-modules.

One of Zope's most valuable resources is its active community of users and developers. Python developers are increasingly turning to Zope to implement their web applications, and Zope has been used as the foundation for a number of commercial products. The primary organ of this community is the Zope mailing list. On this list you can exchange questions and answers and exchange proposals with many Zope users and even the authors of Zope. The Zope mailing list is archived at http://www.zope.org/mailman/listinfo/zope.

26.3.5   The Web Job Board

Since building web applications with Zope can be complex, we have provided you with a complete working application to show how its done. The Web Job Board is a system for posting job openings online. It demonstrates how Zope, DocumentTemplate, and `Bobo-POS` can work together to form a coherent Web application. The job board consists of

- JobBoard.py   The module that contains the JobBoard and JobLising classes
- job_app.py   The module published by Zope
- job_board.dtml   A DocumentTemplate file used by the JobBoard class to display itself
- job_listing.dtml   A DocumentTemplate file used by the JobListing class to display itself
- job_add.dtml   A DocumentTemplate file used by the JobBoard class to gather information to create a `JobListing` object
- confirm.dtml   A DocumentTemplate file used by the JobBoard class to give the user confirmation

In addition, when the application is run, it will create a job_board.db file to store the persistent objects.

The most import part of the job board application is the JobBoard.py module that defines the JobBoard and the JobListing classes. The JobListing class describes a job—what the job title is, a description of the job, and when the job listing closes. The JobBoard class is a collection of JobListing objects along with methods for adding job listings and getting rid of old ones. Notice that DocumentTemplate objects are used to create the web interface methods of the classes. Notice also that both classes are persistent, so that they can be stored in a `BoboPOS` object store.

Let's look at how Zope will map URLs to these objects. A JobBoard object functions as a mapping object and holds `JobListing` objects. For example:

```
# my_board is a JobBoard instance
# my_listing is a JobListing instance
my_board["listing"]=my_listing
```

If, for example, the URL of the `my_board` object is http://www.mydomain.com/cgi-bin/board, then the URL of `my_listing` would be http://www.mydomain.com/cgi-bin/board/listing.

This is the simple magic of Zope at work. Given the URL of a root object, it is easy to know the URL of its subobjects. Our application takes advantage of this by never using absolute URLs, but merely using relative URLs to create hyperlinks from the JobBoard object to JobListing objects and back. To facilitate this process, each JobListing object has an `id` attribute which should be the same as its key in the JobBoard mapping object. So in effect, every JobListing object knows its own URL.

You may also notice that there is very little web-specific code in the JobBoard.py file. This arrangement will make it much easier to maintain your application as it grows and changes. This arrangement also makes it easier to give your application an HTML facelift without messing up its guts.

Figures 26.1-26.4 are screen shots of what the Web Job Board looks like in action. Notice how the URLs map to methods of the JobBoard and JobListing objects. In these screen shots, the base URL of the Web Job Board is http://localhost/scripts/jobboard.py.

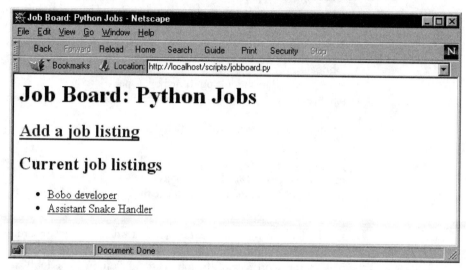

Figure 26.1 The JobBoard object's default method, index_html

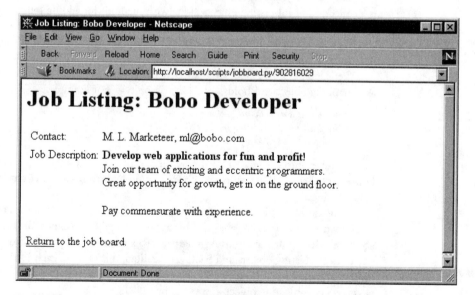

Figure 26.2 A JobListing object displaying itself with its index_html method.

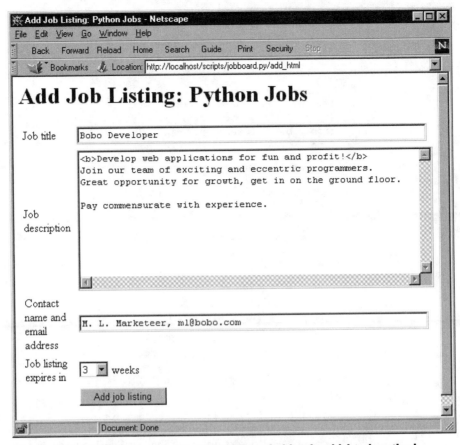

Figure 26.3 The form created by the JobBoard object's add_html method.

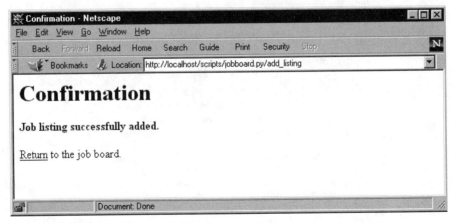

Figure 26.4 The confirmation screen that is returned after a JobListing is created

```
"""JobBoard - An example Zope application
JobBoard.py  - The module which defines the job listing
                 and job board classes
"""

from DocumentTemplate import HTMLFile
from BoboPOS import Persistent
from BoboPOS.PersistentMapping import PersistentMapping
import time
```
 # location of dtml files
```
dtml_loc="D:\\Zope\\JobBoard\\"

class JobBoard(PersistentMapping):
    """A collection of job postings"""

    def __init__(self,title):
        PersistentMapping.__init__(self)
        self.title=title

    def values(self):
        self.expire_listings()
        return PersistentMapping.values(self)

    def expire_listings(self):
        "delete old job listings"
        for key,job in self.items():
            if job.expired():
                del self[key]

    def add_listing(self,title,description,
                    contact,weeks,REQUEST=None):
        "add a new job listing - called by add_html"
```
            # figure out listing expiry time
```
        expires=time.time()+weeks*60*60*24*7
```
            # pick a unique id
```
        id=self.unique_key()
```
            # create new listing object
```
        listing=JobListing(id,title,description,contact,expires)
```
            # add new listing
```
        self[id]=listing
        if REQUEST is not None:
```
                # if this method is called by Zope,
                # return a confirmation message
```
            return self.confirm_html(
                message="Job listing successfully added.")

    def unique_key(self):
        key=int(time.time())
        while self.has_key(key):
            key=key+1
        return str(key)
```
    # default HTML method

```
    index_html=HTMLFile(dtml_loc+"job_board.dtml")
```

 # add a listing HTML form
```
    add_html=HTMLFile(dtml_loc+"job_add.dtml")
```

 # confirmation HTML
```
    confirm_html=HTMLFile(dtml_loc+"confirm.dtml")

class JobListing(Persistent):
    """A job listing"""

    def __init__(self,id,title,description,contact,expires):
        "create a new job listing"
        self.id=id
        self.title=title
        self.description=description
        self.contact=contact
        self.expires=expires

    def expired(self):
        "is this job listing stale?"
        return time.time()   self.expires
```

 # default HTML method
```
    index_html=HTMLFile(dtml_loc+"job_listing.dtml")
```

File job_app.py

```
"""JobBoard - An example Zope application

job_app.py - The module which is published by Zope
"""

import BoboPOS
import JobBoard
```

 # location of the object store
```
db_loc="D:\\Zope\\JobBoard\\"

def create_job_board():
    "creates a new job board"
    db["python_jobs"]=JobBoard.JobBoard("Python Jobs")
    get_transaction().commit()
```

 # define the object store
```
db=BoboPOS.PickleDictionary(db_loc+"job_board.db")
if not db.has_key("python_jobs"):
```
    # if the object store is empty,
    # create a new job board object
```
    create_job_board()
```

 # defines the job board as the
 # only object published by this
 # module
```
bobo_application=db["python_jobs"]
```

 # show the tracebacks for debugging
```
__bobo_hide_tracebacks__=None
```

File job_board.dtml

```
<html>
<head><title>Job Board: <!--#var title--></title></head>
<body bgcolor="#FFFFFF">
<h1>Job Board: <!--#var title--></h1>

<h2><a href="add_html">Add a job listing</a></h2>

<!--#if values-->
<h2>Current job listings</h2>
<ul>
<!--#in values-->
<li><a href="<!--#var id-->"><!--#var title--></a>
<!--#/in-->
</ul>
<!--#else-->
<h2>There are currently no job listings.</h2>
<!--#/if-->
</body>
</html>
```

File job_listing.dtml

```
<html>
<head><title>Job Listing: <!--#var title--></title></head>
<body bgcolor="#FFFFFF">
<h1>Job Listing: <!--#var title--></h1>

<table>
<tr><td>Contact:</td><td><!--#var contact--></td></tr>
<tr valign="top"><td>Job Description:</td>
<td><!--#var description fmt="multi-line"--></td></tr>
</table>
<p><a href="../index_html">Return</a> to the job board.</p>
</body>
</html>
```

File confirm.dtml

```
<html>
<head><title>Confirmation</title></head>
<body bgcolor="#FFFFFF">
<h1>Confirmation</h1>

<p><b><!--#var message--></b></p>

<p><a href="index_html">Return</a> to the job board.</p>
</body>
</html>
```

```
<html>
<head>
<title>Add Job Listing: <!--#var title--></title>
</head>
<body bgcolor="#FFFFFF">
<h1>Add Job Listing: <!--#var title--></h1>

<form action="add_listing" method="post">
<table>
<tr><td>Job title</td>
<td><input type="text" name="title" size=60></td></tr>
<tr><td>Job description</td>
<td><textarea name="description:text" cols=60 rows=10>
</textarea></td></tr>
<tr><td>Contact name and email address</td>
<td><input type="text" name="contact" size=60></td></tr>
<tr><td>Job listing expires in</td>
<td><select name="weeks:int">
<option>1
<option>2
<option>3
<option>4
<option>5
<option>6
</select>
weeks
</td></tr>
<tr><td></td>
<td><input type="submit" value="Add job listing"></td></tr>
</table>
</form>
</body>
</html>
```

CHAPTER 27

What else can Python do?

The preceding chapters have described what I consider to be the Python necessities, those elements that are basic to the language, or which are useful in so many circumstances that almost everyone should be aware of them. However, Python provides many other abilities that are helpful in specialized circumstances. This chapter describes some of the most outstanding of these. While it won't teach you to use these extended abilities, it will let you know of the Python packages out there that might solve your problem immediately.

Some of what this chapter covers comes in the standard Python package, and all you need to do to use that is to read the appropriate section of the *Python Library Reference*, and import the appropriate module. Other capabilities are provided by extensions or outside packages. For these, I'll tell you where to look on the web for the most recent versions.

A major Python effort now under way is the development of the NumPy numeric extension package. The aim of this effort is to give Python users direct access to highly-optimized numeric matrix processing libraries typically used in scientific computing or other number-crunching environments. The NumPy package is not yet complete, but is already highly useable. Eventually, it will probably be incorporated into the Python distribution; for now, you can obtain the most recent version from the Python home page, http://www.python.org.

The Python Imaging Library (PIL) is a project aimed at providing fast, easy-to-use direct Python access to image data, both for processing and display purposes. Like NumPy, it is not yet complete, but is highly useful. Get it from http://www.python.org.

The standard Python distribution ships with several modules which are useful in conjunction with the World Wide Web and the Internet.

The `cgi` module makes the task of writing cgi scripts considerably easier, by automatically parsing URLs and form specifications, and providing various Python classes and functions to operate with the cgi specification in a high-level manner.

The `urllib` module can be used to fetch files or other data across a network, in a manner similar to reading a file using the built-in open and file-reading functions. It supports HTTP, FTP, and Gopher protocols.

The `httplib` module provides an interface to the low-level HTTP protocol. It is used by `urllib`, and may also be used directly for specialized tasks.

The `ftplib` module provides an interface to the FTP protocol, and can be used to implement any sort of FTP-related application. For example, you might use `Tkinter` and the `ftplib` module to write a GUI-based FTP client.

The `nntplib` module provides a full interface to Internet news services; it can be used to implement newsreaders, automated downloaders for newsgroups, and so forth.

The `htmllib` module provides services for parsing HTML. The `xmllib` module does the same thing for XML, the eXtended Markup Language that might replace HTML.

Various other modules provide more specialized net-related functions; MIME-related utilities, email utilities, and so forth.

Of course, for serious web use, you probably wish to make use of the free `HTMLgen` and `Bobo` packages, which are not part of the standard Python distribution, but which are readily available and have already been described in this book.

Python supports multithreaded programming through use of the `threading` library module which is on most systems whose native operating systems support threads. This includes Windows 95 and NT, and most UNIX variants. On some UNIX systems, you may have to recompile or reconfigure to get the `threading` module working. This module provides threads based for the most part on the Java threading model. There is a lower-level `thread` module available as well.

A P P E N D I X

The Quick Python reference

This appendix contains a mini-reference for the Python core language and a few aspects of the standard Python libraries, arranged by functionality. It is intended to be concise and to provide all information needed to begin using Python in a significant manner, but it is not a complete or detailed reference. The most significant omission is that many of the standard Python libraries, excepting just those that are critical to using the language in any real sense, have been omitted. In addition:

- Extremely obvious elements of the language (such as how to add two numbers) are often presented without explanation, to keep the reference manageable.

- Features that are documented here are not necessarily completely documented. Particularly obscure aspects of a Python command, for example, might be omitted to keep the reference concise.

A.1 Reference conventions

The functionality available in Python is mostly explained through a combination of example, semiformal specification, and explanation. Depending on what is being described, one or more of these may be employed.

Semiformal specifications for functions are different from any convention employed previously in the book. They are employed to give a concise representation of the function being discussed, its arguments, results, and exceptions raised. The general format is something like:

```
fun(string, list1, list2, index, size) → result
      ⇒ exception1, exception2…
```

The following points apply to semiformal specifications:

- The syntax of the function or feature being discussed (fun in this case) is presented in bold.
  The arguments are italicized, and their names can either be indicative of the type of argument expected (string, list1, list2), or can be a more specific name which indicates type by association. (I typically associate names like index and size with integers, and I hope you do too.)
- The result is given only if it is meaningful.
  If present, it follows the thin arrow →, and its name will indicate the type of the result.
- If the function can raise exceptions, the exceptions it might raise are given following the thick arrow ⇒.
  However, only exceptions of specific interest to that function are given. For example, many functions expect arguments of a given type, and will raise a TypeError exception if arguments of the wrong type are given. But this is not usually of particular interest—such exceptions indicate a program error rather than an exception that is intended to be used in conjunction with that function.
- Sometimes it will be desirable to include examples along with function specifications. These are given after the semiformal specifications, and consist of a typical application of that function, followed by a right-arrow, followed by the result of that call.

For example:

A Typical Reference Entry: **Semiformal specification of string.split, giving arguments and result type.** ●

```
string.split(string, splitstring, max) → listOfStrings
string.split("How    are \t\tyou?") → ['How', 'are', 'you?']
string.split("date::amount::balance", '::') → ['date',
    'amount', 'balance']
string.split("1.2.3.4.5", '.', 3) → ['1', '2', '3', '4.5']
```
❶

Use *splitstring* as a delimiter, on which to split *string* into a list of substrings. *splitstring* is optional and, if not given, `string.split` will use runs of whitespace as delimiters. *max* is optional and, if present, defines a maximum number of splits to be performed.

❶ Examples of `string.split` in action—calls on left side of arrow, results on the right.

A.2 Special identifiers

Python's keywords

```
>>> import keyword
>>> keyword.dwlist
⇒   ['and', 'assert', 'break', 'class', 'continue', 'def',
    'del', 'elif', 'else', 'except', 'exec', 'finally',
    'for', 'from', 'global', 'if', 'import', 'in', 'is',
    'lambda', 'not', 'or', 'pass', 'print', 'raise', 'return',
    'try', 'while']
```

Built-in functions in Python

```
>>> import builtin
>>> filter(lambda x: type(eval(x)) is type(abs),
    dir(__builtin__))
⇒   ['__import__', 'abs', 'apply', 'buffer', 'callable', 'chr',
    'cmp', 'coerce', 'compile', 'complex', 'delattr', 'dir',
    'divmod', 'eval', 'execfile', 'filter', 'float', 'getattr',
    'globals', 'hasattr', 'hash', 'hex', 'id', 'input', 'int',
    'intern', 'isinstance', 'issubclass', 'len', 'list',
    'locals', 'long', 'map', 'max', 'min', 'oct', 'open', 'ord',
    'pow', 'range', 'raw_input', 'reduce', 'reload', 'repr',
    'round', 'setattr', 'slice', 'str', 'tuple', 'type', 'vars',
    'xrange']
```

A.3 Operators

Below is a concise table of Python operators. The most obvious are not given any further explanation. Operator semantics which are not common outside of Python are explained in the reference and/or main book sections covering the relevant data types.

User-defined classes can define their own methods to be invoked whenever an instance of that class is used with a standard operator. See the chapter on *Special method attributes* for details.

Logical operators

and	Logical 'and', e.g. `if (x>y) and (m==n)` …
not	Logical unary not, e.g. `if not (x==y)` …

or	Logical 'or', e.g. `if (x>y) or (m==n)` …

Comparisons

Comparisons are valid on all Python types, not just numeric objects. See the next reference section for an explanation of how comparisons order objects of various types.

<	Strictly-less-than test.		>	Strictly-greater-than test.
<=	Less-than-or-equal-to test.		>=	Greater-than-or-equal-to test.
==	Equality test.		<>, !=	Not equals test (`<>` is obsolete).
in	x in y asks if x is equal to something in the sequence y.		**not in**	Converse of `in`.
is	x is y asks if x and y are the same object, i.e. not just equivalent, but actually the same object in the computer's memory.		**is not**	Converse of `is`.

Bitwise operators

These operators work with binary numbers on a bit-by-bit basis.

<<	`integer << n` returns `integer` shifted left n positions. It works with long integers too.		>>	Like `<<`, but shift right instead of left.
&	m & n is the bitwise 'and' of integers m and n. m and/or n may be long integers.		|	m | n is the bitwise 'or' of integers m and n. m and/or n may be long integers.
^	m ^ n is the bitwise 'exclusive-or' of integers m and n. m and/or n may be long integers.		~	~m is the bitwise negation of the integer m, defined to be $-(m+1)$. m may be a long integer.

Arithmetic-Style operators

Not all of these operators are restricted to numeric arguments. Some have meaning with lists, tuples, and so forth.

+	Numeric addition, sequence (tuple, list, or string) concatenation.		-	Numeric subtraction, numeric unary minus.
*	Numeric multiplication, list, or string replication.		/	Numeric division. Division involving only integers produces an integer.
**	Numeric exponentiation.		%	Numeric modulus (remainder), string formatting operator.

Precedence

The precedence of operators is shown below with the ordering going from lowest to highest. Those on the same line have the same precedence.

```
or
and
not
<, <=, ==, >=, >, !=, <>, is, in, is not, not in
|
^
&
<<, >>
+, -
*, /, %
**
unary +, unary -, unary ~
```

For example, the following conditional:

```
if x<y<m+n*n and not k or x is 2+y**2:
```

would be evaluated as

```
if (x<y<(m+(n*n))) and (not k) or (x is (2+(y**2)))):
```

A.4 *Comparison ordering*

Any two Python objects can be compared using the standard comparison operators, and give a meaningful answer. The following table describes briefly how this works.

Numbers	Numbers are generally compared exactly as expected, i.e. "0.1 < 3L" is a true statement. The one exception is that complex numbers are not compared in a mathematically meaningful way. They are compared by size of their real part first and then by their imaginary part.
Strings	Strings are compared with one another using a standard character-based ordering. 'aaa' < 'aab' and 'aa' < 'aaa' are both true. Uppercase comes before lowercase, i.e. 'Aa' < 'a'.
Sequences	Any two sequences of the same type may be compared element-by-element. Given two lists, list1 and list2, the first elements of each list are compared against each; if one of those elements is less than the other, the corresponding list is less than the other list. If both first elements are equal, the comparison moves to the second element of each list, and so on. If the comparison reaches the end of one list (all elements to that point being equal), the shorter list is the lesser. If both lists have exactly the same elements, they are equal. For example, [1] < [1, 2] is true, [0, 1] < [1, 1] is true, and [1, 2] == [1, 2] is true, and similarly for tuples. Of course, the elements of sequences may be arbitrary Python objects; comparison rules are invoked recursively. Note: a list and a tuple are considered objects of different types, and are not compared in this manner; see "Basic objects of differing types" later in this explanation of comparison rules.
Dictionaries	Two dictionaries are compared by sorting their elements by key, and then comparing the elements, one by one. Practically speaking, you'll probably never want to do more than find out if one dictionary is equivalent to another, which works exactly as expected—two dictionaries are equivalent if they have equivalent objects stored under equivalent keys. The rules for determining ordering are more complex. See the Python core documentation if you need to make use of this.

Basic objects of differing types	Comparison between two objects of different basic types is done arbitrarily but consistently; for any given version of Python, strings are either always less than lists, or lists are always less than strings. Your program can always assume this consistency during any run, but it's possible (though unlikely) that efficiency considerations might mandate changing the sense of the comparison in some future version of Python. This version of Python says that numbers are always less than lists, but the next version might say lists are always less than numbers.
Other types	For efficiency reasons, Python defaults to comparisons of most other objects (fileobjects, functions, classes) based on their memory address. This gives results which are consistent within a program, but arbitrary. The case of class instance is special, because the default method is often not what is desired.

```
>>>
class myclass:
def __init__(self): self.x = 1
a = myclass()
b = myclass()
a == b
0
```

We would normally expect a and b above to be considered equivalent, because they are of the same class and contain the same data. However, Python compares them by memory address, and since they are different objects in different memory locations, Python says they are not equal. To fix this, define an appropriate __cmp__ function in the class; Python will then use that as the comparison function, when comparing members of the class.

A.5 Numbers

Functionality related to numbers is provided by a mix of built-in functions and operators, and functions from the math module. Numeric functions are shown here; see the reference section on operators for explanation of numeric operators.

Number creation

```
1, -3, 44              # Integers (are based on the C long data type). Maximum allowed
                       # value is sys.maxint.
0xBF12, 0x1E           # Integers (hexadecimal)
0717, 012              # Integers (octal)
3.2, -31e12            # Floats (are based on the C double data type)
999999999L, 41         # Long integers (are of unlimited precision)
3j, 5+4J, 3.2 +2.1j    # Complex numbers
```

Numeric functions and constants

abs(*num*) → *num*
    Returns the absolute value of a number.

math.acos(*num*) → *num*
math.asin(*num*) → *num*

math.atan(*num*) → *num*
> Arc cosine, arc sine, arc tangent functions.

math.atan2(*x, y*) → *num*
> Returns `math.atan(x/y)`.

math.ceil(*num*) → *num*
> Ceiling of a number.

cmp(*obj1, obj2*) → *integer*
> Returns a negative integer if *obj1* < *obj2*, 0 if *obj1* == *obj2*, a positive integer if *obj1* > *obj2*. Not restricted to numbers.

coerce(*x1, y1*) → (*x2, y2*) ⇒ `TypeError`
`coerce(3, 5.0) → (3.0, 5.0)`
> Given two numeric objects *x1* and *y1*, coerce attempts to produce a tuple containing two values *x2* and *y2*, such that *x1* == *x2*, *y1* == *y2*, but *x2* and *y2* have identical types.

math.cos(*num*) → *num*
math.cosh(*num*) → *num*
> Cosine, hyperbolic cosine functions.

divmod(*numerator, denominator*) → (*quotient, remainder*)
> Returns a tuple containing both the quotient and remainder obtained by dividing *numerator* by *denominator*. However, *numerator* and *denominator* are not limited to integers—this function really performs modulus division.

math.e → *num*
> The constant value *e* = 2.71828...

math.exp(*num*) → *num*
> Returns `math.e` raised to the power num.

math.fabs(*float*) → *float*
> Absolute value function for floating-point numbers. (Calls the standard C function.)

float(*obj*) → *float* → `ValueError`
> Coerces a numeric value to be a floating point number, or tries to convert a string to a float.

math.floor(*num*) → *num*
> Returns the floor of the argument.

math.fmod(*num1, num2*) → *num*
> Nominally the functional equivalent of the operator call `num1 % num2`. Differs in that it will always return a float, negative `num1` with positive `num2` returns a negative answer, and positive `num1` with negative `num2` returns a positive answer.

hex(*integer*) → *string*
> Returns a string giving a hexadecimal representation of the integer argument.

math.hypot(*num1, num2*)
> Returns `math.sqrt(num1**2 + num2**2)`. Remember the Pythagorean Theorem?

int(*obj*) → *integer* ⇒ ValueError
   Coerces a numeric object to an integer, or tries to convert a string to an integer.

math.log(*num*) → *num*
   Log base *e*.

math.log10(*num*) → *num*
   Log base 10.

long(*obj*) → *long* ⇒ ValueError
   Coerces a numeric object to a long integer, or try to convert a string to a long integer.

max(*listOfObjs*) → *obj*
min(*listOfObjs*) → *obj*
   Returns the maximum or minimum in a list (or other sequence) of objects. This is not restricted to numbers.

math.modf(*num*) → (*fracPart*, *intPart*)
math.modf(-3.2) → (-0.2, -3)
   Returns a tuple giving the fractional part and integer part of the original number. Summing the fractional and integer part will result in the original number.

oct(*integer*) → *string*
   Returns a string giving an octal representation of the integer argument.

math.pi → *num*
   The constant value *pi* = 3.14159…

pow(*x*, *y*) → *num*
   Returns *x* raised to the power of *y*. If both *x* and *y* are of the same type (e.g., integer), the result will also be of that type, which means that pow(1, -2) will not do what you probably want it to—so be careful!

round(*float1*, *integer*) → *float2*
   Rounds *float1* to *integer* decimal places, to produce *float2*. To "break ties," rounding is done *away from zero*, which means that 0.5 rounded to zero decimal places gives 1.0, while –0.5 rounded to zero decimal places gives –1.0.

math.sin(*num*) → *num*
math.sinh(*num*) → *num*
   Sine, hyperbolic sine functions.

math.sqrt(*num*) → *num*
   Square root.

math.tan(*num*) → *num*
math.tanh(*num*) → *num*
   Tangent, hyperbolic tangent functions.

Complex numbers

complex(*num1, num2*) → complexNumber

> Returns a complex number with real part *num1* and imaginary part *num2*. If *num2* is not present defaults to zero. Returns *x* raised to the power of *y*.
>
> Access the real or imaginary parts of complex numbers with real or imag:

z.**real** → *float*
z.**imag** → *float*

> Built-in operators handle complex numbers correctly. The functions in the math module do *not* understand complex numbers; instead, use the following functions found in the **cmath** module:

acos, acosh, asin, asinh, atan, atanh, cos, cosh, e, exp, log, log10, pi, sin, sinh, sqrt, tan, tanh

> Comparisons of complex numbers are not mathematically valid. They are compared by their tuple (real, imag). If the real part of one is larger than that of the other it is taken as greater (regardless of the size of their repective imaginary parts).

A.6 Strings

Quoting strings

```
u = 'This is a string, with a newline at the end. \n'
v = "So is this, with a tab at the end. \t"
w = '''This is a triple single quoted string'''
x = """Triple double quoted-strings can
        contain real newlines (and tabs)
        (and can also function as a 'documentation string')"""
y = "Any set of strings separated by whitespace " \
        'will be concatenated into a' "single string. Thus" \
        """ this is how to define a long string without """ \
        """ newlines in it (or break a long string " \
        '''across multiple lines of input).'''
raw1 = r"In a raw string \t is a backslash and a 't', NOT a tab. "
raw2 = R"Raw strings are often used for regular expressions."
```

Escape sequences and special characters

The following escape sequences can be used in strings to denote the given special characters:
> \n—newline, \t—tab, \\—backslash, \'—single quote, \" —double quote, \a—bell, \b—backspace, \f—formfeed, \r—carriage return, and \v—vertical tab.

In addition, any ASCII character can be given by specifying its ASCII value as an octal escape sequence *nnn*, or as a hexadecimal escape sequence \x*hh*, where the *n* and *h* characters represent octal and hexadecimal digits, respectively.

Basic operations

```
len(string) → length
string[n] → character
string[m:n] → substring
string1 + string2 → string
string * integer → string
string1 == string2 → Boolean
```
Can also compare using !=, <>, (both preceding mean "not equal"), <, >, <=, >=. String comparison is done in a standard lexical order, so "aaa" < "aab" is true.

Miscellaneous functions

```
chr(integer) → string
```
Given an *integer* representing an ASCII character, returns that character as a one-character string.

```
ord(string) → integer
```
Given a one-character string returns the *integer* that it is represented by in ASCII.

```
string.lstrip(string) → string
string.rstrip(string) → string
string.strip(string) → string
```
These functions strip whitespace off the ends of strings. string.lstrip removes whitespace from the left end of the argument string, string.rstrip removes whitespace from the right end, and string.strip removes whitespace from both ends.

```
string.split(string, splitstring, max) → listOfStrings
string.split("How    are \t\tyou?") → ['How', 'are', 'you?']
string.split("date::amount::balance", '::')
                              → ['date', 'amount', balance']
string.split("1.2.3.4.5", '.', 3) → ['1', '2', '3', '4.5']
```
Uses *splitstring* as a delimiter on which to split *string* into a list of substrings. *splitstring* is optional, and, if not given, string.split will use runs of whitespace as delimiters. *max* is optional, and, if present, defines a maximum number of splits to be performed.

```
string.join(listOfStrings, joinstring) → string
string.join(['I', 'am', 'fine']) → 'I am fine'
string.join(['date', 'amount', 'balance'], '::')
                              → 'date::amount::balance'
```
Converse of string.split. Joins strings in the list *listOfStrings* into a single string, by putting *joinstring* between them and concatenating. *joinstring* is optional, and, if it is not given, a single space will be used as the *joinstring*.

Search/Replace-type functions

```
string.find(string, substring, start, end) → integer
string.rfind(string, substring, start, end) → integer
```

```
string.index(string, substring, start, end) → integer
                                          ⇒ ValueError
string.rindex(string, substring, start, end) → integer
                                          ⇒ ValueError
```

All of these functions look for an instance of *substring* in *string*, and, if found, return the position in *string* of the first character of the found substring. The *start* and *end* values are optional, and, if present, constrain the search to take place within the section of *string* defined by *string[start:end]*. string.find and string.index both search from the left end of *string*, while string.rfind and string.rindex search from the right end. The find functions return a −1 on failure, while the index functions raise a ValueError exception.

```
string.count(string, substring, start, end) → integer
```

Functions similarly do the searching functions above, but instead of returning the position of a substring within *string*, return the number of (non-overlapping) occurrences of *substring* in *string*.

```
string.replace(string, substring, newsubstring, maxtimes)
                                               → string
```

Replaces (non-overlapping) occurrences of *substring* in *string* with *newsubstring*. If the optional *maxtimes* argument is given, a maximum of *maxtimes* replacements will be done, starting from the left end of *string*.

```
string.maketrans(stringOfLengthN, stringOfLengthN)
                                        → translationTable
string.translate(string, translationTable, deleteChars) → string
string.translate('([-1.+2.*3])', string.maketrans('()*', '<>/'), '.-')
                                        → '<[1+2/3]>'
```

string.maketrans and string.translate work together to provide character translation for a string. string.maketrans takes two strings of equal length, and returns a translation table which maps occurrences of the nth character of the first argument to the nth character of the second argument. string.translate takes a string, and a translation table from string.maketrans, and applies that translation table to the string, converting given characters in the string to what the translation table maps them to. string.translate may also take an optional third argument. If present, this argument is a string giving characters which should be removed entirely from the given string.

The **re** module provides more powerful ways to achieve the same effect as some of the operations described above.

Data type conversions

```
`object` ' string
repr(object) → string
str(object) → string
```

Converts arbitrary Python objects to strings. backquotes and repr are identical; they return a full string representation of a Python object. str returns a more human-readable representation, which may not be complete for large objects.

```
integer(string) → integer ⇒ ValueError
string.atoi(string) → integer ⇒ ValueError
float(string) → float → ValueError
string.atof(string) → float⇒ ValueError
long(string) → long integer ⇒ ValueError
string.atol(string)→ long integer ⇒ ValueError
complex(string) → complex number ⇒ ValueError
```

Converts strings to numbers. The string module integer conversion functions can take an additional argument specifying octal or hexadecimal.

String formatting — '%' operator

```
formatString % obj → string
formatString % (obj1, obj2, . . .) → string
formatString % dictionary → string
```

```
"Can have a single %s on the right-hand side" % "object"
          → "Can have a single object on the right-hand side"
"%s is %.2f" % ("Pi", 3.14159) → "Pi is 3.14"
"Pi is %(pi).2f, e is %(e).4f" % {'pi' : 3.14159, 'e' : 2.718}
          → "Pi is 3.14, e is 2.7180"
```

Each *formatString* contains one or more string conversion sequences, which define how data from the object, tuple, or dictionary on the right-hand side of the % is to be substituted into the left-hand side, to produce the result string. The most general form of a Python string conversion sequence is

```
%[(name)][flags][fieldWidth][.precision]type
```

The *[]* above indicate optional elements. The meaning of these elements is given below.

type   Required, one of %, c, s, i, d, u, o, x, X, e, E, f, g, G, with the meanings given below. Defines what is substituted for the string conversion sequence. Here are the commonly used type characters (in approximate order of utility):

s   Substitutes an object as a string. (Uses repr to convert the object to a string first, if necessary, and then substitutes.)

d or i   Substitutes an integer in standard (i.e., base 10) format.

f   Substitutes a number in floating-point notation, (e.g., 3 substitutes as '3.000000').

e   Substitutes a number in scientific notation, (e.g., 3.14 substitutes as '3.140000e+000').

E   Like %e, but use a capital E instead of a small e in the result string.

g   Substitutes a number like %f if the number can be printed reasonably well in the given field width using that format, otherwise substitutes like %e.

G   Like %g, but substitutes like %E instead of %e.

%   Includes a percent sign at this point, in the result string. (i.e., '%%' in the *formatString* means "include a single percent sign".)

These type characters are useful only in specialized cases:

c   Substitutes a character.

u   Substitutes an integer, printing it as an unsigned integer, (e.g., –3 prints as '4294967293').

o   Substitutes an integer, printing it as an unsigned octal number, (e.g., decimal 16 prints as octal '20').

x   Substitutes an integer, printing it as an unsigned hexadecimal number using 'abcdef' as additional base 16 digits, (e.g., decimal 15 prints as hexadecimal 'f').

X   Like %x, but use ABCDEF instead of abcdef.

fieldWidth   If present, should be an integer specifying a minimum number of characters to use in performing the substitution—the string that is substituted will take up at least that many characters. If necessary, the substituted string is padded on the left with spaces to take up the requested width. If the right-hand side of the string modulus operator is a tuple, `fieldWidth` can also be specified as *, in which case the next unused value in the tuple should be an integer giving the field width.

.precision   If present, should be a decimal point followed by an integer. This specifies how many digits of precision should be printed in floating-point or scientific notation substitutions, that is, how many digits should appear after the decimal point when these formats are being used. If the right-hand side of the string modulus operator is a tuple, `.precision` can also be specified as .*, in which case the next unused value in the tuple should be an integer giving the precision.

flags   If present, are one or more of –, +, <space>, #, or 0, in any order. If present, they have the following meanings:

–   In conjunction with fieldWidth, puts padding to the right of the substituted string, instead of to the left.

+   Always prints numbers with signs.

<space> (a single whitespace character.) If the first character of a number is not a sign, a space will be prefixed.

0   For numbers, pads with leading zeroes instead of spaces.

Changes the meaning of some of the type substitution specifiers. For %o, prefixes the substitution with a leading 0. For %x or %X, prefixes with leading 0x or 0X (except if value is 0). For %e, %E, %f, %g, and %G, always includes a decimal point. For %g and %G, don't remove trailing zeroes.

(name)   Can only be used if the right-hand side of the string modulus operator is a dictionary, in which case it must be used in all string conversion sequences. It consists of parentheses enclosing a string, which is used as a key to obtain a value from the provided dictionary. The obtained value is substituted into the string according to the rest of the elements in the string conversion sequence.

String formatting—other functions

string.expandtabs(*string, tabsize*) → *string*
   This function produces a new string by replacing all tabs in its first argument with spaces. The screen is assumed to have a tab set every *tabsize* character, and enough spaces are substituted for each tab character to preserve screen formatting under that assumption. string.expandtabs correctly handles newline characters, but may not return a correct result if other special characters (besides tabs and newlines) are in the string.

```
string.ljust(string, width) → string
string.rjust(string, width) → string
string.center(string, width) → string
```
Each function justifies the string given as the first argument into a field whose width (number of characters) is given as the second argument, by returning a new string of length `width`, created by padding the original string with spaces. `string.ljust` justifies the string to the left (by adding spaces on the right), `string.rjust` justifies the string to the right, and `string.center` centers the string in the field. If the original string is longer than the given `width`, the string is returned unchanged.

```
string.zfill(numstring, width) → string
```
Pads the numeric string given as the first argument with leading zeroes, giving a result `width` characters in length. If the argument string is a signed number, the sign will be correctly placed as the first character of the resulting string.

Case conversion

```
string.capitalize(string) → string
```
Capitalizes the first character of the argument (if the first character is a letter).

```
string.capwords(string) → string
string.capwords(' hello\t, \t  there !!') → 'Hello , There !!'
```
Capitalizes the first characters of all words in the string (first characters which are not letters are left unchanged). This is equivalent to `string.join(map(string.capitalize,string.split(string)))`, and so doesn't preserve runs of whitespace.

```
string.lower(string) → string
string.lower('HELLO, There!') → 'hello, there!'
```
Converts a string to all lowercase characters. Non-alphabetic characters are not affected.

```
string.upper(string) → string
string.upper('HELLO, There!') → 'HELLO, THERE!'
```
Converts a string to all uppercase letters. Non-alphabetic characters are not affected.

```
string.swapcase(string) → string
string.swapcase('HELLO, There!') → 'hello, tHERE!'
```
Converts lowercase to uppercase and uppercase to lowercase. Nonalphabetic characters are not affected.

String constants

```
string.whitespace
```
A string containing all of the characters considered to be whitespace.
```
string.digits
```
A string containing '0123456789'.
```
string.hexdigits
```
A string containing '0123456789abcdefABCDEF'.

string.octdigits
>   A string containing `'01234567'`.

string.lowercase
>   A string containing the lowercase alphabetic characters a-z.

string.uppercase
>   A string containing the uppercase alphabetic characters A-Z.

string.letters
>   A string containing the letters a-z and A-Z.

A.7 Lists

List creation

```
x = []                     # Creates an empty list
x = [1, "two", 3, 4]       # Creates a list already initialized
[1, 2] + [3, 4] → [1, 2, 3, 4]
[None] * 4 → [None, None, None, None]
```

list(*sequence*) → *list* ⇒ TypeError
```
list('hello') → ['h', 'e', 'l', 'l', 'o']
list((1, 2, 3)) → [1, 2, 3]
```
>   Uses the list function to create a list from a sequence of some other type (i.e., a tuple or string). Using list on a list creates and returns a copy of the original list.

List access

list1[*n*] → *object* ⇒ IndexError
>   Returns the *n*th element of the list, counting from 0 as the first element. If n is negative, counts from –1 as the last element, –2 as the second-to-last element, and so on.

list1[*i:j*] → *list2* ⇒ IndexError
```
x = [0, 1, 2, 3, 4]
x[2] → 2
x[-2] → 3
x[1:3] → [1, 2]
x[:-2] → [0, 1, 2]
x[3:] → [3, 4]
```
>   Returns a list consisting of elements between points *i* and *j* in the accessed list. *i* not specified means take *i* equal to 0, *j* not specified means take *j* equal to the length of the list.

list[*i*][*j*] → *object* ⇒ IndexError
>   Returns the *j*th element of the *i*th element of a list. Counts from 0 as the first element. If i and/or j are negative, counts from –1 as the last element, –2 as the second-to-last element, and so on.

List modification

`list[n] = obj`

Replaces the *n*th element of the list with the given object. This follows the same position rules as single-element list access, when calculating which element is the *n*th element.

`list1[i:j] = list2`

Replaces the elements between points *i* and *j* of `list1` with the elements in `list2`. This follows the same rules as multi-element list access, when calculating the list points indicated by *i* and *j*. `list1` will grow or shrink if the number of elements in `list2` differs from the number of elements being substituted.

`list.`**`append`**`(obj)`

Adds *obj* on to the end of `list`.

`list1.`**`exend`**`(list2)`

Adds `list2` on to the end of `list1`. This is an experimental addition to Python version 1.5.2.

`del` `list[n]` ⟹ `IndexError`

Deletes the item at position *n* of `list1`. The list shrinks by one.

`del` `list[i:j]`

Deletes the items between *i* and *j* in `list`.

`list.`**`pop`**`(n)` → `object` ⟹ `IndexError`

Removes the *n*th element of the list and returns it. Counts from 0 as the first element. If *n* is negative, counts from –1 as the last element, –2 as the second-to-last element, and so on. If called with no argument, removes and returns the last element of the list. This is an experimental addition to Python version 1.5.2.

`list.`**`insert`**`(n, obj)` ⟹ `IndexError`

Inserts *obj* at position *n* in `list`. `list.insert(0, obj)` puts *obj* immediately before the first element of the `list`. The size of the list increases by 1 as the result of an insert operation.

`list.`**`remove`**`(obj)` ⟹ `ValueError`

Looks for the first element of the `list` equal to *obj*, and deletes it. If no such element is found, raises a `ValueError`.

`list.`**`reverse`**`()`

Reverses the list in place.

`list.`**`sort`**`()`

Sorts the elements of the list into ascending order, using Python's built-in comparison rules. This is an in-place sort—the list is modified.

`list.`**`sort`**`(fun)`

Sorts the elements of the list into ascending order, using a user-provided sort function. *fun* should be a two-argument function which returns –1 if the first argument is less than the second, 0 if the first argument equals the second, and 1 if the first argument is greater than the second. This is an in-place sort. Note that sorts using user-provided functions are much slower than sorts which use Python's built-in comparison rules.

bisect.insort(*list*, *obj*)

Places *obj* in *list* so as to maintain the list in sorted order if it already is sorted.

Other list operations

bisect.bisect(*list*, *obj*) → *integer*

Returns index where *obj* would be added to *list* so as to maintain the list in sorted order if it already is sorted.

list.**count**(*obj*) → *integer*

Returns the number of elements in *list* which are equal to *obj*.

obj **in** *list*

Returns true (1) if *obj* equals some element of *list*, according to Python's built-in comparison rules. Returns false (0) otherwise.

list.**index**(*obj*) → *integer* ⇒ ValueError

Looks for the first element of *list* equal to *obj*, and returns its position. If no such element is found, raises a ValueError.

obj **not in** *list*

Returns false if *obj* equals some element of *list*, according to Python's built-in comparison rules. Returns true otherwise.

len(*list*) → *integer*

Returns the number of elements in the list.

max(*list*) → *obj*

Returns the element of the list which has the maximum value.

min(*list*) → *obj*

Return the element of the list which has the minimum value.

A.8 Tuples

Tuple creation

```
x = ()                    # Creates an empty tuple
x = (1,)                  # Creates a one element tuple
x = [1, "two", 3, 4]      # Creates a tuple already initialized
(1, 2) + (3, 4) → (1, 2, 3, 4)
(1,) * 4 → (1, 1, 1, 1)
```

tuple(*sequence*) → *tuple* ⇒ TypeError
```
tuple('hello') → ('h', 'e', 'l', 'l', 'o')
tuple([1, 2, 3]) → (1, 2, 3)
```

Uses the tuple function to create a tuple from a sequence of some other type (i.e., a list or string). Using tuple on a tuple creates and returns a copy of the original tuple.

Tuple access

tuple1[n] → *object* ⇒ IndexError

> Returns the *n*th element of the tuple, counting from 0 as the first element. If n is negative, count from –1 as the last element, –2 as the second-to-last element, and so on.

tuple1[i:j] → *tuple2* ⇒ IndexError

```
x = (0, 1, 2, 3, 4)
x[2]    ‡ 2
x[-2]   ‡ 3
x[1:3]  ‡ (1, 2)
x[:3]   ‡ (0, 1, 2)
x[-2:]  ‡ (3, 4)
```

> Returns a tuple consisting of elements between points *i* and *j* in the accessed tuple. *i* not specified means take *i* equal to 0, *j* not specified means take *j* equal to the length of the tuple.

tuple[i][j] → *object* ⇒ IndexError

> Returns the *j*th element of the *i*th element of a tuple. Counts from 0 as the first element. If *i* and/or *j* are negative, count from –1 as the last element, –2 as the second-to-last element, and so on.

Other tuple operations

obj **in** *tuple*

> Returns true (1) if *obj* equals some element of *tuple*, according to Python's built-in comparison rules. Returns false (0) otherwise.

obj **not in** *tuple*

> Returns false if *obj* equals some element of *tuple*, according to Python's built-in comparison rules. Returns true otherwise.

len(*tuple*) → *integer*

> Returns the number of elements in the tuple.

max(*tuple*) → *obj*

> Returns the element of the tuple which has the maximum value.

min(*tuple*) → *obj*

> Returns the element of the tuple which has the minimum value.

A.9 Dictionaries

Creating dictionaries

```
dict = {}
```

```
dict = {1 : "one", 2 : "two"}
```
Creates an empty dictionary by giving an empty pair of curly braces. Creates a dictionary with some elements already initialized by including *key* : *value* pairs in the braces, with each such pair separated from the succeeding pair by a comma.

Dictionary access

`dict[key]` → *obj* ⇒ IndexError

Returns the object in *dict* which is indexed by the given key. If *dict* does not have any value associated with the given key, raises an IndexError exception.

`dict.get(key)` → *obj*
`dict.get(key, default)` → *obj*

Returns the object in *dict* indexed by the given key, if such an object exists, otherwise returns a default value. If the optional second argument is not given, then None will be used as the default value, otherwise whatever was passed in as the second argument will be used as the default value.

`dict.has_key(key)` → *Boolean*

Returns true if *dict* contains a value indexed by *key*, false otherwise.

`dict.keys()` → *listOfKeys*

Returns a list of all keys currently known to the dictionary. This is useful for iterating through all elements of a dictionary.

`dict.values()` → *listOfValues*

Returns a list of all values currently stored in the dictionary.

`dict.items()` → *listOfTuples*

Returns a list of tuples, one for each key/value pair stored in the dictionary. The first element of each tuple is a dictionary key, and the second element of the tuple is the corresponding value.

Dictionary modification

`dict[key]` = *obj*

Inserts *obj* into *dict*, indexed by *key*. If some other element was already in *dict* and accessed by *key*, it will be forgotten.

del `dict[key]` → KeyError

Removes the key and the value associated with it from *dict*. If the key does not exist in *dict* before the del, a KeyError exception will be raised. After the del, the key will no longer exist in dict, that is, *dict*.has_key(*key*) will return false. You cannot remove a key from a dictionary by saying *dict[key]* = None. That simply changes the value associated with the key to None.

`dict.clear()`

Removes all key/value pairs from *dict*. Differs from *dict* = {} as an object is not created.

```
dict1.update(dict2)
```
Updates *dict1* with the key/value pairs of *dict2* (modifies existing or adds new pairs as necessary).

Other dictionary operations

```
dict.copy()
```
Returns a shallow copy of *dict*.

```
len(dict)
```
Returns the number of elements in *dict*.

A.10 Statements, control flow, and function definition

The following are *compound statements*. Their *body*s are *blocks* that contain one or more statements separated by newlines or semicolons. The lines must all be at the same indentation level. The parser uses this indentation to delimit them. A line containing the single word pass can be used as a do-nothing placeholder anywhere a statement is necessary. A compound statement can contain one or more *clauses*. The general form of a compound statement is:

```
compound statement clause:
        block
compound statement clause:
        block
```

Compound statements can appear in blocks, which will result in nested indentation. It is also legal to have a single line block on the same line as a clause directly after the colon:

```
compound statement clause: one-line-body
if x > 0: y = 1; z = 2
```

Splitting statements across multiple lines

A statement can be explicitly split across multiple lines by ending a line with a slash (\). It can also be implicitly split between any two tokens which are within (), [], or {} brackets. Any indentation of the continued line is legal.

```
x = [1000, 2000, 3000,
    4000, 5000]
y = ( 600 + 1200/12 -56 +
    32 - 60)
max(100, 3000, 300,
    4000, 5)
z = "This will be one string" \
    " which will be automatically concatenated"
max("This will return the longer of this first"
    " concatenated string", "And this second short string")
```

if-elif-else statements

```
if condition1:
        body1
elif condition2:
        body2
elif condition3:
        body3
        .
        .
elif condition(n-1):
        body(n-1)
else:
        body(n)
```

Everything after *body1* is optional. The *body* of the first *condition* to evaluate to true will be executed and flow will continue after the construct. The body after else will be executed if none of the conditions evaluates to true.

while loops

```
while condition:
        body
else:
        post-code
```

The else clause is optional and very rarely used. As long as *condition* is true, *body* will be repeatedly executed. A break within *body* will immediately terminate the loop (skipping the *post-code*). A continue within *body* will cause the rest of *body* to be skipped and control flow to return to the top of the loop for the next evaluation of the *condition*. When *condition* evaluates to false, *post-code* is executed.

for loops

```
for variable in list:
        body
else:
        post-code
```

The else clause is optional (and very rarely used). The *body* will be executed once for *variable* set to each value in *list*. A break within *body* will immediately terminate the loop, skipping the else. A continue within *body* will cause the rest of *body* to be skipped and the flow to return to the top of the loop with *variable* set to the next value in *list*. After the body has been executed with *variable* assigned to the last value in *list*, *post-code* is executed.

Functions

A function is defined by

```
def name(parameterList):
        """Optional documentation string (name.__doc__)"""
        body
```

and called by

```
name(argumentList)
```

If the statement "**return** *value*" is encountered in *body*, the function will exit and return *value*. If *value* is not included, a value of None will be returned. Similarly, if there is no return statement, control flow will exit at the end of *body* with a value of None.

An *argumentList* is a comma-separated sequence of zero or more arguments. An *argument* can be of the form:

expression	The positionally corresponding *parameter* is set to the result of the evaluation of *expression*.
name = expression	The *parameter* with name *name* is set to the result of the evaluation of *expression*. This is a keyword argument.

The *parameterList* is a comma-separated sequence of zero or more *parameters*. A *parameter* can be of the form:

variable	*variable* will be assigned to the value of the corresponding argument in the argument list. This correspondence is either based on position or keyword.
variable = value	*value* will be the default given to *variable* if that variable is not given as an argument in the call to the function. Parameters of this form must come after all other parameters of the previous form.
*variable	*variable* will be created as a tuple and assigned any extra positional arguments in the call to the function. Only one parameter may be of this form and it must come after all other parameters of the previous forms.
**variable	*variable* will be created as a dictionary and assigned any extra keyword arguments in the call to the function. Only one parameter may be of this form and it must be the last parameter.

Examples

```
def function1(a, b, c =9, *tup, **dict):
    return [a, b, c, tup, dict.items()]
function1(1, 2, 3) # positional arguments, all present
[1, 2, 3, (), []]
function1(b=1, a=2) # keyword arguments, not all present, so the default is used
[2, 1, 9, (), []]
function1(1, c=3, b=2, d =4, e=5) # extra keyword arguments present
[1, 2, 3, (), [('e', 5), ('d', 4)]]
function1(1,2,3,4,5,6,7,8,9) # extra positional arguments present
[1, 2, 3, (4, 5, 6, 7, 8, 9), []]
```

A lambda expression can be used to create simple unnamed functions:

```
lambda parameter1, parameter2, . . .: statement
```

Example

```
x = lambda a, b, c=9, *tup, **dict: [a, b, c, tup, dict.items()]
                                    # This is the same as function1 above.
x(1, c=3, b=2, d =4, e=5)
[1, 2, 3, (), [('e', 5), ('d', 4)]]
```

A.11 Modules, scripts, and packages

Module and script creation
The basics of defining a module and script are given in the template.

File mymodule.py

```
#! /usr/bin/env python
"""Optional module documentation string (mymodule.__doc__)."""
```

 # Other modules used by this module should be imported first.
```
import neededmodule1, neededmodule2
```

 # Variables assigned to immediately are globally accessible externally
 # and to the functions in the module
```
externalVariable1 = something1
```

 # Variables prepended with an underscore are internally accessible to the functions in the module.
```
_moduleVariable1 = something2
```

 # Functions can be made 'private' by beginning their name with an underscore.
```
def _privateFunction(arg1):
    body
```

```
def publicFunction(arg1, arg2=None):
"""Optional function documentation string
        (mymodule.publicFunction.__doc__)"""
    body
```

 # Controlling function which is executed if the file is started as a script from a command line
```
def main():
    body    # sys.argv[1:] will contain the command line arguments as a list of strings.
```

```
if __name__ == '__main__':  # This will be true if the file is called as a script.
    main()
else:
    moduleSpecificInitializationBody
```

Importing modules
Modules are imported using the `import` statement, which has the three forms:

```
import modulename1, modulename2, . . .
from modulename import name1, name2, name3, . . .
from modulename import *
```

The first is the preferred. When using it, access the functions and variables by prepending them with the module name:

```
a = modulename1.variable2 * modulename1.function3()
```

The second and third allow direct use of the names without qualification with the module name. The second brings in the specified functions and values, the third brings in all functions and variables in the module that are not prepended with an underscore.

```
a = name2 * name3()
```

Uses **reload** to reload a previously (successfully) imported module, whose code you have changed.

```
reload(modulename1)
```

Modules are searched for in the directories given in the variable **sys.path**.

Packages

Packages allow the grouping of modules together in a directory or directory subtree and importing and hierarchically refering to them using a *package.subpackage.module* syntax.

A package or subpackage name is that of a directory in which an initialization file __init__.py has been placed. The code in this possibly empty file is executed when the sub-package is imported (which occurs when an import statement names it or one of its sub-packages). It can contain a __all__ variable set equal to a list of its public modules which are files in the directory.

A module can import another module (i.e. *module1*) from within its own subpackage (directory) by simply referring to it as *module1*.

Interpreter options

The Python interpreter is called at the operating system prompt using a command line of the form:

```
python [options] [ -c cmd | - | file ] [arguments] [ < infile ]
   [ > outfile | >> outfile ]
```

(where [ ] enclose optional items and | separate alternatives) .

If *file* is present, its name is placed in sys.argv[0] and it is executed. If *-c cmd* is present, -c is placed in sys.argv[0] and the command *cmd* is executed (see table below for an example). In both cases, any *arguments* (i.e. *arg1, arg2 ... argN*) are placed as strings in sys.argv[1] to sys.argv[N]. If neither *file* or the -c option are present, the interpreter opens in interactive mode.

When present, standard input is read from *infile* and standard output is written to *outfile*. For > the file is overwritten, while for >> the file is appended to. It is also possible to pipe input in from or output out to another command (i.e., python script.py arg1 | python script2.py)

The following table introduces the possible options for the interpreter.

Option	Description
-d	This is not for end users. It's for the language designers in their testing of the generation of the Python parser. Same as setting PYTHONDEBUG=1.
-h	Displays a description of interpreter options and environment variables.

Option	Description
-i	Enters the interactive interpreter after running script file. Same as setting PYTHONINSPECT=1.
-O	Optimizes generated bytecode. Sets the flag __debug__ to zero whch disables assert statements. Compiled modules will be placed in .pyo rather than .pyc files. Same as setting PYTHONOPTIMIZE=1.
-OO	Same as for the -O option but also removes all document strings.
-S	Don't import site module on startup (i.e., .pth files will not be read).
-t	Issues warnings for any inconsistent usage of tabs.
-u	Reads and writes standard input and output in binary, unbuffered mode. Same as setting PYTHONUNBUFFERED=1.
-v	Uses verbose mode. Prints trace messages for import statements, displaying the full file paths from which modules are imported, and whether they needed to be recompiled. Same as setting PYTHONVERBOSE=1.
-x	Skips the first line of the input file. For allowing a system-dependent file header line.
-X	Disables built-in class-based exceptions (i.e., use string exceptions). For backward compatibility. You shouldn't need to use this.
-c cmd	Executes the given command in a Python interpreter. Must be last option. i.e. python -c "print 'Hello'; print 'World!' ".

Environment variables

Python can use a number of environment variables. How and where these are set depends on the operating system. On UNIX it depends on what shell you are using. If you are using the *C-shell* these can be placed in the .cshrc file:

```
setenv PYTHONPATH /usr/local/python:/home/ramona/python
setenv PYTHONUNBUFFERED 1
```

On Windows they can be placed in autoexec.bat:

```
set PYTHONPATH=c:\mydocu~1\python;c:\mydocu~1\scripts
set PYTHONUNBUFFERED=1
```

Setting any of these variables is optional. The following table lists them.

Variable	Description
PYTHONDEBUG	Same as invocation using python -d.
PYTHONHOME	Alternate directory prefix for setting up the module search path. See the Python documentation for details.
PYTHONINSPECT	If true, stay in the interpreter after running a script. Same as invocation using python -i.
PYTHONOPTIMIZE	Same as invocation using python -O.
PYTHONPATH	Directories to prepend to the module search path (sys.path). Uses the syntax of the PATH variable.
PYTHONSTARTUP	File of Python commands to read and execute before issuing the first prompt in the interactive mode. Note that this is read for interactive sessions only.

Variable	Description
PYTHONUNBUFFERED	Same as invocation using `python -u`.
PYTHONVERBOSE	Same as invocation using `python -v`.

A.12 *Files and directories*

Path-related functions and constants

os.curdir

String giving the string representation meaning current directory under the current operating system. This variable is always equal to '.' under Windows 95/NT and UNIX.

os.pardir

String giving the string representation meaning parent directory under the current operating system. This variable is always equal to '..' under Windows95/NT and UNIX.

os.getcwd() → *path*

Returns a string giving the path to the current working directory.

os.path.join(*string1*, *string2*,...) → *path*

Joins one or more strings into something that is a valid filesystem path on the currently executing system. The result is a string, but should generally be used as if it were an abstract path object. Try to avoid using string operations directly on it, as this will make your code less portable. Each of the arguments should be a valid file/directory/ path name on the given platform.

os.path.split(*path*) → (*dirname*, *basename*)
os.path.split("dir/subdir/file") → ('dir/subdir', 'file')

Splits a filesystem path at the point of its last delimiter.

os.path.basename(*path*) → *string*
os.path.basename("dir/subdir/file") → 'file'

Convenience function which returns the last element of *path*; this is equivalent to os.path.split(*path*)[1].

os.path.dirname(*path*) → *parentPath*
os.path.dirname("dir/subdir/file") → 'dir/subdir'

Given a path to a file or directory, returns the path to the parent directory of the original file/directory.

os.path.splitext(*path*) → (*mainString*, *extension*)
os.path.splitext("dir/file.txt") → ('dir/file', '.txt')

Given a path, this function returns a two-tuple of strings. The first element of the tuple, *mainString*, is all of *path* except for any dotted extension at the end of *path*; the second element is such a dotted extension, if it exists.

os.path.exists(*path*) → *Boolean*
os.path.isfile(*path*) → *Boolean*

os.path.isdir(*path*) → *Boolean*

These three functions return true if, respectively, *path* indicates something which actually exists in the filesystem, is a normal file, or is a directory. They return false otherwise.

os.path.islink(*path*) → *Boolean*
os.path.ismount(*path*) → *Boolean*

On UNIX systems, these functions return true if the given path is, respectively, a mount point or a symbolic link, and false otherwise.

os.path.isabs(*pathString*) → *Boolean*

Returns true if *pathString* is a string in the form of an absolute path, false otherwise.

os.path.getsize(*path*) → *integer*

Returns the size of a file in bytes.

os.path.getmtime(*path*) → *integer*

Returns the last modification time of a file. Note that this can be converted to a human readable string using `time.ctime`.

os.path.getatime(*path*) → *integer*

Returns the last access time of a file. Note that this can be converted to a human readable string using `time.ctime`.

os.path.samefile(*path1*, *path2*) → *Boolean*

Returns true if *path1* and *path2* both point to the same filesystem location. This does not necessarily mean that *path1* and *path2* are the same string.

os.path.commonprefix(*path1*, *path2*,…) → *path*

Finds and returns the longest common prefix for the argument paths.
`os.path.commonprefix('dir/mypath/subdir/file',`
`'dir/mypath/dir2')`
would return `'dir/mypath'`.

os.path.expandvars(*pathString*) → *path*

Finds environment variables (prefixed with '$') in the *pathString*, and expands them to produce *path*, by substituting the environment value associated with each environment variable. This only makes sense on operating systems which support environment variables, such as UNIX or Windows NT. For example, `os.path.expandvars('$HOME/docs')` would produce `'/usr/mcdonald/docs'`, assuming the value of the HOME environment variable in the current execution context was `'/usr/mcdonald'`.

os.path.normcase(*path1*) → *path2*

On UNIX, *path2* will be the same as *path1*. On case-insensitive platforms, *path2* is *path1* converted to all lower case. On Windows, slashes (/) are also converted to backslashes (\).

os.path.normpath(*path1*) → *path2*

path2 will be *path1* with redundant separators removed and up level references collapsed.

os.path.splitdrive(*path1*) → (*driveString, path2*)
```
os.path.splitdrive("c:\\My Documents\\images")
                        → ('c:', '\\My Documents\\images')
```
Given a path, this function returns a tuple containing two strings. The first element of the tuple is the drive and the second is the rest of the path.

glob.glob(*path*) → *pathList*

Returns a list of pathnames that match *path. path* may contain character sequences as well as the wildcards * and ?. A * in *path* matches any sequence of characters. A ? in path matches any single character. A character sequence (i.e., [h,H] or [0-9]) matches any single character in that sequence. These are the same as the UNIX shell rules.

Opening and closing files

open(*filename, mode, buffersize*) → *fileobject*

Opens a file for reading or writing, and returns a file handle to that file. *filename*: the name of the file being opened. *mode*: is. 'r' for reading, 'w' for (over)writing, and 'a' for appending. For binary mode use 'rb', 'wb', or 'ab'. If *mode* not present, defaults to read ('r'). Optional *buffersize* argument.

fileobject.**close**()

Close the file. You should do this when finished using a file, to free up system resources.

Reading and writing files

fileobject.**read**() → *string*
fileobject.**read**(*size*) → *string*

Reads bytes from a file and returns them as a string. If the *size* argument is given, read will attempt to read that many bytes, but will read fewer if not enough data is available. Regardless of how many bytes were read, it will return the read data in a string. If the *size* argument is not given, read will read all remaining data from the file and return it as a string.

fileobject.**readline**() → *string*

Reads a single line from a file, returning it as a string. A newline on the end of the string is retained, if present. The last line in a file may not always have a newline at the end. This means that if readline() returns an empty string, the end-of-file has been reached.

fileobject.**readlines**() → *listOfStrings*

Reads all the lines from a file, and returns them as a list of strings. Newline characters on the ends of lines are retained.

fileobject.**write**(*string*)

Writes the given string to the fileobject. No carriage returns or other characters are added.

`fileobject.`**`writelines`**`(listOfStrings)`
> Writes a list of strings to the fileobject, one-by-one. Only characters in the strings are written. No separators or other additional characters are added.

`array.`**`fromfile`**`(fileobject, n)` → `EOFError`
> Reads up to *n* values from the `fileobject`, appending them to the end of the given `array` object. (See *Python Library Reference* for standard module `'array'`.) If fewer than *n* values are available from the file, Python will read in and append as many values as possible, and then raise an `EOFError` exception. The type of the array determines exactly how data is read in, so this operation can be used to read in data from C binary files.

`array.`**`tofile`**`(fileobject)`
> Writes all of the values in the `array` to the given `fileobject`, in a binary format according to the declared type of the array. See the notes above for `fromfile`.

Screen I/O and redirection

`print` *expression1, expression2, …*
> Evaluates the expressions, converts them to strings if necessary and prints them (separated by spaces) to the standard output. A newline (\n) is added at the end, unless the print statement ends in a comma.

`input``(string)` → `value`
> Prints the optional `string` to the standard output. Then reads in a line from the standard input and returns it evaluated as a Python expression.

`raw_input``(string)` → `string`
> Prints the optional `string` to the standard output and reads in a line from the standard input. Returns it as a string.

`sys.stdin`
> Special standard input file object with `read`, `readline`, and `readlines` methods.

`sys.stdout`
> Special standard output file object with `write` and `writelines` methods.

`sys.stderr`
> Special standard error file object with `write` and `writelines` methods.

`sys.__stdin__`
`sys.__stdout__`
`sys.__stderr__`
> The original settings at the start of program execution for `sys.stdin`, `sys.stdout`, and `sys.stderr` respectively.

Other file I/O operations and constants

`fileobject.`**`seek`**`(offset, relativeTo)`
> Sets the position the fileobject points to in its file. `offset` is a number which specifies a number of bytes by which to change the position of the fileobject. If `relativeTo`

is 0 or omitted, the fileobject is positioned *offset* bytes from the beginning of the file. If *relativeTo* is 1, the fileobject is positioned offset bytes from the current position. If *relativeTo* is 2, the fileobject is positioned *offset* bytes from the end of the file.

fileobject.tell() → *integer*

Converse of seek—returns the current position of the fileobject within its file, as the number of bytes from the beginning of the file.

fileobject.flush()

Forces any buffered output to be written to the file represented by fileobject.

fileinput module

Provides a class that allows you to easily iterate through the lines from the standard input or from one or more files. It is also possible to subclass this functionality. See the *Python Library Reference* for the details.

fileinput.input() → IOERROR
```
for line in fileinput.input():
for line in fileinput.input(['file1','file2'], inplace=1,
                            backup='.old'):
```

If called in a for loop with no arguments will take the strings in sys.argv[1:] as the input file names and successively iterate through their lines. If this is empty, will read from the standard input. If an entry is -, standard input will be read at that point.

If a single file or a list of files are entered as an argument, they will be used as the input files to iterate through.

If keyword argument inplace=1 is present, when an input file's turn to be processed arrives it will be moved to a backup file, using extension .bak, and standard output will be directed to the original filename and the backup file will be removed after processing the file (i.e., a filter mode). If the keyword argument backup='.<extension>' is also present, the given extension will be used for the backup files and the backup files will not be removed.

fileinput.filename() → *string*

Returns the name of the file that is currently being processed.

fileinput.filelineno() → *integer*

Returns the number of lines that have been read out of the file currently being processed.

fileinputlineno() → *integer*

Returns the total number of lines that have been read.

fileinput.isfirstline() → *Boolean*

Returns true if the last line read is the first line of the current file.

fileinput.isstdin() → *Boolean*

Returns true if the last line was read from standard input.

fileinput.nextfile()

Closes the current file so that the next line read will be the first line of the next file.

fileinput.close()

Closes the entire input sequence.

struct module

Provides functions for converting between Python objects and C structures.

struct.pack(*formatString, value1, value2, …*) → *string*

Returns a string with the values packed according to the format given in *formatString*. For converting Python objects to C structures. See the *Python Library Reference* for details on the format strings.

struct.unpack(*formatString, string*) → *tuple*

Unpacks *string* into a tuple of values according to the format given in *formatString*. For converting C structures to Python objects. See the *Python Library Reference* for details on the format strings.

struct.calcsize(*formatString*) → *integer*

Returns the size of the record (string) according to the format given in *formatString*. See the *Python Library Reference* for details on the format strings.

Persistence support

cPickle.dump(*object, fileobject, Boolean*) → PicklingError

Stores a Python object into a file. If the optional third argument is true, a more efficient binary storage format is used rather than the default text format.

cPickle.load(*object, fileobject*) → *object*

Retrieves (loads) a previously stored Python object from a file.

shelve.open(*filename*) → *shelf*

Opens an existing shelf or, if necessary, creates a new shelf object in file *filename*.

shelf.**close**()

Closes a shelf.

shelf[*key*] → *obj* ⇒ IndexError

Returns the object in *shelf* which is indexed by the given key. If *shelf* does not have any value associated with the given key, raises an IndexError exception.

shelf.**has_key**(*key*) → *Boolean*

Returns true if *shelf* contains a value indexed by *key*, false otherwise.

shelf.**keys**() → *listOfKeys*

Returns a list of all keys currently known to the shelf. This is useful for iterating through all elements of a shelf.

shelf[key] = obj

Inserts *obj* into *shelf*, indexed by *key*. If some other element was already in *shelf* and accessed by *key*, it will be forgotten.

del *shelf*[*key*] ⇒ KeyError

Removes the key and the value associated with it from *shelf*. If the key does not exist in *shelf* before the del, a KeyError exception will be raised. After the del, the key will no longer exist in the shelf; that is, `shelf.has_key(key)` will return false. You cannot remove a key from a shelf by saying `shelf[key]` = None. That simply changes the value associated with the key to None.

len(*shelf*)

Returns the number of elements in `shelf`.

Filesystem operations and constants

os.environ

A dictionary whose keys are the names of operating system environment variables, and whose values are the values of those environment variables.

os.name

A string indicating the type of OS the programming is running on, for example, `posix`, `nt`, and so forth.

os.listdir(*path*) → *listOfStrings*

path should point to a directory in the filesystem. `os.listdir` returns a list of the files/subdirectories in that directory.

os.mkdir(*path*)

Makes the indicated directory. If the path argument is an absolute path, the parent directory must already exist.

os.makedirs(*path*)

Makes the indicated directory. Will create parent directories if necessary.

os.remove(*path*)

Removes the indicated file. For safety reasons, this will *not* work with directories. Use `os.rmdir` instead.

os.rmdir(*dirPath*)

Removes the indicated directory. For reasons of data safety, this will work only if the directory is empty. To remove a directory containing files or subdirectories, you must walk through the directory removing everything explicitly.

os.chdir(*path*)

Changes the current working directory. In general, the argument is a string giving the new directory, and can be either relative to the previous current working directory, or absolute.

os.rename(*path1, path2*)

Changes the name of a file or directory, by moving from a location given by *path1* to a location given by *path2*.

os.path.walk(*dirPath, function, arg*)

Recursively walks through the given directory, applying the supplied function. See the main text for details.

`shutil` module

Provides a number of functions for making copies of files with or without their stat information (i.e., mode and access times) as well as the ability to recursively make a copy of or remove a subdirectory.

shutil.copyfile(*srcFile*, *dstFile*)

Makes a binary copy of *srcFile* in *dstFile*.

shutil.copymode(*srcFile*, *dstFile*)

Sets the mode permissions information for *dstFile* equivalent to that of *srcFile*.

shutil.copystat(*srcFile*, *dstFile*)

Sets the *stat* information (i.e., mode permissions and access/modification times) for *dstFile* equivalent to that of *srcFile*.

shutil.copy(*srcFile*, *dst*)

Makes a binary copy of *srcFile* with the same mode permissions. If *dst* is a directory, the copy is placed in *dst/srcFile*, otherwise it is placed in *dst*. This is equivalent to `cp srcFile dst` on UNIX.

shutil.copy2(*srcFile*, *dst*)

Makes a binary copy of *srcFile* with the same stat information. If *dst* is a directory, the copy is placed in *dst/srcFile*, otherwise it is place in *dst*. This is equivalent to `cp -p srcFile dst` on UNIX.

shutil.copytree(*srcDir*, *dstDir*)

Makes a recursive copy of all files and subdirectories of *srcDir* in *dstDir* (using `shutil.copy2`). If an optional third argument is true, files or subdirectories pointed at by symbolic links will be left as symbolic links; otherwise full copies will be made of them.

shutil.rmtree(*dir*)

```
shutil.rmtree("c:\\my documents\\tmp")
```
→ *An error will result in an exception being raised.*
```
shutil.rmtree("c:\\my documents\\tmp", 1 )
```
→ *Any errors are ignored.*

Recursively removes a directory and all its files and subdirectories. If an optional second argument is true, errors in attempts to remove a file or directory will be ignored, otherwise such an error will result in an exception being raised.

A.13 Classes

Basic class definition

The basics of defining a class are given in the template below:

```
class MyClass(inheritedClass1, inheritedClass2,…):
    """Optional class documentation string (MyClass.__doc__)."""
    # Variables assigned to immediately in the class are class variables.
    classVariable = something1

    # All classes should start with an __init__ function, which is the constructor.
    def __init__(self, arg1, arg2,…):
```

```
"""Optional method documentation string
   (MyClass.__init__.__doc__)."""
# Instance variables are stored as attributes of 'self'. They can be made
# private by starting them with a double underscore.
self.__privateVar = arg1
self.publicVar = arg2

# Methods are defined as functions in the class body which take a class
# instance as their first argument (named 'self' by convention). Method
# definitions may make use of any of the argument-passing abilities
# available to "standard" function—in the method below, 'arg2' will
# be given a default value of 'None' if a value is not provided for it by
# the invoking call.
def publicMethod(self, arg1, arg2=None):
    """Optional method documentation string
       (MyClass.publicMethod.__doc__)"""
    body

# Methods can be made 'private' by beginning their names with a double
# underscore.
def __privateMethod(self):
    body

# An instance is created by using a class name as a function.
obj = MyClass(arg1, arg2, …)
# Methods can be invoked in a standard manner.
obj.publicMethod(value1)
```

Special method attributes

The following table gives the Python special method attributes which may be defined within a class. Most of these attributes permit instances of that class to "emulate" built-in Python types, that is, to respond to infix operators, indexing, and so forth. Entries are roughly grouped by relation. The most general special method attributes are at the front of the table.

`__init__(self, arg1, arg2, . . .)`	Called whenever an instance of a class is first created, with the new instance as the first argument. Any arguments given to the creating call of the class name are passed in as subsequent arguments. No return value.
`__del__(self)`	Called when an instance of a class is about to be destroyed by the Python garbage collector. If you want to use this special attribute, carefully read the main Python documentation.
`__repr__(obj)`	Called whenever the expressions `obj` or **repr**(obj) are evaluated. Should return a formal string representation of the object, one from which the object may be rebuilt. Python provides an appropriate `__repr__` function for all objects, including instances of user-defined classes. You should not normally need to or want to define this function.
`__str__(obj)`	Called whenever the expression **str**(obj) is evaluated. This is often done automatically by Python. Should return an easily readable string representation of the object.

__cmp__(*obj, right*)	Comparison. Called whenever *obj* is compared with some other Python value. For example, *obj != right* or *obj > right* should return −1 if *obj* is less than *right*, 0 if *obj* is equal to *right*, or 1 if *obj* is greater than *right*.
__hash__(*obj*)	For immutable objects only. Can be used to return a *hash value*, making the objects usable as dictionary keys. Only objects which define a __cmp__ method should define a __hash__ method, although they do not need to define a __hash__ method just because they define a __cmp__ method. The only hard and fast rule for defining __hash__ is that two objects which test equal using __cmp__ should return identical results from __hash__. For adequate performance, __hash__ methods should attempt to ensure that the returned value reflects all of the contents of the hashed object.
__getattr__(*obj, name*)	Called when an expression of the form *obj.name* is evaluated, only if that expression cannot be satisfactorily evaluated by normal means. In other words, if *obj.name* can be meaningfully evaluated without invoking __getattr__, it will be; only if evaluating *obj.name* would cause an error (because *obj* does not possess an attribute named *name*) will __getattr__ be invoked.
__setattr__(*obj, name, value*)	Called whenever an assignment of the form *obj.name = value* is attempted. This is true even if the assignment is from within __setattr__; so if your __setattr__ method wishes to assign to any instance attributes (including *name*), it must do so through a statement of the form self.__dict__[*attr_name*] = *whatever*, assuming self is the local parameter name for the invoking object. This trick makes use of the fact that Python class instances store their attributes in a dictionary which can be accessed by the special __dict__ attribute.
__delattr__(*obj, name*)	Similar to __setattr__, but called whenever a statement of the form **del** *obj.name* is evaluated.
__call__(*obj, [arg1, arg2, . . .]*)	If defined, this neat little method permits objects to be used as functions. Basically, if *obj* is of a class which defines a __call__ method, then an evaluation of *obj(arg1, arg2,…)* (i.e., *obj* used as a function in a function call) will result in the invocation of __call__(*obj, [arg1, arg2,…]*). The original function arguments are passed into __call__ as a single list argument. Among other things, this can be used to easily create very powerful callback functions for use in GUI programming.
__len__(*obj*)	Called whenever the expression **len**(*obj*) is evaluated.
__getitem__(*obj, key*)	Called whenever the expression *obj[key]* is evaluated, either explicitly, by your code, or implicitly, such as during execution of a for loop over a list. Should return the value in *obj* which is accessed by *key*.
__setitem__(*obj, key, value*)	Similar to __getitem__, but called whenever a statement of the form *obj[key] = value* is executed.
__delitem__(*obj, key*)	Called whenever the statement del *obj[key]* is executed. Should delete the value accessed by *key* from *obj*. No return value.

__getslice__(*obj, start, end*)	Called whenever the expression *obj[i:j]* is evaluated. If i is not present, then *start* is 0; if *j* is not present, then *end* is sys.maxint; if i < 0 then start is i + len(obj); if j < 0, then *end* is j + len(obj); and in all other cases, start == i and end == j.
__setslice__(*obj, start, end, sequence*)	Similar to __getslice__, but called whenever a statement of the form *obj[i:j] = list* is executed, with *sequence* bound to *list*.
__delslice__(*obj, start, end*)	Similar to __getslice__, but called whenever a statement of the form **del** *obj[i:j]* is evaluated.
__add__(*obj, right*	Called whenever the expression *obj + right* is evaluated. Should return a value which is the sum of *obj* and *right*. This need not be a number; the sum of two sequences should be the concatenation of them. If the expression *obj + right* is evaluated, and *obj* is an instance of a user-defined class which does not define __add__, then Python will attempt to find a special function attribute called __radd__ in the classes associated with *right*, and invoke that. See the description of *__radd__* for further details.
__radd__(*robj, left*)	Called whenever the expression *left + robj* is evaluated and there is no __add__ method defined in *left*'s class. This is a sort of last chance to handle the + operator. All of the other binary operator special method attributes (__sub__, __mul__, etc.) also have corresponding right-versions (__rsub__, __rmul__, etc.) even though the right-versions are not listed in this table.
__sub__(*obj, right*)	Like __add__, but called whenever the expression *obj – right* is evaluated.
__mul__(*obj, right*)	Like __add__, but called whenever the expression *obj * right* is evaluated.
__div__(*obj, right*)	Like __add__, but called whenever the expression *obj / right* is evaluated.
__mod__(*obj, right*)	Like __add__, but called whenever the expression *obj % right* is evaluated.
__divmod__(*obj, right*)	Like __add__, but called whenever the expression **divmod**(*obj, right*) is evaluated.
__pow__(*obj, right*)	Like __add__, but called whenever the expression **pow**(*obj, right*) is evaluated.
__lshift__(*obj, right*)	Like __add__, but called whenever the expression *obj << right* is evaluated.
__rshift__(*obj, right*)	Like __add__, but called whenever the expression *obj >> right* is evaluated.
__and__(*obj, right*)	Like __add__, but called whenever the expression *obj & right* is evaluated.
__xor__(*obj, right*)	Like __add__, but called whenever the expression *obj ^ right* is evaluated.
__or__(*obj, right*)	Like __add__, but called whenever the expression *obj	right* is evaluated.

`__neg__`(*obj*), `__pos__`(*obj*), `__invert__`(*obj*)	Called whenever the unary minus, plus, or inversion operators are used on the object. That is, whenever *-obj*, *+obj*, or *~obj* are evaluated.
`__abs__`(*obj*)	Called whenever **abs**(*obj*) is evaluated.
`__int__`(*obj*), `__float__`(*obj*), `__long__`(*obj*)	Called whenever **int**(*obj*), **float**(*obj*), or **long**(*obj*) are evaluated.
`__oct__`(*obj*), `__hex__`(*obj*)	Called whenever **oct**(*obj*), or **hex**(*obj*) are evaluated.
`__nonzero__`(*obj*)	Called whenever *obj* is evaluated in a Boolean context—should return 1 if *obj* can be considered to be true, and 0 if *obj* can be considered as false. If *obj* is evaluated in a Boolean context but does not define __nonzero__, Python will attempt to use __len__ for the purpose, where a value of 0 returned by __len__ means false, and anything else means true.
`__coerce__`(*obj, other*)	This is called automatically by Python under certain circumstances, namely when Python is attempting to perform numeric arithmetic with *obj* and *other*, but does not know how to coerce these two objects into objects of the same numeric type. Your implementation of __coerce__ should return either a two-tuple consisting of *obj* and *other* converted to a common numeric type, or None if you cannot perform this conversion. The full rules governing the use of __coerce__ are rather complex. Refer to the *Python Language Reference* for full details.

A.14 *Exceptions*

The try-except statement is used to *catch* and *handle* an exception:

```
try:
        body
except exceptionType1, variable1:
        exceptionCode1
except exceptionType2, variable2:
        exceptionCode2
                .
                .
                .
except:
        defaultExceptionCode
else:
        elseBody
```

Everything after *exceptionCode1* is optional. If an exception is thrown during execution of *body*, the except clauses are searched. For the first matching *exceptionType*, the exception's argument is placed in the associated *variable* (if there is one, this *variable* is optional) and its *exceptionCode* is executed. An except clause with no *exceptionType* is a default and will catch any remaining exception. If there is no corresponding except clause in a try statement, the current code segment will be aborted and the exception will be thrown up the calling stack. If it reaches the top level without being handled, the program will abort, printing out a traceback. If no exception is thrown during the execution of body, the *elseBody* will be executed and flow will continue normally after the construct.

Another form is the `try-finally` statement. It can be used to ensure that a cleanup action is always performed regardless of how or from where a segment of code is exited.

```
try:
      body
finally:
      cleanupBody
```

The `cleanupBody` is executed when the body finishes normally or when an exception occurs. In the latter case the exception is thrown to the next higher level after the execution of `cleanupBody`.

The `raise` statement is used to throw an exception:

```
raise exception(arguments) or raise exception, argument
```

The *argument* or *arguments* are optional. In the first of these, the single argument associated with the exception will be a tuple containing *arguments*. In the second the argument associated with the exception will be *argument*.

The `assert` statement is a specialized form of the `raise` statement:

```
assert expression, argument
```

An `AssertionError` expression will be raised (with the optional argument) if the *expression* evaluates to false while the system __debug__ variable is true. The __debug__ variable defaults to true. It is turned off by either starting up the Python interpreter with the -O or -OO options or by setting the system variable PYTHONOPTIMIZE to true. The code generator creates no code for assertion statements if __debug__ is false.

A basic user-defined exception is created by inheriting from the top level `Exception` class:

```
class exception(Exception):
    pass
```

The following is the hierarchy of the exceptions classes defined in Python.

Exception
SystemExit
StandardError
   LookupError
      IndexError, KeyError
   ArithmeticError
      OverflowError, ZeroDivisionError, FloatingPointError
   EnvironmentError
      IOError, OSError
   RunTimeError
      NotImplementedError

KeyboardInterrupt, ImportError, IOError, EOFError, RuntimeError, NameError, AttributeError, SyntaxError, TypeError, AssertionError, ValueError, SystemError, MemoryError

This table summarizes when the above exceptions are raised in Python. It is derived from the *Python Library Reference* which gives more details. You can also look at the code implementing these.

Exception	Parent of all exceptions (user-defined exceptions should subclass off of it).
StandardError	Parent of all built-in exceptions.
ArithmeticError	Parent of **OverflowError**, **ZeroDivisionError**, and **FloatingPointError**.
LookupError	Parent of **IndexError** and **KeyError**.
EnvironmentError	Parent of **IOError** and **OSError**.
AssertionError	An `assert` statement failed.
AttributeError	A reference or assignment to an attribute failed. Note that, if an object doesn't support attribute references or attribute assignments at all, a `TypeError` would have been raised instead.
EOFError	An end of file condition was encountered by `input()` or `raw_input()`.
FloatingPointError	A floating point operation failed.
ImportError	The `import` statement was unable either to find the module definition or a requested name from a module.
IndexError	The index on a list, tuple, string, dictionary, or struct was out of range. Note that, if the index was not an integer, a `TypeError` would have been raised instead.
IOError	An I/O operation failed. Possibly because a file could not be found or the disk was full.
KeyError	The key used for a dictionary (or struct) was not found among the existing keys.
KeyboardInterrupt	The user entered the interrupt key (normally CTRL-C or DEL). Note that checks are made for interrupts regularly while the Python interpreter is running.
MemoryError	An operation ran out of memory. The value is a string describing what type of internal operation ran out of memory.
NameError	A name is not defined (was not found in the namespaces of the execution frame). The value is the name that wasn't found.
NotImplementedError	The method has not been implemented. Abstract methods in user-defined base classes, should raise this exception when they expect derived classes to override the method.
OSError	Error from outside Python. Usually has an error number and associated message.
OverflowError	Result of an arithmetic operation is too large to be represented. Most floating point overflows will not be reported. All integer overflows (other than for left shift operations) are reported. Long integers are unlimited precision and do not overflow.
RuntimeError	Error that doesn't fall into another category occurred. Value is a string indicating what went wrong. This exception is rarely raised.

SyntaxError	The parser encountered a syntax error. Has attributes `filename`, `lineno`, `offset`, and `text`. For an improper indentation will return point where encountered.
SystemError	The interpreter found an internal error. The value is a string indicating what went wrong. *This exception should be reported to the maintainer of your Python interpreter. Include the version string of the Python interpreter (`sys.version`), the exact error message (the exception's value), and, if possible, the source of the program that triggered the error.*
SystemExit	Exit exception. When it is not handled, the Python interpreter exits.
TypeError	A built-in operation or function was applied to an item of the wrong type. The value is a string giving details of the mismatch.
ValueError	A built-in operation or function was given an argument of the right type but inappropriate value.
ZeroDivisionError	The second argument of a division (or modulo) operation was zero. The value is a string with the operation and types of the operands.

A.15 Regular expressions

Regular expression objects and match objects

Following is an abridged description of some of the most frequently used regular expression methods. Note that there are more methods and these methods have more options than shown here. For further details see the section on them in the *Python Library Reference*. There is also an excellent tutorial written by Andrew Kuchling found at the Python web site.

re.compile(*pattern*) → *reo*

```
re.compile(r"H|h")              # Create a pattern to match any "h" or "H" in a string.
re.compile(r"h", re.I)          # Create a pattern to match any "h" or "H" in a string.
re.compile(r"^h", re.I | re.M)  # Create a pattern to match any "h" or "H" at the
                                # beginning of any line in a string.
```

Creates a regular expression object (*reo*) from the given *pattern*. Also takes an optional second argument containing one or more flags. Possible flags are:

> re.I (or re.IGNORECASE)   ignores the case of *pattern*;
>
> re.L (or re.LOCALE)   makes the metacharacters \w, \W, \b, and \B depend on the current locale;
>
> re.M (or re.MULTILINE)   makes the metacharacters ^ and $ match beginning and end of every line rather than just the beginning and end of the entire string;
>
> re.S (or re.DOTALL)   makes metacharacter match newlines as well.

Multiple flags can be combined using "|" as a separator between them.

reo.findall(*string*) → *list*

Returns a list containing the non-overlapping occurrences of the regular expression in *string* (if the regular expression contains more than one group, each occurrence found will be represented as a tuple of the matched groups).

reo.**sub**(*string1, string2, integer*) → *string*

Returns a string where all non-overlapping occurrences of the regular expression in *string2* have been replaced by *string1*. The optional third argument is the maximum number of occurrences to replace.

reo.**split**(*string*) → *string*

Uses the regular expression as a delimiter, on which to split *string* into a list of substrings.

reo.**search**(*string*) → *MatchObject*

Searches the string for the first occurrence of the regular expression, returning a *MatchObject* if it's found and *None* if it isn't.

reo.**match**(*string*) → *MatchObject*

Returns a *MatchObject* if the entire *string* matches the regular expression and *None* if it doesn't.

MatchObject.**group**(*string*) → *string*

Returns the matched group with name *string* in the *MatchObject*.

MatchObject.**groupdict**(*string*) → *string*

Return a dictionary containing the named groups in the match in *MatchObject*.

Examples

```
>>> import re
>>> reo1 = re.compile(r"\d+")          #one or more occurences of a digit
>>> reo2 = re.compile(r"[\t:, ]+")     # one or more occurences of tab, colon, comma
                                        # and/or space characters
>>> st = "11:03:1962, 05:30:1930 , 10:28:1957"
>>> reo1.findall(st)
⇒ ['11', '03', '1962', '05', '30', '1930', '10', '28', '1957']
>>> reo2.split(st)
⇒ ['11', '03', '1962', '05', '30', '1930', '10', '28', '1957']
>>> reo2.sub(":::",st)
⇒ '11:::03:::1962:::05:::30:::1930:::10:::28:::1957'
>>> reo3 = re.compile(r"(?P<month>\d\d):"   # a regular expression with three named
           r"(?P<day>\d\d):"                # groups
           r"(?P<year>\d\d\d\d)" )
>>> mo1 = reo3.search(st)
>>> mo1.group('year')
⇒ '1962'
>>> mo1.groupdict()
⇒ {'month': '11', 'year': '1962', 'day': '03'}
>>> reo3.findall(st)
⇒ [('11', '03', '1962'), ('05', '30', '1930'), ('10', '28',
   '1957')]
```

Metacharacters

The following is a table of regular expression metacharacters for use in *patterns*. While I've done some formatting and editing, this table is the product of many people who contributed to the Python documentation effort, and is used with the kind permission of Guido van Rossum and Andrew Kuchling.

!!!   In examples in the table, strings which are intended as regular expressions are underlined, not quoted. All other Python strings are quoted.

Character	Meaning
.	In the default mode, this matches any single character except a newline. If the DOTALL flag has been specified, this matches any character including a newline.
^	Matches the start of the string, and in MULTILINE mode also matches immediately after each newline.
$	Matches the end of the string, and in MULTILINE mode also matches before a newline. *Example:* foo matches both 'foo' and 'foobar', while the regular expression foo$ matches only 'foo'.
*	Causes the resulting RE to match 0 or more repetitions of the preceding RE, as many repetitions as are possible. *Example:* ab* will match 'a', 'ab', or 'a' followed by any number of 'b's.
+	Causes the resulting RE to match one or more repetition of the preceding RE. *Example:* ab+ will match 'a' followed by any nonzero number of 'b's; it will not match just 'a'.
?	Causes the resulting RE to match none or one repetition of the preceding RE. *Example:* ab? will match either 'a' or 'ab'.
*?, +?, ??	The *, +, and ? qualifiers match as much text as possible. Sometimes this behavior isn't desired. *Example:* If the RE <.*> is matched against "<H1>title</H1>", it will match the entire string, and not just <H1>. Adding ? after the qualifier makes it perform the match in non-greedy or minimal fashion; as few characters as possible will be matched. Using <.*?> will match only <H1>.
{m,n}	Causes the resulting RE to match from *m* to *n* repetitions of the preceding RE, attempting to match as many repetitions as possible. *Example:* a{3,5} will match from 3 to 5 'a' characters.
{m,n}?	Causes the resulting RE to match from *m* to *n* repetitions of the preceding RE, attempting to match as few repetitions as possible. This is the nongreedy version of the previous qualifier. *Example:* On the six-character string 'aaaaaa', a{3,5} will match five 'a' characters, while a{3,5}? will match only three characters.
\	Either escapes special characters (permitting you to match characters like '*?+&$'), or signals a special sequence. If you're not using a raw string to express the pattern, remember that Python also uses the backslash as an escape sequence in string literals; if the escape sequence isn't recognized by Python's parser, the backslash and subsequent character are included in the resulting string. However, if Python would recognize the resulting sequence, the backslash should be repeated twice. This is complicated, so it's highly recommended that you use raw strings for all but the simplest expressions.
[ ]	Indicates a set of characters. Characters can be listed individually, or a range of characters can be indicated by giving two characters and separating them by a '-'. Special characters are not active inside sets. **Example**: [amk$] will match any of the characters 'a', 'm', 'k', or '$'; [a-z] will match any lowercase letter and [a-zA-Z0-9] matches any letter or digit.

Character	Meaning
	Character classes such as \w or \ S (defined below) are also acceptable inside a range. If you want to include a] or a - inside a set, precede it with a backslash. Characters not within a range can be matched by including a ^ as the first character of the set (i.e. [^a-z] matches any character which isn't a lowercase letter); ^ elsewhere in a range will simply match the '^' character.
|	A|B, where A and B can be arbitrary REs, creates a regular expression that will match either A or B. This can be used inside groups (see below) as well. To match a literal '|', use \\|, or enclose it inside a character class, like [|].
(...)	Matches whatever regular expression is inside the parentheses, and indicates the start and end of a group; the contents of a group can be retrieved after a match has been performed, and can be matched later in the string with the \number special sequence, described below. To match the literals '(' or ')', use \(or \), or enclose them inside a character class: [(] [)].
(?...)	This is an extension notation (a '?' following a '(' is not meaningful otherwise). The first character after the '?' determines what the meaning and further syntax of the construct is. Below are the currently supported extensions.
(?iLmsx)	(One or more letters from the set 'i', 'L', 'm', 's', 'x'.) The group matches the empty string; the letters set the corresponding flags (re.I, re.L, re.M, re.S, re.X) for the entire regular expression. This is useful if you wish include the flags as part of the regular expression, instead of passing a flag argument to the com-pile function.
(?:...)	A nongrouping version of regular parentheses. Matches whatever is inside the parentheses, but the text matched by the group cannot be retrieved after performing a match or be referenced later in the pattern.
(?P<name>...)	Similar to regular parentheses, but the text matched by the group is accessible via the symbolic group name *name*. Group names must be valid Python identifiers. A symbolic group is also a numbered group, just as if the group were not named. So the group named 'id' in the example above can also be referenced as the numbered group 1. *Example:* if the pattern is (?P<id>[a-zA-Z_]\w*), the group can be referenced by its name in arguments to methods of match objects, such as m.group('id') or m.end('id'), and also by name in pattern text (e.g. (?P=id)) and replacement text (e.g. \g<id>).
(?P=name)	Matches whatever text was matched by the earlier group named *name*.
(?#...)	A comment; the contents of the parentheses are ignored.
(?=...)	Matches if ... matches next, but doesn't consume any of the string. This is called a lookahead assertion. *Example:* Isaac (?=Asimov) will match 'Isaac ' only if it's followed by 'Asimov'.
(?!...)	Matches if ... doesn't match next. This is a negative lookahead assertion. For example, Isaac (?!Asimov) will match 'Isaac ' only if it's not followed by 'Asimov'.

Special sequences

Special sequences in regular expressions are substrings beginning with a backslash, which have a special meaning to the regular expression parser. Using raw strings (i.e. r"string") avoids \t, \b, and \n being interpreted as tab, backspace, and newline, respectively. These special sequences are listed below.

Sequence	Meaning
\t	matches a tab.
\n	matches a newline.
\b	matches the beginning or end of a word.
\B	matches a location which is not the beginning or end of a word.
\d	matches a digit.
\D	matches any character that is not a digit.
\s	matches any whitespace character, same as the RE [\t\n\r\f\v].
\S	matches any nonwhitespace character.
\w	matches any alphanumeric character, as well as the underscore character.
\W	matches any nonalphanumeric character.
\\	matches a backslash.

A.16 Other useful statements, functions, and modules

Statements

```
exec string in globalDict, localDict
exec fileObject in globalDict, localDict
exec codeObject in globalDict, localDict
exec "print 1, ; print 2" → 1, 2
exec "print x" in {'x':1} → 1
exec "print x" in {'x':1}, {'x':2} → 2
f = open("xx",'w'); f.write("print 1, ; print 2"); f.close();
      exec open("xx") → 1, 2
codeObj = compile("print 1, ; print 2", "<string>","exec");
      exec codeObj → 1, 2
```

Executes *string*, the contents of the given file, or the byte-compiled *codeObject* as Python code. Uses the optional *globalDict* and *localDict* as the local and global namespaces, respectively.

Built-in functions

This is an abridged presentation. More details can be found in the *Python Library Reference*.

apply(*function, tuple, dictionary*) → *value*

Calls *function* with positional arguments of *tuple* and keyword argument from the optional *dictionary*. *function* can be a function, method, or a class instance for which __call__ has been defined.

compile(*string, filename, kind*) → *codeObject*
```
compile("print 1+2, ; print 2", '<string>', 'exec')
compile("print 1+2", '<string>', 'single')
compile("1+2", '<string>', 'eval')
```

Creates a byte compiled code object out of *string*. The convention is to use "<string>" for *filename* when the string does not come from a file. *kind* must be set to `'exec'` if *string* contains a sequence of statements, `'single'` if it's a single interactive statement, and `'eval'` if it's an expression. Code objects of all three kinds can be executed by either the `exec` statement or the built-in `eval` function.

dir(*object*) → *list*
    Returns the list of attributes of `object`. Returns the names in the local symbol table if no argument is given.

eval(*expression*) → *value*
eval(*codeObject*)
    Evaluates *expression* or *codeObject*. Can take optional second and third dictionary arguments to be used as the local and global namespaces for the evaluation. Use the built-in `compile` function to create code objects.

filter(*function, list*) → *list*
    Returns the members of list for which function returns true.

globals() → *dictionary*
    Returns the current global namespace.

isinstance(*object, class*) → *boolean*
isinstance(*object, type*) → *boolean*
    Returns true if *object* is an instance of *class* or an instance of a class that inherits from *class*. Or returns true if *object* is of the given type.

issubclass(*class1, class2*) → *boolean*
    Returns true if *class1* is a subclass of *class2*.

locals() → *dictionary*
    Returns the current local namespace.

map(*function, list1, list2, …., listn*) → *list*
map(max, [0, 2, 0], [1, 1, 1]) → [1, 2, 1]
map(None,[1,2,3], [1,2,3]) → [(1, 1), (2, 2), (3, 3)]
    Returns a list of the results of successively calling function with the "i"th elements of each of the input lists as arguments. That is, `map(f,[a0,a1], [b0,b1], [c0,c1])` is the same as `[f(a0,b0,c0), f(a1,b1,c1)]`. Any lists of shorter length are padded with `None`s. Also, if `None` is entered as the function, tuples of the transpose of the list will be returned (see the example).

range(*integer1, integer2, integer3*) → *list*
range(6,15,3) → [6, 9, 12]
range(6,15) → [6, 7, 8, 9, 10, 11, 12, 13, 14]
range(15) → [0, 1, 2, 3, 4, 5, 6, 7, 8, 9, 10, 11, 12, 13, 14]
range(6,-15,-3) → [6, 3, 0, -3, -6, -9, -12]
    Returns a list starting at `integer1`, increasing in steps of `integer3` and stopping before reaching `integer2`. If `integer3` is not present, it steps by increments of 1. If only one argument is present, defaults to start at 0 and step at increments of 1.

reduce(*function, list*) → *value*
    Successively applies a binary function to elements of a list. That is:
    `reduce(f,[a0,a1,a2])` is the same as `f(f(a0,a1), a2)`.

type(*object*) → *type*
>   Returns the type of the given *object*.

Library modules

The following is a small sampling of some of the library modules available. For more details see the *Python Library Reference*.

`cmd module:`
>   Provides support to easily develop basic command-line interpreters.

`copy module:`
>   Provides functions to generically make either shallow or deep copies of any Python object.
>
>   **copy.copy**(*object1*) → *object2*
>   Returns a shallow copy of the object.
>
>   **copy.deepcopy**(*object1*) → *object2*
>   Returns a deep copy of the object.

`getopt module:`
>   Provides support for parsing command-line options and arguments. It provides support both for UNIX single letter and GNU style long options.
>
>   **getopt.getopt**(*argumentTuple*, *optionString*, *longOptionList*)
>   → (*optionList*, *argumentList*) ⇒ error
>   python script.py -v --type=1 --high -f ab arg1 arg2
>   getopt.getopt(sys(sys.argv[1:], 'f:vx', ['type=', 'low',
>   'high']) → ([('-v', ''), ('--type', '1'), ('--high', ''),
>   ('-f', 'ab')], ['arg1', 'arg2']
>   The *longOptionList* is optional. A ":" after a letter in optionString indicates that argument requires an argument. Similarily an "⇒" after a word in *argumentList* indicates that long option requires an argument. Will raise error if an invalid option is found or an option requiring an argument does not have one.

`operators module:`
>   This module allows the standard Python operators to be used as functions (i.e., such that can be used with the built-in map, filter, and reduce functions).

`os module:`
>   Beyond those already described, there are a number of other functions here for platform-specific operating system interactions. One of these is:
>
>   **os.system**(*string*) → *integer*
>   Executes the string as a command on your platform's subshell (i.e., an MS-DOS Prompt window in Windows). Returns the exit status of the command.

`StringIO module:`
>   Allows strings to be encapsulated such that they can be written and read as if they were files (i.e., using read, readline, write and/or writeline methods).

sys module:

Beyond those already introduced, there are a number of other Python system functions and constants here. One of these is

sys.exit(*object*) → SystemExit

Raises a SystemExit exception. Calling this function will cause the interpreter to exit unless you catch the exception. The optional argument is usually an integer giving the exit status.

tempfile module:

Provides support for creating unique names for temporary files.

time module:

There are a number of functions here for obtaining and manipulating dates and times. Some of these are

time.sleep(*integer*)

Suspends program execution for a period of *integer* seconds.

time.time() → *float*
time.time() → 927513723.01

Returns the current time, in elapsed seconds since the system-specific origin time.

time.ctime(*float*) → *string*
time.ctime(time.time) → 'Sun May 23 20:43:07 1999''

Converts time in elapsed seconds to a human readable string. See the time module documentation for functions with other formatting options.

types module:

Gives the list of Python's type names.

UserDict and UserList modules:

Provide support for subclassing dictionaries and lists.

whrandom module:

There are a number of functions here for the generation of pseudo-random numbers. Some of these are:

whrandom.random() → *float*

Returns a random float in the range 0.0 to 1.0.

whrandom.randint(*integer1*, *integer2*) → *integer*

Returns a random integer in the range between *integer* and *integer2*, inclusive.

whrandom.choice(*sequence*) → *element*

Randomly chooses an element out of the *sequence*.

A.17 Python interactive mode summary

On UNIX

There is command-line editing and command history functionality available on the UNIX version. You can move back and forth through the previous lines sent to the interpreter, either singly or via a search, then edit any line before hitting carriage return to have it sent to the interpreter. The following table gives the default key bindings:

Action	Key
Moves cursor one character right	CTRL-F
Moves cursor one character left	CTRL-B
Moves cursor to beginning of the line	CTRL-A
Moves the cursor to end of the line	CTRL-E
Deletes the character right of the cursor	CTRL-D
Deletes the character left of the cursor	\<backspace\>
Erases rest of line right of the cursor	CTRL-K
Yanks last erase string back	CTRL-Y
Undoes last change made (repeatable)	CTRL-_
History - moves up one line in buffer	CTRL-P
History - moves down one line in buffer	CTRL-N
History - searches forward in buffer	CTRL-S
History - searches back in buffer	CTRL-R
History - sends current line to interpreter	\<return\>
Interrupts execution of the interpreter	CTRL-C

Sequential use of the undo key will undo multiple previous changes. Adding the two lines

```
import rlcompleter, readline
readline.parse_and_bind('tab: complete')
```

to the file that is pointed at by $PYTHONSTARTUP variable (`pythonrc` in your home directory) will enable an optional command and variable completion mode. The \<tab\> key will be the completion function. Hit it twice for the options.

In the Python tutorial that comes with Python there is a section on this interactive mode with more details as well as a pointer to more information. See it if you want to change the default key bindings.

On Windows 95/98

There is no command-line editing or command history on the Windows 95/98 versions.

- The \<backspace\> key will delete the last character typed,
- a \<CTRL-C\> will interrupt the interpreter's execution, and
- a \<CTRL-Z\> typed at the prompt will quit the program.

To copy to the clipboard, first click the Mark button. Then select the desired rectangular section with the mouse. Finally, click on Copy button to send it to the clipboard. You can select text directly (without having to first click Mark button), if you enable the Quick Edit option under the Misc tab of the Properties window (which is brought up by clicking on the Properties button).

To paste from the clipboard, first copy the desired text to the clipboard on the source program, then click on Paste button. Note that on at least some Windows 98 machines, Paste doesn't work properly with the default settings as it can take tens of seconds to paste multiple lines into the buffer. This can be fixed easily by *deselecting* the fast pasting option found on the Misc tab of the Properties window (the Properties window is brought up by clicking on the Properties button.

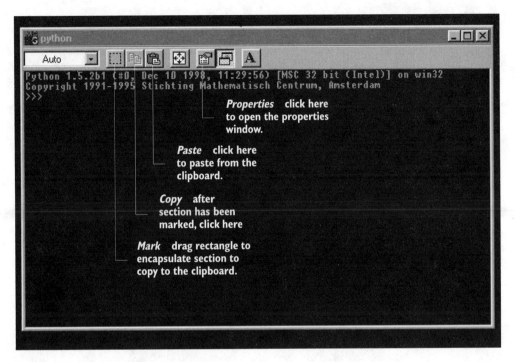

Figure A.1 Working with a clipboard

index

dictionaries (continued)
    representing sparse matrices with 88
    retrieving values from (get) 86, 367
    subclassing (UserDict module) 395
    tuples as keys for 87
    valid keys for 87
    values in (values) 85, 367
    writing to a file (cPickle.dump) 138–141,
        379
dir (display attributes of an object) 393
dir (display names in a module) 117, 220
directories
    changing (os.chdir) 123, 380
    copying recursively (shutil.copytree) 381
    creating (os.mkdir, os.makedirs) 129, 380
    deleting (os.rmdir) 129, 380
    getting the current working directory
        (os.getcwd) 122, 374
    listing the files in (os.listdir) 123, 128, 380
    obtaining from a pathname
        (os.path.basename) 125, 374
    obtaining the access time of
        (os.path.getatime) 375
    obtaining the modification time of
        (os.path.getmtime) 375
    obtaining the name of
        (os.path.dirname) 125, 374
    processing files in a directory tree
        (os.path.walk) 129–130, 380
    renaming (os.rename) 128, 380
    testing the existence of (os.path.isdir) 127,
        375
distributing Python programs 171
division operator (/), for numbers 47
divmod (find quotient and remainder) 355
DLLs
    calling from Python (calldll) 267
documentation string (__doc__)
    for built-in functions 118
    for classes and methods 179–180, 381
    for functions 100, 369
    for modules 371
DOS, Python support on 22
double-quote character (") 69

E

elif (statement)
    with if-else constructs 91, 369
else (statement)
    with exceptions 150, 385
    with for loops 92, 369
    with if-else constructs 91, 369
    with while loops 91, 369
empty value. See None
endian, converting when reading and writing
    data 138
environment variables (os.environ) 126, 380
environment variables, summary 373
EnvironmentError (exception) 387
EOFError (exception) 387
equal to (==), comparison operator 97, 352
equality tests
    based on identity (is, is not) 98
    based on value (==, !=, <>) 98
errors. See exceptions
escape sequences
    basic (\', ", \\, \a, \b, \f, \n, \r, \t, \v) 69, 357
    hexadecimal character representation
        (\xFF) 70, 357
    octal character representation (\777) 70,
        357
eval (evaluate an expression or code
    object) 393
Excel
    guidelines for using a Python client
        with 264
    possibilities for as a client for a Python
        COM server 261
    retrieving data from a Python COM
        server 259
    setting up a workbook with a server 259
    started by a Python client and receiving
        data 263
    starting a Python COM server from 259
    using as a client for a Python COM
        server 258
except (statement) 150, 385
Exception (parent of all exceptions) 387
exception types
    ArithmeticError 387

Windows 95/98, copy and paste 396
Windows 95/98, fixing paste problem 396
interpreter development, command line (cmd
    module) 394
IOError (exception) 387
is (identity operator) 98, 352
is not (identity operator) 98, 352
isinstance (built-in function) 222, 393
issubclass (built-in function) 223, 393
items (dictionary contents method) 85, 367
iteration. See for loops, while loops

J

Java
    comparison with Python 4, 6
    difference in memory management for 190
    integration of Python with (JPython)
      279
    JPython 280–296
      __builtin__ class 291
      calling compiled Python code from
        Java 291
      compiling to Java bytecode (jpythonc) 293
      development approaches when using with
        Java 295
      downloading and installing 283
      example applet ('Hello World') 281
      example java class (general ledger) 286
      example java class extension (general
        ledger) 287
      extending (subclassing) Java classes
        in 287
      Java Bean property mappings 286
      Java proxy classes 285
      jpythonc (compile to java byte code) 293
      Py.java2py method 290
      PyDictionary class 289
      PyList class 290
      PyLong class 290
      PyObject class 290
      PySequence class 290
      PyString class 290
      Python Server Pages (PSP) 296
      PythonInterpreter class 289

PyTuple class 290
speed of 281
using from within Java
    (PythonInterpreter) 289
using java classes from within 285
using special method attributes
    (PyObject) 290
using to test java classes 287

K

KeyboardError (exception) 387
KeyError (exception) 387
keys (dictionary indices) 84, 367, 379
keyword arguments 370
keyword arguments (for functions) 102
keywords in Python 351

L

lambda expressions 100, 370
Latteier, Amos xxi
legal restrictions on use, lack thereof 12
len (length function)
    for dictionaries 84, 368
    for lists 52, 365
    for shelves 142, 379
    for strings 68, 358
    for tuples 63, 366
    use in for loops with the range function 92
    use of __len__ 383
less than (<) 97, 352
less than or equal to (<=) 97, 352
library modules 113
lines, splitting statements across 96, 368
links, testing for (os.path.islink) 128, 375
Linux, installing Python on 22
list (conversion function)
    for converting a string to a list 66, 77, 363
    for converting a tuple to a list 66, 363
list(s) 52–62, 364–365
    appending an element to (append) 54, 364
    bulk initialization of (*) 59, 363
    comparison rules for 353
    concatenation (+) 59, 363
    copying 54, 62

list(s) (continued)
  copying, deep (copy.deepcopy) 394
  copying, shallow versus deep 62
  creating (=) 52, 363
  creating with the range function 93, 393
  delimiters [] 52, 364
  element deletion, by position (del) 55, 364
  element deletion, by value (remove) 55, 364
  empty [] 64
  extending a list (extend) 364
  finding sorted position in (bisect.bisect) 56, 365
  finding the maximum value of (max) 59, 365
  finding the minimum value of (min) 59, 365
  index notation 52–54, 363
  inserting an element in sorted order (bisect.insort) 56, 365
  inserting an element into (insert) 55, 364
  length (len) 52, 365
  making an object behave like one (special method attributes) 228
  matches in (count) 60, 365
  membership determination (in) 58, 365
  modification of 54
  multidimensional 60, 363
  multiplication operator (*) 59, 363
  nested 60, 363
  packing and unpacking 65
  pop an element out of (pop) 364
  reading from a file (cPickle.load) 138–141, 379
  representing matrices with 60
  reversal of (reverse) 56, 364
  searching in (index) 60, 365
  slice notation for 53, 363
  sorted order, insert element in (bisect.inorder) 56, 365
  sorted, partitioning (bisect.bisect) 56
  sorting (sort) 56, 364
  sorting with a custom ordering function 57–58, 365
  subclassing (UserList module) 395

  writing to a file (cPickle.dump) 138–141, 379
Lloyd, Brian xxi
local namespace 114
locals (obtain the local namespace) 115, 393
logical operators (and, or, not) 97, 352
long (conversion function)
  for converting a float to a long integer 47, 356
  for converting a string to a long integer 73, 360
  for converting an integer to a long integer 47, 356
long integers (unlimited precision) 46, 354
LookupError (exception) 387
loops. See for loops, while loops

M

Macintosh, installing Python on 22
map (built-in function) 393
map objects. See dictionaries
match (determine if a string matches a regular expression) 389
match objects (regular expression match)
  obtaining a named group from (group) 389
  obtaining the named groups in (groupdict) 389
math module 48
  math.acos (arc cosine) 355
  math.asin (arc sine) 355
  math.atan (arc tangent) 355
  math.atan2 (arc tangent) 355
  math.ceil (ceiling) 355
  math.cos (cosine) 355
  math.cosh (hyperbolic cosine) 355
  math.e (e constant) 355
  math.exp (value raised to e) 355
  math.fabs (absolute value of a float) 355
  math.floor (floor) 355
  math.fmod (modulus of floats) 356
  math.hypot (hypotenuse) 356
  math.log (log base e) 356
  math.log10 (log base 10) 356
  math.modf (modulus of a fraction) 356

Purchase of *The Quick Python Book* includes free Author Online support. For more information on this feature, please refer to page xxii.